MW00336014

At the Table

At the Table

Food and Family around the World

KEN ALBALA, EDITOR

An Imprint of ABC-CLIO, LLC

Santa Barbara, California • Denver, Colorado

Library of Congress Cataloging-in-Publication Data

Names: Albala, Ken, 1964- editor.
Title: At the table : food and family around the world / Ken Albala, editor.
Description: Santa Barbara, California : Greenwood, an Imprint of ABC-CLIO, LLC, [2016] | Includes bibliographical references and index.
Identifiers: LCCN 2015037311 | ISBN 9781610697378 (alk. paper) | ISBN 9781610697385 (ebook)
Subjects: LCSH: Food habits. | Cooking, International. | LCGFT: Cookbooks.
Classification: LCC GT2850 .A83 2016 | DDC 394.1/2—dc23 LC record available at http://lccn.loc.gov/2015037311

ISBN: 978-1-61069-737-8
EISBN: 978-1-61069-738-5

20 19 18 17 16   1 2 3 4 5

This book is also available on the World Wide Web as an eBook.
Visit www.abc-clio.com for details.

Greenwood
An Imprint of ABC-CLIO, LLC

ABC-CLIO, LLC
130 Cremona Drive, P.O. Box 1911
Santa Barbara, California 93116-1911

This book is printed on acid-free paper ∞
Manufactured in the United States of America

Contents

Preface

This book is designed to showcase the dinner table and what it looks like in countries spanning the globe, both visually in a snapshot photograph and in an accompanying richly descriptive text. Each entry illustrates various features of the eating event from start to finish, including who does the shopping, who cooks, who sits at the table and how they eat, what customs or rituals they observe, how the food itself is cooked and served, and even who cleans up in the end. Recipes are also included. The ultimate purpose is both ethnographic and to provide a base for broad comparison across cultures, religions, and social settings. Some accounts stem from the contributors' personal lives and some are more fly-on-the-wall accounts of objective observers, but all are based on direct experience with the culture covered.

Eating habits are said to be in flux given the changing nature of the family itself, owing to shifting work schedules and the advent of convenience foods and take-out. For many people the breakdown of the family dinner table is seen as directly connected to the demise of the fabric of society. This book is designed to see if this perception of radical change is true and see how, despite so many challenges, people manage to hold on to the family dinner. In some cases they do not. In some cases a family may be construed quite differently than we might expect, and in many cultures there is no table at all. What might be considered proper table manners in one place hardly passes muster in another, and, of course, utensils vary widely from place to place; fingers often work perfectly fine. This is the beautiful diversity of our experience in eating.

Other variables considered include the time of dinner, where people physically eat (in a dining room, in the kitchen, in front of the TV), and whether everyone eats the same food. Dieting, allergies, aversions, and preferences according to age sometimes make serving a common meal an extraordinary challenge for the person in charge, which nowadays is not necessarily the mother of the family. The dynamics of dinnertime conversation are equally as fascinating: some families discuss how their day went, others bicker and fight, and some eat as quickly as possible so they can attend to other things. The purpose here is to examine why these dynamics differ so widely from place to place and what it reveals about each culture.

The examples are in no way meant to be representative of each country, as if that were even possible. Rather, they are simply snapshots of unique, sometimes quirky ways people eat dinner. Nor could we cover every place on the globe. Some stories are located in prosperous cities, some in rural settings. There is a broad range of socioeconomic circumstances featured across the entries, and there are even two contrasting examples from one country precisely for the purpose of detailed comparison. Regarding the culinary landscape, the intent is not to highlight exemplary fine dining and certainly not to stereotype any particular set of customs or eating habits or even feature so-called typical dishes. Rather, the intent is to celebrate the panoply of human experience. The same goes for the structure of the family itself, and the majority of examples here are anything but the perceived norm of a heterosexual couple with 2.5 children. Families are made up of a wide array of relatives, friends, and even solitary individuals. And we must not forget that pets are also often an integral part of the family, even if not fed directly from the table.

At the center of all controversy over dinner is cooking itself. There is a widespread perception that people in the past few generations have lost basic cooking skills and have succumbed to the enticements of mass-produced convenience food that promises to be quick and easy but offers little in terms of gastronomic pleasure or sound nutrition. Moreover, food specifically marketed toward children is thought to be corrupting their palates toward nuggetized, overly salted, and sweet mass-produced food that steers them away from ever appreciating fresh fruits and vegetables and simply prepared dishes made from fresh whole ingredients. Modern industrial food has little respect for culinary traditions, which many see as in danger of being lost. This is thought to be a process begun in the more prosperous nations that has begun to affect the entire globe. We shall see if this perception is true. People may indeed cook differently than in the past, but by and large they are still cooking. One also has to wonder if our perception of a golden past where mom did the cooking from scratch and everyone sat down every night to a quintessential family dinner has more to do with our hopes of what should be rather than what ever really was the norm. The entries that follow provide some evidence that our perceptions are rarely borne out by actual experience. Naturally these accounts offer a tiny statistical sample, but they do show that we should resist making quick judgments about general trends in eating habits and that while the evolution of dinner is inevitable, it is not always so negative.

Another feature that is particularly interesting is how the cooking is done and what technologies are employed. Do families increasingly rely on frozen or canned foods, or is everything fresh and prepared from scratch? Is food purchased once a week and stored in a refrigerator, or is shopping a daily affair? Even the physical layout of the kitchen can be very revealing. Expensive trophy kitchens may rarely be used, while some people seem to manage fine with a tiny burner, a few pots, and a minuscule workspace. It is also amazing that while in one part of the world life seems inconceivable without plastic wrap, tin foil, and plastic containers for leftovers; in other places there aren't even refrigerators. We tend to forget that modern modes of eating are not even a century old, and in some places on Earth they are still unheard of.

On the other hand, one feature of home cooking around the world that might be surprising is the extent to which it has become internationalized. Although people may be straying from traditional recipes and ways of eating, they are increasingly experimenting with new ingredients and flavors. The popularity of Asian food, cooked from scratch, appears to be almost universal. Who could have guessed that curry is enjoyed in the far-flung corners of the world? So too, unsurprisingly, we find pizza, hamburgers, macaroni and cheese, and other dishes, many of which have ceased being associated with their country of origin. There is no doubt that as the world becomes increasingly connected via trade and media, peoples' palates expand and their willingness to try new techniques at home increases. Even more interesting is the way local ingredients and techniques are used to make "foreign" dishes, adapting them to local preferences. I think that this should not be seen as adulteration or bastardization but rather as a natural process that has always been involved in the evolution of cuisine.

Many of the entries also seem to suggest that the dominant mode of shopping for almost exactly the past century may be waning: the supermarket. People seem to have a distaste for shopping, so farmers' markets, delivered community-supported agriculture boxes, and increasingly home delivery of groceries, especially in cities, seem to be proliferating. One can imagine that someday all our groceries will simply be ordered online, which makes sense if retail space is at a premium; they can just be shipped directly from a warehouse. Why make the customer wait on interminable lines at the bulk grocery outlet or shopping club when they can order and have a truck drop everything off?

In gathering together and editing this volume I have incurred many debts, foremost to the authors themselves. Many are dear old friends whom I know from previous projects, from the Oxford Symposium, or from the Association for the Study of Food and Society. Apparently these people simply wanted to work with me again. Some are people I have never met but who proposed outstanding entries that fit in perfectly. Many signed on from the very start, while others signed on at the 11th hour, as happens with every project of this nature. Regardless, the entries fit together beautifully, and the end product is exactly what I had hoped it would be when it was first envisioned. Also, as I look back on over a dozen years editing projects of this type, first for Greenwood Press, which later merged with ABC-CLIO, I realize that this work is not only the culmination of 20 or so books in the Food Culture Around the World series and the *Food Cultures of the World Encyclopedia* I edited but is also the collaborative work of all the marvelous people at ABC-CLIO, foremost Kaitlin Ciarmiello. This project was really her idea, though I might claim that I thought of it one night years ago at a bar in Boston when we two spun book ideas for several hours.

Ken Albala

The Family Dinner: An Introduction

From our vantage point in the 21st century, it is easy to look back and imagine the concept of family dinner as a natural, inherently good, and perhaps even necessary part of life. For Americans, the dinner table is central to our most revered traditions and is enshrined in Norman Rockwell's iconic image of Thanksgiving dinner, where everyone is happy to be together as a giant turkey is presented at the table by family elders. There is a perception that this is how families are supposed to be and how they always have been since time immemorial, and this applies equally to all cultures on Earth. It seems that there is something fundamentally human about sharing food within the family unit—that we would never have evolved as social beings, never even survived as a species, had not our first priority been feeding children and family members, a simple biological necessity. Without families eating together there could be no communities and no political order, and if life were even possible under such conditions, it would be unbearably solitary.

This habit of thinking stems ultimately from Aristotle, who viewed the world as it is and assumed that because something functions well to achieve its ends, it is therefore natural and necessary. For him, the subjection of women, the enslavement of inferiors, and the patriarchal family unit itself are all indispensable parts of how we succeed as humans. This same logic assumes that the erosion of any part of our social arrangements is likely to threaten the entire system. Taking this theory to the extreme, we might even conclude that much of what is wrong with the world today stems from our not eating together as a family anymore.

Sitting at the table for dinner, we learn manners, discuss our aspirations and fears with those close to us, and learn to communicate, negotiate, and behave as political beings. We learn to help others through the habitual setting and clearing of the table, washing dishes, etc. Without the family table, it seems possible that these positive behaviors and values would fail to develop, leading us to wonder if the breakdown of society could be connected to the demise of the family dinner.

There is no denying that people must be fed to survive, but whether this has always universally been in the context of the family unit, let alone at a table, is not so clear. Early humans appear to have moved in small bands that cooperated in hunting, shared food among a few dozen people, reared children together, and even enjoyed sexual relations freely among the band. Some anthropologists speculate that we were originally more like our peaceful ape cousin, the bonobo, than the aggressive chimpanzee. Sharing food among the roving band was the only way to survive, but the social arrangement was nothing like the monogamous coupling or family that we imagine to be natural. This was merely the new social arrange-ment of humans after the advent of agriculture about 10,000 years ago. The ques-tion remains, though, can we thrive as a species eating and living as solitary be-ings? However we define the social and reproductive unit, is a quality life without a family dinner even thinkable? Years ago in a short seminar taught by the anthro-pologist Colin Turnbull, we were presented with this quandary. The readings in-cluded two books he had authored: *The Forest People,* about the Mbuti with whom Turnbull lived, and *The Mountain People,* about the Ik of Uganda whom he studied some years later. The former were perfectly functional, happy, lovable people who shared everything and thrived as hunter-gatherers. In fact, for impressionable un-dergraduates, the Mbuti way of life seemed infinitely preferable to our own. The story of the Ik was not so happy. For purely political reasons they were unable to range widely across their traditional territory to hunt and forage, and their entire society fell apart; people became solitary, stopped sharing, and ate alone. Many died of starvation, especially children. The lesson, although not put so simply, was that humans are in constant interaction with their environment, resources, and fellow humans. Disturbing any crucial element of their means of living can bring disaster to the whole society. One crucial element was indeed sharing food.

One might argue that in settings where people live in a delicate balance with their natural resources or in extreme climates such as the desert or the Arctic, life is more precarious, and various social arrangements are merely adaptations to these extreme situations. Thus, we have thriving bands in the Congo, harems in the Middle East, and a wide array of social arrangements that enable people to survive. But today in modern society, adults certainly can live alone, eat alone, and thrive as autonomous solitary units. A 2014 study by the NPD Group found that 57 percent of all eating occasions among Americans take place alone. Granted, many of these events include snacking or eating lunch at the work desk. But 27 percent of all households consist of a single person, wherein most meals are solitary. The study also found that 32 percent of all dinners in the United States take place alone. Whether these figures have any bearing on the global situation cannot be determined, but suffice to say that the concept of family dinner has been in decline. Whether this is important or should somehow be reversed is another question entirely.

There are various angles from which one can approach this question. First, there are purely aesthetic considerations. In some cultures, a long relaxed dinner with others can be an essential part of the good life. The French believe that good wine, good conversation, and good food should be priorities in daily living. Meals should be eaten slowly in order to fully appreciate and experience the tastes and flavors. Alternatively, the great gastronome M. F. K. Fisher once wrote that eating alone can be the highest form of culinary pleasure. There is no conversation to distract you, no hedging your opinion based on your dining partner's reactions, no trying to impress with your knowledge. You can simply focus on the food—its texture, aroma, flavor, and feeling in the mouth. However, Fisher's high-end solitary experience is not really comparable to the quick meal eaten mindlessly in front of the TV. Interestingly, the TV and computer screen do constitute a kind of techno-logical company, giving the impression that a solitary meal is shared among others. Fascinatingly, in Korea to give the impression of commensalism, there are popular websites on which you can watch people eat. You could argue that it is explicitly a form of sharing when people post pictures of their meal on social media, which often earns words of praise and encouragement. This practice might actually reveal a prime function of eating together: to talk about the food and give praise to the person who has cooked the meal to feed others. The pleasure in eating is therefore more than mere gastronomic sensation; it is also a positive social event and also extends equally to the family members or company who have the distinct pleasure of knowing that someone went out of her or his way to provide for their suste-nance. It becomes especially meaningful when the meal is more than routine, such as including a special ingredient or involving a particularly difficult cooking pro-cedure. The labor expended is congealed in the object produced, which is literally consumed, creating a bond between people that simply cannot be purchased.

There is nothing inherently better about food that is shared at a communal din-ner table. However, when people do eat together, there is a tendency to cook from scratch, spend time preparing food, and eat at the table. Quite the opposite, there is a tendency toward eating prepared and convenience food when eating alone and often not at the actual table. Eating alone can also lead to mindless consumption. This means much more than simply consuming without giving much thought to what you eat. It involves a kind of ethical detachment from food as an object sim-ply to provide calories, energy, and a little taste. In 2013 it was announced that a product called Soylent would provide all the nutrition one would need in pow-dered form, and instead of ordinary meals one could remain in front of the com-puter and simply drink a few shakes a day. One can only imagine what effect this

De-Skilling: Introduction

With the proliferation of convenience foods, there was a fear that housewives, for they did most if not all the cooking, were forgetting basic skills once mastered by their moth-ers or grandmothers. Cake mixes, which gave the appearance of cooking since one had to add eggs and oil, were an easily identified culprit. Those who depended on them could no longer make cakes from scratch, which were perceived to be healthier and cheaper. The time saved, so the manufacturers convinced consumers, was more important than any pleasure or reward from having baked the cake oneself. Actually, there is little concrete evidence that housewives did have extensive cooking skills or even that there were housewives, so to speak, since many women worked outside the home. The idea of de-skilling has nonetheless been a powerful tool in the rhetoric argu-ing for the breakdown of the family unit.

would have on the teeth, being unused. More disturbing was the very idea that this could free you from having to eat with others. Getting necessary nutrients would become mindless. The great farmer/poet Wendell Berry, in an essay titled "The Pleasures of Eating," speculated that in the future we would simply be hooked up to tubes that feed us directly from the factory without our having to think at all. That's only one small step beyond Soylent.

Soylent is simply an exaggerated example of what has already happened to our food supply. Most people rarely have any idea of where ingredients come from, what chemicals may have been added, what pesticides have been sprayed on the ground, or what kind of environmental and social effect our food practices may have. The effects of our food habits are all hidden, despite the mandatory nutrition facts labels that purport to inform us. The more processed the food, the less we really know about it and the more vulnerable we become to corporations whose principal goal is to make a profit. Hiding the ethical ramifications of highly processed food and, of course, getting us to eat more and more of it has led to one of the strangest situations in human history: we spend less on food than any civilization that has ever existed and yet we eat more in aggregate than any civilization has before. Malnutrition and obesity exist side by side.

There is no guarantee that a family meal would make us any more cognizant of our food choices from an ethical standpoint. But at the very least, having to shop for ingredients, cook them, and actively think about what will taste good is good for us, leaves less of a footprint on the environment, and makes us engaged as consumers. Better yet, it makes us *mindful* eaters. When we are forced to weigh various considerations such as cost, freshness, and impact on health, as we do when preparing food for others, we tend to make better choices. Unfortunately, the move toward processed food eaten while on the go is one that much of the Western world has been taking over the past century, and it sometimes feels as though there is little hope of turning back the clock. Every day these rushed, unhealthy habits are spreading around the globe. We see culinary traditions, much like indigenous languages, vanish every day. Part and parcel of the industrial mode of food production and feeding is to expand to new markets, ship food farther, and make it quicker and more convenient to consume. This means that people will eat together less often, meals will become episodic and perfunctory, and the kind of anomie we see pervading much of the developed world will infect the rest. This is not to say that there is no hope. Nor is it particularly helpful to command people to get in the kitchen and force families to sit down for dinner. It is more productive to look at the root causes of dinner disjuncture. Obviously, our daily commutes and work schedules are a major factor in the decline of the dinner table. In the post–World War II suburban communities spread across the United States, commuting parents left for work early and got home late. Family dinners were reserved for special occasions, while on weekdays children often ate alone in front of the TV. Parents' hectic schedules today are only half the story, though. Years ago, after-school activities were just that: they took place at school, and there was a bus to take children home by dinnertime. This rule seems to have disappeared, as sports, music, theater, and a vast variety of children's activities take place in the evening, making a sit-down dinner impossible. How do we combat the elements of modern-day life that seem bent on impeding a family meal? One solution might be to cultivate cooking as an activity pleasurable in itself. People watch a lot of food programs on TV. Magazines and cookbooks sell really well. But study after study shows that each year people spend less time in the kitchen preparing food. We need to focus more on teaching basic skills rather than cooking as competition. We need to value time spent in the kitchen as a creative outlet, not as a chore to be hurried through as painlessly as possible. Everyone has to eat, so why should food preparation be marginalized as something less important than work or other activities? For a great part of the world, simply getting enough food regardless of the way it is eaten is a more serious challenge. There are grave inequities in the distribution of food across the globe that overshadow the minute details of the dinner table. Nonetheless, the question of whether people eat together is crucial for every household, from the most opulent to the most meager. Sharing food is undeniably an essential part of being human, as the entries in this book amply demonstrate.

Ken Albala

Afghanistan

Helen Saberi

Afghanistan is a landlocked country situated at the very heart of Asia, at the meeting place of four major cultural areas: the Middle East, Central Asia, the Indian subcontinent, and the Far East. Afghanistan's turbulent history is perhaps better known than that of its food and cooking. It is this history as well as the diversity of Afghanistan's geography, climate, and ethnic groups that has given rise to a rich and varied food culture.

Although many people in Afghanistan are poor and their diet is generally very basic, most eat three meals a day, albeit often very simple food. Bread (*nan*) is the staple and is eaten with most meals. The midday meal (*nan-e-chosht*) usually consists of a main dish such as soup, noodles, or rice. The evening meal (*nan-e-shab*) might consist of leftovers from lunch, but for many families it is the main meal of the day, and as with the midday meal, dishes such as a soup, a pilau, or rice with korma will be prepared.

Ali and Rabia live in a small two-bed apartment in southwest Kabul. They have five children—two boys and three girls—ranging in age from 10 to 19 years. Ali works as a chauffeur. Rabia's sister and two of her children are coming for dinner, so for this occasion a more elaborate dinner is prepared. Rabia decides to make *mantu* to be followed by *ketcheree quroot* and *kofta*. *Mantu* in Afghanistan is a sort of dumpling stuffed with chopped meat and onion, flavored with spices, and steamed. Variations of *mantu* are found in countries all along the Silk Road, from the steamed bread of China to the stuffed *manti* of Turkey. The *mantu* will be followed by *ketcheree quroot*, a sticky rice and lentil dish very similar to *kichri*, popular in India. It is served in a mound on a large platter. A hollow or well is made in the rice and then is filled with a yogurt sauce. Rabia will serve this with small meatballs (*kofta*) in a rich sauce, although some families make a meat korma to go with it. She will also make a salad (*salata*). Grapes from the north of Kabul will be served after the meal followed by tea.

Shopping used to be the responsibility of men, but recently this role has been taken on by women or children. Many women when they go out cover up under a full burka or *chadri*, as it is known locally. Rabia prefers to wear a *chador*, a sort of open cloak, or sometimes just a veil or scarf to cover her hair. Sometimes she takes one of her children shopping with her to help carry the purchases. To shop for the dinner, she sets off early in the morning to the local bazaar to buy fresh meat from

An Afghan family in Kabul, Afghanistan, eating their evening meal in the traditional style and sitting on cushions and sharing the food communally. (Courtesy of Nasir Saberi)

the butcher for her meatballs. She buys lamb, which is the most popular meat for Afghans. At the same bazaar she also purchases onions and ingredients for a salad from a vegetable stall. Staples such as rice, flour, pulses, and cooking oil are normally bought in large quantities once a month and stored at home.

Preparation and cooking of many Afghan dishes can be laborious, and for this meal it will take about three hours even though she will be helped by her sister and one of her daughters. This is the time-honored way young girls learn how to cook from their mothers. Recipes and techniques are learned through practice and experience.

Rabia has a small basic kitchen. She, like many Afghans, does not have an oven. She cooks on a couple of burners fueled by bottled gas. Although refrigerators are still rare throughout the country and food is traditionally kept fresh and cool in a range of clay pots and containers, Rabia is lucky enough to have a small refrigerator.

Like most Afghans, she does not have sophisticated equipment such as an electric mixer but does have a range of pans in different sizes, some quite large, for cooking rice and a steamer for making *mantu*. She has a pressure cooker that speeds up the cooking of any meat that may be tough. She also has a hand mincer for mincing meat and onions. Families who do not own one get the butcher to perform this task. All Afghan homes have an *awang* (pestle and mortar), an essential piece of equipment for crushing garlic, onions, and herbs and for grinding spices. Most will also have a large slotted spoon called a *kafgeer,* used for stirring dishes and dishing up rice. Most families also have at least one colander for washing and draining vegetables and also for draining rice. They will also have a rolling pin (*aush gaz*) to roll out dough for noodle dishes such as *mantu*. Afghans rarely measure their ingredients, although they usually have a range of pots with handles called *malaqa* that are used as measuring aids, as are ordinary cups, glasses, and spoons.

Rabia starts preparing the meal by making in advance the meatballs to be served with the *ketcheree quroot* (see the recipe below). Meanwhile, her sister makes the yogurt sauce by reconstituting *quroot*. *Quroot* is dried yogurt made by adding salt to strained yogurt (called *chaka*), which is then dried and formed into round balls that harden and resemble grayish-white pebbles. For use in cooking, the *quroot* is reconstituted with water in a special bowl with a rough bottom surface called a *taghora-e-qurooti.* The yogurt is then flavored with plenty of crushed garlic.

Next, together with her sister and daughter, Rabia prepares the *mantu*. First of all she makes the dough with flour, water, and a little salt and kneads it until smooth and shiny. The dough is formed into balls and covered with a damp cloth for about an hour. The lamb meat is then cut up finely and mixed with finely chopped onions, chopped chilies, black pepper, cumin, and salt and all mixed together thoroughly.

Rabia rolls out the dough very thinly on a clean, lightly floured surface. Her sister cuts out four-inch (10-centimeter) squares, while her daughter places a spoonful of the chopped meat mixture into the center of the square and then deftly nips together the dough, not sealing completely so that the steam can penetrate and cook the filling. The shelves of the steamer are thoroughly greased to prevent the *mantu* from sticking. The *mantu* are then placed on the shelves, ready to be steamed later.

They then prepare the rice and mung beans for the *ketcheree quroot* and start cooking it. Meanwhile, Rabia's daughter prepares a mixed salad of finely sliced onions with chopped cucumber, tomatoes, lettuce, and fresh coriander and tosses it all with some salt and lemon juice. All the while the three of them chat and gossip about all sorts of things, such as marriage (the daughter has just gotten engaged) and about their dreams and aspirations.

The *mantu* is put on to steam for about an hour before serving. Meanwhile, one of the sons goes to the local bakery to buy fresh *nan,* as the family does not have its own tandoor for baking bread.

The traditional mode of eating in Afghanistan is on the floor, although in major cities some Afghans sit at a table, Western style. Everyone sits on large colorful cushions called *toshak,* with large pillows (*bolesht*) behind for support. Just before the food is ready to be served, one of the children lays out a large cloth or thin mat

---

Eating on the Floor

In many cultures, especially in the Middle East and India, people eat seated on the floor on a rug. The food might also be placed on the floor and eaten from common trays or might be served at a squat table as in Japan, where people kneel on tatami mats. It takes a lot of practice, and Westerners often find it difficult to sit and eat without getting fidgety or having their legs fall asleep. In some places the men will eat first, and then the women and children eat afterward. These varieties in practices are merely a useful reminder that eating at a table is very much a modern Western phenomenon, though it is spreading around the world.

---

called a *disterkhan* (sometimes called a *sofreh*) on the carpet. Hands are washed before eating. Sometimes especially for guests, a special jug and bowl called *haftawa-wa-lagan* is brought. Water is poured from the jug over the hands, the bowl being used to catch the water. Rabia and her family wear their ordinary day clothes for family meals. The boys wear jeans and T-shirts, and the girls and women a dress over long trousers. Sometimes they wear a veil covering their hair if there are male guests present. Shoes are not worn. Indeed, shoes are taken off when entering the flat. Sometimes slippers or socks may be worn, especially during the cold winter months. No one changes for dinner unless it is a special occasion and there are many guests, in which case everyone wears their best clothes.

All the dishes are served at the same time. There is no formal sequence of courses, although any dessert or fresh fruit will usually be eaten after the savory dishes. Many Afghans share the food communally. Three or four people eat from one large platter of rice with smaller side dishes of korma, salad, chutneys, pickles, and so on, but Rabia and her family prefer to eat off their own individual plates. Bread is passed around for everyone to tear off a piece.

Guests are offered food first. If the father is present he will then take his food, followed by his wife and children. Guests are encouraged to take second helpings. In some large extended families in Afghanistan the men sometimes eat separately from the women and children, who eat when the men have finished.

The traditional way of eating for most Afghans is with the right hand using no cutlery, but many people do use a spoon and sometimes a fork. Bread (either *nan* or *chapatti*) is used by many instead to scoop up food, which is then popped into the mouth. Rice is scooped up with the right hand and formed dexterously into a small ball, which is then popped into the mouth. Spoons are used for eating soups and some desserts such as *firni,* and teaspoons are used for stirring tea. Rabia and her family sometimes eat with their hands, but when there are guests they eat with a spoon.

Most people in Afghanistan are very poor, so any kind of cutlery, crockery, pots, and pans are treasured items. Today most of these articles are mass-produced, and most come from China. Paper serviettes or napkins are sometimes used, especially for guests, but in many households, including Rabia's, a box of tissues is placed on the *disterkhan* for people to help themselves and wipe their hands and mouths as necessary.

Everyone is polite when sitting and eating, even the children, although young children sometimes fidget and play with their food. They are usually tolerated, even by the father if he is present. They are often so hungry that they will just get on with eating anything they are given, but believe it or not, even in Afghanistan some young children are picky and have to be coaxed into eating. Sometimes they get bored, especially if they have finished eating, and leave the table. Some even fall asleep while eating, as dinner is sometimes served late. Rabia and her family at the meal talk a lot. They talk about the children and their studies, problems, and the news of the day, especially about politics. At this meal the talk centered around the small kiosk the boys have bought for selling phone cards, cigarettes, bottled water, and so on. Rabia and her family have a TV but do not watch it while eating their meals, nor do they talk or play on their mobile phones. Should someone call, however, the phone will be answered.

The family does not have any pets, and their flat, by Western standards, is quite bare. In the room where they eat there is no furniture nor are there pictures on the walls, but they do have a traditional Afghan carpet on the floor and cushions to sit on. Most families in Afghanistan do not have lamps or lampshades, just bare light-bulbs for lighting (when they have electricity, that is). Electricity is not available 24 hours a day, so eating meals has to be finely timed to fit in with this. Sometimes the electricity goes off suddenly and unexpectedly, and candles will be lit.

Often, especially if there are guests, some snacks are served before the food. A bowl of nuts such as almonds, walnuts, pine nuts, and pistachios and dried fruits such as red and green raisins might be provided. Other predinner popular snacks are roasted chickpeas and a snack called *seemian* (*sev* in India). *Seemian* are small pieces of crunchy noodles made from chickpea flour paste, which is seasoned with turmeric and red pepper before being deep-fried in oil.

When the food is ready Rabia, her sister, and her daughter will dish up the food in the kitchen. Although all the dishes are placed on the *disterkhan* at the same time, traditionally *mantu* is eaten first as an appetizer. Rabia is serving her *mantu* with yogurt and a sprinkling of fresh coriander, although some families serve it with a carrot korma or a tomato sauce. It is the most traditional of all Uzbek dishes popular all over Afghanistan, especially for guests and special occasions such as engagements and weddings.

After the *mantu* everyone will have some *ketcheree quroot* and *kofta* with some salad on the side.

Desserts are a luxury and are usually only made for special occasions, such as feast days and parties. However, fresh fruit in season is served at the end of every meal. In the winter oranges and bananas are available, but in the summer and autumn the variety of fruit is staggering—cherries, pomegranates, apples, pears, peaches, nectarines, melons, watermelon, and grapes. There are many varieties of grapes grown all over Afghanistan, and for this meal a friend gave Rabia four different kinds of grapes from his land in Deh Sabz (often called the "Vineyard of Kabul") just north of Kabul. He sent small, sweet white ones called *kishmishi;* round, green plump ones called *ghola don;* long, very sweet green ones called *Husseini;* and oval reddish-purple ones called Kandahari.

No alcohol is served. Afghanistan is a Muslim country, and the dietary laws forbid the consumption of alcohol. Rabia and her family drink bottled water poured into glasses with their meal. Fizzy drinks such as locally produced Coca-Cola, Fanta, and Sprite are only served for very special occasions.

When everyone has finished eating, the plates, glasses, etc., are cleared away by the two daughters. Leftovers are put in the fridge to be eaten the following day. They also make the tea. They make green tea (although sometimes they make black tea). The tea is made in a teapot and poured into little glasses called *istekhan.* They sprinkle the tea with a little bit of ground cardamom, as this is considered to aid digestion. Sugar is provided for those who want it. Some people soak sugar cubes (called *qand*) in the hot tea, then hold the cubes in their mouth while sipping the hot tea. Milk is not added. Recently a new trend of tea drinking has emerged. Saffron has always been used to color and flavor many desserts in Afghanistan, but now tea is sometimes flavored with this exotic spice for special occasions. Farmers are being encouraged to cultivate saffron instead of poppies. This has brought down the price of saffron, which used to be imported from Iran and was very expensive.

When everyone has finished drinking their tea, the two daughters clear away the tea dishes and ingredients. They wipe the *disterkhan* with a damp cloth and fold it up, ready for use the next day. Together they do the washing up in the kitchen while the others continue chatting or watch TV.

Ketcheree Quroot

Serves 4

Many Afghans, for quickness, often substitute strained yogurt, as in this recipe.

For the rice:

1 cup (8 oz.) short grain rice

¼ cup mung beans (or green split peas)

salt

6 tablespoons vegetable oil

1¾ cup strained yogurt

2 cloves of garlic, peeled and crushed

2 teaspoons dried mint

red pepper

For the meatballs:

1 pound minced beef or lamb

1 medium onion, minced or ground

2 cloves of garlic, peeled and crushed

1 egg

2 teaspoons ground coriander seeds

1 teaspoon *garam masala*

½ teaspoon black pepper

1 tablespoon finely chopped fresh
coriander

For the sauce:

6 tablespoons vegetable oil

2 medium onions, finely chopped

1 tablespoon tomato puree

water

salt

red or black pepper

1. Wash the rice and mung beans. Boil the latter in plenty of water until soft, then add the rice and enough water to cover by about 2 inches.
2. Add the oil and a teaspoonful of salt; stir; bring to a boil; cover with a lid, slightly ajar; and cook gently over a medium-low heat until the rice is soft and the water has evaporated (about ½ to 1 hour). Turn the heat to low and continue cooking for 20–30 minutes, stirring from time to time. The rice should have a thick, sticky consistency.
3. While the rice is cooking, prepare the meatballs and sauce. Combine and mix together all the ingredients for the meatballs and knead the mixture with the hands until it becomes smooth and sticky. It is essential that the mixture should be really well mixed and kneaded to give the meatballs their characteristic smooth texture and also to prevent them from breaking up while being cooked.
4. Shape into balls about 1–2 inches in diameter. It is best to use wet hands to form the balls into smooth shapes by dipping them from time to time into a little salted water. Some Afghans use egg white to smooth the balls into shape. This also helps prevent the meatballs from breaking up.
5. To make the sauce, heat the oil in a pan over a medium to high heat.
6. Add the chopped onions and fry, stirring continuously until they are reddish-brown.
7. Add the tomato puree and stir and fry briskly until the sauce turns brownish. Stir in a little water. Add salt and pepper according to taste.
8. Bring to the boiling point and then add the meatballs, one at a time, in a single layer. Add more water as necessary to just cover the meatballs.
9. Now cover with a lid, leaving it slightly ajar. Turn down the heat to low and simmer gently for about 45 minutes to an hour or until the meatballs and sauce are brown and the sauce is thick.
10. Combine the strained yogurt with the garlic, a little salt, and red pepper to taste.

11. When all is ready, mound the rice on a large dish and shape it with the back of a spoon. Make a well in the top and fill this with the strained yogurt, reserving some to serve separately. A little of the sauce from the meatballs can be spooned over the rice. Finally, sprinkle with dried mint, and serve the meatballs with their sauce separately.

FURTHER READING

Dupree, Louis. *Afghanistan.* Princeton, NJ: Princeton University Press, 1973.

Richards, Caroline, and Juls Stewart, comps. *Afghanistan Revealed.* London: Frontline Books, 2013.

Saberi, Helen. *Afghan Food and Cookery.* New York: Hippocrene, 2000.

Australia

Lara Anderson

Living in a part of Melbourne with a strong Middle Eastern influence, this family, like many others in the area, eats Middle Eastern food of some sort most weeks. Tonight, the meal is made up of a mix of takeout and homemade food. The mother—who in this house does the lion's share of the cooking—has prepared some dishes she has sought out in one of her favorite cookery books, *Abla's Lebanese Kitchen*. It was Abla Amad who, arriving in Melbourne in 1953, pioneered the now legendary transformation of the Australian foodscape. Until the first waves of immigration after World War II, Australian cuisine was considered bland and insipid. The richness of this transformation is clear in the smells and sounds emanating from the houses along the family's street especially at this time of day, when the sun begins to lose its sting and children are called home from nearby parks. This family's mealtime began then, before dinner, walking home from the playground, the father carrying a child's bike, the four kids running and calling out behind him, all of them anticipating dinner and enjoying the smells of other meals being prepared. For many now, one of the best things about Australia's foodscape is its ethnic cuisines; Melbourne is a city especially renowned for its multicultural culinary offerings.

For many Australians, there is also (and somewhat paradoxically) a growing emphasis on buying and eating local ingredients. This family—like many in the neighborhood—does most of its shopping each Saturday at a farmers' market. Their favorite market is held at the local primary school, which sells Victorian food and seasonal produce. The mother buys what is in season before deciding what she is going to cook, adapting recipes to fit in with what she's been able to purchase at the market. In winter, the youngest two children sometimes miss the tropical produce—mangos and avocados—that is trucked down from Queensland and sold in the supermarkets, but the pleasure of eating locally grown fruits after the long wait for summer to hit is unbeatable. Anyway, the children have learned about the seasons and their effect on food; the mother hopes they are learning to respect that slow, nourishing process. She wants as much as possible for the family to be semi–self-sufficient: they have fresh herbs growing in the garden (lots of mint, parsley, thyme, and coriander), some fruit trees (olives, figs, lemons), and a grape vine as well as their own laying hens.

Like a growing number of families in Australia, this family eats a primarily vegetarian diet. For tonight's meal, the mother is making salad, pan-fried

A summer evening family meal, consisting of locally grown produce, homemade dishes, and some of the neighborhood's local Lebanese food. (Courtesy of Cathy Greenwood)

cauliflower with tahini sauce, and a lentil dish and rice. She has bought most of the ingredients from the farmers' market, and she adds the homegrown parsley and lemons to the tahini sauce. The lentils are the blue French ones, which need to be soaked all day but can be cooked quickly after coming home from work. While the lentils are cooking on the stove top, she prepares the cauliflower, soaking it in boiling water and then frying it in some locally made olive oil. She keeps the water used for the cauliflower boiling on the stove and measures out a cup of basmati rice. Once it is tender, she drains it, pours it into a dish, and sprinkles over it a few handfuls of slivered almonds. The tahini sauce is similarly quick to make. She tosses together the nutty paste, a good pinch of salt, and a peeled piece of garlic, then as she slowly pours in water and a squeeze of lemon with one hand, she whisks it all together with a no-fuss handheld blender in the other. For the salad, she measures out a few handfuls of spinach leaves into a ceramic dish and grates carrot over the top. At the last minute when all is ready to be served, she will mix through a treat: a bag of sesame-glazed walnuts, bought at the deli on the way home from work.

To supplement the meal and also to serve something her younger children will readily eat, she has bought a dozen miniature meat pies from one of the Lebanese bakeries she passes between her tram stop and her street. She also bought gluten-free falafel from one of the nearby shops, which only need heating up in the oven. The falafel are especially for the father and for the daughter's school friend, who is a guest for the evening while her parents go out to see a play. The other children tend to prefer the pies. They are made out of a white bread outer layer with a tomato and minced meat mix in the middle. When they are served at the Lebanese bakery-café, they come with lemon and a chilli dipping sauce, but at home the kids prefer to dip them into a little bit of bottled tomato sauce that they pour out from a jug onto their plates. The mother is careful to ration the sauce so they don't eat too much of it.

All the food is brought from the kitchen to the dining room at the same time and put in the middle of the table. One of the twins helps carry the salad. Each dish has its own serving implement, and everyone joins in passing plates and bowls to each other so that everyone can serve themselves. The mother offers food first to her daughter's friend and then helps her two youngest children with their servings. While she needs to make sure they eat more than just the pies and sauce, the older children know that they need, at the very least, to try a bit of everything. They eat more of the lentils and rice than the younger children, and the adults eat the biggest proportion of vegetables. None of the children like the cauliflower; they can't help comparing it to broccoli, which is a favorite. The father has celiac disease, so he avoids dishes with wheat content and eats only the rice, lentils, and vegetables. Partway through the meal he decides to supplement his plate with some cheese, which he slices in the kitchen and brings to the table with some rice crackers. The bread that the rest of the family eats is kept on a separate dish, since the father is very allergic and even the smallest amount of gluten makes him ill. The children have learned this and often stop to check that food is gluten-free before offering it to him. Celiac disease, or gluten intolerance, is increasingly common in Australia, so the kids have also been made aware of this issue at childcare and school, where they have learned to be careful about sharing food with friends. Fortunately, gluten-free foodstuffs are not uncommon and can be easily sourced at the local supermarkets, but they continue to be niche products, which makes them more expensive than their gluten-based counterparts.

After the kids have eaten their main meal, one of the adults normally tries to get them to eat a little bit more of their vegetables or salad before passing around a platter of fruit, to which everybody helps themselves. Tonight—a warm Melbourne

---

Food Allergies

There is a widespread perception that food allergies have become much more acute in recent decades, making the simple act of serving dinner fraught with apprehension, especially when guests are present. It may simply be that these are more consistently diagnosed and that in the past people simply dealt with discomfort or in the distant past simply never survived. Others contend that it is the chemicals, processing, and antibiotics in food that have triggered the proliferation of food allergies. Whatever the cause, food manufacturers offer gluten-free, dairy-free, nut-free, and other dietary products.

evening—refreshing watermelon is well received by the children, while the adults continue to enjoy the cheese plate and rice crackers with their fruit. They talk to each other in snippets of conversation between eavesdropping on the children, who talk happily with each other about their plans for the next day together (a Saturday) and make constant jokes. Their excitement about all being together and having a guest is clear in the way they can barely sit still to enjoy the sweet melon. In the past, male adults tended to be served first and apportioned the best part of the meal, but this arrangement no longer holds sway—if anything, adults often wait until the children have taken or been served what they wish to eat. Tonight after the children have finished their fruit, a cake is brought to the table. Particularly in summer, dessert is normally just fruit and maybe a few pieces of chocolate from a shared shop-bought block. But since there is a visitor, the mother offers everyone (except the dad) a piece of coconut cake with raspberry and coconut icing that she made with her children yesterday. Making the cake took longer than any other part of the meal, since the younger children like to be involved in the baking, and they take longer to do their bit. The cake has been waiting on the kitchen bench all day, and now the mother is pleased to try it and find that it is a very satisfying end to the meal: the in-season raspberries really lift its flavor, and their sharp tang offers a delightful contrast to the richness of the coconut and butter.

Sometimes food is cut for the younger children, who are still learning table manners, and during the meal they are often reminded that they need to stay seated until everyone is finished. The older children know this rule well and don't ask to leave the table until then. Often, they will go outside to play or into another room to watch television while the adults finish talking. At the table, conversation normally focuses on the meal itself and encouraging the kids to eat properly without making a mess. The parents ask the kids about their day and what they've been learning. Increasingly, the children also ask after their parents who, like many of their generation, are both kept busy working full-time outside the home. Mealtimes are therefore also often a space for planning the practical arrangements of school drop-offs, extracurricular activities, and playdates or sleepovers. Very occasionally, if there is something on the news the adults want to watch, then the television is put on. There is also the occasional Friday night when the children enjoy a more casual dinner while watching a movie or children's programs on ABC.

As with about 90 percent of the meals eaten in this house, this meal takes place at the dining table. The table is found in the living area of the house, with a sitting area on one side of it and an open-plan kitchen on the other. This means that the table naturally tends to be a focal point for anyone first entering the space from either side, and it is where the family gathers most frequently to talk, do homework, and play games. The table was a gift to the family from the children's paternal grandmother, who had no room for it in her home when she downsized to an apartment. It is an Australian teak extension table from the 1970s and is not dissimilar in style to the 20th-century Scandinavian furniture in vogue at the moment. Not just aesthetically pleasing, the table is also very practical. It can be extended to seat 10 or 12 and has been made to do so many times in the past for dinner parties and children's birthday smorgasbords. The dinnerware the family uses tonight is also special to them. It is a Royal Doulton Morning Star dinner set passed down from the same grandmother, who received it as a wedding present in the 1960s. At that point in Australia's history, the country's Anglo-Celtic roots were felt much more strongly. Owning an English dinner set such as this one was then seen as desirable, as it represented an important connection with English culture. Many of the pieces are faded or have utensil marks, but the original pattern is beautiful and clear on those that have been used less and hand-washed rather than put through the dishwasher (like the jugs and big serving platter). Over the years one piece or another has been dropped or lost, taken out into the garden for play tea parties, or lent, carrying leftover cake, to a neighbor. So the set is supplemented with colorful and more child-friendly pieces, bought from IKEA or other cheap houseware shops. The mother also uses a mix of serving bowls and dishes that she has bought over the years during trips to different countries, especially to Spain, where she has spent a great deal of time.

The adults drink wine from sturdy wineglasses; the older children drink water out of the same glasses. The younger children are not yet allowed to use these glasses and eat and drink out of the colorful plastic crockery. The children normally only drink water; lemonade and orange juice are treats, and this reflects an increasing emphasis in the many primary schools in the area on healthy ("nude") eating. The adults normally have one or two glasses of wine with dinner; tonight, they have poured themselves ice-cold New Zealand pinot gris. An aromatic white often with a touch of sweetness, pinot gris pairs nicely with the smoked paprika in the lentils and the richness of the tahini sauce accompanying the cauliflower.

During mealtimes, the cat—who otherwise would constantly try to jump on the table—is kept outside. If there is any meat left over, he is fed that before being given his packaged cat food. Other nonmeat leftovers on the kids' plates are fed to the five hens out the back, which eat ravenously! The parents might also take some leftovers to work tomorrow for lunch. The oldest child takes leftovers as well—she attends a primary school with an ethnically diverse demographic, so the Anglo-Australian tradition of taking a cold sandwich for lunch is not observed by all of the students. The school has installed microwaves where the kids can heat up their curry, noodles, rice, or pasta. While the younger children clear the table and the older ones sweep up under it and wipe it over, the dad does the dishes, tidies the kitchen, and puts everything away, ready for use again tomorrow. The younger kids in particular can still make quite a mess at the table especially with rice, which gets into everything. The mother does the majority of the cooking in this house simply because she is the better cook of the two adults, but this means that after the meal is done she has time to herself while the others are busy with chores. She often uses this time to go to the study to read, to watch the news, or to get some work done.

Sometimes the kids need cajoling into helping with the meal, but for the most part they see the importance of pitching in. It is important to the parents that everyone understands that the domestic duties must be shared as equitably as possible, especially given that both parents work full-time. For this reason too, as nighttime sets in and all the work of the day comes to a close, the family members spend their time quietly, unwinding: reading, watching TV, practicing piano. Often they stay in the same room together. This north-facing living area is an extension, which was added to the original house when the twins were born and the children's maternal aunt came out from New Zealand to live with the family. It was added to a simple weatherboard house, built at the same time as many others in the 1950s in an area that, at that time, was considered to be outer suburban Melbourne. Modest and unadorned, normally with just two or three bedrooms, these houses enabled owners to live and raise a family in a suburban setting during a period of escalating building costs. The new room is light and bright and features a couple of paintings on the walls plus pictures drawn by the eldest daughter, who appears to be a budding artist. There is also an abstract painting by an Australian artist from the 1970s, another present to the family from "Nanny Judith," as the kids call their grandmother. The dining table is in the center of this room, and the mother has arranged it this way. As they eat at night, she can see that every seat at the table offers a different view of the walls' colorful paint marks and pencil strokes. There are plenty of opportunities here for the family to remember the various milestones and experiences as well as the loved ones who have brought them together over the years to share food with each other.

Fried Cauliflower with Tahini Sauce

This recipe serves cauliflower with the sauce, which is too often considered a bland vegetable. However, any favorite vegetable or fried fish can be substituted.

To prepare the cauliflower:

1 cauliflower, separated into small pieces	½ teaspoon of salt
	2 cups olive oil
Boiling water, for soaking	

1. Put cauliflower in a bowl, cover with boiling water, and leave for 5 minutes. Drain and pat dry with paper towel, then rub in salt.
2. Heat the oil in a frying pan for 3–4 minutes. Add the cauliflower pieces and fry for 6–7 minutes. Remove with a slotted spoon and drain on paper towel. Serve hot or at room temperature with tahini sauce.

To prepare the tahini sauce:

½ cup of tahini	¼ cup of water
½ teaspoon salt	¼ cup of lemon juice
1–2 cloves garlic	1 tablespoon of chopped parsley

1. Place the tahini, salt, and garlic in a bowl and slowly add the water, stirring continuously.
2. Gradually pour in the lemon juice and stir until smooth, then mix in the parsley. Add more water if you prefer a thinner consistency.

FURTHER READING

Gallegos, Danielle, Suzanne Dziurawiec, Farida Fozdar, and Loraine Abernethie. "Adolescent Experiences of 'Family Meals' in Australia." *Journal of Sociology* 47(3) (2011): 243–260.

Haden, Roger. *Food Culture in the Pacific Islands*. Santa Barbara, CA: ABC-CLIO, 2009.

Lupton, Deborah. "'Where's Me Dinner'? Food Preparation Arrangements in Rural Australian Families." *Journal of Sociology* 36(3) (August 2000): 172–186.

Austria

Katerina Nussdorfer

Nina knows: however busy the day, however crazy the traffic, however crowded the shops before Christmas, a calm, unhurried, and warm setting awaits her at home in the evening—dinner with her family. That Nina is the center of this story is no surprise—it is she, after all, who will cook the meal tonight as well as most other meals for the family. The family is her husband, Oliver, and their two children, ages 10 and 2½. They live in a suburban house in the 22nd district of Vienna, and though food shopping habits in Vienna are made easy by the proliferation of supermarkets, bakeries, and fast food on every street corner, living in this part of town means having to plan ahead when it comes to groceries. The nearest supermarket is only reachable by car or public bus that departs every half hour in the evening, and most supermarkets will be closed after 7:00 p.m. and on Sundays. So for this evening, when Nina planned to make spaghetti Bolognese, she had to procure all the ingredients for the dinner ahead of time. Getting ingredients for a dinner as simple as spaghetti with sauce could still be a challenge when one has to cater to the different needs of family members: her family, though not vegetarian, rarely eats meat (they have "chili con soya," for example, instead of chili con carne, as Nina reports), her 10-year-old daughter is the pickiest of eaters and will eat no visible carrots, onions, garlic, etc. Her toddler will not eat much in quantity. In order to make this meal in a way that it meets everyone's needs and requirements, Nina cooks the sauce with meat bought from the butcher, which means more expensive but also better in quality and freshly minced in front of her eyes. To compensate for the lack of flavor-boosting garlic and onion, she cracks open a jar of ready-made, store-bought, supermarket-brand sauce—*sugo* with herbs—and adds it to the pan where the meat is already sautéing in Croatian, or more specifically Dalmatian, olive oil, the rare but still present immigrant flavor in their kitchen. That the sauce from the jar is laced with additives, modified starch, glucose syrup, acidifying agents, yeast extract, and too much sodium does not seem to be of any concern. This sauce will go over spaghetti—a special kind made of spelt flour. Spelt generally is a really popular choice in Austria, considered healthier, tastier, and preferred over plain wheat products. Nina opens the small pack of pasta. Most dry pasta in Austrian supermarkets is sold in two-pound packs unless it is a specialty or Italian brand of pasta. Nina measures the amount needed by consulting Oliver, then slides a handful of beige-grayish spaghetti out of the pack and puts it

A family in Austria enjoying an informal dinner of Spaghetti Bolognese. (Courtesy of Katerina Nussdorfer)

in the already boiling salted water. She doesn't normally buy this kind of pasta, and both she and Oliver wonder out loud how it will taste and, most important, if their daughter will accept it, especially since, as Nina comments, it is rather pricey. Most likely they will continue eating regular dry pasta in the future, with occasional treats of other varieties, since price is an important factor when buying food, even for middle-class families. When it comes to shopping for food, the errands are divided, with Nina buying the ingredients when she needs to cook a particular meal and Oliver shopping for bulkier pantry staples and drinks. They normally shop in Spar and Billa and sometimes in the discount store Hofer, with the choice mainly influenced by the convenient location of the supermarkets (they go shopping by car) and by good produce and competitive prices.

Curious about all the hustle and bustle in the kitchen, the toddler comes to see what is going on, and Nina props him up on a stool. Together they fish out a long string of spaghetti in order to test it for doneness. Not so curious is the 10-year-old girl, who sometime into the cooking process comes down from her room upstairs where she was playing computer games. She shows no interest in cooking despite being a picky eater, which means that a lot of the food choices are made around her needs. She doesn't come down because of inviting smells and intriguing sounds coming from the kitchen or because of hunger but because she says she was bored with the game. Sometimes she doesn't come down at all during dinner, especially if she has eaten a snack before, which for many schoolchildren means a roll with cold cuts and/or cheese and pickles (*Wurstsemmel*), or she will eat later on in the evening. And that is okay with her parents. Though they always try to come together at the dinner table, they don't want to have the clock decide when to eat. Even so, the regularity and familiarity of the evening family meal carries a lot of emotional meaning for both parents involved. As Oliver reports, he grew up with his only hot meal being cooked for lunch by his grandmother and with a usual dinner of cold bread, sausages, and snacks, so this new family dinner ritual is something he has come to really appreciate and cherish, especially since he himself rarely cooks it. Nina says that they try to eat together every night, which they consider an achievement and luxury, especially since everyone eats their lunch alone, either at work, in school/kindergarten, or at home or out (Oliver is a stay-home dad at the moment), and breakfast is a rushed affair if it happens at all. Oliver's childhood story is not so unusual, though, since most Austrians used to eat their big warm meal at lunchtime and would only have a light supper or an *Abendbrot* (buttered bread, cheese, and cold cuts). Things have changed a lot in the last two decades, mainly due to altered schedules and prolonged working hours that allow for no big family lunch break; the dispersion of workplaces and their distance relative to the home also means that working and oftentimes tired parents come back home only around or after 6:00 p.m. And when they are home, that much-romanticized cooked meal has to be cooked by someone!

Nina, luckily for her family, is that someone, and tonight she will treat her husband and children to spelt spaghetti with store-bought sauce Bolognese and a salad to accompany it all. For this dinner, she chose Napa cabbage that she bought in the local supermarket. She picked it based on two factors: locality and seasonality. The other salads on offer, she says, came from Italy or Spain, and this deterred her from buying them because of the carbon footprint but mainly because they would probably be full of chemicals and taste like nothing as well. Nina insists that salad be present at their table, and regardless of the kind, it is always seasoned with a simple oil and vinegar lemon dressing, but she uses various oils and vinegars to achieve different tastes, though one oil—the homemade Dalmatian olive oil—seems to prevail. For tonight's salad she chose the Dalmatian olive oil and mixed it with a vinegar infused with rosemary and mixed herbs.

The one cooking task that the children and husband help with takes place while Nina is finishing up the sauce and the pasta. The children help Oliver cut the salad and place it in a large plastic salad bowl. The seasoning, however, is still left to Nina. The children do not normally help with preparing the food, Nina says, and they, the parents, do not insist on involving them in the process. For them, it is more important that the family comes together that one time a day, around the dinner table, in an act of commensality in which the focus is not only on the food but just as much on the social aspect of communicating, sharing the daily events, and providing a nurturing familial atmosphere for the children.

Nina takes special pride in the fact that she tries to cook every day, and while one could argue that very little and quite simple cooking takes place for this particular

Stove-Top Range

It was not until the proliferation of cast-iron ovens in the 19th century that cooking on a stove top became common in households. These were replaced with gas and electricity, but we now take for granted that one cooks facing the stove. In wealthy households, the size and complexity of the stove became a mark of social status, and often a so-called trophy kitchen would be outfitted with a Viking range or Aga cooker but rarely if ever actually used. Interestingly, the kitchen became more important as a site for entertaining or a performative space for men than a place for the daily routine of cooking.

dinner, one could also see how easily *that* cooking might be replaced by other available shortcuts, such as ready-made meat sauces, microwavable pasta dinners, etc. Austrian households as a rule do not have microwave ovens, and it is not unusual for households to not have an electric kettle or a toaster; the latter is especially seen as a specialty item. Since Austrian bread is among the best in the world, bakeries are an essential part of Austrians' daily food habits, and sliced, bagged supermarket toast bread is considered a special bread item rather than an everyday staple. Nina herself cooks her meal on a glass-ceramic stove top that has a fitted oven underneath as well. While it is true that this particular meal does not take longer than half an hour to prepare, perhaps because some shortcuts are used—ready-made sauce instead of vegetables and herbs that would take somewhat longer to prep (chop, cut, fry)—there is still cooking being done and the bulk of it by Nina too. On days when she comes back from work especially tired or doesn't feel well—she works part-time 25 hours a week but also helps her sister's newly opened business—the family simply eats what is in the fridge, sandwiches, cold cuts, leftovers, or snacks. Nina doesn't mind that all the cooking falls on her; in fact, she insists that she enjoys doing it and finds it calming after a long day away from the home. They very rarely order food to be delivered, though they used to order more (mainly pizza) when they lived together in the inner city and had no kids. Oliver hardly ever cooks; still, there is a current shift in gender roles when it comes to the house and kitchen chores of young Austrian families, with more and more men cooking not only sporadically and for fun but also on a steady basis, helping or sometimes even replacing the woman's traditional role in the kitchen. Whether this is a trend and to what extent family background, upbringing, and social class influence these practices is still open to research. When it comes to Nina's kitchen, she is the one who reigns there, but Oliver does make up for not cooking by taking over the clearing of the table and loading the dishwasher and before that for setting it as well.

For this Oliver engages the children, and they help him bring the plates and set the table. No special attention is given to the rules for setting the table—everything is rather relaxed and easygoing. The dishware is chosen specially for the occasion—they always eat pasta in these spaghetti bowls. There is no tablecloth, but there are paper napkins. The cutlery is set in such a way that the spoons are on the left and the knives and forks are together on the right. This is done by Oliver at the very beginning, shortly after Nina starts cooking and way before the children help set the rest of the table. The dishware and cutlery are ordinary and are also not viewed as special or valuable, though they are somewhat special in function (spaghetti bowls). There are knives set on the table, and though not traditionally used for eating spaghetti, they are later on used to cut up the pasta in smaller pieces. There is a heavy accent on convenience, and the fact that there is a family sit-down cooked meal is cherished above all, with the other details kept at a bare minimum in order to make things easier for Nina and simpler for everyone else. There is a always something decorative on the table that Nina adds from behind the stove, and this time one can notice two votive candles in star-shaped holders and a tiny Christmas tree, which is season appropriate, it being the beginning of December and Advent, though both parents agree that religion itself plays no role whatsoever in the family's eating practices. There is no special dress; everyone is in their daily clothes, and the toddler is in his tights. There is no music. The TV is off this time, but sometimes it does stay on in the background.

The meal is served and eaten on the dinner table, which is between the open-plan kitchen and the living room/seating area, and all meals, unless they are snacks in front of the TV/computer, are eaten there. In summer the room opens to the garden with huge French windows and makes it feel like al fresco dining. Nina plants a lot of herbs and vegetables in the garden, and these are an important part of their meals as well. There is a cozy feeling in the dining area because of the nearby cooking island and bar that displays fruit, various bottles, tea boxes, and other food and family items, and the lighting is kept soft and low.

Once everything is cooked, the sauce is brought to the table in the pot in which it was cooked, and the pasta is served in a big ceramic bowl, part of the spaghetti set. There is a plate in front of everyone. Almost immediately everyone helps themselves, though Oliver puts the spaghetti in the children's bowls, especially since the toddler, who sits in a high chair, cannot reach very far. The salad is served in a large plastic bowl, but no additional salad bowls are used—everyone eats directly from the salad bowl, which is only the parents actually. There is also a freshly opened chunk of Parmesan cheese placed on the table on a small plate with a large four-sided grater next to it, and everyone grates their own cheese. There is a lot of reaching for the cheese but little passing; there are no (austere) table manners, neither observed nor implied, and none have been taught to the children. The only serving is done by Oliver not because of hierarchy but because of convenience, and the passing is only of the cheese and grater. It is difficult to see how much the manners would change if the occasion was more formal, but the assumption is that these would only superficially change, with perhaps more thank-yous and more polite, contained manners. But at this very dinner—which, according to both Nina and Oliver, is how they usually eat—there is no order or hierarchy; everyone eats when and as much as they want, which for both children means very little. The daughter is done in 5 minutes. She mainly picks at the food and then, without asking to be excused, leaves the table and disappears upstairs, while the toddler doesn't linger much longer either. Within 15 minutes it is only the parents left at the table. The atmosphere is exceptionally informal, and there are no taboo topics—mostly, the daily events around school, kindergarten, work, and family are discussed without any particular order or attention.

Interestingly enough, there are no drinks during the meal, not even tap water, and it is only after the kids have left that Oliver gets up to bring soda, an herbal Austrian drink, of a generic supermarket brand. Ordinary water tumblers are used. The drinks are served after the meal so that the children avoid having them, because, Oliver says, the drinks are high in sugar and not good for them, but they do not want to bring any attention to this in front of them. During the rest of the meal, which goes on for another 10 minutes, Oliver gets up and already starts clearing the table while Nina is still seated eating. She decided that she will have some more salad later on in the evening and tells Oliver to take it away. He does some small chores in the kitchen, goes to his study for a while, and then comes back and sits down. They continue talking for another half hour, while one or the other occasionally gets up to clear a remaining plate or napkin from the table. The table is not cleaned in any particular way. The leftovers are simply put aside to be had later on or the day after. About 20 minutes after the meal, Oliver rummages in the cupboards, unwraps an already open milk chocolate bar (big 300-gram supermarket brand), and eats a few pieces. He doesn't offer any to Nina, who in the meantime has gotten her iron supplement and, after stirring some into a tall glass of water, sips it through a straw while sitting down and chatting away. Oliver, in the meantime, has started eating blanched almonds with a spoon, directly from the bag. It almost appears as if there is a metadinner taking place, a less structured but a more focused and intimate one whereby the relationship between man and woman and the comfort of familiar food is stripped of social expectations and norms, all the while remaining entirely and even charmingly human.

Dinner is done, and tomorrow, regardless of what the day throws at every one of them, in the evening they will all come together around the table, where Nina will treat them to yet another cooked meal with the hope that years from now even if they don't remember exactly what they had to eat that very night, they will remember that they had it together, as a family.

Quick Spaghetti Bolognese

Serves 4 people

⅔ pound minced beef   olive oil
⅔ pound spaghetti (spelt)   salt and pepper to taste
1 jar of sugo (tomato sauce) with herbs

1. Start by heating some olive oil in which to fry/sauté the minced beef. Cook for about 20 minutes or until the meat is cooked.
2. Add the sugo sauce, stir in, season to taste, cook for another 5 minutes, and remove from heat.
3. Serve over spaghetti, already cooked in salted boiling water.

FURTHER READING

Anderson, L. C. *Breaking Bread: Recipes and Stories from Immigrant Kitchens.* Berkeley: University of California Press, 2010.

Davis, G. *Fanni's Viennese Kitchen: Austrian Recipes and Immigrant Stories.* Milwaukee, WI: October 7th Studio, 2014.

Halkier, Bente. "Suitable Cooking: Performances and Positionings in Cooking Practices among Danish Women." *Food, Culture & Society* 12(3) (2009): 357–377.

Visser, M. *The Rituals of Dinner: The Origins, Evolution, Eccentricities, and Meaning of Table Manners.* Toronto: HarperCollins, 1991.

Belgium

Charlotte De Backer

The people in the photo in this entry are a typical young Belgian family having a meal on an average weekday. Charlotte surprised them on an ordinary day at the end of the workweek with a visit around dinnertime to see what they were eating and how. This way, she was able to get an accurate glimpse of daily life and week-day meals in Belgium.

The family in this picture consists of Sofie, Tom, Emma, and Victor. Sofie is a good friend of Charlotte's and a magnificent cook. She and Tom care a lot about healthy foods, home cooking, and knowing where the food on their plate comes from. They grow some vegetables and herbs in their city garden. During the weekends they often help out at local farms, together with their kids, Emma and Victor. This way, the children learn where food comes from at an early age. Both Emma and Victor are fond of food too. They are picky, which is not unusual at their young age, but have learned to give all foods a try and only judge after having taken a bite. This family represents a well-educated young family from a higher-than-average social class, liv-ing in the city. Their eating habits may well represent the eating habits of single par-ents and lower-social-class families as well, as many people in Belgium have always cared about healthy food and home cooking and increasingly do today. The fact that they live in the city does set them apart from families living in the countryside. Both groups of people cook and care about food, but in the past decades the awareness about sustainable food consumption has grown among city people and not so much among people living in the countryside. The latter also tend to stick more closely to a classical Belgian meal consisting of meat, vegetables, and potatoes, while city peo-ple tend to be more adventurous in their food choices, partly due to the fact that they also live together with people from diverse cultural backgrounds.

As can be seen from the picture, this family is having stir-fried vegetables with noodles today. When Charlotte asks Sofie for the recipe, she looks confused, as this meal does not come with a recipe other than "I just tossed together all the leftover vegetables from our weekly vegetable package with some curry, coconut milk, and cooked noodles."

To understand what Sofie is talking about, we will decipher their meal and any other average meal on a typical weekday in Belgium today. We will start with the plan-ning and cooking, turn to the consumption of the food along with all the social activities surrounding a meal in Belgium, and finish with the cleaning of the table.

A Belgian family of four enjoys a meal scrambled together from vegetable leftovers. It is important to them to prepare fresh meals from scratch, even after a full day of work and school. Dishes are placed centrally on the table, and foods are shared. The children take the lead in serving everyone. (Courtesy of Charlotte De Backer)

PLANNING AND COOKING A SIMPLE WEEKLY FAMILY DINNER IN BELGIUM TODAY

Cooking a meal from scratch on a weekday is no exception in Belgium. Although time spent on cooking a meal has declined, cooking is still strongly embedded in Belgians' daily rituals today (Daniels et al., 2012). It is a tradition that young people inherit from their parents and grandparents (De Backer, 2013). It is not an easy task for many, given the fact that most families consist of either two working parents or a single working parent. Most people work full-time or at least four days per week. An average workday ends between 5:00 p.m. and 7:00 p.m., and most people still need to commute 30 minutes to 1 hour before they arrive home. Consequently, having a family dinner with all members may not be a daily option for everyone, yet still an average Belgian family takes the effort to make this happen at least three to four days a week. It may be a daunting task, especially for those who do their grocery shopping on a daily basis. However, many people in this country aim to concentrate their grocery shopping on Saturday. Saturday is the busiest day for food shopping, and this is partly due to the fact that supermarkets close between 7:00 and 8:00 p.m. on weekdays, and smaller food shops even close at 6:00 p.m. And all shops are closed on Sunday except for some smaller local stores, night shops, and local food markets. Food markets in Belgium are usually very small, with a couple of dozen of stalls. When they are bigger, they include a lot of

Cookbooks

Most people around the world for most of history never needed a cookbook or recipes. They learned to cook directly from family members. There were manuscript cookbooks in ancient and medieval times, but they were largely written for professionals as an aid to memory. The book as a means of teaching cooking was invented with printing, and the first printed cookbook appeared in the 1470s (Platina's *On Honest Pleasure*). From that time to now, people, increasingly literate, have used cookbooks to explore new recipes, ingredients, and techniques and expand their culinary horizons. The digital age may change all that, as interactive forms of education will help people learn through seeing, hearing, and experiencing instruction rather than receiving it via the written word. Today we are in a transitional period, and cookbooks are still among the most viable sectors of the publishing industry, but that may change in the future.

nonfood stalls as well. Food markets may be organized on weekdays or weekend days. In general they are not at all comparable to the farmers' markets in the United States, where food can be bought straight from the food producers. In Belgium, food traders in between the production and consumption process occupy food markets. It more or less ends up in an open-air space where small shops open up their business temporarily. They are popular among older generations but do not attract a lot of young people except when genuine farmers' markets are being organized, which only happens a few times a year, when local producers come to promote their produce in a small organic market in town. On these exceptional occasions, young families fill the scene and hope that these markets will become embedded in a weekly tradition some day. Up until now, most young families plan their weekly groceries on Saturday, and supermarkets become very busy. Alternatives to the weekly trip to these overcrowded supermarkets are on the rise and include online shopping, weekly fruit and/or vegetable bags, and home-delivered ready-to-cook packages. Online shopping can nowadays be done at most supermarkets. You place your order online, and a day or more later your groceries are ready to be picked up—a convenient solution at a small extra cost. Observing the people lining to pick up these groceries in the past few months, Charlotte noticed that it is a man's task. Young children, eager to help load the groceries into the trunk of the car, often accompany their dad.

Next, increasingly people opt for weekly fruit and/or vegetable bags, the equivalent of what in the United States is called a community-supported agriculture box. These can be collected once a week at a central pick-up spot, and often families open up their garage once a week to become a collection point for people in their neighborhood. These bags are most often part of a food co-op system whereby local producers are merged together. Therefore, the fruits and vegetables bought via this system are local and seasonal, which also motivates many young families in Belgium today to opt for this. The family portrayed in this picture makes use of this system. Every week they collect a bag of fruits and a bag of vegetables from a collection point near their house. The food co-op they are part of also offers extra foods that can be ordered online: cheeses, bread, and some meat. Using this system, Sofie and Tom can save a lot of time on shopping for fresh produce. As with most of these systems, they cannot choose their weekly fruits and vegetables, but what they will receive is announced on the food co-op's website a few days in advance. Moreover, the benefit of this system for Sofie and Tom, and many other families, is that it relieves them from the weekly and daily burden of planning a meal. By opting for these packages, someone else plans which foods will be served on the table in the upcoming days. Often these food co-ops will hand out some recipes, so families only need to follow the instructions to cook a fresh meal based on fresh produce. Very comparable to this system and taking it even one step further are companies that deliver packages of ingredients for cooking dinners. These packages may or may not include meat and can be ordered for one person up to a family of five or more for only a few days a week or every day of the week. There are many options, and whatever you choose, your package is home-delivered on an evening during the week. The number of companies offering this service is rapidly increasing, and even though it comes at an extra cost, these boxes are becoming very popular. Many of Charlotte's friends and colleagues opt for this system, and all laud the fact that they no longer need to waste time thinking and planning what to serve and are being freed from the weekly trip to the overcrowded supermarket. In addition, these boxes offer healthy balanced meals, and many customers even lose some weight or at least feel healthier when switching to this system.

Incidentally, the stir-fried meal from this picture is vegetarian. This family does eat meat but not on a daily basis. Cutting down on meat to become flexitarian or vegetarian is heavily promoted in Belgium, and one of the campaigns promotes "Meatless Thursdays," asking people not to eat any meat on Thursday. Several schools engage in this project, and families pick up on it too. In practice, people schedule vegetarian meals on different days of the week. Sofie admits that it often happens toward the end of the week, to cook up any leftovers from the vegetable package. Stir-fried meals or quiches then become a quick solution to avoid leftovers. The ready-to-cook boxes also tend to schedule vegetarian meals toward the end of the week because of practical reasons: fresh fish and meat in Belgium only last for a few days and can best be consumed early on in the week when the box is delivered.

The meal in this picture was prepared by Sofie. It is not uncommon in Belgium today for women to take the lead in everyday cooking practices (Daniels et al., 2012; De Backer, 2013). Men cook too not only on special occasions but on weekdays as well, but this still seems an exception rather than a general rule. In some families men do all the cooking, but again these are the exceptions. In an average Belgian family, women still do most of the daily cooking.

"AAN TAFEL!" ("TO THE TABLE!"): DECIPHERING THE FAMILY HAVING A MEAL TOGETHER

In this picture, the children and parents eat together at a dinner table in the kitchen. Having dinner at a dinner table is standard in Belgium. Eating in front of the television is an exception to this rule, and most families will have their children seated at the dinner table until they have finished their plate and been excused from the table. As a result, children sometimes eat faster to be able to have time to watch television or play video games, and in some families children even seem to skip meals to have time for media consumption, but these are exceptions (Van den Bulck and Eggermont, 2006; Custers and Van den Bulck, 2010). Generally, and especially in families with children who can stay up later than 8:00 p.m., the sound of "Aan tafel," which can be translated as "Dinner is ready," being shouted through the house announces the start of an almost daily ritual: the family being seated around the dinner table together.

Parents and children are seated around the table together in this picture. As mentioned earlier, this is a daunting task to achieve if both parents work and often work late. Therefore, this may not happen every day of the week, but most families try to make this happen most days of the week (Mestdag and Vandeweyer, 2005; Mestdag and Glorieux, 2009). In Belgium, the time spent at the table together has declined in past decades from about an hour to about half an hour (Mestdag and Glorieux, 2009). Then again, half an hour a day is sufficient for families to catch up on what happened that day. It used to be the case that people ate in silence, as our grandparents can still recall. Nowadays, however, family meals are moments to talk about what happened at school or at work and to exchange other information that needs to be shared with the entire family. Of course, these family conversations might as well take place during other activities, but no other activity enlightens a conversations as much as a meal. It is part of Belgium's tradition that having a meal is about so much more than the intake of your calories. Having a meal stands for being in good company, having a good conversation and a good laugh as well. Mealtimes are very much still the social glue in Belgium today, both at home and at the office.

When this picture was taken, the meal was used as an opportunity to teach the children about food practices in different cultures. The meal could broadly be labeled as "Asian," and the children were given chopsticks to eat like Asian people. Emma was quite keen about this, although Victor was not convinced about the "unpractical" utensils and quickly grabbed a fork again. They both knew that in Asia food sharing is a common practice, and they explained to Charlotte how people sometimes even eat out of one bowl, which they demonstrated with great enthusiasm. The scenery soon became quite hectic, with the children picking food out of the bowl and each other's plates, but Sofie and Tom did not mind. This way they playfully learn something and eat their vegetables too, they joked. Moreover, it is also typical for a Belgian meal that all food is placed centrally on the table, and portions are served. It is not necessarily the cook who needs to serve the food. In this family everyone serves everyone. There is only one rule: you never serve only yourself but always serve other people first. This food-sharing practice is part of a typical Belgian food culture whereby dishes are shared with multiple family members. "Eten wat de pot schaft," which can be translated as "Eat what is being served," is an expression that signifies a typical Belgian dinner. A person eats what is being served, whether he or she likes it or not. The person who prepared the meal invested a lot of time, energy, and caring into preparing the dinner, and by eating the foods, one expresses gratitude for all this effort. Moreover, by sharing food people are primed into thinking about fairness, equal portions, who is being served first, and so on. And Belgian young adults who report that they often consumed food this way as children tend to score higher on a self-report altruism scale compared to young adults who said they didn't often eat this way as children (De Backer et al., 2015). The latter, of course, implies that not all families in Belgium share home-cooked meals on a frequent basis. True, there are exceptions. People eat out or opt for convenient ready-made meals to be consumed at home in Belgium (Daniels et al., 2014). One of the benefits of eating out or ordering ready-made meals is that families can cater to individual preferences: a salad for mom, macaroni and cheese for the kids, and a steak with fries for dad—all are possible. It would be crazy to try to prepare all these different meals to cater to the individual preferences of each family member. And still, some Belgians do seem to be that crazy. Some parents do prepare different home-cooked dishes for their children. These so-called children's meals can range from simply being some bread with fillings (sweet or savory) to warm meals liked by children, such as macaroni with ham and cheese or other popular pasta dishes. Most families who eat this way include one of the parents working late, so children are served at an earlier hour than their parents. One of the parents will cook a very simple meal for the children around 6:00 p.m., and together the couple will cook a different meal for themselves when the children are asleep. Another common option in families with young children in Belgium is that the parent who gets home first will eat some leftover foods from the day before with the children and cook a fresh meal when the children are asleep. This is how Sofie's family survived the first years with their kids, finding a way to be able to make fresh home-cooked meals that could be served at different times of the evening.

In this picture everyone is drinking water. Water is a healthy choice for the children, and the Belgian government promotes having water with food. Soft drinks are kept for special occasions or when having a drink outside the house. Adults drink water with their food as well, but most will also have some wine or beer. The choice for wine or beer often depends on what is being served. Fish is traditionally accompanied by white wine, most other dishes are accompanied by red wine, and only a few dishes are served with beer traditionally. However, serving beer with food is on the rise in Belgium. It has a strong and long-standing tradition of being a beer-brewing country, where hundreds of different beers are found. Yet until recently, beer was served in bars, at parties, as an appetizer, or at other occasions in between meals.

People had snacks with beer, but it was not that common to serve beer with a main dish. This changed when a few well-known Belgian chefs started to serve beer with their menu, and beer-food pairings became trendy. This is a smart choice, because with all the beers being produced in our small country, the options for pairings are plenty. Among the easiest beer-food pairings are dishes made with beer, which have traditionally always been served with beer. Recently voted the most typical Belgian dish, best liked by most Belgians today, is *stoverij,* which can be translated as "Belgian stew." The recipe is below, but be careful in selecting the beer: good-quality Belgian beer is a necessity; if you trade it for a cheaper beer, the recipe will fail.

NEVER TAKE AWAY A BELGIAN'S PLATE TOO SOON: CLEANING AND LEFTOVERS

When people have finished their meal in Belgium, they often sit around the table for a while with dirty plates and dishes still in front of them. Moreover, Belgians feel appalled if their plate is taken away too early. Taking away the plates is equal to taking away part of the pleasure. With your plate still in front of you, enjoying the aftertaste and the good conversation is as important as having the meal. Then, when do you take away the plates? It is hard to answer this question; one needs to feel when the moment has come. Often this happens when the conversation becomes less lively, when the glasses and bottles are getting empty, or when the time has come to serve the next part of the meal. While it used to be the mother or the host who did all or most of the clearing back in the old days, nowadays the entire family helps to clear the table. Parents and children will put dirty dishes in the dishwasher or the sink and help clean everything.

On special occasions a dessert will automatically follow the dinner, but even on weekdays families might have a small sweet snack at the end of the meal. Sofie's cabinet is always filled with some good-quality Belgian chocolate. A small sweet treat at the end of the meal is also used to make sure the children will finish their plate or at least have tried everything that was on their plate. The adults might have a cup of coffee or some alcohol with this final treat to celebrate the end of the meal and the start of the rest of the evening.

Stoverij (Belgian Stew)

For +/– 4 people

2.2 pounds beef, cut into pieces

2 onions, sliced into rings

Salt and freshly ground black pepper, to taste

¼ cup flour

1–3 bay leaves

+/– 2 cups good-quality dark brown Belgian beer (e.g., Leffe, Orval, Westmalle)

Slice of brown bread with strong mustard

2 tablespoons dark brown sugar (or replace the slice of bread with 2

slices of gingerbread, the Belgian *peperkoek*)

Butter to bake

1. Season beef with salt and pepper in a bowl; add flour and toss to coat. A quick and easy trick from my grandmother: throw everything in a clean plastic bag and shake well.
2. Cook the beef in butter, and do this in small batches; the meat needs to be crisp and brown on the outside and may still be raw on the inside.
3. In a Dutch oven or large cast-iron pan, cook the onions in butter very slowly so they do not burn.
4. Add the meat to the onion, and add the bay leaves.
5. Pour the beer over the meat so that all the meat is covered with beer.
6. Put the bread and mustard on top.
7. Bring to a boil and then simmer for 2–3 hours without a lid, stirring occasionally.

Serve either with boiled potatoes and freshly made applesauce or with home-cooked fries and a salad.

FURTHER READING

Books

Scholliers, P. *Food Culture in Belgium.* Santa Barbara, CA: Greenwood, 2009.

Van Waerebeek, R., and M. Robbins. *Everybody Eats Well in Belgium Cookbook.* New York: Workman Publishing, 1996.

Articles on Cooking Habits in Belgium

Daniels, S., I. Glorieux, J. Minnen, and T. P. van Tienoven. "More Than Preparing a Meal? Concerning the Meanings of Home Cooking." *Appetite* 58(3) (2012): 1050–1056.

Daniels, S., I. Glorieux, J. Minnen, T. P. van Tienoven, and D. Weenas. "Convenience on the Menu? A Typological Conceptualization of Family Food Expenditures and Food-Related Time Patterns." *Social Science Research* 51 (2015): 205–218.

Articles on Family Meals in Belgium

De Backer, C. J. "Family Meal Traditions: Comparing Reported Childhood Food Habits to Current Food Habits among University Students." *Appetite* 69 (2013): 64–70.

De Backer, C. J., M. L. Fisher, K. Poels, and K. Ponnet. "'Our' Food versus 'My' Food: Investigating the Relation between Childhood Shared Food Practices and Adult Prosocial Behavior in Belgium." *Appetite* 84 (2015): 54–60.

Mestdag, I., and I. Glorieux. "Change and Stability in Commensality Patterns: A Comparative Analysis of Belgian Time-Use Data from 1966, 1999 and 2004." *Sociological Review* 57(4) (2009): 703–726.

Mestdag, I., and J. Vandeweyer. "Where Has Family Time Gone? In Search of Joint Family Activities and the Role of the Family Meal in 1966 and 1999." *Journal of Family History* 30(3) (2005): 304–323.

Articles on Media Interfering with Meals in Belgium

Custers, K., and J. Van den Bulck. "Television Viewing, Computer Game Play and Book Reading during Meals Are Predictors of Meal Skipping in a Cross-Sectional Sample of 12-, 14-and 16-Year-Olds." *Public Health Nutrition* 13(4) (2010): 537–543.

Van den Bulck, J., and S. Eggermont. "Media Use as a Reason for Meal Skipping and Fast Eating in Secondary School Children." *Journal of Human Nutrition and Dietetics* 19(2) (2006): 91–100.

Brazil

Scott Barton

A FAMILY DINNER WITH AYRSON HERÁCLITO, JOCEVAL "VAL" SANTOS, AND TIAGO SANT'ANA

While Scott was visiting Salvador da Bahia de Todos os Santos, Brazil, his local friends, Ayrson and his husband Val, invited him to dinner in their home. Both Ayrson and Val are in their 40s. Ayrson is a nationally acknowledged fine artist, curator, university art professor, and Candomblé practitioner. Val is a Pai de Santo or Candomblé priest and is on staff at the federal university. They have been together for about 15 years. For many years they have shared their home with another dear friend and artist, Tiago, who is in his mid-20s and is a photographer, art curator, and researcher for graduate-level academic standards for the National Ministry of Education.

Cost-of-living economics are difficult in Brazil. Rising monetary inflation has been a major factor in the last few years. Prices are at their worst in urban areas. Therefore, traditional nuclear families, blended families, adult children living with their parents or blood relations, and nontraditional family units are all common (Globo, 2014; Sinterp, 2014).

The evening's dinner was only one course and was somewhat atypical for a Bahian meal, which usually centers around rice, beans, some form of manioc, small amounts of animal protein, vegetables/salad, and often another carbohydrate (Hamilton, 2005; Wilks and Barbosa, 2012). Ayrson prepared an Asian-style stir-fry that, although not part of the standard regional repertoire, did reflect a Bahian culinary sensibility. Strong Afro-Brazilian culinary traditions and technical methodology predominate in this state and throughout most of the northeast (Vianna, 1955, 1979; Cascudo, 1977; Freyre, 1976).

Since all three men of this household work both for themselves and for an outside entity, time management with meal preparation and dining is important to all of them. Once or twice per month they tend to take time to plan and prepare a celebratory meal with multiple courses or dishes. Often the meal is geared to local popular or religious festivals. Then the menu is often planned relative to the nature of the holiday and its customary foods. Otherwise, they tend to prepare 30-minute meals; one-pot dinners; occasionally purchase street food, such as *acarajé* (black-eyed pea fritters) or pizza; make do with leftovers; or simple sauté, as in this case (Fajans, 2008; Hamilton and Hamilton, 2007).

A creative family of Brazilian men relax after a dinner of Bahian *Carne do Sol* "Stir-Fry" Cuz-Cuz Timbale and Caju do Nordeste, an artisanal fermented soft drink. (Courtesy of Scott A. Barton)

There are some households and restaurants that update traditional dishes. Lately there has arisen a growing minority of foreign options such as sushi, pasta, pizza, and multinational quick-service establishments. While the dinner had a foreign gloss, the manner in which it was made—with local ingredients and native techniques and in deference to local tastes—reflected its Bahian rootedness. Instead of using fresh beef, *carne do sol,* a preserved beef similar to corned beef that dates back to colonial cookery, was chosen (Frade, 2012). The group drank Cajuína with dinner. Cajuína is a regional artisanal soft drink made from cashew fruit with a natural effervescence and light sweetness. Cashews grow with a soft custardy fruit attached to the nut. It can be fermented and has a slight similarity to *kombucha,* though not as fizzy (James, 2010). After dinner, beer and coffee were served.

That day and evening Val had some responsibilities at his temple and with a film project in which he was involved. Tiago was out when Scott arrived at their home. Therefore, Ayrson was the designated chef for the meal. While he was cooking, Ayrson offered a snack of boiled peanuts that he had purchased at the open-air market where he had shopped for dinner. Throughout Salvador, particularly in the city center and in working-class neighborhoods, there were several markets frequently with outdoor stalls for selling produce, fruit, regional prepared products, and fish. Meat is frequently purchased from butcher shops. Several of the local markets and their stalls became a hub anchoring activities and traffic flow for various neighborhoods, causing this shopping method to be quite commonplace (Ickes, 2013).

Farmers' Markets

Although there have always been markets for produce around the world, the idea of a farmers' market is a little different. The implication, though not always the reality, is that the produce is grown locally and sold by the person who grew it or the employees of that person. This ensures that the profit doesn't go to retailers or middlemen. Interestingly, these markets have also become social occasions, complete with music and entertainment. Shoppers go as much to meet people as they do to buy food. Farmers' markets have expanded exponentially across the United States, often opening in urban areas where fresh produce might be otherwise difficult to obtain.

Alternatively, Walmart has built a national chain of American-style supermarkets named Bom Preço (Good Prices). Perini is a smaller upscale local chain for gourmet regional, predominantly Iberian, products and some Central European products. In the past several years a few health food stores have begun to crop up on the local landscape in middle- to upper-middle-class districts of the city.

Ayrson is quite deft in the kitchen. This apparently comes from both his teaching from his mother and grandmother growing up, sacred culinary training as a Candomblé practitioner, and his aesthetics and skill as a practicing artist. To prepare himself and his work area, he had set out a variety of small bowls to contain his *mise en place,* those partially prepared or measured ingredients for his recipe. Everything was neatly arranged to organize his work and facilitate the procedural steps of cooking. Their kitchen is quite large, containing a small dining table and several long countertops. The surfaces were either of ceramic tile or stone, the norm for the tropics where molds and bacteria could easily grow if consistent cleaning and scrubbing were left undone. A large pile of large institutional stockpots, *gamelas* (wooden bowls), and serving dishes were stacked in the far corner of the room. These items were used for their large parties and for the preparation and serving of religious meals and offerings that Val often prepared for his temple. Between the stove and the sink they have a lazy Susan that holds olive oil, vinegar, salt, pepper, hot sauce, a head of garlic, a lime or two, an onion, a piece of ginger, and a few types of chili peppers. In the kitchen and at the stove Ayrson's work style was neat, orderly, and precise.

SERVING AND EATING

Although the meat was preserved with salt and there was also soy sauce in the recipe, the preparation did not taste saltier than it would have in an average Chinese restaurant. Ayrson decided to plate each of the dinners to add a flourish and bit of formality to the meal. This allowed him to equally portion out the food and reserve a plate in the kitchen for Tiago, who had not yet come home, in anticipation of his return. Home-based meals were the norm for most people, particularly for dinner. Local foods are relatively reasonably priced, yet the overall rising cost of living and the familial nature of local commensal habitus fostered shared family meals. Tiago arrived halfway through the meal, collecting his plate and joining the group at the table.

Ayrson indicated that he and Val tended to cook individually or collectively, sharing the food preparation and cleaning tasks. Tiago also helped but in a more ancillary role. Both Ayrson and Val are quite adept in the kitchen and are deeply grounded in the local regional cuisine. They seemed to have achieved an equitable balance in the division of labor and planning around their three respective working lives and responsibilities.

While drinking and eating habits vary from house to house, there are certain commonalities. Many Brazilians do not drink tap water. They have a two-chambered terra-cotta water filter, or in some circumstances they have a water cooler. Many people drink bottled soda, usually purchased in two-liter bottles. These soft drinks are often American standard brands, frequently in diet versions, although similar local options exist for less money. The most popular local soft drink is *guaraná,* a very sweet soda based on the highly caffeinated seeds of an Amazonian viny plant. If soda is not offered, fresh fruit juices generally sweetened with sugar and diluted with water, cheap local beer, and coffee, iced or hot, are the norms. Thus, the luxury of the 480-milliliter bottle of Cajuína was a treat either for a Sunday meal or for company.

TABLEWARE AND DESIGN

Since these men all have an affiliation or direct relationship to both Afro-Brazilian secular and sacred culture and the fine arts/design fields, their home decor and the material culture therein is reflective of the synthesis of folkloric traditions and modern design. In their home it is just as common to be served from industrially produced unglazed terra-cotta, either artisanal handmade wooden *gamelas* or ceramic *alguidás* bowls/dishes, as it is to see a modern-style manufactured plate. Locally, in addition to a history of handmade utilitarian ceramics, there are several styles of simple lines of inexpensive everyday china, silver, and glassware that are geared to commercial use, working-class, and marginally employed or alternative consumers (Querino, 1928).

Within the native Bahian culture, there are some foods that are served and eaten as handheld snacks or do not require utensils, such as *acarajé* and *beiju* (manioc flour crepes). Some people, often those who identify as black and are over 50 years of age, will often prefer to eat with their hands. In this case any soupy or broth-based preparations are served with *mingau,* a manioc porridge created from the broth, thickened by the addition of *farinha* (toasted manioc flour) or *farofa* (a seasoned version of *farinha*). The stew can be shaped into a ball and relatively gracefully consumed out of the hand. Otherwise, standard utensils are set at all tables. Meat is often not trimmed of gristle, silver skin or fat to the degree that it is trimmed in United States. Poultry tends to run free, yielding a flavorful and some-times stringy product. Therefore, toothpicks and inconspicuous teeth cleaning at the table occur in almost every home and in restaurants (Cascudo, 1977; IPHAN, 2005; Vianna, 1955).

Local table decor frequently reflects the folkloric lace-making handicraft traditions within the state and the larger northeastern region. Many homes of varying incomes use either lace tablecloths or runners to adorn dining tables. As Scott, the visitor, prepared to set the table, he was told that there was a runner that he could lay out on the table. Since the group was not initially sure if they would truly all eat together (in Tiago's absence), they elected to leave the stone tabletop free of embellishments. Napkins were made from folded paper towels. At larger, more festive meals, cloth napkins are often used. The only other table decoration was a tall water pitcher that had been filled with local greens and a few cut flowers.

Simple, utilitarian glass globe wineglasses were placed on the table for drinking. In addition, there was one inexpensive white mass-market ceramic bowl to serve the stir-fry from, tropical-themed bamboo and stainless cutlery, and four hip rec-tangular white ceramic plates. The medium-sized bowl was the only serving plate on the table. Chopsticks were also an option since the meal itself was Asian, but the group opted to use the cutlery. All of these objects used to serve and eat the meal were utilitarian and quotidian.

The one tool that clearly reflected regional gastronomy was the *cuscuzeira* for cooking the rice. In Bahia a version of couscous (*cus-cuz*) was made as a savory accompaniment from coarsely ground cornmeal or as a sweet dessert from tapioca, coconut, and sugar. In this instance, a bain-marie was used to steam the rice. The main dish was cooked in an aluminum sauté pan that mimicked a wok in shape. To serve the rice, it was tightly packed into one of the small bowls and inverted as a half-sphere of rice onto each of the square plates. When the group sat down, the stir-fry was equally divided between the four plates.

COMPORTMENT

Although this was somewhat of a casual dinner, the act of plating the food and having the Cajuína served in a stemmed wineglass added a level of pomp to the meal. Val had telephoned with his estimated arrival time during the food prepara-tion period, thus anchoring the dinner hour. When he came home the two men greeted each other with a kiss and an embrace and shared brief accounts of their respective days. Val washed up and changed quickly into more comfortable cloth-ing for dinner. Ayrson smoked a cigarette while waiting. Once the group sat down to eat, a brief blessing in a manner consistent with Candomblé worship was made to ancestral spirits, ending with the Yoruba synecdoche *ajeum* (concurrently, "food, eat, sustenance").

Baianos are rife with local customs and superstitions. One of the most common is that when leaving someone's home as an invited guest, you must not touch or open the door(s) to leave the house. If you do, the implication is that you will never return again. Thus, the act of being served and cared for within someone's home is quite prevalent. Because Scott is the guest tonight, most everything is done for him. Simple tasks that could be easily managed—making one's plate, obtaining or filling a glass—are generally completed for the guest as a gesture of hospitality (Vianna, 1979; Souto Maior, 1988).

Midway through the meal Ayrson's cell phone rang. He answered it, briefly excusing himself from the table. He let the caller know that he was eating and agreed to call later on. The dinner was full of good humor and laughter. The conversations ranged from Val's current independent film project as an actor to *terreiro* (the ceremonial shed where rituals are performed) and Candomblé temple affairs to Ayrson's final exhibition opening for the recent Bahian art biennial, *Bienal da Bahia: É Tudo Nordeste*. He explained that whereas the bulk of the show had been hung in town between galleries, community centers, and public spaces, this final exhibition was in Cachoeira, the former colonial center of sugarcane and tobacco plantation agriculture. The show's themes reflected this connection to colonialism and slavery. Ayrson had a singular focus as a curator on this phase of the larger project. All other exhibits had been defined by a hierarchal collaborative structure built on consensus. By the time Tiago had arrived, the conversation had moved on to the recent visit of Lamidi Olayiwola Adeyemi III, the *alaafin* (emperor) of the Oyo state in southwestern Nigeria. This had been the first dignitary of West African royal extraction to visit Bahia. The visit had a great deal of cultural significance vis-à-vis economic incentives and politicking that affected the local national and religious communities.

When Tiago came in, he washed up and changed his clothing before sitting down. He ate some of his food, got up, and paced in front of the window. The other two men used this interlude to share a cigarette. It was lit at the table. In courtesy to the diners, it was immediately carried away to the large bay window that looked down the hillside to the multilane pretzel of streets and traffic below. They took turns leaving the table to smoke a bit, passing it between themselves as they moved from one side of the room to the other. On a table/desk along one wall in the middle of the room opposite a small sofa was a disc player/radio. It was silent throughout the meal.

The layout of the physical living/dining areas was a large, open rectangular room with no partitions. The front door opened onto this space in the southern corner of the room, with the doorway to the kitchen along the same wall at the opposite corner. The large window dominated the wall on the other side of the room. There was a clear view of A Fonte Nova, the recently rebuilt stadium and entertainment venue that hosted the local World Cup soccer competition. Ayrson's sculpture, photography, and paintings as well as some work of colleagues/friends and numerous folkloric objects reflecting regional culture, Afro-Brazilian identity, and Candomblé religious practice accented the room. The floor was simple, made of worn wooden parquet. The walls were alternately painted red or orange, and the ceiling seemed to be 12 feet in height.

Once Tiago finished eating, he went into his room for a brief period. The sharing of the cigarette seemed indicative to how this couple shared the household chores in an egalitarian manner. The two collectively decide what the menu will be for shared meals and who will shop, cook, and clean up. Tonight, Val cleared the dishes from the table and began to wash things in the kitchen. Tiago worked on straightening the dining area. There was no dishwasher. Ayrson returned the phone call he had received earlier. He then offered coffee and beer. He and Scott chose coffee, and the others split a liter bottle of beer. The group returned to the table to consume these beverages. Now that no one was eating, smoking was allowed at the table.

In homes where there are women, gender tends to define the cooking and cleaning roles in these settings. Often an older woman will work alongside a teen or young woman, apparently imparting knowledge and obtaining help for those tasks that require greater stamina, agility, or energy. In Candomblé culture, while there are hierarchies in the kitchen and a designated chef, usually a woman, there is a fairly egalitarian division of labor that can expose both men and women to the daily culinary workload, with certain tasks skewed by gender. The exposure of a shared work ethic in the sacred environment and the quality of the relationships that exist among these three men created a harmonious dynamic in the kitchen and at the table (Moura 2004; Lima 2003).

A Brazilian feast of Bahian Carne do Sol "Stir-Fry" Cuz-Cuz Timbale. (Courtesy of Scott A. Barton)

Carne do Sol Stir-Fry

For 4 people

3 tablespoons virgin olive oil

1 tablespoon diced ginger

1 clove of garlic, sliced

2 *pimentas de cheiro,* thinly sliced (Trinidad aromatic peppers are an equivalent. These very fragrant chilies are cousins to habaneros without their bite.)

¾ pound Carne do sol, cut into thin strips across the grain

1 large onion, thinly sliced

1 large carrot, peeled and sliced into ¼-inch rounds

1 large green bell pepper, seeded and thinly sliced

1 medium *aboborinha* squash, washed and sliced into half moons (you can substitute zucchini)

3 ripe tomatoes (about ½ pound) washed and coarsely chopped

3 scallions, thinly sliced; separate the white from the green portions

3 tablespoons soy sauce

Juice of 1 lime

2 cups short grain rice, sorted, rinsed, and steamed or boiled, then tossed with:

3 tablespoons soy sauce

3 tablespoons toasted sesame seeds

1. Heat a large sauté pan, skillet, or wok over medium-high heat.
2. Add the oil, and then add the ginger, garlic, and *pimentas de cheiro.* Cook, stirring until fragrant without browning.
3. Increase the heat and add the beef. Cook, stirring rapidly until just browned.
4. Add the onion, peppers, and white of the scallions. Cook for about 3 minutes, stirring until the onions have softened and are translucent yet not limp.
5. Add the chopped tomatoes and soy sauce. Cook, stirring until the tomato juices nearly evaporate, allowing the liquid to reduce and coat the vegetable-meat mixture.
6. Remove from the heat, add lime juice, taste, and adjust seasoning. Serve with steamed seasoned rice.

FURTHER READING

Cascudo, Luis C. *Antologia da alimentção no Brasil.* Rio de Janeiro: LTC, 1977.

Dawson, Allan Charles. "Food and Spirits: Religion, Gender, and Identity in the 'African' Cuisine of Northeast Brazil." *African and Black Diaspora: An International Journal* 5(2) (2012): 243–263.

Fajans, Jane. 2008. "Can Moqueca Just Be Fish Stew?" *Anthropology of Food,* Special Issues (2008): S4, http://aof.revues.org/3623.

Flavors of Brazil, http://flavorsofbrazil.blogspot.com/2010/03/cajuina-northeastern-brazils -own-soft.html

Frade, Pedro. "As diferenças entre carne de sol, charque, e carne seca." Petit Gastro: Gastronomia de Primeira, May 27, 2012, Available at: http://www.petitgastro.com.br/as-diferencas-entre-carne-de-sol-charque-e-carne-seca/.

Freyre, Gilberto. *Manifesto regionalista.* Recife: Ministério da Educação e Cultura, Instittuo Joaquim Nabuco de Pesquisas Sociais, 1976.

Hamilton, Cherie Y. *Brazil: A Culinary Journey.* New York: Hippocrene Books, 2005.

Hamilton, R. G., and C. Y. Hamilton. "Caruru and Calulu, Etymologically and Sociogastronomically." *Callaloo* 30(1) (July 2007): 338–342.

Ickes, Scott. *African Brazilian Culture and Regional Identity in Bahia, Brazil.* Gainesville: University Press of Florida, 2013.

IPHAN. Ofício das Baianas de Acarajé: Bens Registrado, 2005, http://portal.iphan.gov.br/bcrE/pages/indexE.jsf#.

Lima, Vivaldo da Costa. *A família de santo nos candomblés jejes-nago s da Bahia: Um estudo de relaço es intragrupais.* Salvador: Corrupio, 2003.

Moura, Carlos Eugênio Marcondes de. "*Culto aos Orixás: Voduns e ancestrais nas religiões afrobrasileiras.*" Rio de Janeiro: Pallas, 2004.

"Preço da cesta básica sobe nas 18 capitais pesquisadas durante 2013." Jornal da Globo, September 1, 2014, http://g1.globo.com/jornal-da-globo/noticia/2014/01/preco-da-cesta-basica-sobe-nas-18-capitais-pesquisadas-durante-2013.html.

Querino, Manuel, R. *A arte culinaria na baia: Breves apontamentos.* Bahia: Papelaria Brasileira, 1928.

Sinterp. *Custo da Cesta Básica em Salvador segue em queda.* Sinterp: Bahia, 2014.

Souto Maior, Mário. *Alimentaça o e folclore.* Rio de Janeiro: Funarte, Instituto Nacional do Folclore, 1988.

Vianna, Hildegardes. *A Bahia já foi assim (crônicas de costumes).* São Paulo; Edições GRD, 1979.

Vianna, Hildegardes. *A cozinha bahiana: Seu folclore, suas receitas.* Bahia: Fundação Gonçalo Moniz, 1955.

Wilk, Richard R., and Lívia Barbosa. *Rice and Beans: A Unique Dish in a Hundred Places.* London: Berg, 2012.

Canada

Judy Corser

Arlene, age 67, a retired social worker, moved from Canada's East Coast to Vancouver, British Columbia, on Canada's west coast eight years ago to be near her daughter and her family. Arlene bought a three-story duplex in the city's vibrant Commercial Drive area and lives alone, renting out her lower level to vacationers to supplement her income.

The Drive, as it is affectionately known, is still lined with mom-and-pop shops, some of which have been there since the 1960s, including coffee roasters, pasta makers, Italian bakeries and cheese shops, a Polish butcher and charcuterie maker, a food co-operative, various vegetarian bakeries and cafés, greengrocers, and many ethnic restaurants from Salvadorean to Ethiopian to Algerian to Vietnamese,

Arlene's large "family," composed of friends and relations, including two, sometimes three, children and a dog, meets every Sunday at her house for a sit-down family dinner. As Arlene says, "It's a chance to have everyone assembled around the table at least once a week. It's something for the kids to remember." (Courtesy of Julia E. Dykstra)

reflecting Vancouver's multiethnic population. Locals are proud that there are 25 coffee shops in a 12-block stretch, and until recently, the neighborhood has resisted chains moving in. Today, there are 2: a Tim Hortons and a Starbucks.

The Drive residents, formerly mainly artists, musicians, and students along with a core population of Italians and Portuguese, were drawn to the working-class neighborhood because of its relative cheapness and abundance of large houses broken up into rental suites and rooms. Commercial Drive was once home to industrialists and merchants whose fine old multistory frame houses overlooked the port and industrial area on Burrard Inlet, to the north, while their workers' houses were built on the lower ground, nearer the tracks that run through to the western terminus of the Canadian Pacific Railway in the center of Vancouver.

Today, many of those earlier residents can no longer afford the higher rents and gentrification brought about by the general trendiness of the area in the past decade, much of it pressure from better-off West Side residents selling their houses and moving to The Drive for the ambience. There are homeless folks, and the area has its share of drug users and petty criminals, but The Drive seems to embrace even these residents as part of their eclectic world. As one woman, who often buys a panhandler a burger and fries at Vera's, says, "Yes, we have bums, but they are OUR bums." The Polish butcher regularly hands out sliced meat from his refrigerator case to those who come in and say they are hungry.

Arlene, an only child, was raised by her mother after her parents divorced when she was 11, and she was strongly motivated to institute family food customs with her own family, her daughter, son-in-law, and their two young children and her son, who lives in a nearby city. She began having regular Sunday dinners. Her "family" expanded to people she or her daughter had met in, say, a theater lineup or an extension college class or even the left-behind girlfriends or boyfriends of acquaintances after the relationships broke up.

Arlene met Victor, from Brazil, in a theater lineup. He and his partner, Robert, born in Singapore, became regular weekly dinner guests, and when Victor got a job traveling throughout Asia, Robert continued coming to Arlene's for dinner. Victor attends when he is in town. They are now godparents to Arlene's granddaughter.

Vanessa, age 27, is a relation, somewhat—she is the daughter of Arlene's ex-husband and his second wife. Vanessa brings her boyfriend Marcus, age 26, to the weekly dinners. Both Vanessa and Marcus are recent university graduates and are currently unemployed. Occasionally Vanessa's nephew, age 2, her brother's son, comes to dinner with Vanessa just to give his single mom some time to herself.

These details illustrate the kind of diversity that is often seen at Canadian dinner tables. Canada is a country of immigrants along with First Nations people, and there are many, many "typical" dinner tables throughout the country. It is as "Canadian" for a Dutch-background young woman and her brother to get together regularly with their divorced father, pick up Indian takeout, and sit in the living room watching a hockey game, eating *naan* bread and butter chicken out of cartons as it is for, say, a traveling salesman in a small Manitoba town to stop in at a

---

Dining Tables

It is hard to imagine, but dining tables are a fairly recent invention, as is a separate space for dining itself. In the past people might eat at an all-purpose worktable with benches, or the wealthy might set up a board on trestles in the main hall, a private room, or even outside, weather permitting. It was only in the 19th century that it became common to have a separate space devoted solely to meals. Interestingly, with the growing informality of American meals and living space, another separate breakfast nook or eating space adjacent to the kitchen replaced the formal dining space for most meals and even informal dinners. For many people around the world, there simply isn't enough space for a separate dining table or room devoted to eating, so the couch or another makeshift arrangement in the living room suffices. Actually, of all rooms in the home, the dining room is probably the easiest to dispense with when space is limited.

---

local hardware store around noon—often called "dinnertime" in rural areas—and be taken home and invited to pull up a chair at the family meal. With long distances between towns and villages and a still-living rural memory, Canadian families were always prepared for an extra unexpected guest for a meal.

Today, the small nephew is not present. However, Arlene's daughter Caroline, age 42, a real estate agent, and her husband John, age 44, a lawyer, are present along with their children, Ruby, age 6, and Oliver, age 9. The 1950s-style mahogany table, a secondhand find, can sit 10 or 12 with three extensible leaves, but today Arlene has left one extension out: she is expecting 8. A regular, George, has called to say he is unwell and cannot come.

"I really do this to have everyone around the table," says Arlene, providing a little background to her regular Sunday dinners. "It's a gift to Caroline, who does all the cooking at her house; it's a break for her. And it's a chance to have everyone assembled around the table at least once a week. It's something for the kids to remember."

Robert, who lives about a mile away, drives to Arlene's house. Everyone else walks, as they all live in the neighborhood.

Arlene does all the shopping, preparing, and cooking, usually the Friday or Saturday beforehand. Except for this meal she rarely cooks for herself, relying on prepared and frozen food that can be easily heated in a toaster oven or microwave. Robert always brings dessert with the exception of today, as it is his birthday, and Caroline will bring a cake, purchased at a big-box supermarket, Great Canadian Superstore, a division of Loblaw Foods.

"I listen to CBC Radio while I prepare the meal," Arlene says. "It's just me and Michael Enright [a Sunday morning radio talk show host]. I am not a good cook. I don't really enjoy it. I am good at following a recipe, but I hate confusion, and in my kitchen people stand around and talk to me while I am cooking, which I hate. So I make sure I have everything ready ahead of time, and there is no last-minute preparation beyond putting dressing on the salad and cooking the rice."

Today Arlene has made a recipe from a Canadian cookbook, a simplified Moroccan recipe, Charmoula Chicken (Baird 2011, 115), adapted to the Crockpot (the brand name of a heavy ceramic pot inside a metal casing, heated by an electric element) and now simmering away on a counter in her kitchen. The salad—"I always make a big green salad with lots of things in it"—is in a large serving bowl in the refrigerator, covered with plastic wrap. On the stove waiting to be steamed are prepared sugar snap peas, topped and tailed. Arlene will put on a half-half mixture of brown rice and a blend of wild rice and quinoa to cook when people arrive. She expects everyone by 6:00 p.m.

Wild rice (*Zizania palustris*) is a Canadian Great Lakes plant, not a true rice but a member of the grass family that has a long heritage with First Nations people in Ontario, Manitoba, and Saskatchewan. It also grows in U.S. states south of the border (Wisconsin, Minnesota, and Michigan). Quinoa, of course, is the cereal of the moment everywhere, it seems.

"We eat chicken quite often. Everyone loves meatloaf, and when it's someone's birthday, they get to choose the meal. George always chooses meatloaf." Next week when Victor returns from his business travels in Thailand, they will have ham and scalloped potatoes. Arlene has a recipe for the scalloped potatoes (layered sliced raw potatoes interspersed with sliced onions and a white sauce, similar to *pommes de terre à la Lyonnaise,* sometimes topped with cheese and frequently served with ham) that is a slow-cooker version. And the ham, which she mentions several times? "It is because it is a *roast*," she explains. "A roast is special, and that's why we are having it, because Victor will be here, and he's been away for a long time."

The first person to arrive usually sets the table. Caroline and her daughter Ruby arrive at 5:40 p.m., and Caroline pours herself a glass of wine from the bottle on the kitchen island and sits in the living room to talk to her mother. Vanessa and her boyfriend arrive five minutes later and immediately start laying out place mats, a set of hand-sewn, fish-shaped colorful cotton mats purchased at an artisan shop in Halifax, Nova Scotia, on one of Arlene's twice-annual trips to the east coast. Ruby helps. She puts special place mats on the table for her and her brother, large plasticized paper drawings done by the children when they were younger. Plates are laid out at each chair, and cutlery is added—fork, knife, and spoon. Vanessa and Marcus are clearly very comfortable with this task and know where everything is. They follow a routine. "We have two sets, pink and mauve cloth napkins, for every meal except for Christmas, Easter and Thanksgiving," Arlene says. "Then we have a white tablecloth and white napkins."

Arlene rinses the rice under the tap in a sieve and places it, along with sufficient water, in a pot on the stove. At the last minute, she adds a half cup extra of brown rice and sets a timer. "I always worry there won't be enough food. Leftovers are great, but I want enough food on the table so people get as much as they want." No salt? "No, I never do. I think we eat too much salt. There is salt on the table if anyone wants it." Arlene doesn't eat white rice. She doesn't think it is nutritious, and besides, she heard somewhere that there was arsenic residue in it. Arlene seems concerned about food safety and health. She recently learned from an American friend how to cook turkey and gravy a day ahead of Christmas or Thanksgiving (in Canada, Thanksgiving is a harvest celebration and is the second Sunday of October). "It's too stressful cooking it the same day," she says. "A turkey is too much work. Besides, I always worry that it won't be done and will kill us all, or it will be overdone and end up jerky." (Jerky is dried salt-preserved raw beef or bison, thinly sliced and chewy. It dates back to the prairies in pioneer days and was an old-time outdoorsman staple food.)

Although Arlene has poured herself a glass of red wine earlier, she does not mention wine or appetizers as people arrive. "I pour out the first glass and put it on the counter for people to take if they wish," Arlene explains. "And that's that. If anyone wants more, they help themselves. I don't pour. I cook; I don't serve. I don't do cleanup either. George usually does that, but he's not here today, so someone else will." The dishes, when they are cleared from the table later, will go into the dishwasher with the exception of her $10 Riedel glasses. "Last time someone put them in the dishwasher, I lost $20 worth of glasses!" The wine on her counter—two bottles (she usually provides one) are both red. One is an Okanagan merlot (the Okanagan is a wine-producing valley in the interior of British Columbia) with the hockey legend "Wayne Gretzky" label, and the other a merlot-syrah blend from the Barossa region of Australia. They used to have "appies" (appetizers) but dropped the habit, as the children gorged and then weren't hungry for their dinner. Although the children are older now, the practice was never reinstated.

The wine is from Canada and Australia. The sugar snap peas are from Mexico. The Texas brown rice has been purchased in bulk. The chicken is from Costco, a big-box store; the *tzatziki* (Greek cucumber-yogurt sauce) was purchased; and the quinoa–wild rice is a prepackaged blend. "At this time of year, I buy the vegetables at the store," Arlene says. "In the summer I go to the Trout Lake farmers' market, and whatever looks good, that's what we eat. I buy meat usually at the organic beef store on The Drive." The butcher is a family-run retail outlet for the family's ranch at 100 Mile House in the interior of British Columbia and sells beef, pork, and lamb. Organic meat is more expensive and is a special treat for the family dinners. The farmers' market is about 15 blocks away and closes in the winter.

By now the rest of the family has arrived, John and Oliver along with their dog, Nola, and Robert, age 55, a software engineer. Nola quickly checks out the floor for scraps. When the 2-year-old is included, there is always plenty of dropped food near his chair. "That's what dogs do," Arlene says approvingly, observing Nola sniffing around the floor. "She's just doing her job."

People greet each other warmly, remove their shoes at the door, and hang up their own coats in the hall closet. Arlene busies herself with putting the rice into a serving bowl, the chicken into another serving bowl, and the sauce in a pitcher on the side. There is a bowl of *tzatziki* sauce, and the salad comes out of the fridge and is carefully dressed with some special olive oil and grapefruit-flavored *balsamico* from Halifax. (*Balsamico* is a northern Italian product made since the Middle Ages from Trebbiano and Lambrusca grapes in Modena and Reggio Emilia. Many flavored so-called balsamic vinegars are produced in North America.) Arlene pours oil over the green salad—which is laden with sunflower seeds, dried cranberries, pieces of orange, and toasted almonds—followed by the balsamic vinegar. Salt and pepper are left to the diners to add on their own, to taste.

Dishes of food are placed in the middle of the table, with several people helping to carry the dishes. Robert puts glasses of ice water at each place. Everyone gets their own beverage, some taking wine to the table with them; Vanessa takes a can of San Pellegrino *limonata*. The two children have plastic glasses. As everyone comes to the table, little Ruby calls out, as she usually does, to everyone's amusement, "Places, please!"

Arlene sits at the head of the table, with her daughter Caroline opposite. Vanessa and Marcus face each other at one end, and John and Robert face each other at the other end, with a child in the middle on each side. Oliver's plate is the same as the adults', while Ruby has a luncheon-size plate. She gets up and down several times over the course of the meal to play with toys in the living room or to disappear upstairs for a few moments but always returns, unremarked, and finishes her meal in relays. "We used to insist that the children stay at the table," Arlene says, "John, especially, being English. But we just realized it was easier not to fuss, and in the end it all works out. Oliver sits and listens and even adds his own comments from time to time. He gets the adult humor now, at nine; Ruby doesn't." (There is acknowledgment that allowances should be made for John's background, English, which may include stricter manners at the table.)

By 6:20 p.m., the meal is under way. Conversation is wide-ranging: someone has been to a fine-dining restaurant lately and reports on that experience, they discuss Robert's birthday, and Oliver talks about playing soccer with some friends that morning. "We don't discuss politics or religion," Arlene says. Too divisive? "No, because we all agree!"

Vanessa asks if the meal is chicken; she says she can't tolerate any spices except cinnamon and especially can't eat fennel or caraway. Arlene assures her the chicken is not spicy at all. John, perhaps with a more English palate, gets up and retrieves hot chili sauce from the fridge, which he spoons out onto his plate, as does Robert, who grew up in Singapore. The chili jar remains on the table.

John checks his cell phone, somewhat shielded by the edge of the table. Marcus half-stands to reach something on the other side of the table, but generally the serving dishes are passed hand to hand and people serve themselves, casually and unconsciously. Vanessa dishes up food for Ruby. As Oliver dislikes cucumber, his father picks it out of the boy's salad and puts it on his own plate. There are compliments to the cook, and Arlene reiterates that she is not much of a cook but can follow a recipe. (Such modesty is commonly seen among Canadian women regarding their cooking skills, particularly among former generations.) The slow cooker is extolled as a time-saver in the kitchen, and Caroline says that she buys cheap cuts of meat at Supervalu (a supermarket chain) to put in her slow cooker in the morning, along with some vegetables "so we come home at the end of the day to a nice meal." John, Oliver, and Marcus (who is from Ontario) all eat English style, that is, with a knife in the right hand and a fork in the left hand, tines down, holding the utensils throughout the meal. The rest all eat Canadian or North American style, only using the knife (in the right hand) to cut food and then resting the knife on the edge of the plate and transferring the fork to the right hand, tines up, to eat. Ruby uses a fork sometimes and her fingers other times.

Conversation continues and includes discussion of hiking equipment, a family trip to the country, backpacks for dogs available at a local store, battery-operated camping cookers, and a Chinese dance performance someone had seen that week. Robert takes second helpings of rice, chicken, and sauce; Marcus has seconds and then thirds of salad; and Vanessa helps herself to seconds of sugar snap peas. When they are finished, knives and forks are set across the plate, parallel, to indicate that the meal is over. Marcus begins to clear the plates, helped by Oliver. Marcus shows the boy how to scrape the debris into the garbage and load the plates in the dishwasher. Vanessa helps. While the table is cleared, Caroline shares some cat videos on her cell phone with Robert, both of whom remain seated.

Arlene refrigerates leftover food in covered containers and makes up a plate for the absent George. The plate is piled high with chicken, rice, sauce (no vegetables, as Arlene says that George doesn't care for vegetables), and plenty of the dessert—birthday cake and Nanaimo bars (see recipe) left from last week's dinner. Caroline volunteers to take the meal to George on her way home.

The family returns to the table for dessert—Robert's birthday cake, a sort of flower-shaped cake made from chocolate cupcakes. Ruby has put six candles on the cake with Arlene's help, who counts "Un, deux, trois, . . ." She is in grade one in French immersion school (Canada has two official languages, French and English). Oliver hands Robert a clownlike hat to put on, and everyone sings a humorous version of "Happy Birthday" accompanied by a birthday card with a musical insert that plays Handel's "Halleluljah Chorus" when opened. Although the extended family do not practice any religious rituals at table (such as saying grace or asking a blessing, still a habit with a minority of Canadian families, particularly older generations), they do have their own traditions and rituals: a stylized birthday song and hat as well as a musical card accompaniment used for every birthday; special place mats for the children; established positions at the table, with whoever has a birthday choosing the menu; special food—a roast—to mark a special event; and different table linens used for ordinary meals and for celebration meals.

At 7:20 p.m., Vanessa begins to clear the dessert plates. Robert removes the remaining glasses and cutlery and puts them in the dishwasher. Arlene's prized Riedel wineglasses are taken to the counter near the sink, to be washed later by hand. Robert stacks the place mats neatly, placing the soiled napkins on top. Arlene will later take them up to the second-floor laundry.

By 7:45 p.m. everyone has left, Marcus taking home the remaining salad in a plastic disposable container. Arlene wipes the table again and replaces the everyday cloth runner and table decorations. The weekly Sunday dinner is over.

A Moroccan-style "Chicken Charmoula," green salad, steamed sugar snap peas, and a wild rice-quinoa mixture are served on fish-shaped cloth placemats made in Halifax, Nova Scotia. (Courtesy of Julia E. Dykstra)

Nanaimo Bars

Generally thought to be Canadian because of the name, this dessert ("bar" or "square" in most of Canada, "slice" in Maritime Eastern Canada and the United States) was supposedly included in care packages from Britain to coal miners in Nanaimo, British Columbia. It doesn't seem a very likely story but is one of the legends behind the origin of the squares. The Bird's Custard Powder is definitely a British link, as the custard powder was developed by the Birmingham chemist (druggist) Alfred Bird in 1837 for his wife, as she could not tolerate eggs. It was one of the first industrial food products and is still sold today. Fry's Cocoa, a Cadbury brand, is also originally a British product.

½ cup butter or margarine

¼ cup sugar

1 egg

½ teaspoon vanilla

5 tablespoons Fry's cocoa powder

2 cups graham wafer crumbs

1 cup flaked coconut

½ cup chopped nuts

¼ cup butter

3 tablespoons canned milk

2 tablespoons Bird's Custard Powder

2 cups sifted confectioner's sugar

4 squares semisweet chocolate

1 tablespoon butter

1. Combine ½ cup butter or margarine, sugar, egg, vanilla, and Fry's cocoa powder in the top of double boiler and cook, stirring, over boiling water until the consistency of custard.
2. Add graham wafer crumbs, flaked coconut, and chopped nuts and blend well.
3. Spread in 9-inch square pan and press down firmly. Refrigerate.
4. Cream ¼ cup butter, canned milk, Bird's Custard Powder, and sifted confectioner's sugar and spread the mixture in the pan on top of the refrigerated coconut-cocoa layer.
5. Melt semisweet chocolate, add 1 tablespoon butter, and spread over the custard layer.
6. Refrigerate. Makes 16 squares.

FURTHER READING

Baird, Elizabeth, et al. *Canadian Living: The Slow Cooker Collection*. Toronto: Transcontinental Books, 2011.

Benoit, Mme. Jehane. *Madame Benoit Cooks at Home*. Toronto: McGraw-Hill Ryerson, 1978.

Cooke, Nathalie, ed. *What's to Eat? Entrees in Canadian Food History*. Montreal: McGill-Queen's University Press, 2009.

Cuizine: The Journal of Canadian Food Cultures/Revue des cultures, www.cuizine.mcgill.ca.

Kirkby, Mary-Anne. *Secrets of a Hutterite Kitchen*. Toronto: Penguin Canada Books, 2014.

Nightingale, Marie. *Out of Old Nova Scotia Kitchens*. Toronto: Pagurian, 1971.

Pattinson, Nellie Lyle. *Canadian Cook Book*. Revised by Helen Wattie and Elinor Donaldson Whyte. Toronto: McGraw-Hill Ryerson, 1977.

Schultz, Judy, and Mary Bailey. *The Food Lover's Trail Guide to Alberta*. Calgary: Brindle and Glass Publishing, 2003.

Staebler, Edna. *Food That Really Schmecks*. Toronto: McGraw-Hill Ryerson, 1968.

Stewart, Anita. *Canada: The Food, the Recipes, the Stories*. Toronto: HarperCollins Canada, 2008.

Traill, Catherine Parr. *Female Emigrant's Guide and Hints on Canadian Housekeeping*. Toronto: Maclear and Company, 1854.

Chile

Sally M. Baho

Dishes and dining customs tell the story of this unique, fertile nation that was once a Spanish colony. The cuisine and eating habits of Chile are a reflection of the society that, like much of the New World, is a melting pot of Old World immigrants and indigenous peoples. Corn is a staple along with beef, after cattle raising was introduced and popularized by the Spanish. Viticulture flourishes, thanks to the European influence; in fact, the vast majority of originally French Carménère grapes are grown in Chile.

The photo depicted in this entry is that of a midday weekend meal eaten in Santiago, Chile, and prepared by a young lady, Esmerelda, and her grandmother. It is common for children to live with their parents until they get married or move out of the area for work or school. Extended family, such as grandparents and siblings, live nearby and get together on the weekends for a long, slow, multicourse meal. In this particular household, the eldest daughter Esmerelda has an affinity

A Chilean family sits in the dining room to eat their main meal, a late lunch, with a starter of *pastel de choclo*. (Courtesy of Sally M. Baho)

for cooking and regularly makes meals for the family when she is not studying (she is a graduate student). However, on a daily basis the mother prepares meals, and due to her dislike of food preparation and self-proclaimed inability to cook, meals are often simple: pasta with store-bought sauce, canned soup, bakery-bought empanadas, etc. This is an accurate representation of Chilean families. Although in some households the husband cooks, it is still common to find the women doing the meal preparation.

Every weekend Esmeralda makes lunch for her family, which she learned from her grandmother while living with her while Esmeralda was at university. Esma, as she is called, is the eldest of three children, and being a military family they were stationed outside of Santiago, so when she was ready to start university the logical thing to do was go live in the city at her grandmother's house. Esmerelda loves to cook and bake and does so at every opportunity, on weekends and for holidays and birthdays—a common trend among young women, a resurgence of cooking and/or maintaining the culture of cooking after their mothers abandoned the kitchen for the workplace just a couple of decades ago.

Friday evening is generally shopping night. Shopping lists are made over *onces* ("elevensies" or high tea) on the balcony overlooking the garden. *Onces,* a staple in Chilean culture, is the coffee or tea taken in the early evening along with some crackers and cheese, cookies, pastries, ice cream, or any other small snack to get you through to dinner. The word *once* means "eleven" and stands for the 11 letters in the word "*aguardiente*" (distilled liquor) and is said to come from the time when Chile was a Spanish colony and the Chileans didn't want the Spanish to know they were having a drink in the afternoon.

Athos, the family golden retriever, lies under the table calmed by the soft murmur of mother and daughter sharing stories of the workweek—the intolerable graduate school advisor and the unreasonable manager. Coffee and cookies rejuvenate the tired-from-the-workweek minds and bodies before the ladies drive down the street to the Lider, part of the multinational chain Walmart. Zigzagging in and out of the 20 food isles, Esma and mama do the shopping for the weekend and the week to come: butter, frozen corn, bread, various cuts of various meats, tomatoes, green onions, Coca-Cola, wine, milk, and cheese.

Esma and mama spend time in the kitchen with a bottle of chilled late-harvest Chilean wine as they prepare the *pastel de choclo* (see recipe) for lunch the following day with the family. Esmeralda diced the onions as Frank Sinatra sang from her laptop computer; because her mother detests cooking and never really learned how to do it, she watches as her daughter skillfully prepares the meals passed down from her grandmother, reading off handwritten recipes organized in a three-ring binder.

A good amount of time was spent in the kitchen but over phases. The main course was prepared the night prior and baked for consumption as the *aperitivo* (apertif) was being consumed. The salmon ceviche was made in the morning and allowed to sit and "cook" in the lemon juice until guests (family members) arrived. Ceviche is a raw fish dish that is allowed to sit in lemon juice; the citric acid is said to "cook" (or break down the protein of the fish like heat would). The dessert was made in the morning, grandmother serving as the chef's right-hand helper and giving tips as necessary: "No, the syrup is not quite done yet. Put it back on the stove." Electrical kitchen appliances were used to prepare this meal—a food processor to grind the corn and eggbeaters for the egg whites required in the dessert. A standard gas range was used in the meal preparation, with the accompaniment of an electric water boiler when hot water was needed for the soaking of the sultanas (raisins) or dried peaches.

An *aperitivo* is usually served before eating lunch or dinner with friends and family in the salon or in warmer seasons on the balcony or terrace. Common *aperitivos* include kir royals (champagne or sparkling wine with a splash of crème de cassis) or pisco sours (a drink whose origins are passionately disputed between Peru and Chile). Peanuts, crackers, ceviche, and *jamón* (dry-cured ham) are common accompaniments to the *aperitivo*. Alternatively, a popular first course is empanada, a savory stuffed pastry that can be purchased at any bakery or supermarket or made at home. Main courses, depending on the season, are meat dishes served with cooked vegetables or noodles with tomato sauce; fish is also commonly consumed, as Chile enjoys a vast Pacific coastline. Chile is a country with a diverse geography and climate. In the north is San Pedro de Atacama, the world's most arid desert; consequently, food eaten in the north is complementary to the weather patterns and climate. A great deal of fruit is consumed—mangos, guava, and passion fruit. In fact, the best lemons in the world are said to come from Pica, an oasis town in the desert. The south of Chile is much colder and very windy; *caldos* (stews) are commonly consumed in the south and in the wintertime throughout the whole country.

The dining table is set in advance, typically by someone other than the cook; in this case, mama set the table, as daughter did the cooking, with grandma as her sous-chef. After a leisurely *aperitivo*, everyone is invited to the dining room where the table is set; the hand-embroidered table runner and crystal centerpieces have been removed and replaced with a plastic table covering and a gold-embossed tablecloth. The main course is preplated in the featured meal, the *pastel de choclo*, in its clay bowls and set on top of the weekend china. Standard steel flatware is used, and paper napkins are readily available on the table. *Buen provecho* (enjoy your meal) is announced by the first person who is ready to eat before he or she starts consuming the meal. A simple Chilean salad consisting of tomatoes, onion, olive oil, and salt can be found on most dining tables accompanying lunch, along with a breadbasket of white rolls, generally flat unleavened bread. Depending on the meal, *pebre* is also found on the dining table. *Pebre* is a condiment made of cilantro, onions, olive oil, garlic, and aji peppers. It is usually eaten with bread, but many people add it to their soups for flavor and spice.

Old Spanish love songs played softly in the background as stories were shared of last summer's vacation when mama was intolerable or the time grandma was able to do the whole hike. And then there was that one time when cousin Juan fell while trying to cross the bridge. Chilean culture is casual; everyone sits down to the meal at the same time and eats together. In most families there is no order for who eats first, although in more traditional families the father might be served first. Conversation is fun and light, reminiscing of times past, sharing stories about the week, and planning for the future. Although the meals are taken at home, everyone is dressed. The younger generations will typically wear modern attire (jeans and T-shirts), while the middle-aged and older-generation family members are dressed more formally, the women in dresses or matching tweed suits, their hair done and faces made up. The same trend is found with men. The younger men, in their teens and twenties, typically wear jeans and T-shirts, while the men in their thirties and older can be found wearing khaki-type pants, button-up shirts, polo shirts, and sweaters. Cell phones are not typically brought to the table, as that would be impolite. Wine is the most common beverage consumed with lunch; Chile produces a great deal of wines—from their unique Carménère to cabernet sauvignons, red blends, whites, and *espumantes* (sparkling wine). Coca-Cola is consumed by children or those who do not wish to drink wine. Chile has a zero-tolerance drinking and driving law, and people generally respect it. Furthermore, many government jobs have policies that include job termination if a person is found driving under the influence of alcohol. When children wish to leave the table, they excuse themselves and return to their television watching, video game playing, book reading, etc., while the adults remain at the table for the *sobremesa,* the time spent leisurely after a meal sitting around the table and talking. Oftentimes *bajativos* (digestive drinks) are served, such as herb liquors or, during the Christmas season, *cola de mono,* a sweet, spiced coffee-and-milk liquor.

Dining habits in Chile vary by season to accommodate weather patterns and preference, not because of food availability. Chile is engaged in huge international trade. Being in the Southern Hemisphere, its winter crops are exported to the Northern Hemisphere and vice versa—strawberries are found year-round, as are berries and lemons. In the summer a common snack is *mote con huesillo*, which can be made at home and is sold at supermarkets and from refrigerated carts by street

Leaving the Table

Once it was considered very impolite to leave the table before everyone was finished or even to clear away a plate until everyone was done. Today it seems that children cannot be expected to hang around while their elders continue their conversation or linger over coffee or drinks. For adults the rules are different, especially if there's company; it would be rude for one person to walk away. Within families on an ordinary weekday, this is becoming less of a rule, especially as everyone tends to be distracted by texting, social media, and portable games anyway.

vendors. The dish is a dehydrated peach, cooked in sugar, water, and cinnamon and allowed to cool; a peach in its cooled sauce is then served over cooked wheat in a cup or bowl with a spoon and is a very cooling snack in the hot summer months. Year-round, people sell sopaipillas on the street, an unleavened fried dough made of a mixture of wheat and corn flours.

During the workweek (Monday–Friday) these typical dishes are commonly consumed, but meals are taken at a restaurant or in one's place of work, which is normal in the city. It is common to find restaurants, pubs, and bars advertising the menu of the day, with a salad, main course, and dessert for a fixed price. In the suburbs and in small towns and villages, it is more common for people to go home for lunch, or if they live far from their place of work, meals are provided by employers or taken at restaurants.

Leftovers are saved in the refrigerator and eaten later in the day for *onces* or for dinner. If what is left over can be used as part of a meal, it is exploited that way. For example, a common soup is made from leftover barbeque meat and is said to be great to cure hangovers. Although Chile is a predominately Catholic nation, Catholic practices are not reflected in the dining habits. Most Chileans claim to be observers of Catholicism rather than active practitioners of the religion, and the religion does not affect their dining customs.

The melting pot of Chilean culture can be seen in various dining customs of society. A big wave of German immigrants came to Chile in the early 20th century, and the German influence is apparent in the beer culture; for example, one of the most common Chilean national beers is Kunstmann. Also, merkén is a popular spice; it is a smoked chili pepper used to season meats, fish dishes, stews, etc. It is a traditional condiment used by the Mapuches, one of the indigenous groups of South America, particularly from central Chile. *Onces* is a tradition that was introduced by the Spanish colonizers and has been adapted to fit contemporary Chilean society, with deals on coffee and pastries or small sandwiches found in cafés and malls throughout the country.

In recent years due to globalization and immigration, sushi has become quite popular in Chile. Because ceviche is already a popular part of Chilean cuisine, the idea of consuming raw fish was readily accepted by Chileans. Similarly, pizza is very common, both authentic and Chilean-adapted varieties. Traditional Italian *margherita* pizzas can be found, as can pizzas with Chilean ingredients, such as *choclo* (maize). Fast-food chains are found all over Santiago serving typical fast-food fare, pancakes at Denny's, frapes at McDonald's, donuts at Dunkin' Donuts, etc.

Chilean dining habits are moving in the direction of the modern world; with most adults working outside of the home, there is little time to make multiple meals a day and eat together as a family. Increasingly, fast food and prepared foods are consumed for time-saving purposes; however, there is a movement in the younger generation to preserve their culture and learn the recipes and customs of their forefathers.

Pastel de Choclo (Corn Pie)

Makes 12 individual pies

Pino (ground beef filling)

2²/₅ pounds ground beef

6 white onions

1 tablespoon butter

½ teaspoon cumin

2 teaspoon paprika

Oregano

Black pepper

Salt

Chicken breast (or any part of the chicken)

Leaves of a celery stalk

Choclo (corn crust)

8.8 pounds of corn kernels (i.e., 8 bags of 1.1-pound frozen corn kernels or about 40 ears of corn). If using frozen corn, you will want to take the corn out of the freezer ahead of time and allow to reach room temperature or defrost in the microwave. If using full ears of corn, you will want to use a sharp knife to saw off the corn kernels from their stalk.

Sugar

Salt

Basil, optional

Other ingredients

Black olives (can be pitted or unpitted)

6 hard-boiled eggs, peeled

Sultanas, soaked in water

Turbinado sugar for topping

Equipment

12 shallow clay bowls

1. To make *pino,* the filling for the pie, finely dice the white onions.
2. Place in a medium-sized pot, pour hot water over the onions, and let boil for 1 to 2 minutes.
3. Dump out hot water and run cold water over the onions. Squeeze the excess water out of the onions, taking fistfuls of onion and squeezing well with both hands.
4. In the same pot, melt the butter and add onions. Stir well for 1 or 2 minutes, then add ground beef, spices, salt, and pepper and cook over low heat until the beef is cooked well all the way through and the onions are translucent, about 10–15 minutes.
5. In a separate pot, cover chicken with water and add celery leaves. Bring to a boil and allow to simmer until chicken is cooked all the way through. Both

pino and chicken can be prepared ahead of time and kept in the refrigerator until ready to assemble the corn pie.

6. In a food processor, blend corn well. (If using basil, add in with the corn when blending.)

7. Put the corn in a double boiler (*baño maria*) with the sugar and salt. Cook the corn slowly, stirring constantly in the double boiler for about 20 minutes.

8. To assemble *pastel de choclo*, evenly distribute *pino* in the clay bowls and add chicken, sultanas, half a hard-boiled egg, and a black olive. Ladle the corn mixture into each bowl. Top with turbinado sugar and bake until pie starts to bubble. Carefully remove from the oven and serve; contents will be extremely hot. Serve with sugar alongside, as some people like to add additional sugar on top.

FURTHER READING

Joelson, Daniel. *Tasting Chile: A Celebration of Authentic Chilean Foods and Wines.* New York: Hippocrene Books, 2005.

Waerebeek-Gonzalez, Ruth Van. *The Chilean Kitchen: Authentic, Homestyle Foods, Regional Wines and Culinary Traditions of Chile.* New York: HP Trade, 1999.

China

Willa Zhen

Gong xi fa cai! Gong hay fat choy! As friends, neighbors, and relatives visit the Zhen family apartment to *bai nian,* or greet the new year, they are welcomed with wishes of happiness and prosperity in Mandarin and Cantonese. Today the Zhen family is celebrating the Chinese New Year, starting with preparations for a Chinese New Year's Eve reunion meal.

The lunar new year is considered the most important day of the year, and family reunions occur on the eve of the event. Far-flung relatives are expected to return home and dine with their loved ones. In the past, generations of extended families lived close to one another, sometimes even sharing the same roof. Gathering together for a reunion meal was not so complicated. Today due to schooling, travel, and work demands, families can find themselves spread throughout their home

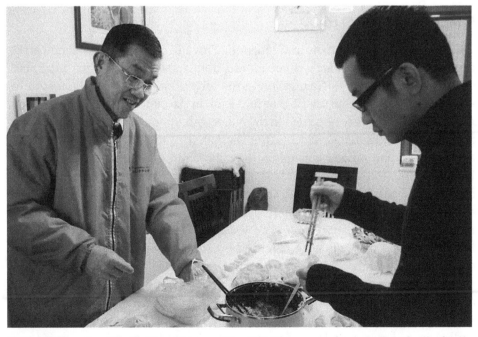

Patriarch Zhen Guo Ping (left) and his son, Zhen Zhi Cheng, prepare dumplings for the family and guests. (Courtesy of Willa Zhen)

province or across the country or even dispersed across the planet. Not all families are as fortunate as this one, which is together to celebrate.

This family reunion takes place in the home of Zhen Zhi Cheng, pictured on the right. He is a successful businessman in his early forties who works as a regional sales manager for a large international firm. This high-rise apartment, which he purchased himself a number of years ago, is located in one of the newer wealthier districts of Guangzhou (Canton), the third-largest city in China. Although relatively unadorned with art or photographs, his spacious three-bedroom home features all the trappings of the upper-middle-class urban lifestyle. New furnishings, many of them from IKEA and other Western brands, fill his home. At the center of his living room is a large flat-screen television with hookups to premium cable channels and high-speed Internet. As an unmarried professional, the only other occasional occupants in his apartment are his parents, Zhen Guo Ping and Lü, and his younger brother, Zhen Jian Cheng. Preferring the hustle and bustle of the big city to the quiet of their home in neighboring Jiangxi Province, they have returned to Guangzhou to celebrate the holidays.

At a cursory glance, this looks like a typical New Year celebration. Family members are gathered around a table wrapping dumplings, preparing food for the most important commensal event of the year, the New Year's Eve reunion dinner. Underscoring this scene are the many changes experienced by urban Chinese society during the 20th and 21st centuries, as captured in the story of the Zhen family.

FAMILY, IDENTITY, AND FOOD

The Zhen family has old roots in Guangdong Province, of which Guangzhou is the capital city. Zhen Guo Ping's father moved from rural Taishan in the provincial countryside to the city of Guangzhou in the early 20th century. As the first to be educated in his family, he was able to find a job in the city working as an accountant in a firm. Eventually he settled in the old neighborhood of Dongshan in Guangzhou, known for its many residents from Taishan. He must have felt at home there, as he married and raised his family of six children in this community. Zhen Guo Ping, born in 1941, is the oldest child. He has since taken over as the family patriarch after the passing of his father nearly a decade ago.

Though a native son, Zhen Guo Ping was forced to move away from the city because of state mandate. Under state socialism (1949–1976), matters of work, family, love, and marriage were regulated by government authorities. Like many other men and women who came of age under state socialism, Zhen Guo Ping was assigned a work unit (*danwei*) and put to work in a factory. He was sent to work in a state-owned sugar factory in Jiangxi Province, located north of Guangdong Province. Separated from his hometown and family, he established a new life. He eventually met and married a local Jiangxi woman named Lü, who bore him his two sons in the 1970s, Zhen Zhi Cheng and Zhen Jian Cheng.

Born in Jiangxi Province, Zhen Zhi Cheng was sent back to Guangzhou to be raised by his paternal grandfather in the old Zhen family home. There he lived in a rickety old southern Chinese Lingnan-style home, with living quarters located on the second floor and a balcony facing the sun. He played with neighborhood children, learned to speak Cantonese and Mandarin, and grew accustomed to local tastes and flavors. By accident of his birth he is not technically a local Cantonese, but through nurture he is every bit a *tudi* (native son) of the city.

His brother, in contrast, was raised in Jiangxi Province. He only learned to understand snippets of Cantonese through the conversations his father had with relatives back in Guangzhou. Instead, he learned to speak the local Jiangxi dialect and Mandarin and adopted the food preferences of his fellow Jiangxi brethren. The lives of the Zhen men show how place and identity have shifted in contemporary China.

Though the roots of this family are in Guangzhou, history and circumstance have spread them to different places. Their multilingual conversations in Mandarin, Cantonese, and Jiangxi dialect, much like their multiregional food preferences, reflect how much Chinese identity and rationality has evolved in the 20th and 21st centuries. Whereas Chinese families once stayed close to one another due to limited social and geographic mobility, the Zhen family has moved from the countryside to the city—from Guangdong Province to Jiangxi Province and back again. While their story does not represent every family, theirs does show the level and depth of social and economic change in China in recent decades.

THE COOKS

Zhen Guo Ping, the patriarch, cooks for his family. Having learned a thing or two during his bachelor days, he enjoys cooking for his family and feeding them. Although his wife, Lü, is a perfectly capable cook, she does less of the family cooking due to protests from her sons. Zhen Zhi Cheng especially is not a fan of her cooking, blaming her copious use of salt, soy sauce, and heavy chilies. These seasonings are typical of Jiangxi cuisine. Because he was raised in Guangzhou, the older son prefers the mild, almost bland, taste of Cantonese food, which favors natural flavors and light seasonings.

Zhen Zhi Cheng, while not much of a talent in the kitchen, cares deeply about the quality, health, and taste of his food. Following food shows on television, he is also a subscriber to *Beitai Chufang* (Betty's Kitchen), a localized adaptation of the popular Swiss cooking magazine. Aimed at urban middle-class women, this magazine highlights the latest culinary trends and is filled with home-style Chinese recipes in addition to Western recipes. Yet he only reads these magazines for inspiration and enjoyment, preferring instead to dine out. Because it is a holiday and his day off, he has joined his father in the kitchen. Today, the two of them have taken the lead in preparing the New Year meal.

PREPARING THE MEAL

Here, father and son are wrapping dumplings together, creating an unusual domestic scene. Often dumplings are wrapped by women or, in the case of a reunion dinner, in the mixed company of men and women as a commensal act. This moment capturing father and son cooking together contrasts against conventions of masculinity in China.

The old stereotype is that Chinese men do not cook. This stereotype is often related to an old saying from the philosopher Mencius (372–289 BCE), who proclaimed that "Gentlemen do not enter the kitchen." This phrase was originally used as an allegory for morality among righteous men. Slaughter, which used to take place in the kitchen, was not a place for men who wanted to maintain moral purity. This phrase has been misused to justify the absence of men in domestic cooking.

It is uncommon, although not unheard of, to find men of Zhen Guo Ping's generation in the kitchen. But for younger men such as Zhen Zhi Cheng, food and cooking are acceptable hobbies among the emerging middle and upper middle classes. Food has become a form of recreation and a way of demonstrating cultural capital and savvy.

Together, father and son have spent much of their day purchasing ingredients and preparing them for the meal. They began their morning around 9:00 a.m. by visiting the wet market for fresh ingredients. Freshly ground pork, Chinese cabbage, scallions, and ginger are purchased from individual stalls at the wet market across the street from their apartment. To save time and effort, they purchased their dumpling wrappers from Watson's Supermarket, a Western-style supermarket owned by a Hong Kong company. This breaks with tradition, as in the past families made their own wrappers with flour and water and rolled them out, one by one. Instead they choose to buy their wrappers, as making them would be "too much trouble."

After shopping to about 11:00 a.m., they set to work around the family dinner table. This dinner table is located in a great room that features a dining room, a living room, and an adjoining enclosed kitchen. The dining room is decorated simply, with clean white walls and a dark black wood dining table. The table has been covered with a cheap disposable plastic tablecloth to protect the table while wrapping dumplings.

The elder Zhen grabs a round tree-trunk cutting board and a Chinese cleaver and sets to work chopping up the vegetables into fine pieces. The vegetables are placed in a cheap plastic bowl and salted to drain out the excess water. Next, the ground pork is placed in a large yellow saucepan. Soy sauce, sugar, salt, ground ginger, scallions, sesame oil, rice wine, and white pepper are added into the mixture for seasoning, folded in with a pair of sturdy bamboo chopsticks. Finally, the vegetables are drained and added into the pork mixture.

As father and son prepare the meal, the other family members occupy themselves with other tasks. Half a dozen relatives and neighbors drift in and out of the apartment. Some have come from neighboring Jiangxi Province and, like the

Zhens, prefer to spend their holidays in the big city. Others are cousins of matri-arch Lü who have origins in Jiangxi but live in Guangzhou. All guests are offered cups of hot tea, served in disposable paper cups for ease of cleanup, by Lü or Zhen Jian Cheng, the younger son. The two of them take turns hosting the guests, offer-ing packaged cookies, fresh Chinese pears, apples and tangerines, and candy. With the diners talking animatedly, the room is abuzz with laughter and stories. The smell of woody incense, lit for good luck, fills the room. The television blasts loudly, showing broadcasts from China Central Television (CCTV), the state-owned television channel. Comedians, singers, actors, actresses, and other celebrities flicker across the screen as they perform lighthearted skits for the amusement of the millions of viewers who are tuned in at the moment.

As father and son are cooking, the guests meander to and from the table to com-ment, observe, and wrap a few dumplings. Lined up along the dining room table like soldiers waiting in formation for inspection, dumplings are scrutinized. Guests argue over which look the best: "It looks like a child made these!" "Good thing you have other talents!" "Is that supposed to be edible?" As the number of dumplings grows, Zhen Zhi Cheng keeps them covered with a moist cloth to stop them from drying out as they wait to be cooked.

Several hundred dumplings later, they are placed aside in the adjoining kitchen. Matriarch Lü rises from her seat on the soft leather couch to prepare them for boil-ing. She dons an old plastic apron and flicks on the two-burner gas stove. Two pots filled with cold tap water are set on each burner, and she waits for them to rise to a boil. She fills a bowl with a mixture of black vinegar and soy sauce, to be used as a condiment for the dumplings. Patriarch Zhen moves to the living room to social-ize with guests and reward himself with a cigarette break. Plop, plop, plop. The dumplings are placed in the bubbling vats and set to boil. Floating to the top, they are scooped out and placed into wide, shallow bowls on the counter.

While the dumplings are cooking, Zhen Jian Cheng excuses himself from his guests. As the younger brother, he has taken the child's task of setting the table. He darts between the kitchen, where the dishes and eating utensils are stored, and the adjoining dining room to grab materials. A disposable plastic tablecloth is placed on the dining table. Ceramic rice bowls, bamboo chopsticks, and ceramic soup spoons for a dozen people are set on a table built for six. The younger brother brings every last stool and chair in the apartment to the table to make room for all the diners. The smells wafting from the kitchen suggest that it is now time to eat.

CHANGING TASTES

It's nearly 1:00 in the afternoon. The hungry mass hovers around the dinner table, sitting in no particular order. Lü claims the seat closest to the kitchen, as she darts back and forth to grab bowls of hot dumplings. Boiled dumplings (*jiaozi*) are the main treat for this family feast. The *jiaozi* are placed in six ceramic serving bowls across the table, and everyone at the table digs in.

It's every diner for themselves. Each eater uses a ceramic spoon to retrieve a few dumplings, which are placed into individual rice bowls. Chopsticks are used to pick up the food, and dumplings are eaten one by one. A few of the women wait patiently for their dumplings to cool down so they don't burn their mouths. Some dip their dumplings into the premixed condiment of black vinegar and soy sauce. Zhen Jian Cheng complains about the lack of spice and retrieves a jar of chili sauce from the kitchen to liven up his dumplings.

These boiled dumplings are not typical of Jiangxi or Guangdong Province. The Cantonese prefer to eat *yau gok*, a golden fried dumpling filled with nuts and sweetmeats. Resembling gold ingots, they evoke joy and festivity. The Zhen family never adopted this tradition, blaming the mess caused by deep-frying with oil. Boiled dumplings are more typical of northern Chinese celebrations, yet the Zhens enjoy them because of their simplicity and their health content. They are certainly a hit at this celebration.

Everyone boasts about the number of dumplings they can eat, with everyone trying to best the other. "Two dozen!" "Only two dozen? I need at least three dozen to feel full!" The animated debates continue in a mixture of Cantonese, Mandarin, and the Jiangxi dialect. There is no pride in eating the smallest amount of dumplings. Bragging rights go to the victor, the one with the largest stomach, as a hearty appetite suggests prosperity and wealth. The dumplings quickly disappear.

After the meal, the younger brother again takes on the child's tasks to clear the table and bring the dirty dishes and utensils to the kitchen. Guests slink off to the sofa to watch more television and sip on tea, for digestion. Lü goes into the back room of the apartment to retrieve a mahjong table from the storage closet and sets up the table for a postmeal game in the living room. Zhen Zhi Cheng slinks off into his bedroom for a postlunch nap. Patriarch Zhen Guo Ping again returns to the kitchen to do the dishes and dry them by hand.

Chopsticks

Chopsticks are said to have been invented in the Han dynasty in China about 2,000 years ago as an expression of Confucian manners that banish all violence from the table, including sharp implements. To cut meat at the table was considered barbaric. Precut meat and vegetables are also much quicker to cook as well, using less fuel. Chopsticks developed very differently in various parts of Asia, though. Chinese chopsticks are blunt on the end, unlike Japanese chopsticks that are shorter and taper toward the end. In Korea, chopsticks are usually made of metal and are used with a long metal spoon to scoop up rice. In some parts of Asia chopsticks are not used; instead, these areas use combinations of utensils, such as the spoon and fork used in Thailand. The fork is used only to push food on the spoon, which goes into the mouth. Chopsticks are only used for noodles, which were imported from China.

Some Cantonese might balk at the traditions and eating habits of the Zhen family table. Regional identity, which extends to regional cuisine and eating habits, in China was once incredibly strong because of limited social and geographic mobility. Today what it means to be of one region, of one place, has become more fluid due to immense social change. The Zhens identify themselves as a proud Cantonese family, in addition to a proud Jiangxi family. Their multilingual and multiregional celebration of Chinese New Year reflects the many changes experienced by urban Chinese in the recent past. Though their dinner table may not be the most traditional celebration, it maintains the spirit of this holiday—of commensality, family, and hope for the coming new year.

Boiled Pork and Cabbage Dumplings

1 pound Chinese or Napa cabbage leaves, finely chopped

1 teaspoon kosher salt

1 teaspoon grated fresh ginger

¼ cup scallions, finely chopped

1 pound ground pork

⅛ teaspoon finely ground white pepper

2 tablespoons Chinese light soy sauce

1 tablespoon Chinese rice wine (Shaoxing wine)

2 teaspoons sesame oil

1 tablespoon cornstarch

½ cup water

2 packages store-bought dumpling wrappers

For serving: Chinese black vinegar (Chinkiang vinegar), chili sauce, light soy sauce

1. Finely chop the cabbage. Remove to a large bowl and sprinkle with salt. Let sit for 10 minutes while you finely chop the other vegetables.
2. After 10 minutes, grab a handful of the cabbage and squeeze out excess water into the sink. Continue until all the water is gone. Place the dry cabbage back into the large bowl and add in pork and the other vegetables. Mix well.
3. In a small bowl, mix the cornstarch and water into a slurry.
4. Gently fold all seasonings, except the slurry, into the pork mixture.
5. To wrap the dumplings, spoon a scant tablespoon of pork mixture into each wrapper. Dot the edges of the wrapper with slurry. Fold up the bottom end of the wrapper and press to shape into a half-moon.
6. Place dumplings on a baking sheet dusted with cornstarch. Keep loosely covered with plastic wrap or a damp towel. Repeat with the rest of the dumplings. Do not let the dumplings touch each other.
7. When all dumplings are wrapped, you can cook immediately or keep refrigerated for several hours. To cook, half fill a pot with water and bring to a boil.

When boiling, slide in a dozen dumplings. Let the water return to a boil, and gently cook for 6–8 minutes. Use a slotted spoon to remove the dumplings when they float to the top and repeat.

8. Serve with black vinegar and soy sauce, or add chili sauce for spice.

FURTHER READING

Anderson, E. N. *The Food of China*. New Haven, CT: Yale University Press, 1990.

Wu, David Y. H., and Chee-Beng Tan, eds. *Changing Chinese Foodways in Asia*. Hong Kong: Chinese University Press, 2001.

Denmark

Caroline Nyvang

In March 2013 Helene learned that she was pregnant, and 13 months ago their boy Lui was born. Welcoming a baby into their lives changed the couple's dinner rituals. Unless they tuck in their toddler early, Christopher, Helene, and Lui usually eat around 5:30 p.m., which is a fairly common time of the day to have dinner in Danish families.

To make room for the family extension, the family recently moved out of their small city apartment and into a roomy house on the outskirts of Copenhagen. The change of scenery also brought about a change of shopping opportunities. Whereas the city center provides a wide array of ethnic groceries, the fringes of the city have

When Helene and Christopher learned that they were having a child, they started looking for a bigger place and soon found a home to their liking. The spacious townhouse on the outskirts of Copenhagen has an open kitchen/dining area that allows the family to tend to their son while dinner is being prepared. (Courtesy of Hans Rasmus Nyvang)

more supermarkets, and Christopher and Helene now mostly shop for food within walking distance of their home. They try to shop for basic groceries once a week, most often on Saturdays. Usually taking along Lui in a backpack carrier, one parent will walk to the nearest supermarket to get staples for a whole week: breakfast cereals, fruit, milk, and coffee.

On Mondays and Tuesdays, Helene and Christopher have dinner with their neighbors. This arrangement has proved to be both cozy and time-saving, as the couples take turn cooking.

Recently, Helene and Christopher have become subscribers to a popular organic food enterprise that carries organic meal boxes. The company delivers to the doorstep once a week, and its boxes contain recipes as well as ingredients for three hot meals for two persons. As it is, this is enough to fill up the small family, and sometimes there are even leftovers that the adults can eat for lunch at work the next day.

In effect, this means that the family's weekday dinners are firmly orchestrated.

With time-consuming careers and a small child, "it's really, really nice that you do not have to worry about what's for dinner," as Helene phrases it. To Christopher, who usually takes great pleasure in the many aspects of preparing dinner, this level of planning took a bit of convincing, but he has since been persuaded by the logistical advantages of having meal kits delivered to their doorstep. Both Christopher and Helene emphasize fresh produce as a key ingredient in a proper meal. All in all, the couple seems to welcome the meal box subscription as a nice compromise between grocery shopping and takeout.

Since starting the subscription, Christopher and Helene have found that they end up throwing out less food than previously. Furthermore, they are both happy that the better part of their diet is organic. According to the couple, buying organic food is not only a healthier and greener choice but also a matter of animal welfare. From her country upbringing, Helene knows a little about raising chickens and is especially keen on buying organic and, preferably, free-range poultry.

Organic Food

In recent decades a national system of labeling has been in place designating organic food, and the market has grown significantly, especially among affluent consumers. The perception is that these foods contain fewer pesticide residues and chemical fertilizers, cannot be genetically modified, have a less negative impact on the environment than conventional agriculture, and are therefore a more healthy choice, especially when feeding one's children. In fact, there is little concrete evidence that organic food is better for health, though long-term in-depth studies may prove otherwise in the future. For the moment, organic food is as much a moral stance and a marker of status as it is a choice among several options, because the cost is prohibitive for those on a tight budget.

Although reducing food waste is environmentally and economically sound, the meal box is not per se a cheaper alternative to doing your own food shopping. By a rough estimate, Christopher and Helene currently spend 20 percent of their disposable income on foodstuffs. This brings the couple up to par with notoriously food-conscious populations such as the French, Italians, and Japanese but sets them apart from the majority of Danes, who on average spend about half as much on food. And in this respect, both Christopher and Helene see a difference compared to their own upbringing, when economic concerns would at times outweigh ecological and gastronomic considerations.

Today, the ingredients for the family dinner are a mixture of leftover meat and produce from a previous meal box. The family is having a duck stew and a spicy vinaigrette salad on the side. In recent years, casseroles have had a revival in Denmark. While the dish is certainly in tune with the current interest in slow cooking, stews have also become a popular everyday dish, with many families pressed for time. Once cooked, the one-pot meal is easy to store in the freezer or refrigerator, and the hearty dish is a quick serve. And as Christopher points out, big-batch cooking doesn't necessarily take longer than cooking one meal.

The duck stew is prepared by Christopher, easily the most epicurean of the two. He is usually the one doing the cooking, while Helene spends time playing with their young son. Preparations normally start around 4:30 p.m., around the time Lui comes home from daycare seeking parental attention. The couple has a large joint kitchen and dining room that makes it easy for the whole family to spend time together, even when one parent is busy at the stove.

Helene and Christopher have a range of kitchen appliances stored in the numerous kitchen cupboards and drawers, but they only use a few select items regularly. Among the perennial favorites is a stand mixer mostly used for kneading dough, a small hand blender for Lui's baby food, and the low-tech salad spinner that was used for tonight's salad. Otherwise, the couple relies on a handful of different knives, which they now agree on have become too dull and need to be sharpened at the butcher shop.

Since starting their meal box subscription, Helene and Christopher rarely buy any convenience food. Almost all meals are home-cooked and based on fresh ingredients. Bread is the only ready-made food item the couple regularly buys. For a while, Helene baked her own sourdough rye loafs—a staple at the Danish lunch table—but after baby Lui was born, she found that it took up too much of her meager spare time.

Lui, already in his high chair and donning a smock bib, is the first to receive a serving. He is clearly hungry and quickly grabs for the fettuccine while he impatiently watches as Helene starts to mash his portion of stew. At the kitchen counter, Christopher is piling pasta and stew onto plates for the adults. Right before bringing the plates to the table, he sprinkles each serving with parsley. Side dishes and the bowl of salad are placed in the center of the dining table so that Helene and Christopher can help themselves to salad throughout the meal.

Helene feeds the stew to Lui, while he digs into the pasta with his hands. Once his initial hunger and fussiness subside, Helene is able to move on to her own plate as her son tries to finish the meal with his own plastic spoon.

As in many other Danish homes, Christopher and Helene's dinning table doubles as a workbench and is scantily set during everyday dinners. There is no tablecloth or decoration, and plates, silverware, and glasses are usually placed at the center of the table along with salt and pepper shakers. The couple drinks carbonated water with every meal. Today—halfway through a long vacation—they will also have red wine, a less frequent indulgence since they had their son.

No overall topic seems to be taboo at the table. The couple, however, has banned phones, tablets, and computers during dinner, a mutual agreement that they both seem keen on keeping. Dinner conversations usually revolve around work, movies, radio shows, and practicalities related to Lui. And clearly their son also has a few things to air as he often chimes in, babbling away between bites.

After having been exclusively breast-fed for 6 months, Lui has slowly been introduced to solids and is now, at 13 months, trying his luck with his own plastic cutlery and plate. This sometimes means that mealtimes become playtime, and food is tossed to the floor. Christopher and Helene have not yet considered any particular table manners they would impose on their young son. But when asked directly, Helene states that she has always assumed that Lui will take part in getting food ready and setting the table once he reaches the proper age.

Ideally, the diners would stay put at the table until all have finished their meals. But after having Lui, the traditional boundaries of mealtimes have been blurred. Lui is often both hungry and tired in the evening, so he is usually given a bit to eat before the rest of his family has a chance to really sit down. Furthermore, one parent often gets Lui ready for bed while the other finishes his or her meal. Tonight, Christopher rises from the table after about 20 minutes, gives Lui a diaper change, and gets him into his pajamas. Meanwhile, Helene finishes her meal.

This, however, is not the last meal for the toddler. Right before Lui's bedtime, the parents always offer supplementary gruel to top him off. Tonight, a generous serving of stew and pasta—even if some ended up on the floor—was apparently enough for Lui, and he shows no interest in the additional serving of rice porridge.

As Helene goes upstairs to tuck Lui in, Christopher starts to clear the table and load the dishwasher. Helene and Christopher have an implicit division of labor. While one parent puts Lui to bed, the other clears the kitchen. That way when their son is finally asleep, the couple will have some time to themselves.

Food has always been an important element in Christopher and Helene's relationship. Despite both of them working full-time in academia, they have usually juggled their busy schedules to make room for a shared evening meal, even if it meant having dinner late in the evening. Furthermore, cooking has long served as a pretext for gathering friends and family in the couple's small apartment in the center of Copenhagen. Christopher is an ardent cook and likes to prepare lavish meals for his and Helene's friends.

A plate of duck stew with Fettucine, with a vinaigrette salad on the side. (Courtesy of Hans Rasmus Nyvang)

Christopher and Helene's Duck Stew with Fettuccine

(Serves 8)

2 small ducks (or equivalent amount of duck parts)

Salt and pepper

Oil

2 tablespoons flour

8 medium shallots, finely sliced

4 cloves of garlic, finely sliced

4 carrots, diced

4 stalks of celery, sliced

2 cups of red wine

3½ ounces tomato puree

2 cups of chicken stock

4–6 thyme sprigs

Fettuccine (fresh)

Parsley

1. Cut up the duck, skin it, and brown the meat in a large pot. Season with salt and pepper.
2. Add the flour along with the shallots, garlic, carrots, and celery. Let it brown for 2–3 minutes.

3. Pour in the red wine, simmer to a boil, and add the tomato puree, chicken stock, and thyme.
4. Let it slow-cook at low heat for at least 2 hours.
5. When the duck is tender, remove the meat from the bones. Skim off the fat, discard the thyme, and season with salt and pepper. Return the duck to the pot and let it simmer for an additional few minutes.
6. Cook the fettuccine and place on a platter. Add the sauce and sprinkle with parsley.

Spicy Romaine Salad with Vinaigrette

(Side dish, serves 4)

1 grapefruit   1 chili pepper (medium hot)
¾ cup red wine vinegar   Olive oil and black pepper to taste
1 head romaine lettuce

1. Squeeze half the grapefruit into a small saucepan.
2. Add the vinegar and cook until reduced to half.
3. Add the finely chopped chili along with 2 tablespoons olive oil and black pepper to taste.
4. Thoroughly rinse and drain the romaine salad. Break it into fairly large pieces.
5. Peel the rest of the grapefruit and slice it into bite-size pieces.
6. Toss the salad and the grapefruit in the vinaigrette. Serve immediately.

FURTHER READING

Notaker, Henry. *Food Culture in Scandinavia.* Westport, CT: Greenwood, 2009.

Ethiopia

Alessandra Grasso

SETTING THE SCENE

A cock crows as the monotonic shrill of morning prayer vibrates throughout the compound. Rediet Tilahun, mother of five, is up before sunrise and getting ready to drive to the market. Approaching the end of September, the rain is starting to subside, and the sun is starting to shine. Bright yellow *meskel* flowers illuminate her compound, just like the hillsides of Addis Ababa, the capital city of Ethiopia. Misrak, the family maid, bought the flowers from a countryman and scattered them on the ground to symbolize freshness and a new year.

It is Thursday, a nonfasting day, which for an Ethiopian Orthodox Christian means that one can cook and eat animal products. For Rediet, it is a special day because her sister from the north of Ethiopia is visiting, and her husband, a moringa farmer who spends a great deal of time away on his farm 310 miles south of the city, returned home for the week. She is also expecting two *forengis* (foreigners) over for dinner, a rare spectacle in the Tilahun home.

Her children are still in bed when Rediet sets off to the market. Three miles away, a man named Mesfin sells the best chicken in the Bole neighborhood. Rediet has been buying chickens from him for as long as she can remember. In her car, she does the sign of the cross as she passes an Ethiopian Orthodox church and arrives at the market, greeted by chicks chirping and kids running around. After exchanging greetings and three kisses on the cheek (left, right, left cheek), Mesfin holds up several live chickens that are tied upside down so Rediet can observe the spur of the chickens' feet to estimate their age. Choosing two chickens that are relatively young, determined by the short length of the spurs, Rediet places the live chickens in the trunk and heads home to begin the culinary journey of *doro wat,* a spicy Ethiopian chicken stew.

The Tilahuns live in a compound composed of two buildings that is shared with extended family, two wild dogs that they've taken under their care, and four puppies. Rediet spends a lot of time in the middle of the compound, which serves as an open-air kitchen for her family. In a room accessible to the middle of the compound, she keeps all of her cooking equipment: an electric *injera* maker (*injera* is the unleavened Ethiopian flat bread or dinner table bread) handed down to her by her mother, an electric food processor, an electric burner, and

The Tilahun's dinner table on a casual night: Rediet (front left) with her daughter Betanya (back right) and husband (head of the table) and two guests right before sharing *doro wat* and *injera*. (Courtesy of Alessandra Grasso)

cooking utensils, such as pots, pans, knives, and a cutting board. Outside, she keeps a charcoal stove that, when it's not burning to cook a pot of *wat* (stew), is burning frankincense, a common ritual especially during Ethiopian coffee ceremonies.

PREPARING *DORO WAT*

For the *doro wat,* Misrak already has the fire going with all the ingredients and equipment needed; the only thing missing are the live chickens in the trunk of Rediet's car. *Doro wat,* a national dish of Ethiopia, is a very spicy chicken stew served with *injera,* which serves as a sponge to soak up all the rich flavors of most Ethiopian dishes as well as a tool to pick up the pieces of food with the fingers of the right hand. Ingredients of *doro wat* include finely minced onions, whole chickens (excluding head, feet, intestines, and stomach), tomatoes, peeled hard-boiled eggs, *niter kibe* (Ethiopian spiced butter), and *berbere* (an Ethiopian spice mixture of chili pepper, garlic, ginger, basil, cardamom, black and white pepper, fenugreek, and rue). Chicken is the most expensive ingredient followed by the onions, since they are not harvested during the rainy season. All of the ingredients except for the chickens were purchased at either a local supermarket or from vendors right next door to their compound. While *injera* can be found at the local supermarket, Rediet makes her own with her electric *injera* maker. She ferments teff for three days at room temperature, using reserved dough as a starter, and then fries a thin layer of dough on the electric griddle. Every three days, she makes 30 large *injera* pancakes and stores them in the maker.

Misrak finely minced about six and a half pounds of onions with the electric food processor and has them cooking in a pot on top of burning coals. The onions become a watery mash after a couple of rounds in the food processor, so it usually takes at least an hour before all of the water is cooked out of the pot. As it sizzles, Rediet takes the chickens out of the car, and her husband, Solomon, comes out of the house to prepare for slaughter. Traditionally in Ethiopia, the man of the house is the one to slaughter the animal, while the woman of the house is the one to cook. Also, it is shameful for a man to take any role in the kitchen; however, Solomon enjoys cooking and helping out and doesn't stick with this tradition, since he has adopted Western practices after living and going to school in the United States.

With a sharp knife in hand, Solomon nods to signal that he is ready for the chickens. In the middle of the compound, he respectfully says a prayer right before he grasps the head of one chicken and quickly severs its neck. He repeats the prayer and motions for the second chicken. Rediet holds the chicken as it is sacrificed and quickly places it under a plastic bucket until the chicken stops flopping around and bleeding out.

Once it is quiet under the bucket, both Rediet and Misrak get down and dirty with work. First, the chickens are placed in a bucket of scalding water to loosen the feathers. Rediet and Misrak take seats beside the bucket and start plucking away. Once all the feathers are in a pile beside the bucket, Rediet burns a piece of newspaper and places the flame under the chickens' skin to burn off its fine hairs. Then it is time to wash and rinse. Washing involves scrubbing the skin with an aqueous solution of *shiro* powder (an Ethiopian chickpea and spice powder mixture) and water, followed by rinsing with water, lemon, and salt. With a knife, Rediet scrapes off the slimy part of the chicken before skinning it and removing the organs. The puppies run over and aggressively fight as the stomach and intestines of the chickens are discarded. The heart and liver are saved for the stew.

Once the chickens are skinned and gutted, Rediet and Misrak cut each chicken into 12 identical pieces. Each piece of the chicken has significance in terms of quality and nutrition. The backbone is the highest quality of meat and is given to the eldest at the table or the guest, followed by the chicken breast, legs, wings, and skin, given to children and finally the wife. Rediet and Misrak work nimbly and fast because they've been preparing chicken since they were children.

As each chicken is cut into the 12 pieces, the pieces are thrown in a pot with water, lemon, and salt.

Once all of the water from the onions is fully evaporated, Rediet adds to the pot the tomatoes that have been through the food processor; a splash of sunflower oil; a generous dollop of *niter kibe;* the 24 pieces of chicken, including 2 hearts and 2 livers; 6 peeled hard-boiled eggs; and a sprinkle of *berbere.* After 40 minutes of butchering, cleaning, and cutting the chicken, Rediet and Misrak get a break as they wait 5 hours for it all to simmer and slowly cook on the hot coals.

THE DINNER TABLE

Each day, there are three typical meals in Ethiopia that last an hour at most: breakfast in the early morning; lunch in the afternoon, followed by coffee; and dinner in the early evening. While breakfast can be toast with butter and jam, scrambled eggs, or *injera firfir* (shredded *injera* mixed with butter and *berbere*), lunch and dinner typically consist of the much heralded Ethiopian staples *wat* (stew), *kitfo* (shredded raw meat), and *tere sega* (sliced raw meat) with *injera*. Unless diners are eating pizza or pasta, *injera* is the foundation of every meal. *Injera* can be made of either white or red teff, corn, sorghum, barley, or a mixture of two or three of these. Rediet makes her *injera* out of teff because her family can afford it, prefers the taste, and knows the nutritional benefits of teff—naturally gluten-free, low in sodium and fat, high in minerals, and rich in protein. For dinner, Rediet peels off four large pancake-shaped *injeras* that were made the day before and stored in her *injera* maker.

As 5:00 p.m. approaches, all of the kids put down what they are doing—books, TV, music—and go to the dining area to help prepare for dinner. Aman, the only son, sets the table with a white plastic tablecloth. Selam and Tigist, the two youngest children, retrieve paper napkins, glass plates, glass cups, and bottles of soda, water, and Ambo (Ethiopian sparkling water) and place them on the table. If it was a holiday, Solomon would take out his strong, thick homemade honey wine, *tej*. Abeba, the second-eldest daughter, helps Rediet unfold one large *injera* and places it onto a metal plate, which is then placed on a colorful straw plate that is covered by a top that looks like a party hat. Betanya, the eldest, is in charge of walking around the family room with a pot of warm water, a tray, and soap. She walks to the guests first, father second, and then all of her siblings and pours warm water over their hands as they scrub with soap. Because they eat with their hands, clean hands are a must.

Solomon sits at the head of the table. His children typically sit beside him; however, because guests are over for dinner, Aman, Selam, Tigist, and Abeba already ate dinner that consisted of *shiro* and *injera*. Tonight Daniel, a *forengi* from the Netherlands, sits at Solomon's right, and Betanya and her aunt sit on Solomon's left. Rediet presents her *doro wat,* still bubbling in a clay pot, with Misrak trailing her with a plate stacked with rolled-up *injera*. I ask Rediet to sit so I can snap a picture of the dinner before our right fingers bathe in the burnt-orange stew of spicy goodness.

After the picture is taken, Misrak brings in the colorful straw plate of *injera* and places it in the middle of the dinner table. One pristine *injera* covers the large round metal plate and is quickly besmirched with a large spoonful of bubbling *wat*. The sauce moves toward the edges of the plate in a capillary motion, and the aroma of *berbere* engulfs the dining room and triggers mouths to water. Six hard-boiled eggs are placed on the edge of the plate, one for each person. Then the chicken is allocated—Solomon and Daniel got the meaty backbone, and the other pieces are placed in the middle for anyone to take. Misrak finishes the presentation of the meal with small spoonfuls of *mitmita* and *berbere* on two sides of the plate for dipping.

After a quick prayer led by Solomon, right hands dive down with deft precision and ensnare the *doro wat* in the net of pristine *injera*. Silence is in the form of happy mouths chewing on tender chicken and soaking in all of the flavorful spices. Small chatter is made about the day—what everyone did and how everyone is feeling—yet there is no need for words. Because she doesn't see her father too often, Betanya asks Solomon for a *gursha*. *Gursha* is when someone feeds another, a gesture no different from a hug between friends. She loves his *gursha* because he always has the right combination of meat, sauce, spice, and *injera*.

When the spice becomes overpowering, one reaches for a cold drink with the left hand since the right hand is serving as a utensil. The rolled *injera* is quickly gone before everyone pulls from the *injera* soaked in the *wat*. It is rude to reach over to someone else's side of the plate, so when Betanya wants the chicken breast that is closer to Rediet, the whole plate is turned for her to reach it. The men at the table eat their portion of chicken plus an extra serving and have at least two rolls of *injera*. Each woman chooses a small piece of chicken and takes one roll of *injera*.

It is expected that everyone is to sit at the table until all are finished eating and that diners do not clean their hands with paper napkins until they are completely full. There are no interruptions other than the occasional complement to Rediet and Misrak. Talking with the mouth full, distractions such as cell phones, and natural yet unpleasant affairs such as burping are forbidden and considered very rude. It is also taboo to speak of anyone who has passed or anything gory, since it is believed that the evil spirit will look down upon them.

Thirty minutes pass until there is no trace of *doro wat* on anyone's plate. Betanya goes around a second time with warm water, soap, and a tray so everyone can wash their hands, and the chatter grows. In the meantime, Misrak clears the table and washes the metal plate and glasses. If there were leftovers, they would be saved for lunch the next day. But it is very rare to have leftovers with *doro wat*.

Slurping and Table Noise

In Japan, it is not a good bowl of noodle soup if you don't noisily slurp it up. The same action is considered rude in Europe. A belch is absolutely disgusting at the table in the West, while in many cultures it is the best compliment one can offer to the host. While singing is usually frowned upon at the table as is any other form of extraneous noise, apparently among the Inuits farting after a meal is grand gesture of appreciation.

COFFEE CEREMONY

Since the night is young, Misrak throws two handfuls of coffee beans onto the plate that is cooking above the charcoal stove. She uses tongs to skillfully pick up two pieces of burning coals and puts them in a small bowl to burn frankincense. The pungent scent of roasting coffee beans mingles with the heady smell of incense. The aroma reaches everyone sitting around the dinner table, followed by the sound similar to pebbles hitting a steel drum. Misrak stirs and shakes the beans until they turn black and shiny. With a pestle and long-handled mortar, she finely grinds the coffee and slowly stirs it into the black clay coffee pot known as a *jebena*. Once ground coffee settles at the floor of the round-bottomed pot, Rediet gracefully pours a thin golden stream of coffee into small decorated glass cups from a height of one foot with impressive precision. Misrak first serves Solomon and then the guests, followed by Betanya and Rediet.

Conversation persists as three cups of coffee with generous amounts of sugar are consumed. The traditional ceremony is a tenet of friendship and respect and consists of three rounds: *abol, tona,* and *baraka*. While the dinner lasted no longer than 40 minutes, the coffee ceremony continues for at least 2 hours. Dialogue transitions from Betanya and her father talking about college in the United States to Solomon describing his faith in miraculous powers of moringa. Rediet joins Misrak in the kitchen to finish washing the dishes. Betanya kisses her father goodnight, and the night comes to an end as the guests, glowing in happiness from a good meal, bundle up in their coats to face the chill of the Ethiopian night.

Doro Wat and *Injera*

Serving for 10–12 people

For the *doro wat*:

10 pounds of onions, finely minced	8 cloves of garlic, minced
Vegetable oil	*Berbere*, as desired
5 pounds of tomatoes, coarsely chopped	2 full-sized chickens, cut

1. Place onions in a large pot on medium heat. Stir until it turns light brown (30–35 minutes).
2. Add a generous amount of vegetable oil until it finely coats the onions.
3. Add tomatoes to the pot; stir occasionally for about 30–35 minutes.
4. Add garlic to the pot.
5. To your liking, add as much *berbere* as you want (the more the spicier) and cook for 20 minutes (rediet normally adds a half pound of *berbere*).
6. Add chicken and leave until cooked and tender, about 1 hour and 30 minutes.

For the *injera:*

2 cups of water

1½ cups of teff flour

Vegetable oil to coat

1. Add water to the teff flour and mix until it is a thin dough mixture.
2. Cover with a cheesecloth or towel and leave it for three days at room temperature.
3. Once there are bubbles on top and you can smell the sour aroma, it's ready.
4. Bring a large pan to medium heat and lightly coat with vegetable oil.
5. Pour batter into the pan to fill the entire surface and cover with a lid.
6. It takes about 5–7 minutes to cook, and you will see the top bubble and start to dry out.
7. Remove with spatula and place on a plate. Repeat until dough is gone.

FURTHER READING

Deresse, Lena. *Cooking with Imaye: Ethiopian Cuisine Straight from Mom's Kitchen.* n.p.: CreateSpace, 2014.

Kloman, Harry. *Mesob across America: Ethiopian Food in the U.S.A.* Bloomington, IN: iUniverse, 2010.

Mesfin, Daniel J. *Exotic Ethiopian Cooking: Society, Culture, Hospitality & Traditions.* Falls Church, VA: Ethiopian Cookbook Enterprise, 1987.

France

Jonell Galloway

Stereotypes of how the French eat are abundant: cream, butter, charcuterie, meat, foie gras, snails, duck confit, cheese, rich pastries, and baguettes all the time, legend would have it. In November 2010, UNESCO even listed the French gastronomic meal on the Representative List of the Intangible Cultural Heritage of Humanity. Although these meals are richer and more copious than everyday meals, the gap is not that wide. There may be fewer courses, but the French still eat three square meals a day and take the time to sit down and talk over meals (Mathé, 2009). Meals generally consist of four courses—starter, main dish, cheese, and fruit—but portions are small. Women working outside the home have simplified some of the more traditional cooking habits, but 66 percent of French

In France, everyone in the family takes part in grocery shopping, preparing meals, and setting and clearing the table. A typical meal consists of a starter, main course, cheese, green salad and dessert, even in today's busy world. (Courtesy of Blake Benton de Roucy)

families still spend an average of 2 hours 22 minutes a day eating, 13 minutes longer than in 1986. One-third of this time is spent over lunch (De St Pol, 2013). It is not unusual for men to take part in shopping, cooking, and washing up, as do children. Tradition prevails but with modern twists. Young people in urban environments are the main exception to this, for example, with 16 percent eating only two meals a day out or in front of the television or while playing a video, but say that they would change their eating habits if they had more money (Riou, 2015).

French home cooking has traditionally been passed down through the generations. Men have always taken a more active part than in other countries, going to weekend markets and to the bakery and even preparing certain special dishes, such as mayonnaise or *cassoulet*. Fresh baguettes or bread with every meal are still the norm when feasible, although specialty breads have developed extensively since the 1980s. The price of standard baguettes remains affordable to everyone. The type of fat used in cooking varies from region to region, with butter in the north, duck and goose fat in the southwest, and olive oil in the southeast, but olive oil has become fairly standard fare in households all over the country. Everyone, even children, knows how to whip up vinaigrette, and green salad is a standard accompaniment to both lunch and dinner.

SCHOOLS

Healthy food was not always a topic discussed in school. In the past, it was assumed that if you ate in the traditional manner, you would get a healthy diet. In the 1990s, the French school system decided to take a closer look at meals, recommending that they be balanced, varied, and distributed over the day, with 20 percent of calories at breakfast, 40 percent at lunch, 10 percent at the 4:00 p.m. snack, and 30 percent at dinner. The school system stresses that meals are a period of relaxation and should be considered a special moment in the day set aside for discovery and pleasure as well as for discussion. Lunch break is 1½ hours, with a minimum of 30 minutes eating. A four-course meal is served: vegetable salad, warm main course with grains and/or vegetables, cheese, and dessert, usually consisting of fresh fruit. It is intentionally referred to as a "school restaurant" so as not to be confused with the traditional terms "canteen" and "cafeteria." But food is not only a question of nutrition: starting in 1991, schools began holding regular tasting awareness workshops where children are exposed to a wide variety of dishes and ingredients and learn about how they are made. Schools even hold tasting competitions. Vending machines are forbidden in schools ("L'école élémentaire en pratique," 2013).

PROCESSED FOODS

The French have always bought certain prepared foods. There is a long tradition of picking up salads from the local pork butcher, which often serves as a deli, along with ham, pâté, sausage, and other prepared foods. Bakers make quiches, sausage rolls, and other savory pastries. Pastry shops sell cakes, cookies, croissants, etc. Butchers often sell salads with bits of meat. Most people go to the bakery to buy bread once a day. There is also a long tradition of preserved foods such as cassoulet, duck and goose confits, and pâtés, often bought in markets or on farms and kept on hand for use when unexpected guests come. Mayonnaise and béarnaise sauce came on the market in the late 1980s and the 1990s. Many resisted, but it is common to buy them at the store today.

WEEKEND VERSUS WEEKDAYS

Weekday meals are less leisurely than weekend meals, when families and friends often linger over the table for two or three hours. Special dishes that require a long time to cook are usually made on the weekends or on holidays. Croissants and *pains au chocolat* are usually reserved for weekend breakfasts and special occasions, as are cakes.

DAY-TO-DAY MEALS

Béatrice and Pierre met in accounting school in Dijon. She is from a rural Périgord family, and he is from an old Lyon family. When they graduated, they got jobs as certified public accountants in Paris, where they lived together and eventually got married. They are now 40 and have three children, twin girls Mathilde and Emmy, age 10, and Geneviève, age 7. A few years ago, they moved from Paris to the suburbs to have more room for the children. Béatrice doesn't work on Wednesdays when the children are off from school.

Before Béatrice and Pierre were married they ate out a lot, trying many of the exotic restaurants available in Paris and traveling to foreign countries. This has somewhat influenced their approach to eating, but both come from regions with strong food and wine traditions, so these traditions remain important in their day-to-day family life. Shopping, planning meals, and cooking are important parts of their weekly routine. There is an open-air market in their village on Wednesday

---

Dinner

The word "dinner" in English has a bizarre history. Originally the larger meal eaten early in the day, in medieval Latin the word was *disjejeunare,* meaning to break one's fast. This became *dejeuner* in medieval French and eventually *disner* in early English. Thus, the word "dinner" actually means breakfast. The meal gradually moved later and later in the day, with dinner eventually becoming little different than supper (the original evening meal). In the 14th century the word, and eventually the meal, "breakfast" was introduced, since dinner no longer broke the evening fast.

and Saturday mornings where Béatrice buys most of the fresh fruit and vegetables. The bakery is a 5-minute walk from their house, so it is easy to buy fresh bread every day and sometimes even twice a day. The butcher is a 10-minute walk, so they drop in every couple of days. They go to the supermarket on Saturday afternoons, loading up on staples for the week.

During the many school and public holidays and vacations, they visit their families in Lyon and the Périgord. Béatrice's parents live on a farm, so they put up cassoulet, duck confit, conserved fruit and vegetables, and jam, which Béatrice and Pierre bring back to Paris with them, adding good-quality homemade meals to their regular local purchases. They also stock up on Beaujolais and Côte du Rhône in Lyon and on Bergerac and Cahors in the Périgord, which they put in their newly equipped wine cellar.

Fitting out their kitchen was important when they renovated their house, so they invested money in it. The Miele dishwasher has a timer so as to run at times when the electricity is cheaper; it is also a water-saving version. The stove is gas with an electric convection oven. Like most French homes, they have a small basic refrigerator, preferring to keep fresh fruit and vegetables in bowls and baskets in the window. The old copper pans are from Pierre's grandmother, as are a set of de Buyer steel frying pans and a crêpe pan. They have a cast-iron Staub stew pot, and a clay Romertopf for roasting chickens, which the children love to have at least once a week. The couple received a set of Cristel saucepans as a wedding gift. They've recently invested in a Swiss Kuhn-Rikon double-wall pan, which they use to steam most vegetables as well as fish. They also have a Kenwood food processor. The yellow and blue kitchen is Provençal in style. It is gay and warm, a real meeting place for the family. The Provençal-style white square kitchen table is used for breakfast and lunch, but they prefer eating dinner in the dining room, where they have an antique table and chairs they bought when they got married.

Pierre jogs every morning before work and on his way home picks up fresh baguettes from the bakery for breakfast before they all set off to school and work. Their kitchen is small, like most French kitchens, but big enough for a breakfast table, so they all eat breakfast together. Breakfast regularly consists of a *tartine* (bread and butter), jam, yogurt, and a piece of fruit except on weekends, when Pierre buys croissants and *pains au chocolat*. The children drink hot chocolate, while Béatrice and Pierre drink café au lait, which is basically half coffee and half hot milk served in a large rounded bowl. They make the coffee with a Bodum French-press coffeemaker and heat the milk in the Nespresso electric milk frother Pierre bought for Béatrice for her birthday.

They drop the children off at school on their way to work. They both work in the city, so unlike many French children who go home for lunch, the children eat lunch at the school restaurant. The children get healthy, balanced meals at school, so that is one less worry about squeezing all their nutritional benefits into the evening meal.

It's Monday. Béatrice picks up the children from school and gives them their 4:30 snack of fruit and yogurt. On her way home, she stops and buys lettuce. Since they eat green salad with every meal, they've already eaten all that she bought at the Saturday market. On Monday, they usually use leftovers of some kind from the weekend. On Sunday Béatrice made a *pot au feu,* using duck, carrots, potatoes, celery, leeks, turnips, and onions. She uses the leftover broth the second day, leaving bits of meat in it, making it like a chunky soup. The children love eating it with *mique,* dumplings made from leftover bread, eggs, corn and wheat flour, and bits of duck and duck fat, a specialty of Périgord. She uses her mother's recipe.

Béatrice gets the children started on their homework and then peels celeriac and grates it in the food processor. She washes the green salad and makes vinaigrette. She checks on the children, helps them with any problems they have, and then starts making mayonnaise to make a celery remoulade, which can last two days. All French children love this salad, so it's always worth the time it takes, plus it's full of fiber. By the time Pierre arrives at 6:00 p.m., Béatrice has already started mixing the dumplings and is warming the broth. The whole family reunites in the living room while the children finish their homework. At 6:45, the children finish and go outside to play while Pierre and Béatrice finish preparing dinner.

Pierre sets the table in the dining room with the Christofle white and blue plates and glasses from IKEA onto a matching blue print tablecloth and takes out the blue cloth napkins with initialed napkin rings. He puts a carafe of water on the table along with a bottle of red Bergerac wine. They think that the children are a bit young to be carrying their good dishes from the kitchen; this will come later, in a few years. The dining room has a view of the garden, and they can often see the sun set during dinner, depending on the time of year.

Béatrice drops the dumplings into the broth, and they are ready to eat. They call the children in to wash their hands at 7:30, Pierre serves the celery remoulade in a large white porcelain bowl from IKEA, and the whole family sits down to eat together. He serves water to everyone and wine to the adults. Emmy talks about the farm expedition her class will be making next week. She's excited. She loves her grandparents' farm in the southwest and wants to be a farmer when she grows up. Mathilde complains about math and says her teacher gives her too much homework. This puts her in a bad mood, so she eats slowly at first but perks up when the dumplings are served. When the starter is finished, Béatrice removes the dishes and serves the *pot au feu* with dumplings in a soup bowl. They talk about Easter, when they are going to Lyon to visit Pierre's family. Emmy wants a fancy dark chocolate bunny from Pierre Hermé like she saw on television, Mathilde prefers the white chocolate ones she saw at the local baker's, and Geneviève wants the kind her Mamie makes in Lyon. They all look forward to seeing their grandparents and cousins and to the feast they always serve for Easter. They can't wait for Mamie's *bugnes,* the hot sugar-coated fritters she serves for their *goûtée* (afternoon snack). Pierre can't wait for her Lyonnais sausage dishes and the local cardoons, while Béatrice is looking forward to the *fromage blanc* with shallots, garlic, and herbs, only found in Lyon and called *cervelle de canut.*

The children beg for seconds of dumplings, and Pierre serves them. Geneviève is getting tired and not sitting up straight. She lays her head on the table, and Béatrice corrects her, telling her to sit up straight and keep her arms on the edge of the table at all times during the meal. Pierre removes these plates and brings more plates and knives and the cheese platter along with the green salad and some leftover chives. He pours on the vinaigrette, mixes the salad and chives, and serves the children, Béatrice, and finally himself. The adults like to eat their salad before the cheese, but the children prefer eating the cheese and salad together. Both ways are acceptable. He passes the platter and lets the children choose. They choose Cabécou de Rocamadour, the one granny always serves, and Gruyère. Béatrice and Pierre eat the ripe Camembert with a bit of Roquefort, which comes from the region she grew up in. Béatrice explains that the Cabecou comes from Rocamadour in the Périgord and shows them the painting on the wall of the goats on her parents' farm.

Emmy asks how many carbohydrates there were in their meal, because her tasting awareness class this morning said it wasn't good to eat too many, and she still wasn't clear as to what carbohydrates were. Mathilde says that carbs are pasta and rice, so they didn't eat any. Béatrice explained that the potato, carrots, celery, and bread all had some carbohydrates but not as much as in pasta or rice and that we need a few carbohydrates in our diet. Emmy feels reassured. Béatrice also thinks of her figure. Like many French women, she avoids carbohydrates as much as possible in an attempt to stay thin. Béatrice removes these plates and brings the fruit bowl. The children choose kiwis, while the parents eat ripe Comice pears. When everyone has finished they excuse the children, and Pierre clears the table and puts the dishes in the dishwasher. Béatrice goes upstairs to give the children their baths and puts them to bed around 8:45.

This French family represents a middle-class family typical of the statistics published by major French research institutes such as the French National Institute of Statistics and Economic Studies and the Research Center for the Study and Observation of Living Conditions. Those with roots in the country and from farms are more likely to stick to the traditional way of eating. For 40 percent of French people, a regular everyday meal is simply a smaller version of the gastronomic meal protected by UNESCO. In urban environments and with young people, these trends differ in that they involve more food prepared outside the home, but even those who buy prepared food in the supermarket or at the deli tend to buy a starter, a main course, cheese, salad, and fruit. Shopping for food is still a family affair, one in which everybody usually takes part. Families cook together and deem the time spent at the table an important part of their social and family life. The traditional French meal is in no danger of disappearing. It has simply adapted to the modern world. Gathering around the table for Sunday lunch is alive and well, and as King Henri IV wished, almost every French family can afford to put a chicken on the table once a week, even if it was roasted by the local supermarket.

Southwest Duck *Pot au Feu*

Prep time: 20 minutes
Cooking time: 3 hours
Serves 4

4–5 duck legs	3 whole cloves
Touch of duck fat	1 clove garlic (with peel)
Salt and pepper	Parsley
2 stems of thyme	2 juniper berries
3 leaves of laurel	2 cups white wine
2 large onions, skin removed	

Cut all into large chunks:

1 pound turnips, peeled	4 stalks celery
3 leeks	8 potatoes, peeled
1 pound carrots or parsnips, peeled	

Note: Save the 3 tablespoons butter or duck fat from frying for tomorrow's dumplings.

Coarse sea salt	Heavy frying pan
Mustard or horseradish	Soup pot

1. Use the end of a butcher knife to make crisscross indentations in the skin of the duck legs.
2. Heat duck fat in heavy frying pan over medium heat. Add duck legs, fat side down. Salt and pepper. Brown on skin side only, saving oil and any bits of skin or meat that fall away.
3. Remove duck legs and put them into soup pot. Add thyme and laurel. Insert cloves into peeled onions. Add garlic clove, parsley, and juniper berries. Pour wine over the mixture, then pour in enough cold water just to cover it all.
4. Slowly bring to a boil. Boil gently for 1 hour and 20 minutes.
5. Add remaining vegetables. Simmer for about 1 hour and 40 minutes or until vegetables are tender.
6. Remove duck legs from broth and drain on paper towels.
7. Bring broth to boil and reduce.
8. Serve duck with coarse sea salt, mustard or horseradish, and vegetable broth.

Mique Dumplings for Leftover *Pot au Feu*

Broth from leftover *pot au feu*

3 tablespoons of duck fat from yesterday's frying

1 crushed garlic clove

2–3 tablespoons of pieces of leftover duck, chopped into tiny chunks, OR bacon bits

1¼ cup leftover bread

3 large eggs

1 clove garlic, minced

3 teaspoons baking powder

¼ cup flour

⅛ cup cornmeal

2 tablespoons fresh parsley, chopped

Salt

Pepper

1. Bring 3 quarts of *pot au feu* broth to a gentle boil.
2. Heat leftover duck fat. Add chopped garlic. Fry chopped duck in hot duck fat until crisp.
3. Cut or tear dried bread into ½-inch cubes and place in a mixing bowl.
4. In another mixing bowl, mix duck fat and crisped duck bits, three or four ladles of hot broth (1 or 1½ cups) from *pot au feu,* eggs, minced garlic, baking powder, parsley, salt, and pepper.
5. Add bread. Mix well, mashing the bread into the liquid until it forms a smooth dough. This will take a while. If the dough is too heavy, mix it with your hands.
6. Add flour and cornmeal. Add salt and pepper to taste. Mix well until it forms a fairly smooth compact ball. The dough should be wet enough to allow you to form dumplings by hand. If not, correct liquid/bread ratio.
7. Form 2½-inch dumplings.
8. Drop dumplings into boiling *pot au feu* broth.
9. Cook for 10 to 15 minutes but before they start falling apart.
10. Serve in a soup dish along with the *pot au feu.*

FURTHER READING

Abramson, Julia L. *Food Culture in France.* Westport, CT: Greenwood, 2006.

De St Pol, Thibaut, and Layla Ricroch. "Le temps de l'alimentation en France," October 2012, http://www.insee.fr/fr/themes/document.asp?ref_id=ip1417.

"L'école élémentaire en pratique: La restauration à l'école," Ministère de l'Éducation nationale, de l'Enseignement supérieur et de la Recherche, October 2013, http://www.education.gouv.fr/cid45/la-restauration-a-l-ecole.html.

Mathé, T., G. Tavoularis, and T. Pilorin. "La gastronomie s'inscrit dans la continuité du modèle alimentaire français," December 2009, http://www.credoc.fr/publications/abstract.php?ref=C267.

Riou, J., T. Lefèvre, I. Parizot, Anne Lhuissier, and Pierre Chauvin. "Is There Still a French Eating Model? A Taxonomy of Eating Behaviors in Adults Living in the Paris Metropolitan Area in 2010." *Plos One* 3(10) 2015. http://journals.plos.org/plosone

/article?id=10.1371/journal.pone.0119161/modele-alimentaire-francais-3-repas
-par-jour-existe-t-il-toujours.html.
Rozin, P., K. Kabnick, E. Pete, C. Fischler, and C. Shields. "The Ecology of Eating: Smaller
Portion Sizes in France Than in the United States Help Explain the French Paradox."
Psychological Science 14 (2003): 450–454.

Germany

Ursula Heinzelmann

Pictured below is the Schmid family at their kitchen table, enjoying lunch on a weekday. They live in a small rural town in the southwest of Germany and have been farming for generations. Today wine is their signature product, but the mixed farming of old prevails with asparagus, potatoes, and, to a smaller extent, other garden fruit and vegetables. Adelheid and Peter, both in their late 30s, have been in charge of the family estate for a decade, with up to four generations living under one roof.

Generally speaking (and in contrast to more urban settings in Germany), the women are in charge of the kitchen and cooking, whereas the men tend vineyards and fields. Also in contrast to city households, where the main meal has mostly moved to the evening, here lunch is the most important meal that brings everybody together around the big kitchen table. Besides Peter's parents, "everybody" includes his centenarian grandmother; Adelheid and Peter's two children, Karl, age 13, and Anna, age 11; Peter's sister and her husband (who live a few houses down the street) and some of their children; and whoever of the Schmids' employees is present that day. Everybody has been up since the early morning, and lunch is served at noon. Hands are scrubbed and dirty shoes left at the door, but otherwise it is pretty much a working lunch, during which the conversation turns to everybody's daily tasks, how things are going out in the fields and vineyards and at the cellar door, and what's up next.

The Schmids start their meal with a clear soup made from boiling beef on the bone, to "fill the stomachs." The broth comes with some leftover pancakes cut into thin strips (*flädle*), finely diced root vegetables, and chopped fresh parsley. It is served in special cups to be eaten with spoons (whereas for the typical Saturday stew a large tureen is used, from which Adelheid serves everybody into deep round plates). The children love to slurp it from the cup but are usually told off for doing so. The main course consists of a pork roast made from the shoulder. Rubbed with mustard, coated in breadcrumbs and herbs, it basically makes itself, comments Adelheid. She is in charge of all administrative matters as well as communications at the estate, and as important as food cooking and eating is, it is not a task that she can devote much time to. She usually makes a rough plan on Monday for the week ahead, devotes the first couple of hours of every workday in the morning to the office, and then spends another couple of hours in the kitchen. Sometimes one of the other women drops in to help or offers to bring along some dish.

A German family living in a rural setting gathers four generations around a big kitchen table for lunch. In contrast to city households, where the main meal is served in the evening, rural families still treat lunch as the most important meal of the day. (Courtesy of Andreas Durst)

Today there are steamed cauliflower and oven-roasted potatoes to go with the meat. It is all served on large dishes and on platters and passed around the table for everybody to serve themselves, including the children. As a general rule, the young ones are expected to eat up whatever they choose to take and to taste everything at least once. But they all love to eat and enjoy getting a few "best bites" slipped onto their plates by their doting great-granny.

The large wooden table with benches running along two sides of it is part of the open-space kitchen. The same wood has been used by some former Schmid for the paneling, and the whole setting radiates coziness without any overly decorous kitsch. There is a radio, but it is only switched on during the rare moments when Adelheid is working here on her own, and the TV in a corner on principle is switched off during meals. On weekdays the wooden table is kept bare, just as everybody is in their working clothes. Rather inexpensive regular china and cutlery are used: a knife and fork for the main course and a small spoon or fork for dessert. In contrast to that, on Sundays when field work is kept to a minimum, the treasured old china from former generations is brought out, together with engraved silver cutlery, a white tablecloth, and napkins.

However, the wineglasses are always the same, modern and functional instead of the colored cut glass of old. This is symbolic: the Schmids belong to the new generation of German wine growers. In the past 25 years German wine has seen a fundamental revival, with many young wine growers leaving the cooperatives their parents belonged to in order to strive for the best possible quality. Adelheid and Peter frequently travel to wine shows and tastings as far away as the U.S. West Coast and Australia, and if school holidays permit, they take the children with them. Anna and Karl are proud to get a tasting sip of each wine served at family meals. On weekdays it tends to be a more regular refreshing dry white such as

---

Cutlery

We might imagine the use of a knife and fork is a simple operation with straightforward rules. Nothing could be further from the truth. In Europe the fork is held in the left hand with tines facing downward, and the knife is held in the right for cutting. Food is conveyed to the mouth on the tip of the fork held by the left hand. In the United States food might be cut up this way, but the fork is then switched to the right hand and used as a shovel to scoop up food. This is a remnant of the early use of the fork in the 17th century—that is, the original way they were used when first introduced. European cutlery use evolved in a different direction.

Gutedel/Chasselas, the local speciality, whereas on Sunday Peter usually brings out one of his excellent Spätburgunder/Pinot Noir or Syrah wines. Effervescent bottled mineral water is always at hand and served in simple tumblers.

To finish the meal, Adelheid serves something sweet: fresh homegrown fruit in the summer or a tub of ice cream if time is particularly short during harvest time. Semolina and rice pudding are big favorites with everybody, as is quark mixed with fruit (like they are going to have today). Finally, the children are expected to clear the table, while one of the men rises to fetch the coffee from the filter machine Adelheid has prepared as well as mugs and some cream and sugar. This is a last moment of relaxing quiet before everybody gets back to work. The women then all join together in cleaning the kitchen, loading the dishwasher, quickly rinsing the pots and pans, and carefully storing away the leftovers in the large fridge, to be incorporated in a later meal. In general, at 1:30 p.m. everybody is back at their work.

A lot of the produce used in the Schmids' kitchen is seasonal and homegrown. The vegetable garden and fruit orchards are right behind the house, next to the sunny patio where the family sits out, weather permitting. The harvest is supplemented by the local purveyors. Similar to the Schmids, the butcher and baker have been around for generations and are surviving because of the strong support of the local population. However, Peter's mother has always baked her own bread every Friday, and Adelheid does a weekly run to the next supermarket to shop for basics, just as she has no qualms about incorporating convenience food such as canned tomatoes into her cooking.

The same is true for the dishes she serves. Whereas the pictured meal is very traditional, the next day might feature pizza, pasta, or a Thai curry. While traveling, all the Schmids are happy to enjoy and taste the local cuisine—although they draw a line at breakfast, which they prefer to be as much as possible what they're used to: filter coffee, a little milk, some kind of bread, butter, and jam or honey. The children like their muesli and hot chocolate, and all of them struggle when faced with a big American-style cook-up or an Asian savory soup at an early hour.

Just as her cooking, Adelheid's kitchen combines traditional elements with very modern technology. One part of the oven range is fired with wood, of which there are ample provisions. The fire makes for a cozy kitchen in the winter, and some dishes such as fried potatoes and baked apples are particularly delicious when prepared that way. On the other hand, Adelheid is glad to be able to switch on the gas burner as well. She uses a pressure cooker to speed up some procedures, while she is happy to let a roast cook very slowly in an old earthen crock she inherited from her mother. There is a microwave that is mostly used to reheat small portions or leftovers. Like a lot of farming households, Adelheid owns a Thermomix, a highly sophisticated machine that combines a food processor's functions with that of a cooker operated on a touchscreen and with an integrated scale. It can be preset to mix a mayonnaise or heat the mixture for a sauce hollandaise to go with the asparagus in late spring but also to make a cream dessert, and Adelheid finds it most convenient and well worth the significant investment.

By and large, the techniques used to prepare food in Germany are the same as in other Western cultures. Pasta, potatoes, and dumplings in all variations are boiled in large amounts of water, as are some kinds of vegetables such as cauliflower and larger cuts of meat (called *Siedfleisch*). More tender ingredients such as fish are kept just under the boiling point. The energy and time-saving *Schnellkochtopf* (pressure cooker) uses steam, but Adelheid also owns a woven bamboo steamer basket bought at an Asian store. The pork roast uses a combination of dry and wet heat to tenderize and yield some sauce. In the winter ragouts, *gulash* and large meat cuts are braised: the meat is browned, and vegetables such as carrots, celeriac, and onions are added and lightly sautéed as well before a little liquid is added. A lid then goes on the pan, and the meat is slowly finished, often in the oven, where it yields the sauce deemed essential for a traditional real meal. Somewhat paradoxically, the finished dish is still called roast (*Braten*), although strictly speaking roasting would involve only dry heat, with a little fat but no liquid, either on the stove or in the oven. That is how *Schnitzel* are made, often but not always covered in breadcrumbs. Although the Schmids' kids love fries as much as everybody else, Adelheid has no deep fryer; in general, deep-frying is not very common in private households in Germany. Her pans are mostly of stainless steel; the aluminum widely used after World War II today is deemed a health risk, but there is the odd cast-iron or copper pan. An array of cake tins and baking sheets completes the kitchen equipment, some enameled white or black, some in glass, some earthen and in all kinds of traditional and modern shapes.

Undoubtedly food preparation, which entails chopping, pounding, and the like, used to be a more physically demanding task for former generations and has been made much easier today with the aid of electricity. Adelheid's drawers contain a handheld blender and an electric whisk, whereas the standing blender and the food processor with all kinds of functions have been made obsolete by the Thermomix. Besides that, there are herb and garlic cutters, egg cookers, can openers, knives, knife sharpeners, lemon squeezers, bread slicers, and cheese graters, and someone even gave them an electrically powered pepper mill. As recipes are in (kilo)grams and (milli)liters, there is a liter measure as well as an electronic scale. Adelheid uses a large wooden cutting board but also has smaller ones made of plastic. A whole battery of knives live on a magnetic holder fixed to the wall, whereas other tools such as wooden spoons, slotted spoons, sieves, and a rolling pin are kept in a big earthen jar next to the stove. A Swabian relative has given her a *Spätzlebrett,* a handheld wooden board on which an almost liquid egg noodle dough is spread with a palette knife to be scraped in thin strips into boiling water to make spätzle, a kind of egg pasta. However, Adelheid is much more likely to opt for (quicker) mashed potatoes.

If all this sounds very traditional, it is obviously just one facet of the diversity that is German food culture. To capture all of Germany's extremely complex, multilayered dinner culture in a single representative picture and meal is by definition impossible. So many differences and facets have been molded by geography, climate, and the infinite cultural influences from all sides in the course of history: Germany is a country right in the middle of the European continent, situated between the Slavs and the Romans, cold and heat, sea and mountains. Germany has no single national, overarching haute cuisine, not even a national dish. In addition to geographic and climatic reasons, this is mainly due to four factors. First, when populations moved they took some of their food preferences with them (in a similar manner, German emigrants took their foodways with them over the Atlantic to the Americas). Second, the disintegration of the (albeit not very tightly joined) nation into countless small political units following the decline of Charlemagne's kingdom in the course of the ninth century was the basis for a variety of regional cuisines, each itself a complex system of socioeconomic and cultural layers. Third, the reformation movement instigated by Martin Luther and many like-minded innovators in the 16th century set an example for the wider populace that it was possible to be and act differently. Finally, the late but far-reaching and intense industrialization in the course of the 19th century turned a patchwork of agrarian states into one thoroughly urbanized industrial one. It also led to a surge of fears and longings in reaction, back then as much as today. Simply put, the result of that is the organic movement of today.

Having said all that, though, we can zoom out, so to speak, and look at the similarities this picture represents, after all. In a lot of homes, a table in the kitchen is one of if not the most important space: it is often described as used most, with the best atmosphere or feeling, and also used to receive visitors. On the table you'll always find some kind of china, glasses, and cutlery, even if the pizza has been delivered. TV or music might be in the background, but conversation at the table in general is deemed more important. All over Germany it is still women who are mainly responsible for the kitchen and all related tasks (therefore often taking on a double role). As for the food itself, potatoes since the 18th century have played a major role in the German diet. Also, even in nonreligious households, the food tends to be influenced by Christian traditions, serving fish or a vegetable dish on

Fridays (traditionally a lean day) and, for example, carp on New Year's Eve and/or Good Friday. And finally, Germans' meat of preference has been pork for a long time, although steak is now high on the list of favored dishes as well.

Further, it has to be said that in a new trend contrasting the old lure of the rural idyll once young adults started a family, recent statistics see Germans moving back into towns and cities. This changes the urban landscape and blurs the erstwhile clear contrasts between urban and rural communities. As the agricultural sector has been struggling to reinvent itself in an industrially driven environment, one of its most successful offshoots, capable of bridging the gulf between rural production and urban consumption, during the last two decades has been viticulture.

Finally, the southwest of Germany, the Schmids' home region bordering on Switzerland and France and often called "Alemannic," arguably boasts the country's most sophisticated food culture (as well as a very strong accent very close to Swiss German and almost unintelligible to northern folks). In no small part this can be traced to the times of Roman invasion roughly 2,000 years ago, leaving a taste for the generosity of more southern foodways that has combined well with natural resources. The Schmids lead a comfortable life with good food, but they are aware that neither roast nor grapes just fall from the sky.

Schweinebraten/Roast Pork (Based on and Adapted from Mimi Sheraton, *The German Cookbook,* New York: Random House, 1965, 1993, 2014)

8 to 10 servings

5- to 6-pound roast (leg or shoulder)	½ cup fresh breadcrumbs
garlic cloves, cut in half	4 onions, sliced
2 tablespoons Dijon mustard	2 carrots, sliced
Salt and pepper	½ cup water
3 tablespoons butter, soft	½ cup dry white wine
Dried or fresh thyme, marjoram, parsley, and sage	

1. Preheat oven to 350°.
2. Rub meat on all sides with cloves of garlic as well as the mustard and soft butter. Sprinkle liberally with salt and pepper.
3. Roughly chop or break down herbs, mix with breadcrumbs, and roll meat in this.
4. Arrange bed of onions and carrots on bottom of open roasting pan. Lay meat on vegetables.
5. Add water and wine to pan and roast in preheated oven for 2½ to 3 hours, adding more liquid to pan as needed.

6. Remove finished meat to a heated platter, roughly strain the pan juices to re-
    move the (exhausted) vegetables, and serve with the meat.

Milchreis (Rice Pudding)

8 dessert servings

2 cups white short grain rice

2 quarts whole milk

pinch of salt

Zest of 1 lemon

4 tablespoons butter

Granulated sugar and cinnamon to taste
for sprinkling over finished pudding

1. Wash rice.
2. Bring to boil with milk and seasonings, stirring all the time.
3. Cover and cook in oven at very low heat for 45 minutes to 1 hour until rice is
    soft, stirring occasionally.
4. Stir in butter (more if you wish). Serve warm, sprinkled liberally with sugar
    and cinnamon. Stewed fruit or applesauce is very good with this.

FURTHER READING

Heinzelmann, Ursula. *Beyond Bratwurst: A History of Food in Germany.* London: Reaktion
    Books, 2014.
Heinzelmann, Ursula. *Food Culture in Germany.* Westport, CT: Greenwood, 2008.

Great Britain: Wales

Annie Levy

Tea with Jayne and Wyn Evans brings their large family together at the end of each day to share food that is cooked with love. The family includes Thomas, age 2; Annabelle, age 4; Emma, age 6; Freddie, age 13; and Esme, the oldest, at age 15. The Evanses "really like their food" and feel that eating together is an important ritual of daily life. Jayne regards her commitment to cooking as traditional. Wyn's mother cooked, and so did her own mother. It's "just tradition really." "A farm house wife" never stops, she laughs, referring to her "workaholism." Annie, visiting the family, feels as if she has walked into an idyll of rural Welsh farm family life in a contemporary context. Reading Welsh history, one glimpses rural households that are either poor or rich, and this lifestyle feels very middle class in the sense of being comfortable but not excessive, a feeling of plenty that is accompanied by a Christian gratefulness. There's an international awareness too, and many worry that the European Union might change farm subsidies that for now help to stabilize the income of many farming families.

The Evans family lives in a new modern house with a rustic feel that they built in proximity to the land where Wyn raises sheep and cows, not far from a market town where the children go to school. On the days Jayne works in another town, she stops in larger supermarkets such as Aldi and Tesco for club-card points and orders Asda online for many staples; on other days she gives her business in the local town to the proprietor-owned vegetable shop Tonks and the Williams Family Butchers. The shopkeepers all know her and appreciate her regular business.

Jayne and Wyn have built their house themselves with great attention to energy efficiency (with solar, wood, underfloor heating, and plans for future hydro) and physical and aesthetic comfort. They designed their kitchen to reflect the needs of a busy family, and Jayne continually expresses gratitude for the large double-door refrigerator, still an unusual luxury in the United Kingdom, with the outside ice dispenser sitting on top of server freezer drawers and for the large electric Rangemaster with the glass top and the slow-cooker oven feature. The kitchen is large, perhaps a third of it a play area with couches and toys overlooking an inglenook fireplace. In the middle stands an island that functions as a surface for fruit bowls filled with diverse fruit (oranges, melons, apples, grapefruit, bananas) for cooking and as a staging point for serving dinner. On three sides the island is surrounded— the sink/cooker/fridge triangle design.

A Welsh farming family eating a traditional tea. (Courtesy of Susan Bound)

On the fourth side is the long rectangular kitchen table, covered with an oil-cloth tablecloth with a black-and-white kitten motif and surrounded by a combination of chairs, some of sleek black leather or vinyl and others in an updated country-kitchen carved wood style. Jayne's taste reflects her desire for a sense of light and uncluttered space (versus the dark and heavily patterned interiors that were a feature of her parents' generation) while maintaining a feeling of coziness.

Refrigerator

Refrigerators were only made practical for home use in the early 20th century, gradually replacing the icebox, which was just that: a block of ice in an insulated box. Freon was the key component that made refrigerators affordable. Through the 20th century, refrigerators, often combined with freezer units, became bigger and bigger, allowing people to shop for more groceries at a time. They also became the center of the household, its focus, replacing the hearth. Here people would place pictures and notices and often hang out in the kitchen around the fridge rummaging for snacks. Eventually refrigerators were fitted with ice and water dispensers and even smart applications that could adjust the temperature of various sections and suggest when food should be used before spoiling.

Annie was invited for a 6:30 meal (an aspirational rather than exact time). When she arrives at 6:00, Jayne and her two younger daughters are preparing the batter for the Yorkshire puddings. Annabelle and Emma are standing on stools, helping their mum with small whisks in hand, mixing the Dove's Farm gluten-free flour with salt, milk, and eggs in an old-style pottery yellow-ware Mason bowl in the classic 1901 pattern. "The batter feels too loose," said Jayne, adding more flour by feel for "the right consistency." She melts lard from a paper-wrapped block, pours it into muffin tins, slightly smaller and deeper than Yorkshire pans, and pops them in a hot oven. When the fat is hot enough, Jayne adds the batter, and the tins go back in the oven. The secret to Yorkshires is hot fat and a hot oven, she instructs.

The vegetables have been prepared earlier in the day; even the children often help with peeling carrots and potatoes. The roast potatoes are leftovers from Sunday lunch (we're on a Tuesday), some of which have been mashed, and others of which will be served in chunks. The roast went in the oven at 9:00 p.m. the previous evening; it's a special LMC cut (beef "leg of mutton") that is rare to find these days but is specially ordered from the butcher, who has also scored the joint to suggest the correct angle of cutting for optimal tenderness. This cut requires such a long, slow cook that most people won't buy it these days. But Jayne has her slow-cooking oven and cooks the joint with a little stock from vegetables, and a long-time favorite product named Browning that now must be bought at small specialty shops, as smaller supermarkets no longer stock it; it contains salt, glucose, and coloring and gives that good flavor and deep brown hue to stocks and gravies. Jayne shares Wyn's mother's trick for smooth and perfect gravies: dissolve corn flour (cornstarch) in hot water and add to the cooking stock from the vegetables and drippings and pan juices from the roasting meat (plus a little Browning).

"Be careful with the Browning, as it can stain things—a few drops work brilliantly," Jayne tells me later. "My mum used to keep the bottle in a plastic cup to stop marks. I just wipe the drips!!!"

It is difficult to estimate how much time Jayne spends cooking. Jayne's cooking life is one in which food prepared in intentional volume as well as leftovers from one meal form a portion of another. Clearly, she does kitchen tasks throughout the days when she's home and bits of shopping on the days she's working or is otherwise out. She's thinking about food a lot of the time and cooks Wyn "dinner" at midday—always home-cooked, though occasionally she will use curry sauce from a jar, for instance, or recipes from Slimming World. Wyn works hard, and Jayne feels that he has high expectation for meals. And, he expresses his pleasure and gratitude for her cooking. She will sometimes have cooking days and prepare meals in advance, which she stores in the freezer drawers. Jayne and Wyn seem to accept their roles responsibly and appreciate what the other does in a reciprocal relationship, and this forms the basis of home and family in which the food is central.

Jayne speaks with concern about food and health issues. She avoids gluten, is deficient in B12, and requires supplements to keep her levels up. She is wary of adding too much salt, as her family as a history of heart disease, though for Wyn, "Mother likes salt" and believes it's a natural human craving (and why junk food is so successful, because healthy food is nowadays undersalted when it arrives at the table). Jayne gives the little ones apple and orange juices diluted with water—Vitamin C for their runny noses but aware that the acid and sugar are not so good for their teeth. The rest of us will be given large glasses of ice water with our meal.

When Wyn comes in at around 6:30, he begins to help. At the kitchen island, he slices the joint of beef with an old bone-handled carving fork and a modern high-tech designed knife and puts a slice or two on each white porcelain plate, which Freddie had counted out for everyone (except the little ones) and placed on the table. Freddie also had put sturdy contemporary stainless forks and knives and large glasses of ice water on the table. Jayne lays the hot saucepans on well-used laminated cardboard place mats in the center of the table, commenting that if this was a more formal meal, she might use serving bowls. The small children each have plastic Disney character beakers and special plastic bowls that Jayne's mother enjoys giving as gifts, and these are useful because they don't shatter if they fall to the floor. It's a table that reflects an aspiration for things to look nice and somewhat unified but accepts that old items (the trivet place mats) and gifted items might be practical even if not a visual match.

As Wyn carves the meat, he jokes that they should be serving Welsh lamb, since they farm it. He carries the individual plates to the table.

Jayne portions out the vegetables so that everyone is guaranteed a bit of everything and nothing runs out. "My rule is to eat everything on the table, but there's some give and take." At the same time, she cooks so as to please the diversity of ages and tastes in her family, hence the number of separate items. She places careful amounts in the little children's bowls so they eat enough but not too much is wasted. She pours gravy in the little kids' bowls, and everyone else pours their own from a stainless steel gravy saucepan with a special lip for pouring.

Freddie is at one end of the table, and Wyn is at the head, next to Thomas. The rest of the group is sitting around the table, with Jayne closest to the kitchen surfaces in case she needs to get up. She serves me a plate piled with food; the meal feels like Christmas, but they all assure me that there is even more variety, loads more, at Christmas.

While everyone is sitting quietly, Freddie says a brief prayer thanking the Lord for the lovely food and "Jayney" for doing all the cooking and requests good results on his recent exams. Everybody chuckles with him on this.

The vegetables consist of boiled carrots cut in coins, broccoli, peas, roasted potatoes (mashed and others in chunks), and mixed butternut squash and sweet potatoes roasted with garlic granules. But the meat is central, and the gravy unifies everything on the plate with that savory and slightly salty character. Thomas is crazy about broccoli and clamors for more, which his parents are happy about.

Annabelle seems to be feeling tired or poorly and doesn't eat much. The meat is indeed very tender for having slow-cooked for 22 hours!

Slowly the children get up from the table, not having completely finished their bowls. Thomas starts circling the island on his little toy car with wheels and then his blue bouncy cow. Annabelle and Emma are running around too. There's lots of laughter.

Freddie has begun to clear the finished plates and stack them on the side next to the sink. It's the job of the older children to clear and clean at this meal. Esme will rinse and place all the plates in the dishwasher and wash up the saucepans. Jayne feels strongly about the work being shared between children and adults and in this case across gender.

Everyone slowly gathers in their seats again. Or rather, two are on laps, Thomas on Wyn's, who with a fork feeds into his little boy's mouth the remainders from his bowl and some extra broccoli, and Annabelle on Esme's lap, as Jayne tries to get a little more of the potatoes and vegetables into her little girl's tummy.

Jayne gets up and puts little cakes on a plate—treats of gluten-free cornflakes mixed with Nutella, placed daintily in white fluted paper cases. She brings these to the table and gives each diner one as a small sweet to end the meal.

Freddie goes upstairs to shower, puts on his pajamas, and comes back down to finish clearing. Jayne makes a milky, chocolatey Nesquick in a sippy cup for Annabelle; she usually wouldn't offer chocolate at this time—a strawberry milk would be better—but is concerned the girl isn't well and hasn't eaten properly. Annabelle is also munching on carrot sticks, and Jayne will offer these as well as fruit, cherry tomatoes, and red peppers for snacks. Evening eating is not strictly regulated, though it irritates Jayne if Freddie eats standing at the island.

There's not much left over from the meal—some carrots, some gravy, a few potatoes, and some meat—and with these tomorrow Jayne will make a beef and onion pie with choux pastry, gluten free of course. She shows off her well-loved Mcdougall's Better Baking pamphlet, cherished recipes from a large UK flour brand that she's had for so many years its lost its cover, and flips through the pages, showing me all the recipes she needs, good traditional British fare.

Soon after the meal Wyn will go out to tend again to the sheep and cows. He doesn't participate in the clearing or cleaning of the meal. Esme goes upstairs to help the little girls get to bed. Freddie watches the television. Jayne is ready to wind down. This has been an example of a real Welsh meal of meat and vegetables, one that reflects a contemporary economy in which farmers are able to make a middle-class income, especially when supplemented by another income, such as Jayne's in an office. Their traditional foods are prepared with modern notions of healthy eating and convenience products where appropriate. And Jayne, even as a working woman, accepts some gender division for herself and Wyn yet insists that her older children, a boy and a girl, have equal duties in the kitchen.

Gluten-Free Yorkshires (Yorkshire Puddings)

If you're Jayne and have a big family, double all your recipes!

1 teaspoon of lard	4 eggs
½ cup gluten-free flour	¾ cup milk
½ teaspoon salt	

1. Preheat oven to hot, 400°F.
2. Melt the lard from a block in each cup of a 12-cup muffin tin. Place tin in oven.
3. Mix gluten-free flour and salt; beat in eggs and milk. Judge whether the consistency feels correct to you. Remember that you are using a recipe for white wheat flour and adjust your flour quantities accordingly to get the batter to feel similar to pancake batter.
4. Remove the muffin tin from the oven and pour batter equally into the cups. Bake for 20 minutes, hoping your puddings will lighten, turn golden, and rise.
5. Serve immediately.

FURTHER READING

Mason, Laura. *Food Culture in Great Britain.* Westport, CT: Greenwood, 2004.
Tibbott, S. Minwel. *Domestic Life in Wales.* Cardiff: University of Wales Press, 2002.
"What Would You Consider to Be 'Traditional Welsh Food'?" National Museum of Wales, https://www.museumwales.ac.uk/rhagor/galleries/traditional_foods/.

Greece

Nafsika Papacharalampous

A GREEK SUNDAY LUNCH

As Nafsika enters the airy Athenian kitchen, Katerina is taking a glass jar from the cupboard. "You're just in time," she says, opening the oven to remove the tray with the meatloaf, slightly brown on its edges, aromas filling the bright kitchen. "I'm about to put the orzo in the tomato sauce, which means we will be having lunch in 20 minutes," she says, opening the jar. Every Sunday Katerina cooks for the family. She also cooks every day, but Sundays are more special. She usually prepares one of her old recipes that take longer to make, more often than not some kind of meat baked in the oven. It is the one day of the week when the whole family not only eats together but comes together and spends time before and after the meal.

For the Greek family, gathering around the table on Sunday is an unvarying ritual that brings everyone together, often extending beyond the family itself and including other relatives or friends. For these Sunday lunches Katerina spends around two hours in the kitchen, preparing the food and cleaning up the utensils and bowls she uses. After the end of the meal it is Xenofon, her husband, who puts the dishes in the dishwasher, a division of labor that this family upholds, although still in Greece the kitchen is more of a female space.

Katerina explains how she prepares the *rolo,* the Greek version of the meatloaf, as she and Nafsika both sit on wooden stools in the kitchen. Nafsika is offered coffee. In the living room Xenofon is drinking some ouzo accompanied by a few olives and bread, a regular prelunch Sunday ritual for him.

The dishes cooked on Sundays are labor-intensive, and most important, despite the proliferation of convenience foods, these meals are all prepared from scratch, illuminating the sense of duty, pride, and care in the role of Greek women within the household. But while allergies and other health issues are always respected and food preferences are often taken into account by the cook, that is not always the case, especially when it comes to children: they are encouraged and often obliged to learn to eat everything. This can be challenging if you are a teenager who hates grilled fish but had to eat it on a regular basis for Sunday lunch because nothing else was prepared. Yet as children are compelled to taste everything, they often grow up with a natural curiosity for foods that seem appalling at first, which makes the method somewhat successful.

Caterina serves Rolo me Kritharaki to her husband, Xenofon, and daughter, Eirini, as the Pa-pacharalampous family gathers around the table for their weekly Sunday lunch. The meal in-cludes home-cooked food made with the care and love that has been bringing this Greek family together for over 30 years. (Courtesy of Nafsika Papacharalampous)

Katerina explains that the graviera cheese used in her recipe is from a friend who lives in Crete: "This cheese, you know where it is coming from, it is purer." "And it tastes better," Eirini, her daughter, adds as she enters the kitchen and nibbles on some bread. In Greece, friends and family living in rural areas had always been sending foodstuffs into the city, and the link between the countryside and the city still remains strong. These foods, like the graviera cheese, are greatly valued maybe now more than ever, as there is a turn toward rural simplicity and attention paid to local provenance.

The group moves into the family room, a wide bright space where the living room and dining room coexist. The room is wide, now filled with the aromas of meat and tomatoes. There are floor-to-ceiling windows on each side and a door leading to the separate kitchen area. In the living room area there are three couches, the TV, and the fireplace, while the dining room has a wooden round table and four wooden chairs around it, one for each of us. On days when guests are invited, more chairs are brought in. Today everyone is dressed in their casual outfits, jeans and sweatpants; when a family member is joining, the dress code remains the same. However, if there are more people invited, family or friends, then everyone dresses up.

Eirini helps Xenofon set the table with a white crisp tablecloth with small flowers, brown linen napkins, and the everyday cutlery. Four white ceramic plates from IKEA are placed on the table, with knife on the right side and fork on the left. The cutlery—plain, steel, and without any frills—has been in the household for decades, a wedding present given to the couple. On special occasions silver cutlery with a more elaborate design is used, a full set of knives, forks, and spoons of various sizes and for various uses (a fish knife, a dessert knife, and so forth). Xenofon inherited these from his grandparents, and they have been in his family for generations. Similarly, the water glasses placed at the top right corner of each plate are also mass-produced, while on special occasions the family heirlooms, fine glasses with handcrafted elements, are used. It seems that the festive meals remain closer to the past, as items of sentimental and monetary value are used, while for everyday meals mass-produced industrialized items are preferred, creating an important distinction between celebration and everyday life, between the past and the present.

The Sunday lunch, considered somewhere between celebration and everyday life, still remains a ritual for the Greek family, and setting the table plays an important role in this. One may eat on the couch in front of the TV or laptop when alone or use paper napkins, but for the family lunch taking the time to set the table is a way of respecting the food and the family. Brown linen napkins are placed on each plate, a way of commemorating the past, as back in the day only linen napkins were used: "Each person had their own linen napkin, and there was always a tablecloth; this is the way we learned, and this is what we want to teach our children," Katerina and Xenofon agree. Wineglasses are also brought to the table, as is a glass carafe with red wine. If there are children or teenagers present, they do not get a wineglass, a subtle separation of the young from the old. No sodas or other beverages accompany the meal, a jug with crisp tap water placed in the middle of the table being the only drink preferred, as if not to intervene with the bold flavors of the food.

Eirini brings a steel bread basket covered in a red cloth with slices of bread. There used to be bakers, but now the loaf of bread is purchased at the supermarket presliced or is sliced at home. Xenofon and Eirini prefer brown bread, while Katerina prefers white, so there might be either depending on what has been purchased. Today it is brown, which makes Eirini very happy as she loves dipping it into the sauce. On the table there is also olive oil, brought in a large tin container from a village in the southern part of Greece; vinegar bought at the supermarket; and freshly squeezed lemon juice made with lemons from the garden, all poured into small glass bottles with corks that used to contain ouzo. There is also fine sea salt and a pepper mill. All these are there for each person to dress their salad. The salads are brought into the table by Xenofon, boiled vegetables for Katerina and a finely chopped lettuce and grated carrot salad for everyone else.

While the table is being prepared, Katerina moves between the living room and the kitchen to check on the food. "Speaking of ingredients," she says, "we only buy tomatoes in the summer. Xenofon goes to the central market, where he buys many kilos of tomatoes, and we sit together, blend them into a puree, place them in jars, and freeze them. So whenever I want to cook something with tomato, I defrost one of these jars." "I don't like the taste of canned tomatoes," Xenofon says. "It doesn't really taste like tomato." They both agree. Fresh ingredients and seasonality still play an important role in the Greek table. Even though many are now using supermarkets to source their foodstuffs, local networks of bakers, butchers, and cheesemongers are still alive, complementing and coexisting with the convenience of the one-stop shop. No matter where people shop, however, seasonality and locality are still valued, as Greek-origin foodstuffs, which can often be more expensive than foreign ones, are preferred. "We always buy Greek meat," Katerina says. "You know how the animals are raised here. And we have to support our producers." An elusive sense of nationalism is being reproduced in the choice of ingredients for the family lunch especially today, a time of crisis.

As the family sits around the table, Katerina brings the glass baking tray with the brown meatloaf, surrounded by the red tomato sauce, golden orzo, and pieces of melted cheese. Everyone waits for all to be served. Then the group wishes "Kali Orexi" (Bon Appétit) so as to start eating. Katerina serves Xenofon first, then Eirini, and in the end herself. If there are guests they are always served first, older people and men having priority over the young and the women. This order of serving still remains very much alive, embracing and maintaining the family and social hierarchies. Xenofon usually gets a large portion of food, while Eirini and Katerina get smaller portions. After Katerina serves, there is always food left, maybe a couple of servings, which remain at the table for whoever would like to eat more. After the end of the meal, the leftovers are kept in glass containers in the fridge; if there are more than two portions left, they are usually stored in the freezer and used on a weeknight so Katerina doesn't have to think of what to cook every day.

There is no TV in the background or music on; Greeks are very, very loud on their own. The only thing that can be heard is the noise from the knives and forks touching the plates, satisfied "mmm" noises, and always the (often heated) discussions on nothing and everything: from what happened during the week at school or work to the way the food tastes ("What is that herb in the meatloaf again? It is delicious.") and from current affairs and the new government to same-sex marriage. Different generations come together, and the young often clash with the old, debating different life views but also seeking advice. Tradition and modernity are defined and negotiated around the Greek table.

Eirini sprinkles some more grated cheese on her orzo as everyone takes a piece of bread from the basket. Xenofon serves himself some water and passes the jug around. He also serves himself some wine; the rest prefer to just have water. Xenofon puts some salad on his salad plate and dresses it with olive oil and vinegar; Eirini doesn't take any, while Katerina prefers lemon and olive oil for her boiled vegetables.

It is a sunny day in Athens as most days are, and the bright light entering the large windows contradicts the wintery food prepared. But foods change according to the seasons, and despite the sunshine it is still winter. In the summer, the family Sunday lunch will probably be served on the balcony and consist of fresh grilled fish, a *horiatiki* (tomato and cucumber salad with feta cheese and olives), crisp cool white wine or beer, and of course bread.

The meatloaf is tender, and the piece with the yolk from the hard-boiled eggs is the one everyone prefers. Xenofon later asks for a second serving, joking that his first piece wasn't "the good one" because it didn't have much of the egg.

Everyone upholds table manners. Eirini's phone beeps, but she doesn't reply to the text. Although there is not a strict no-phones rule, usually phones are left aside for lunch. The only thing eaten with hands is bread. Xenofon explains that when he was young everyone learned how to "properly eat": elbows close to sides, knife on the right hand, and fork on the left, and this is still how all Greeks eat now, young and old. Xenofon tells a story of when he was a young boy and his father used to put books under his arms when eating so that he kept his elbows close to his body, and at boarding school he had to sit at the table for hours to learn how to peel an orange with a knife and fork, making absolutely no sound at all: "You place the orange peel on your plate so that the knife touches the peel and not the plate, and no sound is made." Learning table manners as such forms part of the greater social changes that happened in Greece after the 1950s. The urbanization created the need for many to integrate into city life and create a new social identity closer to the modernized West, escaping from their rural roots. This was manifested in learning the "appropriate" table manners, often described in cookery books of the time. Today, even though table manners are always taught to and followed by the young, these stories seem so strange and make Eirini laugh as she takes pieces of bread and dips them in the tomato sauce, creating mouthfuls of orzo, cheese, tomato, and bread.

The orzo cooked in the tomato sauce has a risotto-like texture, gooey and smooth, but far beyond al dente: pasta, rice, and vegetables are often very well

Seconds?

In some countries it is considered requisite that the host offer more food, and refusing it is considered impolite. In Greece, for example, it is a compliment to the host, and one easily becomes stuffed. In other countries, the offer of food must be politely refused at first. In some contexts an offer of food should not be accepted. In Chile, it is considered impolite to help yourself to seconds. In Scotland if someone says "you'll already have had your tea," that is not a question but a statement, affirming that you won't be served food, so please don't ask. In some places it is expected that you will take a small portion to make sure everyone is fed and only later take more. Equally fascinating is when food placed at the end of a meal should not be touched, as with rice at the end of a Chinese banquet. Eating it would signal that there wasn't enough food, and you're still hungry.

cooked in Greece, the older generation thinking that al dente is a state of cooking synonymous to undercooked. The saltiness of the cheese balances the sweetness of the summer tomatoes, while the cinnamon, although not apparent, offers an Anatolian twist to the otherwise Western flavors, symbolizing Greece's presence betwixt and between these two worlds: Anatolia (in present-day Turkey) and the West. The salad is crispy, offering the much-needed freshness to a warm and comforting meal, while the bread, a staple at the Greek table, is always eaten dipped in the sauce and in the olive oil and vinegar or lemon that remains in the salad bowl.

Xenofon sips his wine while a heated discussion on the significance of fasting has begun. Although certain days of fasting are usually respected in Greek households, this is now changing, as fewer young people conform to the traditional cycles of fasting and feasting. The discussion moves on to a different topic, as Eirini says that she wants to get a dog and everyone offers their opinion. While discussing potential names for the future dog, everyone is almost done eating. Katerina soon starts clearing the plates. She brings two ashtrays and cigarettes for her and Xenofon. The change in the weather is now the topic at hand and how cold it is expected to be in the next few days. Xenofon and Katerina smoke. No dessert is served today, although usually there will be seasonal fruit. Katerina offers to make coffee, indicating the end of the meal. Only now can everyone get up and move to the living room area where they will have coffee.

Nafsika finishes her coffee and says goodbye to the Athenian family; it has been almost two and a half hours since her arrival at this warm home. As the afternoon sun begins to set, Nafsika realizes that until today she had never noticed how important this Sunday lunch is, even though she grew up with it. Nor did she realize how this ritual and this food prepared with love and care holds families together and how it brings comfort to the soul.

Greek Meatloaf

1 medium onion	½ cup grated graviera cheese (or another salty, mature, hard cheese)
Handful of finely chopped parsley leaves	
Quarter of a loaf of stale bread, crusts removed, cut into pieces	2 tablespoons ketchup
	3 hard-boiled eggs
Milk (enough to cover the bread)	Margarine to grease a pan
1 pound of ground beef	Tomatoes
1 pound of ground pork	1¼ cup orzo
Salt and pepper	2–3 pinches of cinnamon
2 eggs	

1. Preheat oven to 400 degrees F.
2. Gently fry the onion until it becomes translucent and slightly brown.
3. Then add the parsley leaves to the onion and turn off the heat. Let cool.
4. Place the pieces of bread into a bowl.
5. Pour enough milk over it so that it covers the bread. Let it soak.
6. In a large bowl, place the ground beef and ground pork, seasoning with salt and pepper.
7. Add the (now) cooled onions with the parsley to the soaked bread, squeezing out with your hands all the excess liquid; add the 2 eggs, the cheese, and the ketchup. Knead using your hands until all ingredients are well mixed together.
8. Peel the 3 hard-boiled eggs.
9. Arrange the meat mixture on a clean surface, forming a wide rectangular shape.
10. Place the 3 hard-boiled eggs on top of the meat mixture, one next to the other, parallel to its longest side.
11. With your hands, lift the meat mixture from the sides and cover the eggs, creating a meatloaf with "hidden" eggs inside.
12. Butter a rectangular deep glass baking tray with margarine. Place the meatloaf in the center.
13. Pour enough tomatoes (pulsed in a food processor) and a little bit of water all around until they reach the middle of the meatloaf.
14. Bake for 45 minutes or until the loaf browns and the tomato is cooked.
15. Remove from oven and add orzo in the tomato sauce; season with salt, pepper, and cinnamon.
16. Add water so that the orzo cooks in the tomato sauce and water.
17. Stir with a spoon so that the orzo, salt, pepper, cinnamon, tomato, and water are well mixed together around the meatloaf.
18. Turn down the oven to 350 degrees, and when the orzo is cooked about 20 minutes later (you may add some more water if needed), sprinkle grated graviera cheese on the orzo, return to the oven, and bake for another 5 minutes or until the cheese melts.

FURTHER READING

Papacharalampous, N. "'This Is Not Kolokythakia Tiganita!' Or What Greek Cookery Books Reveal about Tradition, Nationality and the Localities." MA thesis, School of Oriental and African Studies, University of London, 2012.

Sutton, D. E. *Remembrance of Repasts: An Anthropology of Food and Memory.* Oxford: Oxford University Press, 2001.

Sutton, D. E. *Secrets from the Greek Kitchen: Cooking, Skill, and Everyday Life on an Aegean Island.* Berkeley: University of California Press, 2014.

Sutton, D. E., and M. Hernandez. "Hands That Remember: An Ethnographic Approach to Everyday Cooking." *Expedition* 45 (2003): 31–37.

Zouraris, C. *Deipnosofistis.* 1991; reprint, Athens: Ikaros, 2008.

Zouraris, C. *O defteros deipnosofistis.* Athens: Ikaros, 2001.

Iceland

Nanna Rögnvaldardóttir

Nanna has thousands of cookbooks on her shelves and has cooked all kinds of meals from them for her family, sometimes wonderful, sometimes weird, and frequently both. But when they are all coming for dinner and she wants to make absolutely sure to make everybody happy, she cooks for them an old favorite, *kjöt í karríi*. And when she announces that this is what is for dinner, there is always applause.

Kjöt í karríi, which translates as "meat in curry," is not a remarkable dish in any way; it is chunks of lamb on the bone, simmered until tender. A mild curry sauce is made from the stock, flavored with curry powder and thickened with flour. This is served with boiled white rice and traditionally potatoes and sometimes carrots, although the potatoes, a remainder of the times when Icelanders refused to recognize anything that wasn't served with potatoes as a proper meal, are often left out

The whole family gathers around the table for one of their favorite old-fashioned dishes. Chunks of lamb and mounds of rice are eagerly heaped on every dish and curry sauce is ladled liberally over the servings, but most of the vegetables remain on the serving platter. (Courtesy of Nanna Rögnvaldardóttir)

now. The dish has been popular in Iceland since the mid-19th century and was probably the spiciest thing many people ever had.

Nanna's family loves it. Today they are coming to dinner—all except her daughter-in-law, who is abroad working on her doctoral thesis and prefers her mother's *kjöt í karrí* anyway, so she won't miss it—and Nanna needs to go out to buy some lamb. Usually she would go to a nearby grocery store, but today a market has been set up in the foyer of the gleaming new Harpa concert hall—not where one would usually expect to find a farmers' market, but this is Iceland, where sometimes things are done differently—and someone there will probably have some nice lamb.

Nanna goes there and browses the stalls, tastes several things, and buys some goat meat, a couple of hanger steaks (hard to find elsewhere), some smoked mackerel, and smoked cod's roe. And then she comes across the farmers from Hrólfsstaðahellir, a farm in southern Iceland. They have some succulent-looking horse steaks, which she doesn't need now; a horse sausage that she tastes but finds a bit too dry; and a cooler full of different cuts of lamb. She browses through the vacuum-packed offerings and finds several promising-looking chunks of sirloin, so she buys roughly four and a half pounds. Icelandic lamb is slaughtered fairly young after having grazed on herbs and hardy mountain grasses in the wilderness for a few months, and Nanna knows that it will be both tender and tasty; these farmers know how to raise meat.

When Nanna comes home it is already time to start the cooking, so she goes into the kitchen, gets one of the larger pans out of the cupboard, and places the meat in it. There is not much external fat so she sees no need for trimming it, as she might have done with regular soup meat from a supermarket. Nanna was brought up in a farm culture where fat, a much-needed source of energy in a cold climate, was highly appreciated, and her mother would never have trimmed it from the meat. The young urbanites she is cooking for on this occasion think differently and generally dislike fat.

Nanna adds cold water to just cover the meat, around two quarts, and turns on the burner. When the meat has boiled fairly briskly for a few minutes, she uses a slotted spoon to skim the broth. She adds powdered lamb stock, a bay leaf,

Supermarket Layout and Shelving

In supermarkets the fresh and refrigerated foods range around the periphery of the store, ostensibly for access to electricity. Actually, the higher-priced packaged goods are intentionally placed in the center aisles for greater access, because they are significantly marked up and last longer on the shelf, yielding higher profits for the owner. The end of each aisle is also key, where one finds snacks and foods bought on impulse. Even the arrangement on the shelves is carefully considered. Eye-level shelves are the most important, and manufacturers sometimes pay to have their products placed there, though foods marketed to children are always at their own eye level.

salt, and some carrots. Then she lowers the heat and simmers the lamb for just over an hour.

There is not much to do in the kitchen during this time, so Nanna goes into the dining room to tidy up—there are tablecloths, runners, napkins, plates, and cutlery everywhere because she has been quite busy recently taking photographs for a book she is working on and was using the dining room as the studio, so she needs to get all the styling paraphernalia out of the way.

When that is done, Nanna pulls out one of the dining table extension leaves, as there will be seven people for dinner. The table is old and full of character, and when there are fewer people and she doesn't need the extensions, she rarely uses a tablecloth. But the extension leaves are of a different color than the tabletop, so she fetches back one of the tablecloths she just put away. The weather has been rather inclement recently, but today is the first sunny day for many weeks, so Nanna decides to use a cheerful green tablecloth that she also thinks fits the food nicely, though she can't be bothered to iron it for this crowd. She does have matching cloth napkins but she's not using them this time, on a weekday.

Nanna also thinks about which plates to use. Her granddaughter's boyfriend is coming, and as he is not quite family yet she is not using the everyday plates—instead Nanna opts for her third-best set of plates. They are white with an embossed floral pattern. She wouldn't use anything more fancy than that for this type of food. She also uses the everyday steak cutlery and plain water glasses that she buys in bulk from IKEA. There are no wineglasses; wine is rarely served with everyday food here, and although she fleetingly thinks about asking one of her wine-buff friends to suggest a matching just for fun, she would never serve anything but water with this dish. Forty years ago, milk would have been the norm; Nanna's family used to drink milk with every meal. Even when she was in college, the jugs that were placed on the tables in the canteen contained milk, not water. You had to ask at the counter if you wanted water.

Nanna's son arrives while she is setting the table, and her daughter and her family—her husband, her two children, and the aforementioned boyfriend—appear while she is cooking a pound of rice to serve with the lamb curry. "Ah, the good rice!" the grandson exclaims when he discovers Nanna is using white rice. His more health-conscious mother always uses brown rice. Out of habit, Nanna also cooks a few potatoes although she knows it is unlikely anyone will want them.

The only thing that is left is making the curry sauce, so Nanna removes the meat and carrots from the pan with a slotted spoon onto a serving platter and keeps it warm. Then she half-fills an old jam jar with cold water, adds several heaped tablespoons of flour and a couple of tablespoons of curry powder (or rather what is left in the box, as she doesn't actually measure it), shakes the closed jar vigorously, and stirs the yellow sludge briskly into the boiling broth to thicken it. If she was preparing a smaller amount of sauce she would make a curry roux, but this time she takes a shortcut. Nanna uses all the broth for the sauce so there is an awful lot of it, but she knows her family. She tastes it and adds a little pepper; then the curry sauce can be left to simmer unattended, so she joins the family in the living room.

Starters are rarely served with everyday meals in Iceland, and there is little if any tradition for them in many homes—Nanna doesn't recall her mother serving a single dish during her more than 60 years as a housewife that could be considered a starter—and Nanna would only offer something to nibble on before a meal of this type if she had been trying out a new recipe and wanted to test the results on the family. But she doesn't have anything now, so the family just chats.

After 10 minutes or so the sauce is ready, and so is everything else. Nanna carries the platter of meat and carrots to the table, along with a big bowl of rice and another of curry sauce, and tells her family to be seated. They almost invariably take the same seats every time, but if someone should decide to switch, that wouldn't cause any trouble—except if someone appropriates Nanna's seat at the head of the table, of course.

Nanna is the matriarch of the family, and there is an unwritten rule that no one puts anything on his or her plate until she sits down and says "gjörið svo vel" (please begin). This is how home meals usually start in Iceland, and if someone sneaked something onto his or her plate before the magic words had been uttered, someone else would probably yell at the person or at least frown. Not even the grandson breaks this rule in this family. But the family does not wait for Nanna to serve herself first or expect her to serve them.

Everyone helps himself or herself, and there is no particular order; however, if there are children who need some assistance with their food, someone usually helps them first before starting on his or her own meal. And if there was an outside guest, most of us would wait for that person to begin serving himself or herself, although the always hungry grandson might not have patience for that. The boyfriend is now such a familiar face at the dinner table that he has lost this status, and no one waits for him to begin.

If something needs to be added to the table, Nanna always gets up and fetches it herself, except that one of the others may go and fill the water pitcher from the kitchen tap. On this occasion she needs to go twice into the kitchen to refill the large sauce bowl, because everyone likes to drench the food in curry sauce. But she is prepared for this.

The granddaughter, usually a rather moderate eater who often can't finish even a normal portion of food, heaps her plate with rice and cut-up meat and pours several ladles of curry sauce over it. "This is how it should be," she tells the boyfriend, who is quick to imitate her. Then they dig in.

The dinner is very informal, as most of this family's meals are. The grownups have mostly come straight from their workplace and are wearing their everyday clothes. Nanna's grandson came directly from track practice, so he is hungry. He always is, but this time he is hungry enough for three large helpings. Most of the others have at least two helpings. The evening meal is always timed to begin at 7:00 unless someone has asked for it to be put forward or backward for some reason. The TV is on in the adjoining living room so they can hear the 7:00 news, but there is rarely anything interesting enough to make anyone leave the table to watch, except maybe sports. But today nothing seems to be happening, so even the grandson makes no effort to leave the table until everyone has finished the main course.

The family talks a lot over dinner and laughs a lot. Anything goes, more or less: politics, which the family fortunately mostly agrees on; work; weather; TV shows, which invariably means that the son needs to use his iPhone to show his sister something he has found on YouTube; dogs, which means that the son-in-law reaches for his iPhone to show some photos of their Labradors; sports; and invariably, food. The granddaughter gets a few text messages that she absolutely has to read and respond to during the meal. The son teases the daughter; the daughter teases the son. The grandson asks for help in cutting the meat off the bone, and although everyone tells him that as he is now a teenager he should be able to do it himself, he still gets the assistance he asked for, along with some teasing. Someone mentions sheep from the Skagafjörður region, and every-one laughs at Nanna's expense except the boyfriend. He looks a bit confused; he is not quite used to the family yet and doesn't know about the running jokes in the family.

The grandson, having eaten more than anyone else, is allowed to leave the table even though the grown males are still finishing their meat and curry. He borrows Nanna's laptop and places himself firmly in front of the TV. By the time everyone has finished the main course, there is one small piece of meat and one carrot left and a little sauce, but the rice bowl has been almost licked clean. No one has touched the potatoes, of course; Nanna has planned to use them in another dish tomorrow anyway. The son collects the plates and carries them to the kitchen while Nanna fetches dessert plates, forks, and spoons.

Nanna often serves more than one dessert, as she does a lot of testing and may have several desserts stored in the fridge or freezer. This time there are three—all sugar free and without sugar substitutes, as Nanna has recently discovered that she is prediabetic and decided to quit sugar, as the daughter did two years ago, and try to develop less of a sweet tooth. They do eat fruit and fruit-sweetened desserts and cakes, however. Nanna is also working on a sugar-free cookbook, so there is a co-conut rice pudding with pineapple and mango; baked apples with nuts, raisins, and almond butter; and fruit-flavored ice cream. Everyone likes at least some of the desserts except the son, who announces that life was better on the whole before his sister and Nanna quit sugar. He gets little sympathy.

The grandson returns to the table for dessert. He devours three large helpings of ice cream and tries to stuff some huge chunks into his mouth. He is told that this isn't polite and that if he behaves like that when Nanna takes him to Rome in the spring, the Italian food police will probably arrest him for bad table manners. "But I'm not in Rome now, am I?" he says gleefully and gobbles up another large bite. The next one is smaller, though.

The family remains at the table for quite some time after they have finished the desserts, all except the grandson, who prefers the TV and the computer to their company. As always, Nanna asks the son to make coffee. As a former barista, he does this dutifully and skillfully and brings the coffee to the table in a coffee press. He also gets out the coffee cups, a typical mismatch from the kitchen cupboard. Nanna does have several sets, but they are only used when there are outside guests. The granddaughter and the boyfriend do not want any coffee, but they remain at the table and take part in the conversation.

The walls of the dining room are covered by rows and rows of cookbooks. Usually it is Nanna who reaches for one of them when something comes up in a dinner conversation, but this time the talk somehow turns to nose sizes, and the son starts to search for something he is absolutely sure he saw in one of the cookbooks—he is adamant that there is a photo of a man with the world's largest nose, somehow connected with caviar. The son goes through all the Russian cookbooks but doesn't find it.

The grandson is competing in a track meet early tomorrow morning and has to go to bed early, so his parents prepare to take him home, and the others decide to leave as well. They all say "takk fyrir matinn" (thank you for the food) as they rise from their seats, as is always done here, and Nanna's reply is "verði ykkur að góðu," which may be translated as "may it benefit you" or something along those lines. It would be considered very impolite to leave the table without thanking the host in this manner.

The son collects the dessert plates and brings them into the kitchen. They all say their goodbyes and go away, and as there are almost no leftovers, all that is left for Nanna to do is to rinse the plates and fill the dishwasher. Then she sits back and relaxes. And somehow her thoughts bring back visions of the farm kitchen of her childhood and her mother cooking *kjöt í karríi* for everyone.

Lamb Curry

Serves 4

1½ to 2 pounds lamb, on the bone

Salt

2 teaspoons lamb stock powder, or to taste

1 bay leaf

3 to 4 medium carrots

1½ tablespoon butter, softened

2 tablespoons flour

2 teaspoons curry powder, or to taste

Freshly ground pepper

1. The meat should be cut into fairly large chunks. Cut away excess fat, rinse the meat in cold running water, and put it into a pan.
2. Add enough water to just cover and bring to a boil.
3. Skim and add 1 teaspoon of salt and the bay leaf and carrots. Simmer for around an hour, or until the meat is tender. Remove it, with the carrots, to a plate and keep hot.

4. Strain the broth into a pitcher.
5. Wash and dry the pan and put it back on the cooker at medium heat. Melt the butter, then add flour and curry powder and stir until smooth.
6. Gradually stir in the hot broth until the thickness of the sauce is to your liking—it should be fairly thin. Alternately, just shake flour and curry powder with some cold water and stir into the hot broth.
7. Bring to a boil and simmer for 5 to 10 minutes. Season to taste.

Serve the sauce with the meat and vegetables, along with boiled long-grain rice and maybe some potatoes.

FURTHER READING

Gísladóttir, Hallgerður. *Íslensk matarhefð*. Reykjavík: Mál og menning, 1999.
Ísberg, Nína Rut. "Migration and Cultural Transmission: Making a Home in Iceland." PhD dissertation, University of London, 2010, http://skemman.is/stream/get/1946/14459/34342/1/thesisseptember10.pdf.
Rögnvaldardóttir, Nanna. *Icelandic Food and Cookery*. New and rev. ed. Reykjavík: Iðunn, 2014.

India

Colleen Taylor Sen

Defining and describing a typical Indian meal is a challenge in view of the enormous physical, climatic, ethnic, and religious diversity of a country of more than 1 billion people, 15 official languages and many dialects, 8 major religions, and innumerable sects, castes, classes, and other social divisions. Most Indian languages do not even have a word for a meal and use circumlocutions. For example, to invite someone to your house for a meal, you would ask them to come and "eat" at a certain hour, the time indicating whether it is lunch or dinner. While an English speaker might ask if you had "lunch" (or "dinner"), a north Indian Hindi speaker would ask "roti khaya?" (Have you eaten bread?), and a Bengali speaker might ask "bhat kheiicho?" (Have you eaten rice?), indicating the importance of these starches in their diet.

Although there are enormous regional and even local variations in the food of the Indian subcontinent, Indian meals share some common characteristics. Generally, a diner never touches the food or plate of another person. Food touched by another person, even a spouse or other family member, is considered polluted and therefore inedible. In the past, leftover food would be given to servants, homeless people, or even cows and birds, but today, with refrigeration, most families reheat vegetables and rice from the previous night's dinner for breakfast or take it to the office for lunch.

Traditionally, people sat on the floor for meals and took their

The traditional way of eating in India is by using one's right hand, as this family is doing. This allows the eater to mix the elements on the plate to his or her personal taste and enhances the sensory experience of dining. (Szefei/Dreamstime.com)

food from banana leaves or *thalis* (round metal plates with a raised rim holding little bowls), using only their right hand to convey the food in their mouths. Today, many middle-class people in cities sit on chairs at dining tables and eat from plates using Western-style cutlery, mainly forks and spoons, since meat and vegetables are already cut into pieces. Those who can afford it have two main meals—lunch and dinner, the former being the most important—and two supplementary meals: breakfast and a light snack in the afternoon, sometimes called "tea" or "tiffin." The core of a meal is a starch (such as wheat, rice, millet, sorghum, or corn) plus boiled lentils (dal), which together provide most of the needed amino acids. They are supplemented by vegetables, meat, and fish and an array of condiments, including sweet chutneys; sweet, sour, hot, and very hot pickles; salads; and yogurt. Vegetarians (who constitute around a third of the Indian population, mainly Hindus, but only around 5 percent of Bengalis) avoid meat, although very few Indians are vegan. However, even nonvegetarians eat relatively little meat for economic reasons since meat is expensive, although meat consumption is increasing with rising incomes. Alcohol is very rarely consumed with a meal; the standard beverage is water.

Indian meals do not normally have a sequence of courses. Everything arrives more or less at once, although certain dishes may appear at different points in the meal. Even in Bengali cuisine, where dishes are served sequentially, they remain on the table throughout the meal and are mixed together on the same plate. The Nobel laureate Octavio Paz, for a decade Mexico's ambassador to India, writes:

> In European cooking, the order of the dishes is quite precise. It is a diachronic cuisine. . . . A radical difference: in India, the various dishes come together on a single large plate. Neither a succession nor a parade, but a conglomeration and

Sharing and Pollution

In some cultures, eating from others' plates is considered rude unless there is a close personal connection. Sharing is not uncommon, but custom dictates that one ask first. This only applies to countries where private plates are the norm, as in Europe and the United States. Strangers eating from another's plate can be a violation of personal space or might be considered a form of pollution, as someone else's fork and saliva touches your food. This can be true even if that person is a person one would normally kiss. In India, even a spouse's plate is polluted. At a family dinner table, siblings or spouses may regularly eat off each other's plates or even surreptitiously snag food. Arguably, private dining space only developed with the idea of private property in the context of capitalism in the West, and in fact the idea of pollution is anything but universal. In Ethiopia, *gursha* is exactly the opposite, a gesture of closeness in which one person picks up food with the flat bread *injera* in the hand and feeds another.

superimposition of things and tastes; a synchronic cuisine. A fusion of flavors, a fusion of times. (Ray, 2004, 28–29)

The following is a description of a meal in the home of a middle-class Bengali family: Ranjit, a colonel in the Indian army; his wife Anisha; and their two daughters Rinku and Tinku (their pet names, used by family members), who are 7 and 15 years old, respectively. They live in a spacious apartment in an army complex at Fort William in Kolkata. The family has their main meal at midday. During the week it takes place around 2:00 or 2:30 p.m. when the girls come back from school, but on weekends it may be an hour or so earlier. Whenever he can Ranjit joins his family for lunch, in which case they eat in the dining room. But when it just the girls and Anisha, they often have lunch in the TV room while watching television. Dinner is typically much later—at 10:00 or 11:00 p.m. or even later in some Kolkata families. The interval between meals is broken by an afternoon tea around 5:30 or 6:00 at which savories, such as samosas, sweets (both Western and Indian style), and tea are served. Tea is served in the British style with milk and sugar, rarely spices.

Anisha, who does not work outside the house, does all the cooking herself, although a part-time male servant does the daily shopping at a nearby outdoor market. It's not uncommon for men to do the shopping in Bengali families, especially for fish. Part-time servants also help with chopping the vegetables, which can be time consuming, and the washing up. In the past middle-class families had live-in servants, but this is becoming rarer. It is common in cities for several families to share the services of helpers.

Anisha's kitchen, like most Indian kitchens, is small by Western standards. She does most of her cooking on a couple of burners fueled by bottled gas. (Ovens are rare in Indian homes.) Anisha sometimes uses a pressure cooker, which speeds up the cooking of meat that otherwise can take several hours. The Indian batterie de cuisine is also relatively small. A common receptacle is a deep stainless steel or cast-iron pot (*karahi*) with two handles and a flat or slightly concave bottom that is used for sautéing and deep-frying. Rice and currylike dishes with a liquid gravy are prepared in a straight-sided pan with a lid. A *tawa*, a flat heavy iron griddle with a long handle, is used for roasting and preparing breads that require little or no oil. A perforated metal spoon is used for frying and draining, and a ladle is used for stirring. In Bengal, a large knife mounted on a wooden board called a *bonti* is used to cut fish and large vegetables. In the past all the preparation was done sitting on the floor, but in modern households such as Anisha's the work is done on granite or marble counters. She grinds the spices by hand using a stone rolling pin on a stone slab.

Today some relatives are visiting, so the midday meal will be slightly more elaborate than usual. Because it is mid-June and the weather is very hot, the menu features some dishes believed to be cooling. Anisha cooks everything in advance and warms the food over the stove before serving. In general, Indian food is not served at a hot temperature: warm or even room temperature is standard. Her first task is to cook the rice, which is the main starch in the Bengali diet and is served throughout the meal. First, she washes the rice carefully, removing any impurities, and drains it well. She brings water three times the volume of the rice to a boil, then adds the washed rice and cooks it over medium heat until each grain is soft yet separate. (In traditional Bengali society, a girl being considered as a bride had to cook rice for her potential in-laws. If the rice was sticky, the candidate was not considered suitable.) Anisha drains the rice to remove excess starch and keeps it warm over the stove.

Today's meal will start with a bitter dish called *shukto* that is intended to stimulate the appetite (just as the French take a glass of vermouth as a digestif). *Shukto* is the traditional first course in a Bengali lunch, especially in the summer because of its cooling properties. Anisha carefully slices the vegetables: potatoes, eggplant, white radish, potol (a small green squash), unripe banana, and bitter gourd; the thickness of the slices depends on how quickly the vegetable takes to cook. She sautés the vegetables in vegetable oil, then mixes them with a paste of ground turmeric, ginger, cumin, and mustard seed and simmers the mixture until the vegetables are cooked. The final touch is a sprinkling of *panchphoron* fried in ghee. *Panchphoron* (meaning "five spices") is the standard Bengal masala (spice mixture), made from equal parts of fennel seeds, *radhuni* (known as celery seeds though actually a different plant, *Trachyspermum roxburghianum*), nigella (black cumin or onion seed, which is actually neither cumin nor onion; in Hindi it is called *kalonji*), fenugreek seeds, and cumin seeds. At the very end she adds a little milk and sugar. Bengalis are famous for their sweet tooth, and a pinch of sugar is often added to vegetable and meat dishes.

Next she prepares dal, a seasoned soupy preparation of boiled lentils. There are many varieties of lentils and many methods of preparation. Today she cooks *urad* (black) dal, which is a typical summertime dish (see recipe) and more complicated to prepare than the *masur* dal (also called red or Egyptian dal), which is the usual dal served in Anisha's household.

Next because there are guests, she prepares three vegetable dishes: one fried, one lightly spiced, and a third that is heavier. Normally she makes only one or two of them. The fried dish is sliced eggplant rubbed with turmeric and salt and then deep-fried in mustard oil. The second is sweet golden mung dal; mung dal is dry roasted, simmered with onions and green chilies, cooked with sautéed bay leaves, and cumin seeds and finally mixed with a little milk and sugar. The third dish is *lau ghanto,* slices of bottle gourd that are sautéed and then simmered with cumin, turmeric, coriander, and chili paste and finally stir-cooked with bori—little pellets of ground dried lentil paste that are bought ready-made.

The centerpiece of a Bengali meal is fish, which is a marker of Bengali identity. "Maccher bhate bangali," says a proverb, meaning "Fish + rice = Bengali." In Bengal, even people who would be vegetarians elsewhere in India eat fish, which is jokingly called "vegetables of the river." Carp is a favorite, cooked in mustard oil (a traditional Bengali cooking medium) or boiled to make a stew called *maccher jhol,* which is what Anisha makes today for her guests. She rubs thick slices of carp with turmeric and salt, then fries them in mustard oil. She sautés *panchphoron* and a paste of aromatic spices in a little oil, then adds water and some potatoes, which were fried earlier. After a few minutes, she adds the fish and cooks the mixture a while longer. However, because her children don't like fish, Anisha makes a chicken curry as well. She sautés sliced onions in ghee, then adds chilies, garlic, and onions ground into a paste and sautés the mixture with chopped tomatoes. She stir-fries chicken pieces, adds water, and simmers the chicken for around an hour. Finally, she adds some quartered potatoes and cooks until the chicken and potatoes are done and the gravy has thickened. Her final task is the preparation of *tok*, a sweet and sour chutney that will act as a palate cleanser before dessert. Tomatoes are often used in this dish, but her children don't like them either, so she makes it with apples.

Anisha sets the table herself in the dining room. She spreads a cloth over the table and puts cotton napkins at each place setting together with a plate, a knife, and a spoon. Anisha serves everyone herself, starting with the guests, then her husband, and finally her children. First she takes around a bowl of rice, putting some on each plate until the person served asks her to stop, often by saying *bas* (enough). Next she brings out the other dishes on their separate serving plates and serves each dish to her guests and the family. Shukto comes first, followed by the dal, the vegetables, the fish, and the chicken curry. However, although the dishes are served sequentially, they remain on the table throughout the meal so that people can take more of a dish they particularly like. A dish of hot pickles is there for those who like to add a bit of piquancy to their food. The rice is constantly replenished as needed. Each guest is served a glass of water, although Indians in general drink very little during the meal.

Anisha sits down and serves herself only after everyone else has eaten. At the very end of the meal she serves a typical Bengali dessert, bought from one of Kolkata's many sweet shops: *mishti doi* (sweet yogurt), a thick, sweet yet slightly sour yogurt made from buffalo milk that is always sold in little clay pots, which help keep it cool. *Mishti doi* is eaten with a spoon. Tea or coffee are not usually served at the end of a meal.

The older members of the family eat with their fingers, mixing a bit of food with the rice and popping it into their mouths. Tinku and Rinku eat solid items with their fingers but use spoons with the dishes with gravy. Some people mix several items together, while others prefer to eat them separately. In an Indian meal, the diner becomes an active participant in the creation of the meal by mixing and matching dishes and flavors to suit his or her individual tastes.

When the family dines alone, the children talk about what happened at school, and Rinku is especially talkative. They aren't allowed to bring their beloved cell phones to the table. When guests are present, the conversation touches on the activities of friends and relatives as well as pending marriages, a favorite topic of conversation.

Urad dal is one of the richest sources of proteins and vitamin B as well as fiber, which makes it easy to digest. (Manubahuguna/Dreamstime.com)

When the meal is over, Anisha clears the table; sometimes the children help her. A part-time maid comes in to wash the dishes in the sink. Leftovers are stored in the refrigerator, to be recycled at a later meal.

Urad Dal

½ pound *urad* (black) lentils

6 cups of water

A pinch of turmeric powder

2 tablespoons of ginger paste (ginger ground in water)

Salt and sugar to taste

1 tablespoon clarified butter (ghee)

½ teaspoon mustard seeds

2 dry red chilies

1. Bring the water to a boil, and add the dal and the turmeric.
2. Cook over high heat until the lentils are cooked (around half an hour).
3. Add the ginger paste, a little sugar, and salt and mix well.

4. Heat the ghee in the *krahi,* and sauté the mustard seeds and chilies until they stop crackling.
5. Pour over the dal and mix well.

FURTHER READING

Banerji, Chitrita. *Life and Food in Bengal.* Calcutta: Rupa Paperback, 1993.

DasGupta, Minakshi. *Bangla Ranna: The Bengal Cookbook.* 2nd rev. ed. New Delhi: UBSPD, 2012.

Ray, Krishnendu. *The Migrant's Table.* Philadelphia, PA: Temple University Press, 2004.

Sen, Colleen Taylor. *Feasts and Fasts: A History of Food in India.* London: Reaktion, 2014.

Indonesia

Amanda Katili Niode

The province of Gorontalo on the island of Sulawesi, Indonesia, is located in the Wallacea, a transition zone between the Oriental and Australian regions. It is a relatively untouched paradise boasting great aquatic life, lakes, forts, and underwater reefs as well as beautiful mountainous scenery and an interesting history. It is a great destination for those who seek natural landscapes of mountains and sea without the crowds. Last but not least, it is also a top destination for food lovers. Gorontalo gained fame as the ancestral land of famous Indonesians, including an Indonesian president, a national hero, singers, and business moguls.

Bordering Sulawesi Sea and the Philippines to the north and Tomini Bay and Molucca Sea to the south, the province of Gorontalo has a population of 1 million people, about 66 percent of whom live in rural areas, while 34 percent live in urban areas. Its capital, the city of Gorontalo, population 180,000, has views of the hills and nearby coastal areas with world-class dive sites. Near the city is Tomini Bay, with a number of small islands spreading around the sea that have abundant coral reefs and an enormous number of ocean species, hence an excellent source of seafood.

The food of this region is generally spicy but rarely includes sugar or artificial flavorings; thus it is said to be honest and natural. Arifasno Napu, a nutrition expert who conducted research on traditional Gorontalo food, identified 15 staple foods; along with rice there are also sago, maize, and cassava. Traditionally there are 10 vegetable dishes with local or vegetable-based ingredients that are common in Indonesia, namely eggplant, water spinach, and fern. There are 35 kinds of snacks that traditionally are not made of wheat flour but of maize, cassava, sweet potatoes, bananas, and rice flour. There are also 15 side dishes with basic ingredients from lakes and the ocean, including freshwater fish and seafood (mostly fish and sometimes shrimp).

The dinner table features a wide array of foods (recipes follow below): steamed white rice and an appetizer of *binthe lo putungo,* which is roasted corn with banana blossom. There is also a *sate tuna* (tuna satay), a fish dish called *bobara bakar* (grilled trevallies), and *Bilenthango* (fish split and topped with herbs and spices) as well as *mujair bakar rica* (grilled tilapia with chili pepper). The table also includes *ayam bakar rica* (grilled chicken with chili pepper) and a kind of black soup with meat called *tabu moyitomo. Tilumiti lo kando* is a dish of stir-fried water spinach,

A father, mother, and three children gather around a dining table in a middle class home in Gorontalo, Gorontalo Province, Indonesia for a family meal. The dishes consist of fish, chicken, water spinach, papaya blossoms, and roasted corn and banana blossoms. (Courtesy of Donald Wahani)

pilitode lo paku is fern with coconut milk, and *pilitode lo-poki poki* is eggplant with coconut milk. All these are accompanied by *sambal* (hot condiments), which include *sambal roa* (smoked, crushed, and spiced garfish), *dabu-dabu* (chili, shallot, and tomato condiment), and *sambal cabai* (chili pepper condiment). There are also bananas (*pisang*), and there is mineral water to drink.

The housewife does the daily cooking, assisted by a servant or members of the extended family such as sisters, aunts, or nieces who may live in the same household. The ingredients are purchased at the Central Market that is opened from 6:00 a.m. to 5:00 p.m. Sometimes there are roving fishmongers riding motorbikes or bicycles with rattan baskets full of fish on both sides of the vehicles. The central market in Gorontalo carries all kinds of ingredients, sometimes sold individually or premixed. For example, the coconut used as an ingredient for *tabu moyitomo* (meat in black soup) is grated and then toasted. Customers can buy this prepared coconut to mix with other ingredients to prepare the black soup.

Early in the morning women often go to the fish port, which has a fish auction facility and a fish market, to buy newly caught fish from incoming fishing boats. Besides auctioning, the facility provides stalls that mostly sell fish, some shrimp, and sometimes crabs, scallops, and oysters. Beef and chicken are commonly purchased in the central market. Housewives in Gorontalo prefer to buy their kitchen needs every day at the traditional markets rather than storing food ingredients at home, as it is considered better to have fresh foods.

Some joke that fish from Gorontalo only die once compared to fish that has died five times in landlocked areas, since the fish have to pass through many hands and are stored in freezers before being consumed.

A typical visit to the traditional market is usually around 7:00 a.m. and lasts for about an hour so that upon returning home, women still have plenty of time to cook. To get to the market, they walk if it is within walking distance. But if the market is far away they may ride a *bendi* (horse-drawn cart) or *bentor* (motorcycle modified into a rickshaw). By spending about two to three hours in the kitchen, a housewife with one assistant can finish cooking a number of dishes, as shown in the picture.

The food is cooked from scratch by first cleaning the fish, chicken, or meat to be cooked. Also, vegetables, tomatoes, and onions need to be washed clean and cut, sliced, or chopped. A stone mortar is available to grind herbs and spices. Certain foods such as *morongi* (spiced shredded chicken) take up to seven hours to cook and can be stored for a long time in the refrigerator and then reheated as needed. Grilled food takes about one to two hours, from the time of beginning preparation until ready to serve.

The equipment used for cooking nowadays is semimodern, such as a gas-fired stove. However, certain foods such as satay and corn are prepared using a simple barbecue grill fired by coconut shells, often mixed with candlenut shells. Steamed white rice as a staple food is cooked using a rice cooker. It is more practical and saves a lot of time, as it takes only a maximum of 30 minutes to have the rice cooked. Indonesians eat rice three times a day, and rice is one of the nine necessities for daily living. The others are sugar, cooking oil and butter, beef and chicken, eggs, milk, corn, kerosene/gas, and iodized salt. For some people, although they

Kitchen Tools

There is a surprising array of kitchen implements around the world, some of which are more or less universal, while others are unique to individual places. No Mexican kitchen would be without a blender, which to a great extent has replaced the *molcajete* for making sauces. An Asian kitchen is rarely without a rice cooker, which is unusual in the West. Coconut scrapers are found in Southeast Asian kitchens but almost never in the West. Likewise, toasters are fairly unique among Western bread-eating cultures. Even the standard knife and cutting board arrangement is not as ubiquitous as one might think. In some cultures one cuts up ingredients with a small knife in the hand. In Bengal, India, food is cut on a *bonti*, a stationary knife that one sits in front of, passing the food across the blade.

may have eaten a wide variety of foods and are full, they nonetheless don't consider it a real meal unless there is rice on the menu.

The blender is one modern electric appliance that is present in most kitchens. This tool is only used to grind ingredients to a very fine consistency, while the sauce or seasoning for grilled fish or chicken with chili pepper still uses a traditional stone mortar because this results in a coarse texture with visible herbs and spices.

Dabu-dabu, a salsalike hot condiment, does not need to be cooked, just thinly sliced and seasoned to taste with a little extra salt or other flavorings. Chili peppers, hot chili, lime, grated coconut, coconut milk, and homemade coconut oil are must-have ingredients in every household in Gorontalo. Hot peppers in Gorontalo are unique. In addition to their small size, they have a smooth and shiny skin and are hot beyond belief. Gorontalese take this hot pepper wherever they go, because it is different from chilies in other parts of Indonesia and elsewhere in the world.

Coconut oil is another important ingredient. To make 17 ounces of homemade coconut oil, press coconut milk out of 10 coconuts. Boil for about three hours, constantly stirring, which gives it a distinct and very savory taste and smell. Home-made coconut oil is an ingredient for both hot condiments and stir-fried and deep-fried dishes. Grated coconut is produced by using a traditional coconut grater; one sits on a sort of bench, and in front (connected to the bench) is a sharp coconut grater with metal spikes on which one scrapes the meat out from the coconut shell. Hand-grated coconut has a different texture compared to what is produced by a modern coconut grater.

Dinnertime is 7:30–8:30 p.m. after the Isya prayer. Family members sit on chairs in front of the dining table. All food is placed on the table for sharing, and the tables in middle-class and well-to-do homes are usually filled with food selections. Public officials have food available all day in their homes as guests come and go. Family members take food from the serving plates for themselves, especially food that they like, as each family member may have different preferences. Parents help young children, encouraging those who are not fond of vegetables or just want certain foods.

In the old days, fathers got the best part of food (bigger in volume and prime selection) because they were the breadwinners of the households. Nowadays parents prioritize their children, and fathers today are keener in serving their children. The dinnerware is Western style, but the way the food is placed on the table does not exactly follow Western style. There are serving plates to put food on the table and dinner plates for family members. Cutlery is usually spoons and forks made of stainless steel, and one never finds a knife at the table. The food is already cut into bite-size morsels, so there is no need to cut food anyway. Spicy and hot foods with rice are sometimes consumed with the right hand without spoons and forks. To eat satay, one holds the end of the stick and bites the meat.

Although many residents of Gorontalo eat fish, there are no special small plates for fishbones on the table, as they are just placed on the edge of the individuals' plates. On the table, large spoons are available to take and put food on individual plates. There are rarely individual soup bowls. The soup is poured into a deep dinner plate that will also directly be used for other foods. Soup is often mixed with other dishes.

Food is taken from pots and pans in a kitchen or in the larder, placed in the appropriate plates, and all laid out on the table at once. The plating is like *nasi campur* (rice with side dishes in small quantities surrounding the rice). People can have seconds or thirds as they wish, provided the food is still available. If the food is limited, though, they are careful to share it fairly unless there are family members who do not like meat or chicken, in which case those who do take larger portions. If food runs out at the dinner table, the mother might get some more if there is still some left in the kitchen. Because food is generally spicy, rice is eaten quite a lot, with the portion of rice much bigger than the side dishes. There is also a water dispenser located near the dining table to make it easier for family members to get drinking water.

Table mats are also common at the dinner table, functioning as place mats and to make cleaning the table easier after dinner. A white tablecloth is commonly used as well. Napkins made of cloth or paper are sometimes placed on the table, but diners usually go directly to the sink not far away from the dinner table to wash their hands. In some houses there are small bowls for hand washing, placed next to dinner plates. Those who want to be practical have plastic table-cloths because they are easy to clean, but plastic ruins the beauty of a dining table. Tablecloths are purchased from a specialty store or from a friend who sews them, while the plastic tablecloths are sold in supermarkets or even tradi-tional markets.

Conversation at the dinner table begins as usual with questions from the chil-dren, asking their mother about the day's cooking and whether their favorite foods are on the table. Children sometimes complain about unfamiliar foods and unu-sual tastes. The mother may also complain about ever-rising food costs. The dining room is a special place for eating dinner. Families gather wearing casual attire. They recount what happened during the day. Children tell parents what happened at school. No cell phones or games are allowed at the dining table, nor are pets because an eating place should be clean. The time spent for dining on average is one hour. There should be no shouting or food fights. Children are allowed to speak only after their food has been swallowed so as not to choke. Everyone stays until dinner is finished. Television, radio, and music sets have their own place in the living room, not in the dining room.

The food put on the plate should be finished, respecting our brothers and sisters who cannot afford to buy food. Parents set an example for their children regarding table manners and instantly correct mistakes their children make in how to hold a fork or spoon. There should also be no sound when chewing food.

In general, on the dining room wall there is framed artwork—nature paintings, drawings of vegetables or fruit, and other beautiful paintings that are thought to increase a person's appetite. The dining room looks cozy with a beautiful flower arrangement.

A household assistant or family members help clear the table and wash the dishes. Children do not wash the dishes for fear that they will break ceramic plates and glasses. Dishes are washed with dish soap. Soot at the bottom of pots and pans is scrubbed first with coconut fiber or with ashes. Any leftover food is shared with the household assistant or other families or kept as leftovers for consumption the next day.

Drinking water is always available during breakfast, lunch, and dinner. More than 20 years ago, most people boiled their water before drinking. Nowadays those who have enough money buy large containers of mineral water that are placed on a water dispenser, as mineral water is considered clean and practical. Tea or coffee are consumed in the mornings and afternoons or served if there are guests, so coffee or tea usually does not follow dinner. If coffee is served to guests, called *kopi lo polondulo* in Gorontalo, it is a hint that it is time to end the visit or an event.

Children eat the same food, but there are specially prepared foods that are not too hot or spicy. They also avoid bony fish. Parents try to get their children to eat with the concept of "four is healthy and five is perfect." The four is rice, meat/fish, vegetables, and fruits. The five is milk, although milk is not consumed at dinner.

Fish, chicken, and meat are often presented whole or shredded so that all the seasonings can be absorbed, hence the food will taste better. There are several kinds of condiments for each member of the family with different spiciness. Sometimes in a family there are several kinds of condiments available based on preference, such as soy sauce, tomato sauce, eggplant sauce, chili garlic sauce, chili vinegar (vinegar, red eye chili, and onion), and chili pepper condiment.

Tofu and tempeh, soya-based foods, are popular in Java, where most than 60 percent of Indonesia's population live, but are rarely found in Gorontalo, although due to the increasing number of migrants local markets are beginning to sell tofu and tempeh.

Snacks are common in the morning or afternoon. Quite popular is fried bananas eaten with hot sauce. A combination of bananas and peanuts is consumed by teenagers and couples.

Most of Indonesia's population is Muslim, so there are forbidden foods, including pork, blood, or animals that live in two worlds, such as amphibians (e.g., frogs and turtles). Alcoholic drinks are strictly prohibited.

Because Gorontalo is located near the sea, fish dishes are very popular. Those who grew up there are very sensitive and can distinguish between fresh fish and slightly spoiled fish by the look of fish and the taste. Fresh fish is always very tasty even when cooked without excessive seasoning. Freshwater fish from Lake

Limboto is also very popular. Fish such as tilapia cultured in fish ponds is more common now than lake fish due to the eutrophication of the lake that decreases the number of endemic species.

Offal of chicken, cattle, and goat is not eaten, including oxtail. But in the last 10 years, Gorontalo's eating habits have begun to change due to the increasing number of migrants coming into the city after it became the capital of the province in 2001. Prior to that Gorontalo was just a regency, with the provincial capital located eight hours east by car.

Living in an agricultural area with abundant marine resources, it is unusual for families to go hungry even if they only have minimal income. The food sold has always been mostly local food. But now many chain restaurants are found in Gorontalo, and this has been changing the role of local food so that young people are not familiar with local food and snacks. Local homes are still the best place to find delicious authentic Gorontalo food. Inviting guests to dinner is considered a way to respect people.

Steamed White Rice

Appetizer
Binthe lo Putungo (roasted corn with banana blossom)

For the grilled corn:

Corn	Butter

For the *putungo*:

½ part banana blossom, cut lengthwise	5 cloves of shallot
½ pound shrimp	2 cloves of garlic
About ¾ cup of grated young coconut	Hot pepper to taste
Papaya leaves	Salt to taste

To make the grilled corn:
Peel corn and grill over charcoals or coconut shells while buttered. Do not overgrill.

To make the *putungo*:

1. Thinly slice banana blossom and place in a bowl.
2. Rotate a stick in the middle of the banana blossom pile, down to the bottom of bowl. Clamp the stick between two palms, move one hand forward and one

hand backward to eliminate the sap of the banana blossom; repeat and wash clean.

3. Wash and boil shrimp for about 15 minutes and set aside.
4. Slice green papaya leaves. Wash and set aside.
5. Grind shallot, garlic, hot pepper, and salt and set aside.

To serve:

1. Mix together all the ingredients already prepared: sliced banana blossom, papaya leaves, grated coconut, boiled shrimp, and spices. Stir until evenly marinaded.
2. Place on a plate ready to be served with grilled corn.

Fish

Sate Tuna (tuna satay)

1 pound of fresh tuna	5 cloves of shallot
Homemade coconut oil	7 pieces of chili pepper
Skewers	Hot pepper to taste
2 pieces of lemon	Salt to taste

Make the satay:

1. Cut tuna into bite-size cubes. Pour lemon juice and a little salt over the fish and stir.
2. Stick 5 cubes to each skewer.
3. Grill the tuna satay for about 10–15 minutes.

Make the sauce:

1. Grind shallot, chili pepper, hot pepper, and salt.
2. Boil homemade coconut oil.
3. Pour in a little lemon juice, add salt, and set aside.

To serve:
Put grilled tuna satay on a plate and pour sauce that had been prepared earlier, ready to be served.

Bobara Bakar (Grilled Trevallies)

Trevallies	1 piece of lemon for each fish
Homemade cooking oil	

1. Clean the trevallies and discard the gills.
2. Slice the fish sideways and pour lemon juice on it.
3. Grill fish for about 15 minutes while basting to keep it intact until cooked. Remove and serve.

Bilenthango (Fish Split and Topped with Herbs and Spices)

3 pieces of tilapia fish	2 tomatoes
Cooking oil for frying	2 stalks of scallions
7 cloves of shallot	Salt to taste
Hot pepper to taste	

1. Grind the shallot, hot pepper, and salt.
2. Thinly slice the tomatoes and finely slice the scallions lengthwise.
3. Mix all and set aside.
4. Wash tilapia but do not eliminate all of its scales.
5. Split the fish into two without breaking. Put all the seasoning on top of the fish.
6. Cover a frying pan with banana leaves.
7. Put oil on top and fry the seasoned fish.
8. Pour hot oil, taken from the edge of the fish, on top of the fish in a frying pan. Pour over and over until cooked and the seasoning still looks fresh.

Note: The benefit of scales on *bilenthango* is to keep the fish intact during the cooking process. If all the fish scales are gone, the fish body will be broken in pieces when removed from the pan.

Mujair Bakar Rica (Grilled Tilapia with Chili Pepper)

3 tilapia	5 pieces of chili pepper
Cooking oil for greasing	Hot pepper
2 pieces of lemon	Salt to taste
5 cloves of shallot	

1. Clean the inside of the tilapia fish. Do not remove the scales. Wash.
3. Grill while basting. Do not overgrill.

To make the sauce:

1. Finely grind shallot, chili pepper, hot pepper, and salt.
2. Pour in heated homemade cooking oil.
3. Put in a little bit of lime juice and add salt.

To serve:

1. Put the grilled tilapia on a plate.
2. Pour the sauce over the fish and serve.

Poultry

Ayam Bakar Rica (Grilled Chicken with Chili Pepper)

1 local chicken	7 cloves of shallots
4 cloves of garlic	7 pieces of chili pepper
1 teaspoon of fine coriander	Hot pepper
Salt to taste	Oil to baste

To make the chicken:

1. Clean the chicken and cut into 2 parts (chest and thigh).
2. Boil chicken until half cooked with sliced garlic, coriander, and salt.
3. Drain and grill, basting with oil.

To make the sauce:

1. Finely grind shallot, chilies, hot pepper, and salt.
2. Pour heated oil over and add lemon juice and salt.

To serve:

1. Put grilled chicken on a serving plate.
2. Pour the sauce prepared earlier over the chicken.

Soup

Tabu Moyitomo (Meat in Black Soup)

1 pound of beef or beef ribs	15 shallots
8½ cups of water to boil	5 cloves of garlic
2 tablespoons of cooking oil	15 pieces of chili pepper
1 cup of grated coconut	Hot pepper to taste

1 teaspoon of coriander

1 teaspoon of pepper

½ teaspoon of fine cumin

1 inch of roasted turmeric

5 stalks of lemongrass

3 small slices of galangal

1 inch of roasted ginger

2 tablespoons of tamarind

Basil leaves

Lime leaves

Pandan leaves

Scallions

Salt

To make the beef:

1. Boil beef in a stew pan until cooked.
2. Set aside

Make the soup:

1. Toast shredded coconut in a frying pan until lightly browned.
2. Grind until the oil from the shredded coconut is out. Set aside.
3. Grind and blend shallot, garlic, red chili, hot pepper, coriander, pepper, galangal, lemongrass, turmeric, ginger, cumin, and salt.
4. Mix ground spices with scallions, basil leaves, pandan leaves, and lime leaves.
5. Sauté with the toasted coconut until cooked.
6. Pour the sautéed spices into the stew pan.
7. Simmer until the spices seep into the meat.
8. Ready to be served.

Vegetables

Tilumiti Lo Kando (Stir-Fried Water Spinach)

2 bunches of water spinach

5 cloves of shallots

3 cloves of garlic

Hot pepper

Salt

Homemade coconut oil

1. Slice the spinach and split the stems and the leaves. Wash and set aside.
2. Slice shallots, garlic, and hot pepper. Set aside.
3. Sauté sliced seasoning with a little oil, add a little bit of water, and add salt to taste.
4. At boiling point, put in the spinach stems and leave them in until half cooked.
5. Put in the leafy part of the spinach.
6. Stir-fry until cooked and serve.

Pilitode Lo Paku (Fern with Coconut Milk)

1 cup of papaya flowers	3 cloves of garlic
3 young papaya leaves	Hot pepper
2 bunches of fern leaves	Salt
5 cloves of shallots	Cooking oil

To make the papaya leaves:
1. Boil papaya flower until tender and it has lost its bitter taste. Set aside.
2. Thinly slice young papaya leaves. Wash and set aside.
3. Pick the leaves or stems of young ferns. Wash and set aside.

To make the seasoning:
1. Slice shallot, garlic, and hot pepper.

To finish:
1. Sauté the seasoning. Add salt to taste.
2. Add a little water. Next add the boiled papaya flower, the sliced papaya flower, and fern leaves and stir-fry until cooked. Serve.

Pilitode Lo-Poki Poki (Eggplant with Coconut Milk)

2 bunches of long purple eggplants	2 cloves of garlic
1¼ cup of coconut milk	5 chili peppers
Oil for frying	Hot pepper to taste
7 cloves of shallots	Salt to taste

To make the eggplants:
1. Cut the eggplants lengthwise into 2 parts and wash.
2. Fry eggplants and set aside.

Make the sauce:
1. Grind shallot, garlic, chili peppers, hot pepper, and salt and set aside.
2. Sauté the ground spices with a little oil until fragrant.
3. Pour in coconut milk and stir until boiling.

To finish:
1. Put the fried egg plants in coconut milk. Cook over low heat.
2. Stir until cooked and ready to serve.

Sambal (Hot Condiments)

Sambal Roa (Smoked, Crushed, and Spiced Garfish)

7 smoked roa (garfish)

5 cloves of shallots

Chili pepper

1 tomato

Oil

Salt to taste

1. Clean the smoked roa by separating the mouths and the bones.
2. Finely crush and set aside.
3. Slice shallot, chili, and tomatoes and stir-fry with a little oil.
4. After the tomato is cooked, add the smoked roa and stir until cooked.

Dabu-Dabu (Chili, Shallot, and Tomato Condiment)

5 cloves shallots

Hot pepper

2 tomatoes

1 lime

2 tablespoons of homemade coconut oil

Salt

1. Slice shallot, hot pepper, and tomatoes and place in a bowl.
2. Put lime juice in the bowl add salt to taste, then mix.
3. Pour in boiled coconut oil.
4. Serve.

Sambal Cabai (Chili Pepper Condiment)

5 cloves of shallots

7 chili peppers

3 hot peppers

1 tomato

4 tablespoons of homemade coconut oil

Salt to taste

1. Finely grind shallots, chili peppers, hot peppers, and tomato.
2. Sauté with hot homemade coconut oil.
3. Salt to taste and serve.

Additional Menu

Kerupuk (Chips)
Casual dining is not complete without crackers. Most children like chips as a side dish. A variety of flavored chips are sold in the market, including shrimp, fish, and vegetable flavors. Housewives buy a handful and fry them with hot oil. Crackers can be directly consumed and placed in an airtight jar.

Morongi (Spiced Shredded Chicken)

2 chickens	2¼ cups thick coconut milk
15 shallots	9 chili peppers
9 cloves of garlic	Hot pepper to taste
2 tablespoons of coriander	Salt
1½ tablespoons of pepper	3 tablespoons oil

1. Cut chicken into 4 pieces: 2 parts thighs and 2 parts chest.
2. Finely grind shallots, garlic, coriander, pepper, chilies, hot pepper, and salt.
3. Sauté using a little oil until fragrant.
4. Pour in coconut milk and chicken.
5. Boil for about 1 hour and stir occasionally.
6. When the coconut milk is almost dry, pour some more and stir constantly.
7. Keep doing this until the chicken begins to break down, shredded, and the color is golden brown with no coconut milk left.
8. Stir constantly over medium heat to avoid scorching on the bottom of the pan.
9. It will take about 6–7 hours to prepare this dish until it is ready to be presented.

Note: *Morongi* can last a long time in dry conditions.

FURTHER READING

Allen, Rantje. *Gorontalo: Hidden Paradise*. Photographs by William Tan, Takako Uno, and Stephen Wong. Singapore: Snow Pub, 2006.

Chandra, Mae. *Indonesian: Modern and Traditional Indonesian Cuisine*. Chatswood NSW, Australia: New Holland Publishers, 2014.

Owen, Sri. *The Indonesian Kitchen: Recipes and Stories*. Northampton, MA: Interlink Publishing Group, 2008.

Iran

Saman Hassibi and Amir Sayadabdi

Atefeh hangs up the phone and takes a look at the clock. It's 11:00 a.m. on a Friday morning. The kids are still in bed, but she and her husband, Iraj, are wide awake and have started a relaxed weekend morning. Atefeh has almost three hours to prepare everything for a late weekend lunch. It is a good thing that most everyday Iranian dishes would only require a few pots or pans, even though they tend to take a long time to be prepared thoroughly. The time spent for each dish is generally passive: prepare everything and let the taste of every ingredient combine in a pot over a low heat, then come back in an hour or two ready for a decent feast.

An Iranian family having lunch at Sofreh (the cloth spread on the floor). Mom cooked *Zereshk Polow ba Morgh* (barberry rice with chicken) and prepared *Mast-o-Khiar* (yogurt with cucumber) and *Sabzi Khordan* (fresh herb platter) as two common side dishes. Bread is also present. Bread and rice are two huge staples of the cuisine. (Courtesy of Atefeh Amouheydari)

Dining patterns might vary from one family to another, depending on their jobs, ages, and the number of family members. Atefeh is a teacher and has to be at work at precisely 7:30 every morning. That does not give her much time to prepare lunch every day, so every time she cooks during weekdays, she makes enough food for the family for two days. Although they all prefer the days that the lunch is freshly made, they know that it is too much to ask of a working mom. Not only does she have her full-time job to think about, but she also has cooking, cleaning, and other chores to consider. She also has to care about her children's school performance and help them with their projects. However, Atefeh is quite lucky that Iraj helps her with the children, and they are financially fortunate enough to be able to hire a cleaner once a week.

Every weekday, Atefeh and Iraj wake up earlier than the children. They prepare a light breakfast, and Atefeh rushes to work while Iraj waits until their son, Sina, and daughter, Negar, are on the way to school. Then, he takes care of the dishes and goes to work.

For Atefeh and Iraj's family—as for most of the middle-class Iranian working families—during weekdays dinner has become the main eating ritual shared with all the members of the family. Only on Friday, which is the weekend family day, luncheon is still the main event, whether eaten at home or in a restaurant. Nonetheless, cooking still remains the mother's duty. Sometimes the father may help, but that is a memorable occasion.

It is Friday, and only a few shops are open. Iraj knows this well, so he did the week's shopping the day before, according to Atefeh's list. Traditionally, it is the man's job to provide for his family. So even though Atefeh and Iraj are quite young, they sometimes use the traditional methods to make their life more organized. Therefore, Iraj buys the staples such as rice, meat, chicken, oil, legumes, salt, and pasta based on the list that Atefeh writes. But other food items that need a delicate woman's touch are usually taken care of by Atefeh. According to an old belief or maybe common sense, fruits, herbs, and vegetables need to be bought earlier in the morning, so once a week Iraj drives Atefeh to huge wholesale greengrocers owned by the city hall that provide these at a lower price. They buy the main vegetables that can be stored longer such as onions, potatoes, carrots, cucumbers, sprouts, and broccoli there. They usually do the shopping on Thursdays when Iraj is free and Atefeh and Sina come back home before noon. Fruits and other special greens are bought as needed during weekdays when Atefeh passes by the small private greengrocers. They let her handpick what she wants but charge her extra. This does not sound very economically efficient, but she believes that having some higher-quality ingredients is really worth the price and affects the results of her cooking. Other small items are usually bought by Sina so he can learn to be responsible from an early age and one day do the shopping for his own family.

Atefeh has planned to cook *zereshk polow ba morgh* (barberry rice with chicken) today, as it is one of the family's favorites, does not take much time, and she has everything handy. Each part of this dish (barberry, rice, and chicken) should be prepared separately. Atefeh has cooked enough in her life to know how to manage preparing them altogether. As Iraj buys the staples in bulk and ready to cook, she has the chicken cleaned and cut in the freezer. She takes out two packages of frozen chicken pieces for today's and tomorrow's lunch and then places them in the microwave to defrost. She has already measured and washed the rice and left it in a bowl covered with cold water and some salt to soak. After she prepares the chicken and puts the pot on the gas stove, she makes her barberry topping on another flame and sets it aside. Now is time to make the rice and the *tahdig*. *Tahdig* (meaning "the bottom of the pot"), is a delicious crispy treat that was created to prevent the precious grains of rice from sticking to the bottom of the pot and becoming inedible. A skilled cook such as Ateferh would leave slices of potatoes, pieces of bread (usually *lavash*), lettuce, tomatoes, or whatever she fancies at the bottom of the pot and adds a pile of al dente rice on top of them to steam. The result is an extremely delicious crispy crust on the bottom with fluffy white rice on top. Atefeh has learned a trick from her mother, which is widely used by professional chefs, to finish the leftover rice. She makes a mixture of leftover rice, yogurt, saffron, and eggs to make a special golden batter, which later results in another type of the perfect *tahdig*.

After three hours of nonstop work, within which Atefeh managed to prepare a couple of side dishes, she calls her children to help while she prepares the main dish platters.

In Iranian cuisine, side dishes are as important as the main dish. Atefeh's family tends to have at least one type of side dish with every dinner or lunch. They might be different sorts of salads, pickles, or yogurt. Today they are having two common and very popular side dishes named *sabzi khordan* and *mast-o-khiar*. The *sabzi khordan* is simply a basket of seasonal herbs and greens including pennyroyal, scallion, radish, tarragon, wild leek, parsley, both green and purple basil, cress, dill, coriander, *satureja*, and mint. The *mast-o-khiar* (yogurt with cucumber) is prepared by Negar today. Preparing the *mast-o-khiar* is not very difficult, yet Negar knows how to make hers surprisingly tasty. Grandma taught her to use thickened plain yogurt for the perfect texture, Persian cucumbers for the best taste, dried mint and thyme to have a distinctive aroma, and finally a garnish of some dried damask rose petals and ground walnut.

Sina is setting the *sofreh* on the carpet of the living room. The *sofreh* is a special traditional Iranian mat spread that is set on the floor, and the family sits around it to eat. It is rolled out before eating and then cleaned and folded after every setting. Years ago, it was made of textile; however, nowadays the plastic types are commonly used, as they are cheaper and more convenient, especially for cleaning. Atefeh used to have different sizes of the *sofreh* for when they have different crowds of guests. However, they now have a big dining table for a buffet-type setting hosting bigger groups or just to sit around when having a few guests. Sina has to move the coffee table in order to find enough room on the carpet so everyone can sit comfortably on the warm Persian rug while eating. He usually is responsible for setting the *sofreh* but tries to sneak out when cleaning. Setting the *sofreh* is much easier for him, since he just has to bring whatever mom puts on the kitchen bench and then follow a simple order. After the spread is rolled out, plates, cutlery, and drinking glasses are placed on top. For rice dishes, usually a flat plate and a spoon and fork set are laid per person. They mainly use the spoon to eat, while the fork has an auxiliary place. This setting is almost always the same except for more soupy dishes, which logically require a bowl. Pitchers of drinks are usually filled with tap water and ice, or soda and ice come next. Today they have the *dough* as well, a very popular yogurt drink all over Iran that is a mixture of yogurt, water, and some other optional ingredients such as dried mint or mint water.

Side dishes and any necessary utensils for serving the main and side dishes are also brought to the *sofreh*. It is not considered polite to pick food with one's utensils; therefore, each dish and side dish comes with a proper serving ladle, spoon, or fork. The only things that can be grabbed by hand are the *sabzi khordan* and bread. A salt shaker and bread basket are the other common accessories of the *sofreh*, alongside a package of paper tissue to use as napkins if needed. In less casual settings such as a dinner party, for instance, the package of paper tissue is replaced with proper—and sometimes colorful—paper napkins, while the setting becomes fancier. Iranians usually leave the best of everything for guests: no matter how rich or poor, in rural areas or cities, and regardless of age or gender, the guest always comes first. The best plates and fancy crystal glasses are used when a guest is present. Other times when it is only for the family, more attainable and plain utensils are used—nothing too fancy but more comfortable and replaceable in case of an accident.

Sina is happy that today they are not hosting, because they do not need to dine at the table and can even watch TV while eating. He will not be constantly reminded by mom and dad to watch his manners: "Don't start before the guests!" "Watch your language!" "Don't bring your phone to the table." "You are not going to leave the table before everyone is finished." And so on. However, the primary etiquette must still be followed, such as not speaking with a full mouth, not munching or chewing with your mouth open, not leaving any food on the plate, and not sniveling. Generally, eating within the family follows a set of more relaxed rules. Children are allowed to leave the table when they are done; however, they also need to clean up while leaving the table, which includes taking their own dishes back to the kitchen. When Iraj and Atefeh were children, rules were more strict and in favor of adults, but nowadays they are more relaxed and in favor of children. A rule such as "not eating with the left hand" is almost extinct, as the belief that the left hand is unholy has been disregarded. There is a dress code while hosting guests that prevents the family members from dressing too comfortably. However, when they are dining together they can dress as they desire. For example, Atefeh and Negar never wear shorts or tank tops in front of guests but preferably wear a shirt or blouse with jeans or skirts. And dad never shows up with his favorite sweatpants and a T-shirt, just as he has today, but often with trousers and a shirt.

Table Talk and Manners

There are certain topics that one simply does not mention at the table: politics, presumably to avoid tension, and sex, to avoid embarrassment. And even though we rarely hold these as hard-and-fast rules today, there is still a strong taboo against mentioning anything disgusting or violent. For reasons that are purely cultural, even the thought of bodily effluvia while eating is nauseating. So, the idea of proper table conversation is anything but a thing of the past. Of course, for this very reason children will try to gross out their siblings not merely with words but also with acts calculated to disgust and horrify. Belching and farting at the table are merely one expression of such transgressive behavior.

Iraj is sitting at the *sofreh* picking at the *mast-o-khiar* with some bread. He is very fond of bread. Although rice is thought to be the main staple, he believes that bread is equally important and should not be taken for granted. He respects it and never lets the bread be discarded. Even if it becomes too dry or too old, he preserves it in a piece of cloth to use it later in soups or to feed the wild birds. He learned from his father that bread never should be let fall on the ground. So, if he sees a piece of bread on the ground or the street, he would lift it and leave it on an higher surface. He also believes that there should be enough bread on hand every day, especially for breakfast. This is why on each trip to the bakery he buys one or two extra loaves and asks Atefeh to freeze them for a rainy day. Negar and Atefeh seldom go to bakeries, as they find it very unpleasant to wait in line to buy bread. The lines in the bakeries depend on the baking time that the shops set. Iranian traditional breads are flat, so they need much less time in the oven and taste best while fresh. So, in order to buy a fresh loaf, it is better to wait in the shop for a few moments before the bakers start working and buy a few hot-from-the-oven loaves. In case of emergency, when they need bread Atefeh goes to the neighbors and borrows a few loaves. Borrowing small items is common among neighbors' wives. Atefeh borrows bread, which she returns the next day; her neighbor gets a couple of eggs or onions and returns them later. Occasionally when Iraj goes to buy bread, he picks up a few extra loaves to give to the close neighbors. No one will say no to a fresh loaf of bread!

Atefeh prepares the final step of her masterpiece by assembling all three parts, which she has already made. The rest of her family has gathered around the *sofreh*, which is still missing the main dish because it has to be hot from the stove. Negar places the chicken pieces in a platter and pours the broth on top of them, while Atefeh mixes the rice with the barberry topping and garnishes it with almond and pistachio slices. Afterward, she tries to take out the *tahdig* from the bottom of the pot using a colander. The colander that is used in the kitchen is certainly not used for serving; the former is more practical, while the latter is decorative. It is a good thing that the pots are Teflon; otherwise, taking the *tahdig* out is a real inconvenience: Atefeh has to put the hot pot in the sink, which is filled with about an inch of cold water to give the pot a shock so that the *tahdig* comes out more easily. The platter of rice and barberries with the *tahdig* on the side is ready, and she transfers it to the table while Negar brings the chicken and broth.

When the platter is brought to the *sofreh* and everyone is seated, they help themselves to the side dishes. Iraj is usually the first one to be served the main dish if they are not hosting a guest or having the grandparents over. He gives his plate to Atefeh, and she serves rice to him and the children and then helps herself. But the chicken or the stew is there for everyone to help themselves. Sina is still too young to know how to serve, so either of his parents serves him a plate. After all these years, Atefeh knows approximately how much each member of the family eats. Sometimes Negar is on a fad diet of which Atefeh disapproves and tries to correct her daughter's attitude toward food by serving her the amount she thinks is suitable. Another time Sina might be too hungry after having a playdate, so she serves him twice. Atefeh herself is not very fond of cooked red meat, so when they have a stew that calls for red meat, she sets it aside but eats the rest. Iraj is the only one whom she almost always serves without fault. After all, they have been together for a long time. Iraj has gone through the years that Atefeh was dabbling in cooking, and Atefeh has passed the times that Iraj did the shopping wrong. When hosting, the order of serving changes by prioritizing the guests; adult guests help themselves with the main dish first, and then the family starts. When hosting children, Atefeh serves them even before Iraj. Iraj is not a hypocrite, but he is more helpful when they have guests. He knows that with every guest comes a great deal of pressure as to being a proper host, so he does whatever he can to ease the situation for his wife and fulfill his duties. He helps with setting and clearing the table and helps Atefeh in the kitchen as well. He barely does such things when there are just four of them.

The food is finally brought to the *sofreh,* and everyone is seated. Today they just have one main dish, and there is no starter or dessert. These kinds of courses are served when they have guests. On these occasions all courses from soups or salads to any type of desserts are all brought to the table (which sometimes works as a buffet table) at the same time, and the guests are welcome to help themselves with any course they wish. However, today is a family lunch, and therefore only their two side dishes, the *mast-o-khiar* and the *sabzi khordan,* accompany the food. The types of side dishes vary depending on the main dish and the harmony they make. For instance, according to ancient Persian medicine, yogurt shouldn't be eaten with fish, while pickles usually accompany fish dishes; raw onions, basil, and marinated olives often follow kebabs; and salads and the *sabzi khordan* usually go well with stews.

Family members may each eat the food in a different order. Iraj adds a few spoonfuls of the broth on top of the rice with barberries, puts a piece of chicken on top, and digs in with his fork and spoon. He eats a piece of warm *tahdig* first. However, his son does not like the crispy texture, so he always pours a little broth on it to moisten the *tahdig*. Atefeh usually starts with some salad or cooked vegetables. She is concerned about health and keeping her figure but unlike her daughter does not believe in fad diets; Atefeh believes in healthy eating. They both do not eat much rice. Atefeh believes that rice is a bit manly and a tad too heavy, while Iraj and Sina always eat the largest portions of rice.

As they start eating, Iraj comments on how great the food is. He always does that even if he does not enjoy the taste much. He has learned that appreciating food is a gesture of respect to the one who cooked it. He has tried to educate his children with the same kind of manners. However, the parents know that the generation gap is widening, so they do not expect their children to follow the manners that they were brought up with.

As they eat, they talk about the notable events of the past week. The TV is on, and its sound fills some gaps within their conversation. Whatever happened in the day or week is usually the main topic at the *sofreh*. The *sofreh* is probably the main—and sometimes the only—event that could gather this family together. Therefore, they take advantage of this opportunity for sharing their news and sometimes their feelings. However, they all know that discussing sensitive issues should be avoided; Atefeh and Iraj do not talk about the news or politics, Negar does not mention her crush on the neighbor's boy, and Sina tries to forget about the window he had broken earlier this week while playing football. The children both confide in their mother, as she is much softer. Atefeh tends to tell Iraj everything when they are alone, and they both usually share a good laugh about the "big problems" of their children.

After half an hour at the *sofreh,* everyone is almost finished. The children finished much earlier. Sina has left for his room, but Negar remains at the *sofreh* until the end of the meal. There is some rice and chicken left in the main platters, besides what Atefeh has already set aside for tomorrow's lunch. Often Atefeh, just like many other Iranian women, prepares a little bit more food in case an unexpected guest arrives. Hospitality is a way of life in Iran, and guests should never feel unwelcome even if they arrive untimely or without any prior notice or invitation. However, if no guest shows up, there will naturally be some leftovers that will be taken to work or school or will be eaten as a midday snack the following day. Throwing food away is strictly frowned upon.

Atefeh and Negar start clearing the *sofreh*. Iraj is already watching the news, which has just started. Atefeh and Negar take the dishes to the kitchen. Atefeh is usually the one who does the dishes, but today Negar will do that, as she thinks her mom needs some rest. Atefeh checks the kettle that she had put over a low flame before sitting for lunch. The water is boiling, and it is time to have tea. An almost inseparable part of an Iranian course is drinking tea. Tea plays a significant role in Iranian food habits, and many people drink it after their meal and throughout the day. She takes her china teapot, puts a mesh tea infuser inside it to prevent the leaves from going into the cup, and places a few teaspoons of loose black tea in the infuser. Sometimes she adds a pinch of rose petals, a few cracked cardamom pods, or a tiny cinnamon stick to make the tea extra aromatic. Then she adds boiling water to the pot, puts it on top of the kettle, and lets the tea steep for about 5 to 10 minutes. The reason for placing the pot over the kettle is that as the water simmers, the steam keeps the tea warm and helps the brewing process.

Tea is usually considered an adult drink except for breakfast, when the children sweeten it with sugar and have it with their bread and cheese. Negar has already gone to her room, and Atefeh is putting two *estekans*, special tea-drinking glasses, on a small tray. A tea-drinking glass should always be see-through so that the perfect colored tea can glow in it. Iraj likes his tea to be dark and strong, while Atefeh prefers a lighter color. It is customary to ask how light or strong people like their tea to be. Atefeh pours the tea into the *estekans*: she pours the brewed tea first and then adjusts the color by adding the necessary amount of boiling water. She also puts two *nabats* (rock sugar) on the side and takes out a bowl of dried fruits (dates, figs, apricots, and white mulberries) and brings it to Iraj. He changes the channel from sport news to the TV series that Atefeh likes and welcomes her to his side. This is when the two of them could sit together without the kids around and enjoy themselves while having "the finest tea in the world," as Iraj puts it.

Zereshk Polow ba Morgh (Barberry Rice with Chicken)

Utensils:

For polo: 1 large pot with lid, 1 tea towel, 1 colander

For barberries: 1 medium saucepan

For chicken: 1 pot with lid

Ingredients for polo:

4–5 cups rice (medium-grain Persian rice or basmati rice)

Water

3 tablespoons salt

4 tablespoons cooking oil

1 large peeled potato (optional)

2 tablespoon butter or oil (optional)

Ingredients for barberry topping:

1 cup dried barberries

2 tablespoons white sugar

½ cup melted butter

½ teaspoon saffron

2 tablespoons each pistachio and almond slivers (optional)

Ingredients for chicken dish:

1 whole chicken cut into pieces

1 medium onion, chopped

3 cloves garlic, diced

2 tablespoons lemon juice

1 teaspoon turmeric

1 teaspoon black pepper

1 teaspoon salt

2 tablespoons olive or cooking oil

For polo:

Wash the rice with cold water and leave it in a bowl covered with water and 2 tablespoons of salt for at least 1 hour to soak.

Place a large pot on the stove and fill it up with water. Bring it up to a boil and add the remaining salt.

Throw the excess soaking water out and add the rice to the boiling water in the pot. Let it be on a medium heat until the water starts boiling again. Stir only once or twice and let the rice cook until it is al dente (about 7–10 minutes).

Tip: Do not stir the rice too often at this point, as the grains are fragile and may break. That must be avoided when aiming for perfect Persian rice.

Drain the rice and rinse it with some cold water to stop the grains from sticking to each other.

Put the large pot back on the stove on medium heat, add the oil, and place the slices of the potato in a layer on the bottom of the pot. Let it stay over the heat for a few seconds and then set it aside.

Gradually add the rice back to the pot and make a mountain out of it. Add ½ cup boiling water with 2 tablespoon butter to it, put the lid back on the pot, and let it start to steam on medium heat (about 3–5 minutes).

Tip: You can see the steam if your pot has a glass lid, but an expert Iranian mom wets her finger and sticks it to the lower sides of the pot for a millisecond. When she hears a sizzling sound, she knows it's time for using the tea towel.

Turn the heat to low, take off the lid, and wrap it with a tea towel—covering the underside—and place it back on the pot. Leave it for around 45 minutes until the rice is fully cooked and has a fluffy texture with separate grains.

For barberry topping:

Grind the saffron with a pinch of sugar in a mortar to make a fine powder. Place the powder in a glass and add ½ cup of boiling water. Place a saucer on top of the glass and let the saffron brew into a fiery red liquid.

Tip: You can skip the grinding part, but as an Iranian I advise against it. Saffron is expensive everywhere; with grinding and brewing it you can extract every bit of taste and color from this magnificent flower.

Wash the barberries and set aside.

Place a pan on medium heat and add the butter to melt.

Add the barberries, lower the heat, and stir for a minute.

Add the sugar and half of the brewed saffron and stir until the sugar is melted and the barberries are a bit tender.

Set the pot aside.

For chicken:

Wash the chicken pieces and place them in a pot, and add the chopped onion.

In a bowl combine the spices, salt, garlic, lemon juice, and 1½ cups water.

Add the spice mixture to the pot, put the lid on, and let the chicken cook on low heat for about 1 to 1½ hours, until the chicken is cooked and tender with just enough broth left in the pot.

Tip: You can add other vegetables such as carrot, squash, broccoli, or cauliflower to the chicken if you'd like some cooked veggies on the side with your chicken.

Assembling:

Take a plateful of rice and mix the barberry topping with it, using a fork to avoid the rice from breaking. The rice will be golden yellow with the saffron that was used in preparing the barberries. Add the rest of the saffron liquid if you would prefer a deeper color.

Transfer the rest of the rice onto plates or a big platter, and add the golden rice on top. Sprinkle the almond and pistachio slices on top.

Put the chicken pieces on the side of the plates, or put everything on a big platter. Pour the broth in a separate bowl or on top of the chicken pieces.

To eat this dish as a true Iranian, add a few spoonfuls of the broth on top of the rice with barberries, put a piece of chicken on top, and dig in with your fork and spoon. Remember to take a piece of the *tahdig* when it's still warm. Bon appétit, or as we say, *Noush-e-jan!*

FURTHER READING

Batmanglij, Najmieh. *A Taste of Persia: An Introduction to Persian Cooking.* London: I. B. Tauris, 2007.

Batmanglij, Najmieh. *From Persia to Napa: Wine at the Persian Table.* Odenton, MD: Mage Publishers, 2006.

Batmanglij, Najmieh. *The New Food of Life: A Book of Ancient Persian and Modern Iranian Cooking and Ceremonies.* Odenton, MD: Mage Publishers, 1992.

Dana-Haeri, J. *From a Persian Kitchen: Fresh Discoveries in Iranian Cooking.* London: I. B. Tauris, 2014.

Ghanoonparvar, M. R. *Persian Cuisine: Traditional, Regional and Modern Foods.* Lexington, KY: Mazda Publishers, 2006.

Ghayour, S. 2014. *Persiana: Recipes from the Middle East and Beyond.* Northampton, MA: Interlink Publishing Group, 2014.

Gunter, A. C. 1988. "The Art of Eating and Drinking in Ancient Iran." *Asian Art* 1(2) (1988): 7–52.

Nickles, H. *Middle Eastern Cooking.* New York: Time Life Books, 1969.

Shafia, L. *The New Persian Kitchen.* New York: Ten Speed, 2013.

Video Sources

"Americans Try Persian Food with Their Driver." YouTube, https://www.youtube.com/watch?v=ixsNifCLYOA.

"Persian Food Safari." YouTube, part 1, https://www.youtube.com/watch?v=YiZ1z4l7Ny4; part 2, https://www.youtube.com/watch?v=onuhJBBEW7g; part 3, https://www.youtube.com/watch?v=kL1Iv-bDMeI/.

Ireland

Máirtín Mac Con Iomaire

Ireland has transformed in the last 25 years from a relatively monocultural society with heavy emigration to one that is truly multicultural and even experienced waves of immigration particularly during the years of the so-called Celtic Tiger (1992–2007), when the Irish economy was riding the crest of a financial boom. Since 2008 the country has been in recession, with the first green shoots of growth appearing in the economy in 2014. Dining patterns changed during the boom years, with a noticeable rise in dining outside the home and the use of home replacement meals (ready-made meals from supermarkets and takeout meals) for the cash-rich time-poor citizens. Restaurants have managed to survive the recession that followed by reducing their prices and costs, substituting cheaper cuts of meat (pork belly, lamb shanks, brisket), and cooking slowly and creatively. More

An Irish family enjoying a roast chicken dinner with herb stuffing, mashed potatoes, honey roasted vegetables, and peas. (Courtesy of Máirtín Mac Con Iomaire).

expensive prime cuts tended to disappear, and to casualize the dining experience, restaurants dispensed with linen tablecloths and other expensive paraphernalia. Patterns subsequently changed also at home during the austerity years, with citizens not forgetting the gastronomic learning of the boom years but choosing to dine on special meal deals from certain supermarkets, particularly on weekends, as a treat rather than dining out in restaurants. There has been a return to home cooking in Ireland since the recession and also a growth in home baking, influenced by cookery shows such as *MasterChef Ireland* and *The Great Irish Bake Off*. More time is spent cooking meals on weekends than during the week. Irish people have also reembraced Tupperware and are bringing home-cooked food to work and reheating it in microwaves rather than purchasing lunch. Batch cookery of stews and soups once or twice a week and freezing have become popular.

Certain foods such as potato, sausages, ham, bacon, roast chicken, and stuffing are still enormously popular despite the rise in ethnic food such as Thai green curry, lasagna, chicken *tikka masala*, fajitas, rice, and pasta. Annual research on culinary students' best food memories by the author has shown slight changes in recent years toward ethnic foods, but family meals such as Christmas dinner and Sunday dinners containing roast meat and vegetables are still popular although not as pervasive as in the past. The dinner described in this essay is a roast meat dinner, with members of an extended family unit getting together to catch up on life in early September. The responsibility for cooking the meal is shared between the man and woman of the house. Irish men have become more active in the kitchen in the last two decades. Recent research of 4,300 women aged 25 to 44 found that 25 percent say both partners share the cooking responsibilities, with 8 percent indicating that the male partner was the main chef. As in other countries, there are a number of dietary restrictions among the family dining. Two of the children are dairy and gluten intolerant, one of the visiting cousins is a fussy eater, and one of the adults doesn't eat red meat, milk, cream, or butter. All of this is negotiated and catered to in as low-key a fashion as possible to avoid drawing attention to any one individual.

The meal contains traditional Irish foods (chicken, potatoes, carrots, turnips, parsnips, honey, strawberries), but these ingredients are cooked drawing influence from some modern techniques and foreign influence. Some items are fully prepared from scratch, whereas some convenience products or prepreared foods are also utilized (cranberry sauce, gluten-free stock cubes, Birdseye frozen peas, dairy-free ice cream, and meringue shells). Some nontraditional vegetables (butternut squash) are also included among the roast vegetable medley. The meal is also accompanied by wine for the adults and water for the children. Wine consumption and connoisseurship has risen dramatically in Ireland in the last three decades. New world wines, particularly from Australia, New Zealand, and Chile, have captured a large market share due to their marketing by variety and clear labeling. Over 9 million cases of wine were sold in Ireland in 2011 (Murphy, 2014, 170). The white wine served at the meal is a Villa Maria sauvignon blanc from the Marlborough region in New Zealand, and the red wine is a rioja from Spain.

Menu

Leek and potato soup

Roast chicken with parsley and thyme stuffing, cranberry sauce, roast gravy, mashed potatoes, roast potatoes, honey-roasted root vegetables, and petit pois peas.

Fresh strawberries and cream with meringues

All the shopping is done in a large Tesco Supermarket, although there has been a dramatic growth in German supermarket chains such as Aldi (which owns Trader Joe's in the United States) and Lidl in recent years as Irish citizens seek to get better value for their money. The chicken is bought fresh and is a standard three-pound bird that sells at nearly a third of the price of a similar organic free-range bird. The chickens are Irish, although there has been a dramatic growth in the use of cheaper imported chicken breasts from Holland and Thailand particularly in the Irish catering industry, which has resulted in the closure of a number of Irish poultry producers in recent years. Two chickens are bought, as it is a larger gathering than the usual family meal, and any leftovers will form part of another meal.

The house is cleaned and the shopping is done the day before the dinner. The husband does the shopping, while the wife vacuums the house and organizes the material culture for the dinner. Good cutlery and crockery are taken out of storage. The cutlery is an electroplated nickel silver set from Newbridge Cutlery that was a wedding present over a decade ago and is only used for Christmas and special occasions. Some of the crockery serving dishes were also wedding presents and are from Terrence Conran's Habitat shop, which no longer has a branch in Ireland. There are not enough matching plates, so some larger white plates that were purchased a few years earlier in an Irish department store, Meadows & Byrnes, will be used. The sauce boat was picked up in a bric-a-brac store and sits on a matching plate to catch any drips. The salt and pepper grinders are from Cole and Mason and were purchased at TK Maxx, as was the roasting trays used for the chickens and the vegetables.

The chickens will be rubbed in olive oil, seasoned with salt and pepper, and placed on a roasting tray on a bed of roughly quartered onions, celery stalks, and carrots and some thyme and parsley stalks. The chickens will be laid on their sides and placed in a 350°F oven and will be turned every 20 minutes for an even roasting to produce nice crispy skin and keep the bird moist. The chickens will roast for about 80 minutes and then will be removed and kept warm while the roasting pan is used to make the gravy. Excess fat will be removed from the pan, and the pan will be reheated on the stove and deglazed with some white wine and then some gluten-free stock. The gravy will be thickened with a little diluted corn flour once the flavor is adjusted, thus making the gravy suitable for the celiac guests. For the stuffing, a large onion will be finely diced and sweated off in butter until soft; some finely chopped parsley and thyme will be added along with salt and pepper and then some fresh breadcrumbs purchased in the supermarket. This will be placed in the oven for about 20 minutes to cook out in the covered pot. The stuffing will be served separately for the non–celiac disease diners.

The soup will be prepared early and can be reheated before service. For the soup, we sweat off two finely diced large onions and four celery stalks, finely sliced in a thick-bottomed pan, until soft. We add in three leeks that have been halved, washed, and sliced thinly. To this we add some stock made from gluten-free stock cubes and four large potatoes that have been finely diced. When the potatoes are soft, we take half the mix and blend it with a soup gun (immersion blender) and mix back in the pot to produce a soup that is half smooth and half chunky. It is seasoned with freshly milled black pepper.

The potatoes used are of the rooster variety, which is a very versatile potato developed in Ireland about 30 years ago. Roosters account for about 80 percent of Irish potato consumption today, yet we still enjoy new potato varieties such as queens and pinks during the summer months, which are sold on the roadside by farmers, particularly along the east coast of Ireland. For the mashed potatoes, the potatoes will be peeled and chopped into equal-size pieces, boiled until soft, strained, and allowed to dry out a bit before mashing with some heated milk, butter, and salt and pepper. A few will be taken out for the dairy-free diners before mashing! Some potato chunks will be parboiled and then tossed in a hot pan and roasted in the oven along with some garlic cloves, rosemary, sea salt, and pepper. The root vegetables will be peeled, cut into large chunks, fried in a hot pan, transferred into a large roasting tray, and placed in a hot oven. When they are soft in the middle, they will be tossed in honey and roasted for a final 10 minutes to slightly caramelize. The peas will be cooked straight from the freezer just before service, as they only take 5 minutes to cook.

SERVICE

The table is laid with a nice tablecloth, although for everyday meals the oilcloth that covers the table suffices. There are nice colorful paper napkins on the table that were purchased at IKEA, and a knife, fork, and soup spoon are set out in front of each diner. Separate cutlery will be brought to the table for the dessert course. There is a lit thick candle in the center of the table, a jar of Coleman's cranberry sauce, and a salt and pepper set. There are wineglasses for the adults and some normal glasses for the children's water. The soup will be served in soup bowls topped with some finely chopped parsley. The fussy eater will have received a separate Erin Hot Cup oxtail soup discretely as the rest receive the leek and potato soup. As the hostess clears the soup plates and puts them in the dishwasher, the host begins to carve the chicken, which will be served on plates and handed to each guest, ladies first, followed by men and then children and finally the host and hostess. The vegetables, gravy, and stuffing are laid on the table so that the diners can take as much or as little as they wish and according to their dietary restrictions. This creates a bit of interaction as individuals offer to serve each other. Both red and white wines are offered, the white wine chilled and the red wine at room temperature. A jug of water is also placed on the table. The host serves wine to the guests and regularly tops off their glasses.

CONVERSATION

The conversation is mostly lighthearted, centering on the sporting success of the children's various teams and the success or otherwise of the county teams in the Gaelic Athletic Association, Ireland's national sporting organization. Recent books read over the holidays and films seen are also discussed, with children discussing the latest celebrity gossip or YouTube sensation. Few Irish dinners manage to escape the two taboo topics of religion and politics, and after some discussion (sometimes heated) over the discovery of mass graves of young children in a former mother and child home run by the religious orders and the fact that none of the bankers or corrupt politicians and developers who were responsible for the financial collapse in Ireland have yet or probably will ever see jail, the mood eases as some funny stories are shared and old yarns retold, to much amusement. The children asked to be excused when the political discussion started, and they are lured back later with the promise of dessert. Some of the younger children are coaxed to play a tune on their violins or to sing a song they learned in school. Two of the eldest children are tasked with preparing the strawberries while the dishes are cleared from the table and loaded into the dishwasher. The leftover elements of the meal are carefully segregated and refrigerated and will be reconstituted for the following day's dinner. The chicken carcass will be picked clean and placed in a pot with some vegetables to make stock. The bulky dishes and the pots will be stacked neatly and washed by hand by the host after the guests leave as the hostess tidies up the rest of the house.

DESSERT AND COFFEE

The strawberries are washed, quartered, and sprinkled with caster sugar and then served with the prepared meringue nests and a combination of whipped cream or dairy-free ice cream and sometimes both for the children, who want the best of both worlds. There is discussion about the variety of dairy-free ice creams available and also the growing availability of gluten-free breads and cakes.

The hostess offers coffee to the adults from her Nespresso machine, which has pride of place in her kitchen. Some choose espressos, while two choose cappuccinos that are produced using the Nespresso milk-frothing machine. This leads to discussion on which is the diners' favorite Nespresso capsule and that you can order them cheaper online in bulk. It also starts a discussion on the growing trend for specialty coffees in Dublin, with Colin Harmon's 3FE café getting special attention, as he changes his beans every few weeks depending on seasonality and only supplies wholesale beans to establishments that have the apparatus to fully enhance the quality of the beans in the finished coffees. Ireland experienced a phenomenal growth in coffee culture during the boom. Sales of gourmet coffee machines for use in the home have increased since the recession, as Irish citizens who have grown accustomed to barista coffee have become home baristas. As Murphy (2014, 171) suggests, the Celtic Tiger cubs could not unlearn the art of the gastronome:

> He/she has merely retreated to into the lavish kitchen of their negatively leveraged home. They can be found sitting at their "kitchen island" on a Friday night matching wines from a German discount store to Tesco's "Dine-in" meal range while verbally admonishing the men and women who killed our Celtic Tiger.

Honey-Roasted Root Vegetables

1 pound of carrots

1 pound of parsnips

1 pound of turnips

1 pound of butternut squash (optional)

Vegetable oil

Salt and freshly ground black pepper

2 tablespoons of honey

1. Peel and roughly chop all vegetables into 1-inch chunks.
2. Preheat the oven to 400 degrees Fahrenheit and insert roasting pan to preheat.
3. Heat a thick-bottomed pan on the stove top until very hot.
4. Add a spoon of oil and then the turnips first and brown well on each side.
5. Add browned turnips to the pan in the oven and repeat the browning process with carrots and then parsnips.
6. Season the pan of browned vegetables well with salt and freshly ground pepper and return to the oven.
7. After 20 minutes, toss the vegetables in the pan and return to the oven.
8. After 35 minutes when vegetables are soft, add honey, toss in the pan, and return to oven for the final 5 minutes of cooking. Serve hot.

FURTHER READING

Mac Con Iomaire, Máirtín. "Coffee Culture in Dublin: A Brief History." *M/C Journal: A Journal of Media and Culture* 15(2) (2012), http://journal.media-culture.org.au/index.php/mcjournal/article/viewArticle/456.

Mac Con Iomaire, Máirtín. "Ireland." In *Food Cultures of the World Encyclopedia,* Vol. 4, edited by Ken Albala, 197–205. Westport, CT: Greenwood, 2011.

Mac Con Iomaire, Máirtín. "Ireland." In *Street Food around the World: An Encyclopedia of Food and Culture,* edited by B. Kraig and C. Sen, 192–196. Santa Barbara, CA: ABC-CLIO, 2013.

Mac Con Iomaire, Máirtín, and Eamon Maher. *"Tickling the Palate": Gastronomy in Irish Literature and Culture*. Oxford: Peter Lang, 2014.

McGowan, Sharon. "75% Still Dinner Ladies." *Irish Daily Mirror,* October 22, 2014, 17.

Murphy, Brian. "'A Hundred Thousand Welcomes': Food and Wine as Cultural Signifiers." In *From Prosperity to Austerity: A Socio-Cultural Critique of the Celtic Tiger and Its Aftermath*, edited by E. Maher and E. O'Brien, 161–173. Manchester, UK: Manchester University Press, 2014.

Israel

Jennifer Shutek

IFTĀR IN ARRABA: BREAKING THE RAMADAN FAST IN NORTHERN ISRAEL

Ramadan in northern Israel is one of the most vibrant, delicious, and almost claus-trophobically intense times imaginable. Jennifer spent two days and one night with the family of a friend, Farah. Jennifer met her while spending the summer in Jerusalem. Farah's family lives in Arraba, a small, predominantly Muslim-Arab council in the Lower Galilee. She kindly invited Jennifer to travel north with her for a few days and join her family for *iftār*. Usually Jennifer would have been invited to have dinner with them, but she would be visiting during July, which this year meant visiting during Ramadan. This is an Islamic month during which Muslims fast for the daylight hours and break their fast with a large meal after sunset; the word *iftār* is derived from the same Arabic root as the verb "to break fast," or eat breakfast.

The family sits around the table, waiting to break the fast; the window overlooks their garden and the Arab council of Arraba in the Lower Galilee. (Courtesy of Fatina Dahli Photography)

Jennifer was lucky enough to share two *iftār* meals with them. Each meal was unique, and in many ways her experiences throughout the two days that she spent with Farah's family were really stories of two different *iftār* meals, each with its own menu, location, rituals, and ambience.

During most of the year, the preparation and consumption of food occupies an important place in many Palestinian Israeli families. Somewhat paradoxically, however, food becomes almost an obsession during the monthlong fasting of Ramadan. Not only does abstention from foods, beverages, and smoking from sunrise to sunset heighten the attention paid to eating, but each *iftār* meal is also a feast, requiring hours of planning, shopping, and preparation. Appreciating the significance of food during Ramadan requires discussing almost all aspects of the day, since most of people's waking hours are spent purchasing, cleaning, and cooking food.

Food takes on heightened importance for a number of reasons. Not only is it essential for survival, but it is also a source of aesthetic pleasure, an aspect of religious practice (through the consumption of only halal foods and the abstention from alcohol), an integral part of national identity, and a key facet of Palestinian hospitality. This last factor is evident in Arab households throughout Israel, as people invite new acquaintances over for coffee nearly as soon as they have met them. It would be unthinkable to have guests visit—even briefly—without offering Arabic coffee, tea, sweets, or nuts and dried fruits.

Similarly, guests should reciprocate the hospitality when possible by bringing a gift. Jennifer's *iftārs* in Arraba, then, began in Jerusalem. The hospitality of Farah's family required a gift, a thank-you for their generosity and trust—by allowing her into their home, showing her how they prepared their meal, and having her at their dinner table, they were welcoming her into their family.

The day before they set out on the journey to Arraba, Jennifer paid a visit to Jerusalem's Mehane Yehuda market, a bustling, vibrant cacophony of colors, smells, and sounds. She had spoken to other Palestinian Israeli friends about an appropriate gift, and they had instructed her to buy dried fruits, nuts, and, if possible, dried watermelon seeds, which were especially popular snacks. After 15 minutes in the narrow, crowded corridors of the market filled with overflowing stalls of halvah, fish, bagels, manaqeesh, spices, sweets, and olives, Jennifer settled on one of the many dried fruit and nut vendors. She bought bags of soft amber-colored dried apricots, tart rings of dried pineapple, sweet fresh dates, rich walnuts, and cream-colored cashews, which she carried on the three-hour journey from Jerusalem to Arraba.

Upon arriving at the family's house, a white building with a sloping yard containing several olive trees and large picture windows overlooking houses, agricultural land, and a mosque, Jennifer was introduced to Farah's family. Her two younger brothers and youngest sister, Amina, lived at home with her mother, Samar, and her father, Nasim. To Samar's chagrin, Jennifer confirmed what Farah had told her: Jennifer is a vegetarian and would not be eating meat that evening. Three other sisters, all married, lived in nearby councils with their husbands and children and would join the family later in the evening. A newcomer and a guest,

Jennifer was not privy to the dinner preparation to any great extent during the first evening. During the early evening, the family took a ride into town and then talked in the downstairs living room while Samar continued to prepare *iftār*. As the sun began to descend toward the horizon, the sleepy house sprang into action. The women hurried to arrange the numerous plates of food on the table set up on the second floor in time for sunset.

The *adhān*, or call to prayer, emerged from the minaret's loudspeaker and fell over Arraba, signaling the oncoming sunset. A cannon sounded as the evening darkened, indicating that the fast could be broken. Samar and her daughters rushed to finish laying the table, watched impatiently by Nasim, Farah's brothers, and two of Farah's brothers-in-law. The eagerness with which the family watched the last few dishes adorn the table was evident. Their hunger and anticipation were clear in their attentiveness to the food before them and their irritation at any delay in eating.

The table was full of the results of Samar's hours in the kitchen. A deep metal tray of grilled chicken sat in the middle of the table, surrounded by platters of vermicelli-laced cinnamon-scented rice topped with steaming pieces of pan-fried beef, bowls full of creamy hummus drenched in fragrant olive oil, saucières of thin sour yogurt, and a huge pan of kefta (a meatball or meatloaf, in this case made with beef, tomatoes, parsley, and potatoes). Bowls of Arabic salad, made of finely diced tomatoes, bell peppers, parsley, mint, pickles, and kernels of sweet corn, sat beside dishes of corn, mayonnaise, and dill salad, the latter being the only dish on the table that was purchased. Jennifer was also introduced to a green viscous Palestinian soup called *mloukhiya*. This is traditionally made using chicken broth and jute leaves, which are fibrous leaves that give a thick, gelatinous texture to the broth. At the end of the table were two-liter bottles of Coca-Cola, with white Hebrew letters scrawled across the cherry-red labels. Water, a lemon soda drink, tamarind juice, or Coca-Cola, according to each person's preference, was poured into tiny disposable plastic cups. At each setting, the younger women and the children placed a plate decorated with floral patterns, a fork, and a spoon. On top of each plate was placed a bowl of steaming vegetable soup, and large pieces of thick pita and charred *taboon* bread were strewn throughout the dishes.

In theory, those observing Ramadan should break the fast by eating an odd number of dates, as this was reportedly how the Prophet Muhammad broke his fast. Dates hold culinary, cultural, and religious importance for Palestinians and are also said to provide an abundance of energy. Muslims are advised to drink some water with their dates, perhaps eat a small bowl of soup, and wait for half an hour before consuming their main meal of the day. Many will perform their evening prayer between the breaking of the fast and their *iftār* meal. The realities of *iftār*, however, can diverge from these prescriptions, as was the case during that evening's meal.

After hastily inhaling a date, pausing only to quickly remove the pit, everyone at the table ate frantically, a long, hot day of fasting behind them. The men served themselves first, taking huge pieces of chicken with their hands and using a combination of their personal cutlery and chunks of hand-torn pita to scoop rice,

Fasting

Almost all cultures practice some formal variety of fasting, which may mean very different things in various religions. In Catholicism and Orthodox Christianity, it usually means avoiding meat at the Friday evening meal. In Judaism there are special days of atonement, the most important of which is Yom Kippur, when no food is eaten. In Islam the devout abstain from food during the day for the entire month of Ramadan, eating only in the evening. Other cultures have special individual fasts to attain spiritual purity or to promote health and longevity. In all cases these serve to punctuate and divide regular meals in a ritually prescribed fashion, drawing the family and community closer together.

salad, beef, and hummus onto their plates, as the matriarch doled out pieces of kefta. The women and children ate their soup and then served themselves from the communal plates once Nasim and the other men had filled their plates. Several of the men smoked as they devoured their food and talked energetically in between mouthfuls, and tobacco-scented clouds drifted out of the wide window that overlooked the family's small olive grove, the neighboring houses, and, in the stretching distance, a red and purple–streaked sunset.

Farah observed Jennifer watching her family members eating ravenously and said, "This is why we all have a *kirsch* [belly]—we eat so quickly!" Indeed, the entire meal was done in less than 20 minutes, and the men and Samar abruptly left the table as soon as they were finished eating. They descended to the first floor to pray and then smoke and talk over tiny cups of aromatic Arabic coffee, made by pouring scalding water over finely ground coffee beans flavored with cardamom. The women and children lingered slightly longer to finish up their meals before taking on the daunting task of cleaning up after a feast for some 10 people.

Shortly after Samar and the men had left, the women and children cleared the table, emptying all of the scant leftovers, except for the hummus and yogurt, into a large trash bin along with the disposable cups. The sisters divided up the tasks: one continued to clear the table, another stacked chairs and dismantled the table with the help of some of the children, and Jennifer helped a third wash and dry the dishes. Another sister arrived as the cleanup neared completion, and we all moved furniture back into the room, as it had been removed to set up the dining table. The sisters sat in the erstwhile dining room, now a sitting room, while the younger children flitted in and out throughout the evening. One of Farah's nieces came around with plates of succulent watermelon and serving forks. The women lifted pieces of the fruit onto napkins and ate them with their fingers. The eating stretched into the night. Nasim brought in boxes of sweet syrup-soaked pastries from the family's bakery, including *qatayef*, and the traditional Palestinian dessert *knafeh*, both cheese-filled phyllo pastry desserts that were eaten by hand.

As the night wore on, those sisters who were married and living nearby retired to their own homes, while Farah and one of her brothers watched the National Geographic and Discovery channels, both in Arabic, while snacking on ice cream, milk chocolate, grape juice, and seconds and thirds from the box of Nasim's sweets. The last ones to go to bed turned in by 2:00 a.m. While Farah's family did not take this meal, many Muslims will eat *suhoor,* a small meal taken before sunrise and often including many of the same foods as *iftār* but in smaller quantities.

The first evening's *iftār* appeared as if by magic on the table, while the second day's *iftār* revealed the mechanism behind the illusion. While Jennifer had been a more formal guest during the first meal, by the second morning she was family and was taken on a culinary tour of the council.

Jennifer woke relatively early and crept downstairs at 9:00 a.m. to find Nasim and Samar in the living room. During a two-hour conversation in Arabic and English, Samar told Jennifer, "You cannot understand Arabs if you do not understand their food." The previous night's meal and the ensuing day certainly illustrated food's significance in Palestinian Israeli culture. Fasting and feasting created a sense of community, solidarity, and religious cohesion, while sharing food facilitated close ties between family members even as they married and moved into houses of their own. Offering meals to guests such as Jennifer was a warm way in which Samar welcomed guests into her home, providing them with a meal, something universally familiar and comforting. Understanding Palestinian Israeli food, then, meant acknowledging and understanding the density of human life among Palestinian Israeli communities and seeing them as individuals within but also beyond the images of the Israeli-Palestinian conflict that occupies so much space in popular media coverage of the region.

Once the other children had woken up, Jennifer was taken to a dilapidated hut in the backyard that housed a small cement dome, or *taboon,* an oven used to bake thin circular sheets of bread by laying them on fire-heated stones. *Taboon* bread is covered in char marks and infused with an enticing flavor of smoke and is consumed by Palestinians throughout Israel. Nasim proudly told me that this was where his mother used to bake the bread for their family but that it was no longer in use.

Jennifer was then bundled into the family car alongside Farah, Amina, and one of her brothers. Some 10 minutes later, Nasim parked the car outside of a building and led the way to the back, where four women wearing aprons sat around a low table, talking in Palestinian Arabic. Each woman balanced a large bowl filled with akkawiy cheese, cinnamon, and powdered nuts on her lap and had stacks of palm-sized thin yeast pancakes in front of her. As they talked, the women deftly took a pancake in one hand, expertly pinched the perfect amount of cheese mixture with the other, and placed it in the center of the pancake, then used both fingers to crimp it shut to form a soft, plump half-moon dumpling that was then placed onto a massive rectangular baking sheet. These dumplings, or *qatayef,* were snugly placed so that each slightly overlapped the one above it until the pan was entirely full. Inside of the bakery, which was owned by Nasim, these pans were carefully slipped into industrial-size ovens and baked at a high temperature. For the final touch, *qatayef* are boiled in syrup before serving.

After chatting in Arabic with Nasim for several minutes, one of the women approached Jennifer. She slipped an apron over her head, handed her a bowl of *ak-kawiy*, nudged a small stack of the pancakes toward her, and motioned for her to begin churning out the pastries herself, which she did for the next quarter of an hour.

Once two trays had been filled, the tour continued. Nasim's brother, who co-owned the bakery, demonstrated with dexterity how he rolled out six-foot-long ropes of phyllo straws filled with cheese, cutting them into the small delicate cylinders that would eventually be sprinkled with finely chopped bright green pistachios and consumed as *knafeh*. All the sweets were baked in a massive fire-burning oven and then either sold or taken home and enjoyed by the family after *iftār*.

The next stop was a spacious outdoor market where the family purchased much of its produce. Finally, the children brought Jennifer to a *taboon* bakery, where thousands of rounds of *taboon* bread were placed on a conveyer belt, passed for 30 seconds through an intensely hot oven, and pulled out, steaming, to be cooled and then sold.

Back at home they found Samar in the kitchen, where she had been working throughout the afternoon to cut potatoes into wedges for deep-frying, boil and season rice and *freekeh,* and prepare lentil soup, which was simmering over a low flame in an old dented pot. She said that she needed a head of lettuce for the salads, which Amina went to purchase at a nearby produce stand. Meanwhile, Samar continued to cook, chopping mint, bell peppers, tomatoes, and onions to make two bowls of multicolored salad, one dressed with lemon, olive oil, and pungent ground cumin and the other made with mint and *jarj r.* Pointing to the chopped leafy green, Farah grinned and said that it was particularly helpful "for men," eliciting a laugh from her mother. It turned out that the green was arugula, which is believed to help with fertility.

Samar had been working on *iftār* since midday, and the food was nearly complete at around 7:30 p.m. Farah, Amina, and Jennifer helped, sharing the main knife that was used to prepare all of the food and taking turns chopping the vegetables and herbs for the salads on brightly colored plastic chopping boards.

A small table covered in a burgundy tablecloth had been set up downstairs in the kitchen, and places for five were set. This *iftār* had a relaxed and casual air, and Samar was more talkative as she finished up the food preparation. The group fell into near silence as sunset approached while finishing up the remaining food preparation and washing several of the cooking utensils before the *adhān*.

With the call to prayer and the cannon signaling the end to another day of fasting, the four of us worked in comfortable silence to put out the remaining dishes and pour drinks. The two salads, homemade potato fries, a Chinese dish that the family simply calls "chicken," and *freekeh* sat before the group, a huge spread for

One of the family's daughters sits with her husband. The husband is dipping taboon bread into a plate of hummus topped with olive oil. (Courtesy of Fatina Dahli Photography)

four people. *Freekeh,* a hallmark of Palestinian home cooking, is toasted green wheat that is cooked like rice. Samar always prepared it with chicken but had omitted the poultry in Jennifer's honor (although she several times expressed discomfort at this omission, as meat is seen as essential for nutrition in many Palestinian Israeli families). Small individual bowls of vegetable and lentil soup sat at each person's place. Dates, fresh *taboon* bread, and bottles of water, Coca-Cola, lemon soft drink, and Thousand Island dressing finished off the impressive array of dishes. A place was set for Nasim, though he was at the bakery and would not arrive home until after everyone else had finished eating. "Hāthā asghar wa lākin ahsan," Samar said, referring to the smaller meal in comparison to the previous night's more ceremonial table setting: "this is smaller but better."

Mlukhiya (Jute Leaf Soup)*

2 packages frozen minced *mlukhiya* (jute leaves)

4 cups hot broth (typically chicken broth, either fresh or from a stock cube, paste, or powder;

vegetable stock can also be substituted)

2 tablespoon butter or olive oil

10 cloves garlic, halved or quartered

2 teaspoon ground coriander seeds

Salt to taste

1. Remove *mlukhiya* from freezer several hours prior to cooking; thaw.
2. Sauté garlic in butter or olive oil in a small pan until garlic becomes golden brown; add coriander seeds and cook for another minute.
3. In a large pot over medium-high heat, place the defrosted jute leaves and add broth one cup at a time, stirring to incorporate the broth into the leaves before adding an additional cup. Stir well, bringing to a boil, then reduce to a simmer.
4. Add the garlic and coriander mixture to the soup (which should be thick), then season with salt to taste.
5. Serve with a piece of *taboon* bread, hummus, and chopped vegetable salads.

*Recipe compiled in consultation with Laila El-Haddad and Maggie Schmitt's *The Gaza Kitchen,* several Middle Eastern food blogs, and the host family with which I ate *iftār* in the Lower Galilee in northern Israel.

FURTHER READING

Bourdain, Anthony. "Parts Unknown—Jerusalem." Season 2, Episode 1, CNN, September 2013.

Friedlander, Marty. "Tourist Tip #287: 'Ramadan Kareem.'" Ha'aretz, July 15, 2013, www .haaretz.com/travel-in-israel/tourist-tip-of-the-day/.premium-1.535812.

Gvion, Liora. *Beyond Hummus and Falafel: Social and Political Aspects of Palestinian Food in Israel.* Translated by David Wesley and Elana Wesley. Berkeley: University of California Press, 2012.

Vered, Ronit. "Yotam Ottolenghi and Sami Tamimi Talk Jerusalem, Recipes and Passports." Ha'aretz, January 12, 2013, http://www.haaretz.com/weekend/pleasure-hunting /yotam-ottolenghi-and-sami-tamimi-talk-jerusalem-recipes-and-passports. premium-1.493199.

Italy

Judith Klinger

When Judith and her husband first moved to a small hilltop village in Italy and started learning to speak Italian, it seemed as if everyone spoke about food all the time. The couple thought that this was because their vocabulary was mostly food related, but then over time they realized that it was because Italians really do talk about food all the time. You can start a conversation with anyone in Italy by talking about food or the weather. And if you are talking about the weather, the conversation naturally leads to how it affects food.

In the area of rural Umbria, mealtimes give the day its rhythm. Breakfast is usually quick, often a coffee and a small pastry or sandwich at the bar, where greeting your neighbors is as important as the coffee. Around noontime, if you pass someone on the street you wish him or her a *buon pranzo* (good lunch). Kids straggle home from school, shops close down, and many spouses live close to work, so they also come home. Although this is changing, lunch at home is still the norm. The

Dinner with friends in Italy. (Courtesy of Judith Klinger)

Migrant Cooking

Migrant communities have a fascinating relationship to their traditional foods. On the one hand, they are a marker of identity and a reminder of homeland. On the other hand, they can be a stigma of otherness, preventing immigrants from feeling at home among unusual food customs. Special foods for holidays also tend to remain unchanged even when families have become otherwise assimilated. This means that archaic recipes and practices often survive among migrants abroad long after these practices have disappeared in the homeland. One example would be the combination of spaghetti with meatballs, which one never sees in Italy and is considered a purely Italian American phenomenon but actually harks back to much older practices in southern Italy.

village goes from being a buzzing beehive of activity to pin-drop quiet. The smell of frying sweet peppers wafts down the street, mingling with the sounds of cutlery and dishes in use.

The evening kitchen music changes according to the season. In cool weather the smell of wood smoke permeates the town, and the sounds are muted. In the summer, dinners are later and more casual, with an evening trip to the piazza and the bar as part of the ritual.

On Sunday, the tempo changes. The breakfast visit to the café stretches on for an hour or so, as everyone visits and catches up on local news. Card games that involve shouting and slapping cards on the table go on until lunchtime. Going to church is optional, but gathering for a Sunday meal is mandatory. There is an air of anticipation as cooking smells waft through the streets. The family around the table could mean friends who are as close as family, or maybe it means that the grown children drive up from Rome with their children to gather around Nona's table. What is critical is that the matriarch has made a home-cooked meal, that everyone is looking forward to eating together, and that for a precious few hours life is as it should be, lived around the dinner table.

Judith and her husband found themselves very much looking forward to a Sunday dinner at Renata and Alvaro's house. Usually it is Sunday lunch that is the centerpiece of the day, but things are changing, and some of the guests had to work, so the group gathered for a Sunday dinner. The dinner guests were people who had known each other for many years, some who are as close as family and some who, like Judith and her husband, were honored to be included. It was a formal invitation to an informal dinner, and thus everyone knew that Renata would have been working a long time in the kitchen to serve this "casual" feast. The guests also knew that they would eat very well, as Renata has a reputation for being an excellent cook.

The day before the meal Renata made cappelletti, a small stuffed, folded pasta that, when made properly, resembles the round, pillowy belly button of Venus herself. The cappelletti would be served in a *brodo* (broth) made from the bones of the various meats that are used in the filling of the pasta.

While there certainly are convenience foods available in Italy, and there seem to be more and more every year, an invitation to dinner usually means that everything will be homemade. It's a point of honor.

Where you source your ingredients is important. Many people have vegetable gardens, and they are a source of great pride and bragging rights. Gardening methods are hotly debated: should you plant your tomatoes on a mound or in a trough? Over the years, Judith and her husband have learned to simply nod and agree with whatever method is being proclaimed as "the only way" to plant something. They have learned the art of respectful resistance.

The dinner was in the late fall, so most of the vegetables came from the weekly town market. The market is one of the few places where husbands and wives are seen together in public. Selecting the produce, carrying the load, discussing recipes with the vendors, and, of course, chatting with friends are all a part of the market experience.

The meats for the dinner came from a farmer Alvaro knows. The man sells his homegrown and butchered meats to select local people. It's not exactly black market or under the table, but it's not completely legal either. Alvaro has promised he'll take Judith up there in the spring so she can meet the farmer and hopefully become one of the lucky ones who can buy his meat.

While a husband helps procure the ingredients, it's usually the wife who is in the kitchen doing the cooking and the cleaning up. The general exception to this rule is grilling over a fire, which tends to be the man's job (but, of course, all the prep and cleanup chores belong to the woman).

Judith and her husband were the first to arrive for dinner, so they stood around the kitchen table examining and exclaiming over the beautiful platter of cappelletti that was waiting for them. The fireplace was lit and warmed up the cozy kitchen. More guests arrived, and soon there wasn't enough room in the kitchen, so they moved into the living room to wait for the last guests. While they waited they nibbled on a few nuts (no one dared to ruin their appetite!) and sipped glasses of sparkling Prosecco wine. Alvaro travels up to the Veneto region, specifically to the Valdobbiadene area to buy his *sfuso* Prosecco; *sfuso* means "loose" or "in bulk." Most people go directly to the vineyard to buy their wine in bulk and then take it home to bottle it. While buying a sparkling wine is a bit unusual, Alvaro has obviously mastered the bottling technique as well as finding a very delicious wine.

If all this seems like a lot of work—going to the market, the farmer, and the vineyard to gather groceries—it's so woven into the fabric of life that it isn't work at all. Besides, at each stop you talk to people, and you are convinced that everything tastes better because you are connected to the source of the food.

Once all the guests have arrived, they head into the dining room. There are eight this evening, so they can't all fit at the kitchen table. Tonight they will dine in the room that serves as Alvaro's office, where the computer is in the corner, one wall houses the well-filled bookcase, and there are pictures of family and friends on the wall. It is a warm and comfortable room, filled with a beautifully set table. The place settings include water and wineglasses and cloth napkins on a lovely blue tablecloth. The dishes are from Renata's grandmother, fine china with a delicate pattern.

It's obvious the guests are in for an evening of fine dining, and everyone is happy and appreciative to be in each other's company. These are professional people: an architect, a writer, and a few who regularly perform in local theatrical productions. Renata is a talented seamstress, but it is the theatrical productions that bind this particular group of diners.

Everyone in the group is knowledgeable about the history of the area, and the discussions are lively and unpredictable. Over the course of the evening, the computer is fired up a few times to settle an argument or to illustrate a point. No one uses his or her cell phones to fact-check or text, mostly because cell phone service in Umbria is very unreliable. It's also considered rude to text or make phone calls during dinner.

Most Italian meals are served in courses. There is a pattern or ritual that is generally followed no matter what part of Italy or how upscale or lowly the restaurant. Small tasty bites of various foods will be served as the antipasto, or first, course. Then the pasta (primi course) is followed by the meat (secondi course). Vegetables arrive with the secondi course. This dinner was no exception. The meal begins with *affettati* (sliced cured meats). In Umbria, this is a very typical way to open a meal and appetite. The Umbrian region is renown for its cured meats, and this evening's selection is excellent. Platters of the sliced meats are passed around, and everyone takes a few pieces—and then a few more pieces. The meats are eaten with the fingers or with a fork and knife, as you please. Tonight there is a special, golden yellow bread made with cheese. Always praise the cheese bread, but be careful, as huge discussions can ensue over the best cheese bread recipe. You don't want to get caught on the wrong side of this argument!

There is wine on the table, and everyone partakes. When a glass is empty someone is always ready to refill it, but no one will drink too much. One of the guests adds some water to her wine, which is not uncommon, particularly with the strong local wine. Tonight's wines are of excellent quality, and there is a lot of knowledgeable discussion about a particular 100 percent Sangiovese wine that was brought by the architect, who has an extensive wine collection.

Everyone is also drinking a glass of water. Italians are the world's largest consumers of bottled water, and it would be unusual to not have a bottle of still water and a bottle of sparkling water available. The water is usually served at room temperature, or *ambiente*, as cold water is believed to be not good for the health (and ice water on a hot day is considered downright foolish and dangerous).

The *affettati* plates are cleared by two of the women guests, and when Renata appears with the steaming hot pot of cappelletti in *brodo*, the dining room erupts in happy applause. Renata fills everyone's bowl with the fragrant soup, and the group immediately begins discussing the various reasons why Renata's cappelletti is particularly delicious. The small size and thinness of the pasta is highly praised because it is difficult and time-consuming. None of the cappelletti has opened in the broth, which means that each one was perfectly sealed. The filling has just the right amount of nutmeg and the perfect amount of filling, and all of this denotes the work of a true pasta master.

All of this praise wasn't said just to congratulate Renata; it was actually a very thoughtful and occasionally debated discussion on the many merits and details of a finely made cappelletti. This is the rarest of gifts: honest appraisal and praise. While the conversation is flowing, people are seasoning their soup according to their particular tastes. Most like a bit of grated parmigiana added to the soup, although Renata disapproves because she claims that it alters the flavor of the *brodo* too much. The architect stuns everyone by adding a soupspoon of red wine to his *brodo*. He is nonplussed by the general dissent and thoroughly enjoys his soup. Everyone is encouraged to help themselves to seconds (and thirds), and they happily do so until the pot is empty.

Now it is time to move on to the secondi course. The meats that flavored the broth are now brought to the table as a *bollito misto* (boiled mixed meats). In this case there are *zampetti* (whole pig feet), *muscolo* (beef), *gallina* (a thin, bony chicken that is used primarily for *brodo*), and another cut of beef. *Bollito misto* is a classic dish of the northern part of Italy, and tonight two different sauces accompany it: parsley/caper/anchovy and a tuna sauce. The salty umami-saturated parsley sauce is a fresh, lively counterpoint to the rich meats. The creamy mayonnaise-laden tuna purée is rich and unctuous.

The *contorni* (vegetables) are also plentiful, and while simple in preparation, they are scrumptious. Tourists in Italy often complain that there aren't enough vegetables, but at home they are always plentiful and varied. Tonight there are whole sweet red onions that were roasted in foil in the wood fireplace in the kitchen. Broccoli with some garlic was roasted until it was falling apart. Thinly sliced eggplant was oven roasted and then simply dressed in good local olive oil.

While the guests are eating, as if the smell of his mother's cooking had wafted to Bologna, their son Andrea calls on Skype. It's very congenial, as if he had just sat down at the table with us. Andrea knows everyone in the room, and it is a pleasant 10-minute conversation with a son who is missing his mother's cooking and the companionship of the table.

By now, everyone has eaten until they can eat no more, so of course it's time to move on to the dolce (sweet) course. On a daily basis, Umbrians may eat some fruit for dessert or a simple cake, but tonight the guests are in for a treat: a tiramisu-style cake and a strudel.

Everyone at the table is quite full and unsure if they are ready for more food. But there is always a remedy for that overstuffed feeling, and that's when Alvaro brings out the homemade vintage Vin Santo. It is obviously a cherished bottle, and everyone partakes of this sweet wine that smells of dried fruits and walnuts.

Capelleti in *brodo*. (Courtesy of Judith Klinger)

Renata brings a steaming pot of espresso to the table, and the guests contentedly pass around the cups and sugar. Finally, regretfully, the dinner has ended, and it's time for everyone to head home and get ready for the workweek ahead. It's okay, though, because for the three or four hours that they were together, all was right with the world, and the memory of the meal will keep each guest happy—at least until next Sunday, when everyone will be hungry again.

Cappelletti in *Brodo* (Meat-Filled Pasta in Broth)

10 eggs for the pasta + 2 eggs for the filling

Pork, beef, chicken breast (combined, about 2 pounds of meat)

Reserve the bones and additional meat for the broth

1 medium carrot

1 medium hard onion

1–2 stalks of celery

Butter

Lemon peel

Grated nutmeg

Flour, Tipo 00 (a finely ground, soft wheat flour)

For the filling:

1. Finely chop the carrot, onion, and celery (this mixture is called the *soffrito*) and sauté in olive oil over medium heat until the vegetables are soft.
2. Chop the meat into small pieces and cook until done.

3. In a large bowl, combine the meat, 2 eggs, a good-sized knob of butter, freshly grated lemon peel, and abundant nutmeg.
4. Mix well, then feed the mixture through a meat grinder, creating a soft, very finely textured meat paste.

For the pasta:

When you want to determine how much fresh pasta to make, the critical factor is the number of eggs, not the weight of the flour. For example, to make about 370 cappelletti, you will need to make a 10-egg batch of pasta. The rule of thumb is two to one: two parts flour to one part egg. You can easily adjust the amount of flour, but it's much trickier to adjust the volume of egg.

To determine the volume of raw eggs, use a scale. Tare the scale to remove the weight of the bowl, and add the eggs.

1. Weigh out twice that amount in flour, and pour it onto a flat surface. Make a well in the flour and add the eggs.
2. Gently scramble the eggs, incorporating the flour into the eggs. Eventually it will become too stiff to blend with a fork, and you'll knead the pasta by hand until it becomes a coherent ball of dough. Let the dough (and yourself) rest for at least 20 minutes.
3. Using a rolling pin, extend the pasta into a thin, flat sheet. Cut the pasta into 3-inch squares. Cover the pasta with a damp towel as you work so the pasta won't dry out.

Filling the pasta:

1. Place a small amount of the meat filling into the center of the square, fold the filled square into a triangle, and gently seal the edges with a moistened finger.
2. Lift the cappelletti and seal together the two outside corners of the pasta to create a ring.
3. Fold down the top crown of the triangle to form a little cap, or cappelletti.

It takes Renata about 3 hours or a full morning's work to make about 370 cappelletti. Novices should plan on it taking much longer, or they should make smaller batches.

Cappelletti should be either refrigerated (up to one day) or frozen for later use.

The broth:

Using the bones of the meat, make a broth. The broth should be clear, degreased, and very flavorful.

For the broth:

1. Roughly chop 1–2 peeled carrots, an onion, and a few stalks of celery.
2. Sauté gently for a few minutes. Add salt to taste.

3. Add the meat bones and cook for about 2–3 hours over low heat. Bones are for flavor, and Renata likes to use a *zampetto* (pig's foot) to add extra flavor to her broth.

4. When it is time to serve the soup, cook the cappelletti for a few minutes in the boiling broth (when you see them begin to float, they are done) and serve immediately.

FURTHER READING

Capatti, Alberto, and Massimo Montanari. *Italian Cuisine: A Cultural History.* New York: Columbia University Press, 2003.

Parasecoli, Fabio. *Al Dente: A History of Food in Italy.* London: Reaktion, 2014.

Riley, Gillian. *The Oxford Companion to Italian Food.* Oxford: Oxford University Press, 2007.

Japan

Shawn M. Higgins

Iruma City in the Saitama Prefecture is where many Tokyo workers lay their heads at night—not much more than a *beddo-taun* (bed town) as they say in Japanese. But what Iruma might lack in entertainment it makes up for in flavors and scents. Bed towns mean families, and families mean food. After taking the 45-minute express train home from work in Tokyo and driving 10 more minutes from the train station, Shawn parks his car down the street in his rented dirt patch of land adjacent to a cabbage field. If he returns at around 6:00 p.m., he can catch the varied scents of meals being prepared drifting out of the suburban homes. Most restaurants in Tokyo are courteous enough about smell pollution not to let the aromas of their respective cuisines escape from their buildings in excess. The open dining room

Three generations of family members sit down for *kiritanpo nabe*, a hot-pot of chicken, vegetables, and stock. The meal is famously from Akita Prefecture of Japan, the area from which the eldest generation here hails. (Courtesy of Michael Higgins)

windows of Iruma suggest the exact opposite—families are sharing and even showing off what is cooking. Many times, Shawn's family has walked their chihuahua around the block, smelled curry boiling in someone's kitchen, and decided their own family's dinner based on what others were making that evening.

This is the story of Shawn's family, their environment, and their food. There are five family members whose ages span three generations living in a two-story four-bedroom house alongside their dog, Chi. Papa and Mama (as they are called) are both in their 60s and have been married for 36 years. Shawn and his wife are *ara-saa* (around 30) and have been married for 6 years. They met in Riverside, California, as classmates, in a teaching certificate program. In September 2014 they welcomed into the world their first child, Louis, who was born right here in Iruma City, Saitama, Japan.

To fully appreciate the story that Shawn's family offers—one that showcases traditions and changes, age and youth, the local and the transnational—a bit of information about Japanese demographics is needed. Japan is facing an unprecedented demographic outlook in terms of age and nationality of residents. In 1950, the national population consisted of 35.5 percent children under age 14, 59.6 percent people aged 15–64, and only 4.9 percent senior citizens over age 65. By 1980, these numbers had steadily shifted to 23.5 percent, 67.4 percent, and 9.1 percent, respectively, an early warning of the declining birthrate and the graying of the population. In 2013, the senior population of Japan reached a staggering 25.1 percent of the total population, and children under age 14 only made up 12.9 percent. Therefore, while this family's story is fairly common in representing the senior age group, it also offers a glimpse of the few families with little ones at the dinner table.

As for the nationality of residents, the foreign population reached its historical height in 2010, with 2,134,151 people carrying legal documentation as recorded by the census. This number swiftly dropped in 2011 and 2012, presumably due to the combination disaster of the Tohoku earthquake, tsunami, and nuclear meltdown in March 2011. However, the foreign population increased again in 2013, reaching 2,066,445, a number nearly double that of 1990. Even so, this number only represents 1.6 percent of the total population of Japan. Therefore, Shawn's own eating habits as a foreign resident in Japan offer a sample of this small yet present percentage. Along with moving into the house of his wife's parents came some changes or accommodations in terms of table manners, serving style, and general conversations during dinner. For all of these reasons, their multigenerational, transnational family provides an interesting insight into various aspects of Japanese family and food culture.

The type of food served in their house is surprisingly representative of their transnational makeup, although this is not an effect of Shawn's presence in the house. Actually, the meals served in the home of his wife's family have been a mix of traditional Japanese dishes and Western fare ever since she was a child. Breakfast takes place between 6:00 and 9:00 a.m. depending on the day of the week, lasts about 30 minutes, and is always Western-style. This meal normally consists of bread purchased from the supermarket, local bakery, convenience store, or department store; individual plain yogurt cups for everyone; a glass of milk for Papa, who adds a Brazilian bee propolis extract to his drink; and coffee or tea for everyone except Shawn's wife, who is breast-feeding and therefore avoids caffeine when possible. Lunch is eaten between noon and 2:00 p.m. and is much more debatable than breakfast in terms of fare and dining location. Sometimes the family gets burgers from a fast-food chain and eats at home. Other times they purchase prepared Japanese-style bento lunches from the supermarket. On occasion, they indulge Papa's heavy eating habits and go for ramen or Chinese food at a local restaurant. Not infrequently does Mama simply put together something from the hodgepodge of ingredients sitting in the fridge or freezer.

Dinner, however, is definitely the largest and most important meal of the day in this home. Unless someone is attending a work-related function or Shawn and his wife are out on a date, everyone is expected to be home for dinner every night. Dinner preparation begins between 6:00 and 7:00 p.m., and dinner normally begins around 8:00 p.m. Depending on their respective energy levels, dinner lasts between one and two hours. Dinner almost always consists of a main dish, at least one or two side dishes, a soup, and a bowl of rice. If the meal is Japanese, then the soup is without question miso soup. If the meal is Western, then the miso soup might be traded out for corn pottage, pumpkin soup, or cold vichyssoise. The occasional Chinese-influenced dinner might be accompanied by Mama's take on egg-drop soup. Regardless of the type of fare for dinner, freshly prepared rice is almost always present. Both Papa and Mama are from Akita Prefecture of Japan, a region famous for and proud of its rice quality. And while Mama might skip her rice portion due to her lighter eating habits these days, Papa always demands a full bowl of rice—full means more than 100 grams, even though this is the recommended maximum consumption per meal. Dinner is frequently followed by some kind of dessert, which is always complemented by bitter Japanese green tea and sometimes another cup of European tea.

Tonight, dinner is special. Obaa-chan (Grandma), living in the same house in Akita where Mama grew up, sent via temperature-controlled postal service a package of ingredients for making a cherished Akita dish, *kiritanpo*. *Kiritanpo*, the term for cooked rice that is kneaded into a cylinder and toasted around 13.5-inch wooden skewers, is shorthand for a hot pot dish consisting of burdock root, leeks, maitake mushrooms, chicken, and the rice cylinders themselves. These rice cylinders were originally created by woodcutters and hunters in the Akita mountain forests who needed a portable and hearty meal they could roast over a fire. Grandma purchased these dinner items from an Akita co-op that prepares traditional local cuisines. She sent them to the family in a box wrapped in decorative flower-print paper. Today, *kiritanpo* serves as a sort of Tohoku-region soul food that nostalgically brings Papa and Mama back to their childhoods and brings Shawn and his wife back in contact with her eccentric and loving grandmother.

Most cooking in this kitchen is done using either a three-burner gas stove or a 1,500-watt convection microwave. As is true for most Japanese homes, there is no standalone oven, no dishwasher, and no garbage disposal in the sink. Instead, there is a yellow mesh bag in the kitchen sink for all scrap food items that can later be emptied. Mama prepares all meals in the kitchen on a single rectangular white cutting board, forcing her to clean off the cutting board after each use. There is a cotton cloth on the preparation counter used to clean up most spills and condensation. Otherwise, a paper towel roll and another cotton towel hanging from the refrigerator on magnetic hooks can be used. Oils, sauces, and other bottled ingredients are kept under the sink. At the far end of the kitchen are three large white trash bins for burnable items, PET (polyethylene terephthalate) bottles, and all other plastic containers and wrapping. There is a door leading directly out of the kitchen into the side yard, but this door is blocked by these bins and is never opened.

The first step in Mama's dinner preparation is the donning of her green cooking apron, the one with Monet-like watercolor flowers printed on it. In addition, she wears a white medical face mask tonight while she cooks because she has been fighting off a cold and wants to avoid contaminating the food. The last special item of clothing that Mama wears as she cooks is a particular pair of house shoes. Mama is a bit too short for the counter height in the kitchen, so she wears slippers with a slight heel while she cooks.

Mama begins prepping the ingredients for the *kiritanpo* hot pot dinner. First, she washes the Japanese parsley and leeks in a stainless steel bowl with very cold water. Next, she cuts the parsley and leeks into roughly two-inch-long pieces on her white cutting board. She opens the package of *ito-konnyaku*, dumps the contents out into a strainer, then pours the remaining *konnyaku* noodles onto the cutting board for slicing. Mama then takes the *kiritanpo* out of the refrigerator, places them on a large blue ceramic plate, covers them in plastic wrap, and microwaves them at 500 watts for three minutes. While these warm up, she begins bringing the soup mix containing tofu, chicken, maitake mushrooms, and burdock root to a boil. Today she uses a *hinai-jidori* chicken stock made from bones and cartilage that comes in a package, but she reminds everyone that in her childhood it would have been made from scratch. The smell of the boiling maitake mushrooms is really breathtaking. Mama laments that wild mushrooms are becoming much harder to find, reminiscing about picking them with her mother when she was young in Akita. Mama uses long wooden chopsticks to stir the mix as it boils. She samples the soup using a small white soy sauce plate as she prepares the meal, and she approvingly smiles after tasting it. The ingredients might not all be sourced from the same places as those of her childhood, but *kiritanpo nabe* is still delicious. She adds the Japanese parsley, leeks, and *ito-konnyaku* to the broth just before turning the heat off, signaling the end of her cooking.

Meanwhile, Papa has been sitting in the living room watching the weather report on the news, while Shawn's wife has been upstairs taking care of their son. From the kitchen Mama asks Papa where a certain serving dish is, but when he comes into the kitchen and begins looking for it in the cabinets above the stove, she becomes angry, worrying that dust will fall out of the cabinets and into the prepared food. Papa retreats from the kitchen into the safety of his reclining massage chair in the living room while Mama continues plating. She opts for distributing the soup into individual ceramic bowls instead of bringing the hot pot itself to the table. She divides the ingredients into the bowls using the same wooden chopsticks she used for cooking, giving Papa a bit more than everyone else. After pouring the soup into the bowls, she begins handing them over the counter to Shawn and to Papa, who has returned from a quick massage in his chair. Shawn's wife joins the family, bringing their son downstairs with her, and she sets him in his electronic rocking bed in the corner before helping to set the table. As Papa and Shawn continue placing the bowls on the table, Shawn's wife makes minor adjustments to the table arrangement and reminds them of cutlery and wares they have all overlooked. Papa sneaks into the kitchen and grabs four small blue ornate plates used for side dishes and places them on the table. Tonight they are for store-bought kimchi—an odd compliment to traditional Akita cuisine but one the family all enjoys nevertheless. Papa also grabs a bottle of Kubota Manjyu sake from the fridge and places it on the dining table along with small serving cups. Papa cannot drink alcohol due to a negative physical reaction from even a slight amount (sometimes referred to as the Asian flush syndrome), but Mama and Shawn indulge on this special culinary occasion in this sake that is best served cold.

On the table there is a small ceramic soy sauce container, a plastic container of toothpicks, and a small condiment bowl filled with packages of Japanese mustard and tartar sauce. There is also a damp blue towel on the dinner table used to clean up any messes such as sauce droplets. Television is central to this family's meals, and so the remote is placed in the center of the dining table accordingly. There are no place mats on the table, and there are no napkins either. Instead, tissues and paper towels that are set on the adjacent counter inside the bay window are available whenever needed. Looking around the room as the table is set, it becomes clear from the bric-a-brac on the walls how important time is in Japanese culture. There are two calendars mounted on the walls as well as an analog clock that is set 20 minutes ahead, guaranteeing that if you plan your schedule by that clock, you should be prepared by your desired departure time. Since there are exceptionally punctual buses and trains to be caught in Japan, time is truly of the essence.

Before dinner, Papa takes an offering of rice to a small shrine kept inside the house near the front door called *hotoke-sama* (venerable buddhas) that serves as a memorial to the family's ancestors. After he returns, they begin dinner with the phrase *itadakimasu*, which roughly translates as "thank you for the meal and everything that went into it." Everyone picks up their chopsticks and digs in to the *kiri-tanpo nabe*. They talk at the dinner table, but the conversations are mainly about the content of the television program they are watching at the time. They might comment on political or economic news stories, play along with a quiz show, or laugh at a variety show. The family dog used to be in the dining room during

> ## The Elderly
>
> In many nations it is considered polite to serve the elderly first at the table or to reserve the best portions for them. In cultures as disparate as West Africa and China, respect for elders means that they are always given first place, and the youngest are fed last. Fascinatingly, in most modern Western cultures it is children who are fed first, either because they are impatient, might need help, or are considered more important to feed. Since the elderly rarely live in the same household with children in most modern societies, their pride of place has largely disappeared, and in elder communities and homes, cafeteria-style dining replaces the pride of place that respected elders once held.

meals, being fed bits of the meal by Papa and Mama, but since their grandson was born, the dog has been restricted to the living room, mainly out of fear of her biting the baby. The family eats, watches television, and laughs and chats a bit. The meal finishes without any grand announcement or agreement; each person at their own pace simply places their chopsticks over the rim of their bowl with the tips facing 9:00, and the meal is over.

After the meal the whole family helps clear the table, but Mama does all of the dishes. On a night of exceptional plating or proportions, Shawn and his wife might help dry dishes after Mama washes them. Shawn and his wife normally leave the table earlier than Papa and Mama for two reasons: they have to attend to putting their son to bed, and his wife's parents normally stay seated at the table for an additional hour or so after dinner watching television programs that Shawn and his wife are not huge fans of (particularly historical period dramas).

Kiritanpo Nabe (Cylindrical Rice Hot Pot)

(makes 5–6 servings)

10 handmade *kiritanpo* (rice cylinders)

²/₃ pound chicken thigh meat

4 cups *hinai-jidori* soup mix (straight type, not concentrated) or substitute chicken stock and a combination of onion extract and Japanese flavoring ingredient extract (kombu, tuna, sake, soy bean)

1 bundle Japanese parsley (also known as water dropwort or Chinese celery)

1 bundle leeks

1 large burdock root, julienned

1 cup *ito-konnyaku*, noodle-shaped (also known as elephant yam)

1 bouquet maitake mushrooms (also known as hen-of-the-woods, ram's head, or sheep's head mushrooms)

¾ pound tofu, soft

1. Cut the leeks into approximately 2-inch pieces, cut the Japanese parsley and *ito-konnyaku* into 2- to 3-inch pieces, and break the maitake mushrooms apart from the bouquet. Julienne the large burdock root.
2. Wrap the *kiritanpo* individually in plastic and microwave at 500 watts for three minutes. Remove using an oven mitt or cloth for safety.
3. Cut each *kiritanpo* into three equal pieces. Breaking it into pieces by hand is also fine.
4. Prepare the *hinai-jidori* soup mix and add the tofu, chicken thigh meat, maitake mushroom, and burdock root. Bring the mix to a boil and add seasoning, soy sauce, and/or cooking sake to taste.
5. Turn the heat off and add the *ito-konnyaku* to the mix.
6. Add the *kiritanpo*, leeks, and Japanese parsley just before serving.

Be careful not to add the *kiritanpo* to the soup if it is still boiling, as the rice cylinders might easily break apart inside.

Additionally, some people add mochi, udon noodles, or rice to make a heartier meal. These items should be warmed up or cooked prior to adding them to the soup mix and should be added just before serving.

FURTHER READING

"Chapter 2 Population and Households." Statistics Japan: Statistics Bureau, Ministry of Internal Affairs and Communications, 2014, http://www.stat.go.jp/english/data/nenkan/1431-02.htm.

Cwiertka, Katarzyna J. *Modern Japanese Cuisine: Food, Power, and National Identity.* London: Reaktion, 2007.

Ishige, Naomichi. *The History and Culture of Japanese Food.* London and New York: Routledge, 2001.

"Local Cuisine of the Tohoku region." Japan National Tourism Organization, 2014, http://www.jnto.go.jp/eng/attractions/dining/food/jfood_03.html.

Mali

Stephen R. Wooten

COMMENSALITY WHERE THERE IS NO TABLE: THE IMPORTANCE OF EATING TOGETHER IN RURAL MALI

Over the course of 13 months in the early 1990s, Stephen ate almost all his daily meals with one family on the Mande Plateau in central Mali (West Africa). Nene Jara, the leader of Niamakoroni (a community of about 300 Bamana-speaking farmers) welcomed him, as the resident ethnographer, into his large household in a time-honored fashion: by integrating him into a group meal. Nene's family consisted of 59 people, his *dumògòw* (house people). Like most rural Bamana families, his household was an extended family constituted through connections along male lines. Nene's group included his wives and their children and his adult sons and their wives and children as well as his junior brothers and their wives and children. This large group had one central hearth, or *gwa*, and the nine married women living in the household took turns cooking for this family. Each day one *tobilimuso* (cooking woman) gathered grain from the central granary and prepared it for the group. Once the grain was cooked, she meted it out into a set of approximately 10 bowls, added leaf sauce, and then distributed it among the groups. Approximately five eating groups were thus constituted, each with age and gender profiles.

In the intervening years, Stephen has traveled back to Mali numerous times for additional field research with the people of Niamakoroni and in other communities across the country. In the process he has gained an intimate understanding of how commensality helps foster the spirit of family and community—what local people call *badenya* (mother-childness). As one woman explained it, "A united family eats together; they eat *baden* (mother-child) porridge." When family members such as those in Nene's household lower themselves to crouch around bowls of millet or rice and sauce placed on the ground before them by hardworking cooks, they eat and also forge bonds that all depend on for survival and community spirit.

The bond of commensality transcends the family setting as well. On so many occasions while traveling in Mali, people whom Stephen had never met before have called out "Come eat with us!" Such calls are clearly acts of hospitality, but they go further than that; a call to eat is a call to connect. "By inviting someone to join you, you are opening up the possibility for connection, for empathy. If your invitation is taken up, this shows that we are and can be one, which is *badenya*,"

Come and eat. A woman presents a bowl of sorghum porridge with green leaf sauce while her counterparts eat their lunch in Niamakoroni, Mali, June 2015. (Courtesy of Stephen Wooten)

explained Sunje Jara, a quiet but insightful male elder. *Badenya* is something that people in the wider cultural world of Mande-language speakers prize more than anything else. It is the essence of community.

By accepting periodic invitations to come and eat and through sharing regular meals with Nene's family, Stephen learned a lot about who eats together, how, and why—about commensality's role in Bamana life. In addition to nourishing the individual physical body, consuming food with others constitutes and nourishes key social groups among the proud farmers he has come to know. Eating together is a sign of kinship connections, and these bonds are reinforced every day when contemporary residents partake of the food that nourishes them. Kinship ties put people in an eating space, but the act of dipping one's hand into the bowl of grain and sauce that lies before you solidifies these relations.

Anthropologists have, of course, long recognized the significance that the consumption of a communal meal has in the dynamics of community life (e.g., Douglas 1971; Richards 1932, 1939; Weismantel 1989). Stephen argues that commensality is central to an understanding of the nature of social and economic improvisation in Bamana communities in rural Mali. Indeed, the centrality of the collective meal is readily apparent to and spoken widely of by the people of Niamakoroni. The phrases *u bè to dun nyògòn fè* (they eat meals together) and *u tè to dun nyògòn fè* (they don't eat meals together) are important ways of expressing the character and quality of domestic relations within households. A vignette of a daily round of meals in the community will help illuminate the alimentary action that occurs in the process of creating the ties that bind.

PREPARING AND CONSUMING BOWLS OF FOOD: THE POWER OF THE DAILY MEAL

In the village, patterned activities and processes come together to create the *badenya* that characterizes community living. A sketch of the flow of life in Niamakoroni will allow us to appreciate the power of family meals and food-related actions.

Each new day begins with women's early morning activities. Before the sun appears, a married woman in each one of the community's compounds rises in order to prepare the morning meal (*daraka*) for the people of her compound, her fellow *dumògòw*. She will be the day's *tobilimuso*. This responsibility rotates among all married women except elders and new wives.

Her activities begin with the drop of a rubber bucket into the village's common well. She draws in the rope, hand over hand, lifting the water to the surface and emptying it into a metal washbasin. When it is full, she lifts it on top of her head, placing it carefully on a small piece of coiled cloth. Often, the cool water splashes onto the baby who likely rests on her back. She walks carefully to the cooking hut or *gwabugu* (hearth place), where she empties the water into the cooking pots. She repeats the process numerous times so that she will have sufficient water to cook the morning's meal. Interestingly, the *gwabugu* where the meal, the substance of unity, is made is a quintessential women's space among the Bamanas. Men do not typically enter these structures. The literal hearth of *badenya* is a female site.

Once she has the water boiling, she adds millet or sorghum flour. The day before she would have retrieved the whole grain from the group's collective stores held in her household head's meeting space. The grain was harvested the preceding fall from a distant bush family field, or *foroba*, worked in common by the household's adult males during the rainy season (roughly June–September). To prepare the grain for cooking, she processes it using a mortar and pestle, removing the grain from the chaff. With the grain cleaned, she pulverizes it into flour. Through their deliberate individual actions, each *tobilimuso* helps to create the alimentary process that ties household members together in *badenya*.

The morning meal typically consists of a thin sorghum porridge, or *seri*, served to household members in large enamel or plastic bowls, most of which were produced in China. The thin gruel is consumed using a gourd spoon (*galama*). Small groups of family members, organized along lines of gender and age, crouch around and dip gourds into a common bowl. The gourd is then raised to the lips, and the contents are drawn off with a sipping action. This process continues until the bowl itself is emptied. The most junior member of the eating circle delivers the empty bowl to the *tobilimuso* for cleaning.

After the morning meal, all members of the *du* disperse to pursue their day's activities; some head off alone, and others depart in groups. During the rainy season, the adult men typically depart en masse for work in the *du*'s main grain field, the *foroba*, where they stay from about 8:00 a.m. to 3:00 p.m. Except for the *tobilimuso*, who is responsible for the day's cooking, the *du*'s adult women typically head off in the company of their young children to work their own women's fields, the *musoforow*.

After her early-morning activities, the *tobilimuso* turns her attention directly to the task of readying the midday meal (*tilelafana*). This meal is usually a thick sorghum paste called *to*, accompanied by a green leaf sauce called *na*. Each woman gathers the leaves for her sauce from plants in the bush or from crops such as okra growing in the *musoforow*. The midday meal is distributed first to those who typically remain in the village—the young children, the elders, and the sick or injured—and to the women who return to the compound from their nearby fields. Girls and young women usually bring bowls of *to* and *na* to the men working in the distant *foroba*. After the meal, people usually return to their activities.

In the middle of the afternoon, men finish up their day's *foroba* activities and either return to the village or move on to other non-*foroba* production activities, which are often the source of personal income. A good many head off to the garden plots (*nakòw*) in the low-lying stream areas close to the village. Some head into the bush to gather resources for making rope, mats, or bamboo furniture.

Women often finish work in their *musoforow* at around the same time. Many of them also then turn to personal-income activities. They typically immerse themselves for several hours in the demanding task of charcoal (*finfin*) production. People generally spend several hours in these pursuits before returning to their compounds for the main collective meal of the day, *suròfana*.

At about 6:00 p.m., all *du* members reunite for *suròfana*, served in the *du*'s common area as with the morning meal. Usually the fare is identical to the midday meal: *to* and *na*. On some special occasions, rice (a purchased staple) is the grain of choice. Again, separate eating groups form within each *du*, divided first by gender and then within gender by age. However, the oldest man in the group, the *cèkòròba* and *dutigi*, typically eats with several young boys (between four and seven years old), and the oldest woman (*musokòròba*) typically eats with several young girls. Toddlers eat with their mothers.

The *tobilimuso* brings the cooked food out from the *gwabugu* and begins by placing a bowl on the ground in front of the *dutigi*, then placing one in front of the next group of men, and continuing through all the assembled men and women. With their right hands, people take a bit of the *to* and dip it into the *na*, which has been placed in a hollowed area in the center of the *to*. The process continues until each individual is satisfied or the food runs out. If the food in a particular bowl does run out before someone is full, he or she is free to move on to a neighboring group that is still eating.

When everyone has finished eating, the *tobilimuso* collects the bowls. Often she gives the remainders to the compound's dogs, or if food is scarce, the remainders are kept for the following day. She then proceeds to wash the bowls and cooking pots so they will be ready for the next meal. When people are full they say "A barika" (Thanks be), to which the others assembled respond by passing the thanks to Allah with "A barika Allah ye"; even the many non-Muslims in the community use these phrases. They then pull back from the intimate eating circle, licking their hands before washing them off in the same bowl of water they used at the start of the meal.

Interestingly, while all *tobilimusow* produce basically the same meals of grain and sauce, they can do so with individual flair. Regular consumers of household meals can distinguish one woman's sauce from another's. It is not uncommon to hear someone, typically a man, praise a particular *tobilimuso*'s sauce publicly by saying "I ni gwa, I ni na" (You and your hearth, you and your sauce). This statement is a commentary on the woman's distinctive culinary style. In a social world where women typically have few public opportunities to secure status, those who receive such praise find it very empowering.

After eating, the *dumɔgɔw* usually linger in the eating area, talking and making plans for the next day's activities. These discussion groups follow gender lines as well. After a period of conversation, people disperse back into the village, where they meet up with friends or spouses to chat or rest before retiring.

Having consumed the big meal of the day, older people typically are in their huts and asleep by 8:30 or 9:00 p.m. Stephen sometimes joined groups of young people for an hour or two in the early evening. Sometimes they would spend these hours processing produce from an individual's garden—on several occasions, Stephen sat shelling beans until 10:30 p.m. These were very animated sessions, and a good deal of socializing took place. Indeed, young people amazed him by staying up talking and listening to the radio well into the early morning hours, even when they had to head off to a day of labor early the next morning.

As this portrait of the daily round of meals suggests, the people of each household are united by their consumption of food prepared from a common hearth. One of the most common phrases in discussions of food and family dynamics—*du kelen, gwa kelen* (one household, one hearth)—is typically rendered with conviction, as if it communicated a prized social value. The upshot is that the character of meal preparation and the nature of its consumption define households; if you have two hearths and two eating groups, you have two households. Each and every day, *dumɔgɔw* come together to gather around bowls of food prepared in a common kitchen. Instead of a series of discrete eating groups, the households of the village are unified consumption units. Even if the people could eat alone, they choose not to. Instead, they choose to share their meals. Interestingly, on occasions when Stephen was sick or simply overwhelmed with the social intimacy of day-to-day life and chose to prepare meals alone in his house, people often came by to check on him to see if he had a problem—they meant a social problem, not a physical one.

However, there is complexity within this framework and within the "unity." All people do not eat together within the community; and even within households, there are some dividing lines. As families grow over time, distinct groups tend to emerge, groups that over time constitute their own residential units, farming units, and, ultimately, eating units. Naturally, when issues of scale become significant, transformation needs to occur, new eating groups need to be constituted through the construction of new dwellings, and, most important, there need to be new hearths at which women can cook common meals to feed the house-people. This is a normal process, one that replicates rather than replaces the basic ideology.

Another distinction within the realm of eating together occurs between age groups and genders within the household. At all meals, men and women eat separately. The women eat on one side of the public space, and the men eat on the other. Within each gender group, people are further differentiated by age, with rough age mates eating together from a common bowl, the only exception being the aforementioned: when favored boys eat with their grandfather. So in a sense, the unified eating group is actually composed of a set of subgroups.

EXTENDING THE *BADENYA* OF THE SHARED MEAL

As mentioned above, communal eating is also a way of bringing nonkin or outsiders into the social fold. Many times when he traveled to neighboring villages near and far and arrived to find people gathered around bowls of *to* and sauce, Stephen was greeted with "Come, eat. Join us!" This happens day in and day out whenever travelers come by, and it also happens on a more profound level in the case of inviting new families to live in the community. A prominent male once recounted the village history. He pointed out that the original family of settlers invited another family to come live with them, and eating together at the outset was part of the process. Sharing meals until the newcomers could get on their feet was a way of creating new community ties and bonds. By sharing food, the hosts were forging new social relations, expressing and building *badenya*.

Another dimension of this dynamic is apparent in community-wide meat-sharing events. On occasions when one of the village men was successful in his hunt of wild animals in the bush around the village, a windfall of meat would become available. The meat would be cooked and then rather ceremoniously and publicly divided into equal parts, to be distributed to all households in the community and even on occasion to households in nearby villages.

The same dynamic would unfold on those occasions when Stephen procured freshly butchered meat from the market. The package of meat would arrive in the village, and the eldest man present at the time would open it in full view of all the inhabitants. He would then divide the mass into five clear piles, one for each household. A young man would then be dispatched to deliver packets to each family. Once it was received and cooked, the *dutigi* of each household would divide the meat into individual portions for his *dumògòw*.

On a smaller scale, even boys who kill a lizard with a slingshot typically grill it and share it with their playmates. Whenever Stephen passed the leftovers of his sweetened morning porridge along to the nearby children, the bowl fed a large number of young people who gathered around and shared it. The practice of sharing such a prized resource reveals the significance people place on exchanges that tie people together. The acts are reciprocal in nature—one man shares the fruit of his hunt with members of his community; a *dutigi* shares a windfall with his family members. The lines of sharing construct and trace the lines of community.

As noted above, no one, not even a visiting anthropologist, eats alone in the Bamana world. Recall that on Stephen's first day in the community, Nene invited him to be a member of his eating group. Each day he spent in the village, Stephen joined Nene and his *dumògòw* for the evening—there is a local pattern of shared nourishment.

A BARIKA! THANKS BE!

As this brief tour of the alimentary landscape of a Bamana community suggests, groups who eat together are grateful. People united by residence, kinship, and marriage partake of common meals that the women cooked at their group's common hearth with produce from household grain fields (*forobaw*) worked by male *du* members under the direction of their *dutigi*. In a very real sense, members of each of *duw* are linked in a shared economy of life, an economy of collective food. Its most basic aspects are apparent in the course of the most alimentary piece of daily life in the community, the consumption of the *foroba to*. The production and consumption of this shared meal is intimately connected to the organization of food production. Each time a woman cooks and lays a bowl of food on the ground before her family members, she transforms the products of different streams of household labor to present an opportunity to connect their efforts and to solidify their bonds. With each dip of the hand into the collective bowl of *foroba to,* a meal that embodies the fruit of everyone's labors (men's grain and women's sauce), individual family members acknowledge each other's work and signal their social unity. In this way, deep commensality is achieved day in and day out in a place where the Western-style dining table is completely absent.

LEARNING TO MAKE *JABAJI* WHERE THERE IS NO COOKBOOK

When Stephen asked women in Niamakoroni how to make one of his favorite dishes, *jabaji* (onion sauce), the responses were pretty short and direct: "Get some onions, vegetable oil, and salt and cook them all together. You can add some tomato paste or Maggi powder if you have money to buy it." Their elementary guidance actually highlights an important aspect of culinary practice in the area. In the village and most other Bamana communities, cooking knowledge is shared orally and through interactive hands-on learning. From an early age, daughters help their mothers prepare and serve meals. In the process they learn how to process grains and create three or four sauces. They learn what ingredients are included in which

All hands in. A group of boys and men eat a lunch of corn couscous and sorghum porridge with green leaf sauce in Niamakoroni, Mali, June 2015. (Courtesy of Stephen Wooten)

dishes. By watching and assisting, they learn how much of what to add and when and how to produce the intended fare. There is no need for a cookbook or instruction manual in this setting. Such information is transmitted intergenerationally through an apprentice-type relationship. Mothers have the opportunity to share their particular takes on village standards with their daughters, and daughters have the chance to improvise a bit on the received wisdom of their mothers without radically changing the menu.

Jabaji (Onion Sauce)

8–10 small-medium onions, diced
½ cup of vegetable oil
1 6-ounce can of tomato paste

1 chicken-flavored bouillon cube
Salt to taste

1. Add all ingredients to a large pot and simmer over medium heat until onions are soft.
2. Stir and break up onions until they form a sauce.
3. Serve on top of porridge, rice, or pasta.

FURTHER READING

Douglas, Mary. "Deciphering a Meal." In *Myth, Symbol, and Culture,* edited by Clifford Geertz, 61–82. New York: Norton, 1971.

Richards, Audrey. *Hunger and Work in a Savage Tribe.* London: Routledge, 1932.

Richards, Audrey. *Land, Labour and Diet in Northern Rhodesia.* London: Oxford University Press, 1939.

Weismantel, Mary. *Food, Gender, and Poverty in the Ecuadorian Andes.* Philadelphia: University of Pennsylvania Press, 1989.

Wooten, Stephen. *The Art of Livelihood: Creating Expressive Agri-Culture in Rural Mali.* Durham, NC: Carolina Academic, 2009.

Mexico

Cristina Potters

Mexico is the 14th-largest country in the world, with a land surface of more than 770,000 square miles. Due to its size and placement on the planet, Mexico boasts the world's 4th-largest biodiversity. Biodiversity, a concept first discussed in 1985, simply means the variety of species, be they animal or vegetable, that exist in any determined space. The term also refers to genetic variability, to ecosystems, and to regions in a given place. Mexico's enormous biodiversity makes it possible to grow and eat a tremendous variety of foodstuffs, including corn, beans, squash, chilies, cattle, fowl, sheep, goats, and many other species.

In addition to biodiversity, Mexico also boasts wide cultural diversity. Ultramodern urban populations exist elbow to elbow with working-class multigenerational

In Mexico, it does indeed take a village! These Purépecha women from the state of Michoacán wear their traje típico (native clothing) as they prepare hundreds of *corundas*, a regional specialty similar to tamales, for the wedding feast of the daughter of one of their close friends. (Courtesy of Cristina Potters)

families. Households in which all adult family members bustle off to work in an office contrast with households in which no adult has a "real" job; 60 percent of all Mexicans work in the informal economy, earning what money they can and living on each day's earnings. In many instances, the most traditional and yet most economically marginalized people are Mexico's indigenous population. For this group, survival of the ethnic group as well as the individual is paramount. The Ramírez family, of the Purépecha race, lives and works in the state of Michoacán. Today, we will visit their table.

Michoacán, located in west-central Mexico, has a land surface of nearly 23,000 square miles. Its varied topography, ranging from long coastlines to high mountains, and its climate, which includes hot, dry lowlands as well as cool, damp highlands, offers an almost unparalleled number of native species.

Because of Michoacán's varied climate, cultivation of fruits and vegetables is possible all year long. The largest crop in Michoacán is corn, either native strains grown in the *milpa* (family use plot of land) or commercially grown corn. Corn composes nearly 45 percent of Michoacán's agricultural product. In addition, Michoacán is the world's largest producer of avocados, both the commercially grown Hass variety that is exported everywhere in the world and the ancient native *aguacate criollo*.

In addition to the avocado, Michoacán produces huge quantities of broccoli, cauliflower, Swiss chard, lentils, macadamia nuts, coconuts, guavas, plums, strawberries, blackberries, and red raspberries, among other edible crops. Bee culture gives ample honey and other hive by-products.

In Michoacán as in most of Mexico, what many people eat hinges in large part on what is available during any given season. Urban populations tend to have more out-of-season food choices due to the presence of modern supermarkets. Rural populations depend less on purchased foodstuffs and more on food of their own

Globalization of Taste

The global appeal of foods such as pizza, Chinese noodles, and curry appears to be a recent phenomenon; since nowadays information travels so rapidly, restaurants introduce new flavors, and new ingredients are available in grocery stores. Actually, all these foods traveled wide and far many centuries ago. The wheat that went into the pizza and noodles traveled many millennia ago both East and West, and the spices that went into the curry traveled great distances in ancient times. Once the Americas were connected to Africa, Europe, and Asia, it would not be uncommon to find tomatoes in Italy or even China. The ground spices and nuts that one finds in a curry as well as a Mexican mole are not coincidentally similar; they share a common root in medieval Persian cuisine. Thus, taste has always been global but is more apparently so today.

production. In rural areas such as the remote village where the Ramírez family lives, nearly all produce is homegrown or grows wild in the hillsides surrounding the town. Most families keep a pig for slaughter, most raise chickens and turkeys, and many have goats or cows for the family's milk and cheese.

The ancient and current basis for Michoacán's home food production is the *milpa,* a family's parcel of land (usually annexed to the family home) where the millennia-old and still fundamental Mesoamerican triad of corn, beans, and squash is grown. Today's *milpa,* which after thousands of years of cultivation consists of these same plants, usually includes chilies, *quelites* (wild greens), and tomatoes. The *milpa* is the spot where Mexico's rich cultural and agricultural heritage and knowledge join to make use of nature during the entire cultivation cycle. The *milpa* alone has demonstrated its capacity to sustain the healthy and diverse nourishment of large populations, nourishment sustainable from the pre-Hispanic era to current times. The key word is "sustainable": the *milpa* is the living and lasting foundation of Mexico's agricultural biodiversity, renewable with each year's crop cycle.

Far off the beaten path is the mountain village (population fewer than 4,000 souls) where the Ramírez family lives and no near access to modern shopping; the trek via public transportation to the nearest large town takes an hour or more. In the village, there are one or two tiny mom-and-pop storefronts where items such as salt, sugar, canned pickled chilies, catsup, vegetable oil, and loaves of white bread are available, along with a selection of potato chips, cookies, candy bars, soft drinks, and cups of ramen soups, prepared in the store's microwave for carry-out.

Due to custom and preference, nearly all food consumed in the Ramírez home is prepared by Señora Ramírez and her adult daughters. Daily food preparation, accomplished predominately over a wood fire, includes walking the hills to gather fallen branches for the fire; building and maintaining the cooking fire; hauling water; planting, raising, picking, and drying corn; processing and grinding corn daily for human consumption; patting out fresh tortillas and other corn-based foods for each day's meals; planting, cultivating, harvesting, and prepping squash, beans, chilies, and other crops in the *milpa;* collecting wild plants in the forests; feeding pigs, cows, chickens, ducks, turkeys, goats, and other domestic animals; collecting eggs; milking cows and goats; preparing cheeses; and a hundred other daily tasks. The list is long, and food-related chores begin before sunup and only end in time for bed at night.

Given what appear to urban onlookers to be primitive and enormously complex tasks necessary to put daily food on the family table, one wonders: whose responsibility is each task? In the Ramírez family culture—which is nearly identical to the rest of modern Purépecha culture—division of labor is determined by the gender and age of family members. Men's daily labor at home generally consists of caring for the household's animals, gathering wood, and performing the heavier agricultural work. Outside the home, men may work as day laborers or fishermen or in other jobs. Women's daily labor includes taking corn to the mill for grinding;

preparing breakfast for the family; getting the children ready for school; washing dishes; making the day's tortillas; washing clothing; cleaning the house; watering plants; feeding chickens, dogs, and cats; preparing and delivering the midmorning meal (*almuerzo*) to the men working in the fields; and beginning preparations for the family's main meal of the day (*comida*). As children begin to grow up, each takes on tasks suitable to his or her age and gender. Boys help their fathers with the tasks allotted to men, and girls help their mothers with women's work. It is highly unusual for a Purépecha woman to work outside the home. Even today in the early 21st century, there is little change in the gender-oriented division of labor that is based on centuries-old perceptions of roles.

The traditional Purépecha house where the Ramírez family lives is called a *troje*. The *troje* is built of planed logs, fitted together by traditional joining methods so that the house can be dismantled and moved should life require. The *troje* has two levels: the ground level, where the family lives, and an upper level, which is for storage. In general, the lower level consists of several discrete cabin-type buildings that form a family home. The living and sleeping quarters are separate from the kitchen; the *letrina* (outdoor toilet) and an outdoor *pila* (source of cold water for dish and clothes washing) are separate from both the kitchen and the living area. Part of the patio contains the *milpa,* which is the source of the family's corn, beans, squash, *quelites,* and chilies. The patio is also normally home to chickens, cats, dogs, and frequently a pig that is being raised for later butchering. Around the grounds there are guava, orange, banana, loquat, and avocado trees.

The *troje's* kitchen is very simple and usually built on a dirt floor. The heart of the kitchen is the *parangua*—the sacred intimacy of the three-stone rectangular fire space where cooking is done over burning wood. Along one wall or two, *trasteros* (open shelves for dishes and other utensils) hold colorful plates and glasses. Large clay and light-blue enameled metal pots hang on the wall next to the *trasteros.* There is a worktable, a few straight-back wooden chairs, and a shelf hanging from the ceiling that holds staples out of the reach of animals. There are no windows, but the high center peak of the roof has a hole for smoke from the *parangua* to escape. There is also an adobe-brick woodstove, smooth-coated with clay and whitewashed. A clay *comal* (griddle) is built into the stove, as are one or two holes where pots can rest and beneath which wood burns. Outside the kitchen not far from the door is a clay beehive-shaped oven. The kitchen measures about 8 by 10 feet.

The Purépecha community still eats primarily what it grows and raises. Few foods other than some fruits and vegetables and some basic staples—flour, salt, sugar, oatmeal, vegetable oil—are purchased. Watermelon, jicama, pineapple, and other fruits not grown at home are not ordinarily eaten at meals but are consumed between meals. Mangos, oranges, bananas, loquats, and all other fruits grown at home are also snack foods; depending on the season of the year, one can almost always walk into the patio and pick something directly from a tree or bush to eat on the spot. Milk and *pan dulce* (sweet bread, purchased at the town bakery) are also consumed more as a snack than as a meal. The saying in Mexico "Panza llena, corazón contento" (Full stomach, happy heart) is certainly true among the Purépecha community. Those who are more financially comfortable eat when and what they want; those who are financially strapped eat when food is available.

The Ramírez family straddles the two poles: when work is available, money and food are plentiful. When work is scarce, so are money and food. Meat is always scarce unless an animal has been butchered recently. Nevertheless, Señora Ramírez feeds her family at least three times a day, although the usual Mexican meal schedule can call for four or five meals: *desayuno,* meaning "unfast," a small very early meal of *pan dulce* and coffee or hot chocolate; *almuerzo,* a late morning heavier meal, sometimes composed of yesterday's main meal leftovers; *comida,* the midafternoon main meal, the largest meal of the day; *merienda,* a late afternoon or early evening snack that is rapidly going by the wayside; and *cena,* a late evening small meal (a *taco* or two, a *pan dulce* with herbal tea or hot chocolate, or some other similarly small items meant to tide one over through the night until the next morning's *desayuno*).

Señora Ramírez and Yadira, her oldest married daughter, prepared today's *comida* (main meal) for the rest of the family:

- Oldest son Álvaro, his wife Guillermina, and their children Alvarito, Juanita, and Demián;
- Son Gustavo and his new wife Rosa;
- Son Benito, still in secondary school;
- Daughter Josefina, her husband Jorge, and their baby daughter Cynthia;
- Oldest daughter Yadira, her husband Miguel Ángel, and their children Pamela, Vicente, and baby Inés; and
- Señora Ramírez, her husband Marcos, and their adult godchild Samuel, who has Down syndrome.

With twenty at the table, we are a fairly normal-sized group for a Ramírez family *comida.* Today's meal includes *corundas* (a Purépecha specialty, triangular tamales, made today with diced carrots and Swiss chard) served with *churipo* (a traditional Purépecha beef-based soup), and *agua fresca de zarzamora* (fresh blackberry-flavored water). Michoacán produces blackberries for export as well as for local use; Yadira's husband Miguel Ángel works for a regional blackberry grower and frequently brings cultivated berries to the family table. The only ingredient purchased for this meal is the beef, butchered earlier today by a neighbor. Everything else except the blackberries is grown at home. Even the honey that sweetens the *agua fresca* is taken from the family's beehives.

For several hours yesterday, Señora Ramírez simmered a large pot of dried corn in a solution of builder's lime and water and left it to cool. Early this morning, she thoroughly washed the simmered corn and removed each kernel's hard covering. By 10:00 a.m. she is at the local grinding mill to have her corn ground for *corundas.* While Señora Ramírez waits her turn at the mill, Yadira starts preparations for the *churipo,* a rich long-cooked broth with bony chunks of beef, chilies, cabbage, carrots, *xoconostle* (a sour cactus fruit used in savory dishes), and other ingredients.

All of the men and adolescent boys eat first, sitting wherever there is space in the *troje.* Some sit at the kitchen worktable, others sit on wooden chairs just outside the kitchen, and two sit on the porch steps. The women serve them, dishing up clay bowls of steaming *churipo* and passing large oval *bateas* (wooden trays) filled with *corundas.* As the men remove the long corn leaves from their *corundas,* one of the little girls goes through the rooms collecting the leaves in a plastic bucket. Nothing goes to waste in the Purépecha kitchen; the leaves will be used later for a different purpose. The men, hungry from their morning work, eat steadily and talk little. A slight and brief upward jerk of the chin means "bring more *churipo*" or "I need more *corundas.*" Rosa, the newest daughter-in-law, carries around pitcher after pitcher of *agua fresca,* refilling glasses and cups.

When the men finish, they move to the porch to talk of work, weather, the year's corn crop, and the cost and advisability of raising a hog. Some smoke postprandial cigarettes. Samuel dozes.

With the men out of the way, the women relax around the table, serving *churipo* and *corundas* to one another. This is the hour to *comadrear*—talk of women's things, gossip a little, fret that the *corundas* could have been lighter textured, complain about the high cost of everything, commiserate about the men, worry about the state of youths today, and admire the latest babies. It's time to tease newlywed Rosa: how long do we have to wait for your first baby?

Children stand close to their mothers; the older children have their own bowls of *churipo,* their own spoons, their own plates of *corundas,* and a glass of *agua fresca.* Mothers feed the littler ones from their bowls, pinching pieces of *corunda* into the *churipo* broth, lifting the spoon to the child's mouth, offering the glass of *agua fresca,* and wiping a chin or a spill. Baby Cynthia cries; Josefina opens her blouse to feed her.

When the children are satisfied, they stream out into the patio to see the latest litter of kittens, trace a court in the dirt for *avión* (hopscotch), wander among the flowers and talk about school, gossip, and giggle. The boys pause to lean on their fathers' shoulders, listening to man talk.

With only the babies to tend, Señora Ramírez and the other women rest a bit, nibbling at a *corunda* and sipping the last of the *agua fresca.* The conversation curls itself around to encompass a problem with the parish priest, a neighbor's mental health problem, and Guillermina's possible new pregnancy: topics thought to be unsuitable for children's ears.

Soon the shadow in the doorway lengthens; it's time to wash the dishes, feed the chickens, and give the bones from the *churipo* to the family dog. The men rouse themselves from their talk and walk into the *milpa* to inspect the corn and squash. Miguel Ángel decides to stay home; his work with the berries will wait until tomorrow.

The women bring the dishes to the *pila* in the patio. One scrapes, one washes, one dries, and one brings more dishes to be washed and carries clean dishes back to the kitchen. All scraps go into the bucket as feed for chickens, dogs, and cats. The long corn leaves that wrapped the *corundas* are washed along with the dishes; later they'll be used to make ring-shaped bases for round-bottomed clay pots.

The sun sinks lower; Señora Ramírez plugs in the cord for the single unshaded bulb that hangs in the middle of the kitchen. The dishes clatter into their shelves, and the pots hang again on their hooks. Señora Ramírez and the other women sit again at the worktable to sort through a pile of dried beans, picking out the odd straws, the little stones that look just like beans but will break your teeth if you don't get rid of them, and the occasional bug-eaten bean. Once the garbage is removed, the beans are put to soak until the morning. While the women pick at the beans, they talk—scandalized—about a neighbor who doesn't bother to soak her beans.

Dried corn, simmering in its pot of water and builder's lime for tomorrow's tortillas, comes off the fire to cool through the night. The cycle begins again.

Churipo

4+ pounds of beef (with bones), cut into chunks	2 or 3 *xoconostles* (optional if you can't find them)
1 bunch of cilantro, chopped	½ large cabbage, cut into chunks
5 *ancho* chilies; remove seeds and soak chilies in hot water	1 pound peeled carrots, cut into 2-inch sections
5 *guajillo* chilies; remove seeds and soak chilies in hot water	Salt to taste

1. Cook the beef in water to cover until done.
2. Add the chopped cilantro.
3. In a blender, blend the drained, soaked chilies with a little water and strain the mixture into a cooking pot. Allow to simmer for 30 minutes.
4. Add the vegetables and simmer until the vegetables are tender. Add salt to taste.

FURTHER READING

Foster, George. *Empire's Children: The People of Tzintzuntzan*. Washington, DC: Smithsonian Institution Institute of Social Anthropology, 1948.

Kennedy, Diana. *The Art of Mexican Cooking*. 2nd ed. New York: Clarkson Potter, 2008.

Mexico Cooks!, http://www.mexicocooks.typepad.com.

Netherlands

Karin Vaneker

In the Netherlands, almost 40 percent of the population lives alone, and single-person households are expected to grow significantly in the future. Graphic designer Jan de Vries is among almost 3 million Dutch people who currently are living alone. He is single, in his mid-50s, and lives in the center of a city with almost 160,000 people in the eastern Netherlands. Before his early 20s, Jan didn't display a particular interest in food and food preparation. He was born and raised in a small village and in a traditional Dutch family, and his mother did most of the cooking. Being a boy, Jan didn't learn anything about cooking at home. He was in his mid-20s when he prepared his first dish and immediately abandoned typical Dutch food such as potatoes and vegetables with meat, usually pork—which he knew from home. Toward the end of his studies when he was living in a dormitory, he became more serious about cooking and purchased his first cookbook *Ou est le garlic* (1979), written and illustrated by the British spy and cookery writer Len Deighton, because he loved Deighton's thrillers and studied graphic design. From the book Jan learned French cooking and especially how to make sauces. By the time he entered his first serious relationship and his children were born, he was cooking almost every day. Because it was more of the same and due to its focus on meat, he started disliking French cuisine and started watching cookery programs on the British Broadcasting Corporation network. Jan discovered Delia Smith teaching the English how to cook an egg and became interested in authentic Italian cuisine. To improve his culinary skills but also for ideas and recipes, he started buying cookbooks from chefs Nigel Slater, River Café, Dean & DeLuca, Heston Blumenthal, and Jamie Oliver. At the same time Jan became fascinated by reference books with information about food and cooking and started spending money on good-quality kitchen equipment. After his wife passed away a few years ago, he had to find a new approach to cooking. Unless his children from a prior relationship are visiting for the weekend and except for the occasional dinner with friends, on an average day Jan cooks a meal and eats it alone. Although lonely diners are perceived as a tragedy and it is not easy to cook for one person either, Jan enjoys cooking and doesn't mind eating alone. Unlike most Dutch people, he doesn't purchase his groceries in the supermarket either. Jan prefers to shop at the market and in ethnic and specialized stores. He always goes to the same places. Jan is convinced that the owners of market stalls and small stores pay much more attention

Graphic designer Jan de Vries reading while eating home-cooked stir-fried chicken breast with a marinated salad. (Courtesy of Karin Vaneker)

to the quality and taste of the food than to its appearance. For the past 40 years Jan has done most of his food shopping on a Saturday or a Tuesday. On these days there's an open-air market on the city's major square. He'll take his heavy-duty shopping trolley, walk to the close-by market, and buy a weekly supply of fresh vegetables, fruits, fish, and cheese. Jan also likes to shop at the Turk and the Toko, the Turkish and Indonesian grocery stores, respectively, that are very common in Dutch cities. Occasionally he buys some meat at the butcher, but on a regular basis he goes to the poulterer, where he either buys some French corn-fed chicken or regional-raised country grouse (*landhoen*).

Jan likes to prepare his food with fresh ingredients and from scratch. He doesn't like to throw food away and always eats whatever he prepares for dinner. What he prepares largely depends on his weekly supply of groceries and the cooking style and cuisine he fancies. Probably because the Asian, and especially Malayan, style of cooking is close to the cuisine of the former Dutch colony of Indonesia, currently he prefers to cook dishes with a Malayan twist. Through reading cookery books and watching shows on television, he discovered that the wok and stir-frying offer many more possibilities to prepare a meal for a person alone than most cuisines. On average Jan will spend 30 minutes in the kitchen to prepare one main dish with a salad, a nutritious soup or a vegetarian bean stew with lentils. Because there's not much available in the city, on rare occasions he doesn't cook dinner himself but eats ready-made or takeout food. And as he tries to eat about 10.5

grams of fresh vegetables every day, he stocks his fridge with fennel, broccoli, cos lettuce, tomatoes, spring onions, and other vegetables that will stay fresh longer.

In order to prepare a stir-fried chicken breast with a marinated salad, Jan used ingredients from his pantry, fridge, and kitchen shelves and went to the poulterer to purchase a chicken breast. He prepares his food in the galley kitchen of his ground-floor apartment in a spacious living space, with a huge wooden dinner table opposite the kitchen area, a workspace with two large-screen computers, several bookshelves, and a couch in front of the television and fireplace.

On most days Jan eats his first meal of the day around midday, when he prepares a breakfast of Turkish yogurt with some fresh strawberries and ecological (spelt) muesli. Later in the afternoon he snacks on fruits or cheese; dinner is his second and main meal. He mostly eats his dinner between 8:00 and 9:00 p.m. and will either sit down at the dinner table or sit on the couch, and while eating he will read a book or the newspaper or watch television.

Before he starts cooking he always sharpens his one-piece stainless steel Japanese knives on a Japanese water stone and makes a mise en place of the ingredients. For the stir-fried chicken breast with a marinated salad, several knives and most of the ingredients were put on a large wooden cutting board next to the sink. A seasoned carbon steel wok with a wooden handle and a saucepan with a steamer were put on the stove, and a wok spoon, salad spinner, white bowl, and plate were placed on the workspace of his galley kitchen.

When he purchased his apartment, located in a former factory, he bought kitchen components that served his requirements and altered them according to his practical needs. From the countertop to the stove with five burners (one for slow cooking, two regular burners, and a fast burner for a wok), the semiprofessional espresso machine, the coffee mill, the toaster, and seven Japanese knives on a magnetic strip, his self-built kitchen is dominated by a countertop and equipment made from stainless steel. Behind the work top he made a stainless steel shelf for his pepper mill and bottles of oil and vinegar.

Takeout

Takeout is nothing new. The ancient Romans had their *popinae* (food stalls), and many apartments in the ancient world had no cooking facilities. The same was true 19 centuries later in major cities, where people depended on what is the equivalent of takeout. In similar fashion, there are people today, by necessity in thriving sophisticated cities, who never cook food and depend entirely on takeout. Whether this is important is a matter for debate. Arguably, it does take less time and makes cleanup, especially for a family, much easier. On the other hand, such establishments rarely consider health, and takeout usually costs more than cooking from scratch. One undeniable fact is that takeout has greatly expanded familiarity with ethnic cuisines, which are both interesting and usually quite affordable.

Currently Jan uses at least five different types of olive oil, mostly Italian; a bottle of grape seed oil; and four different types of vinegar such as red balsamic, white balsamic, and wine vinegar with tarragon. Beneath the countertop, he stores ingredients such as salt, sugar, flour, and pots and pans in drawers. So apart from making a mise en place, he has easy access to ingredients he might need while cooking. After Jan made a mise en place of the vegetables, he started with the preparations of the marinade for the salad by thinly slicing half a shallot and a quarter of a fennel bulb and cutting a small preserved lemon into small pieces with a medium-sized Japanese knife. He then tore a handful of cos lettuce leaves into pieces and put these in cold water in the bowl of the salad spinner, cleaning the lettuce by hand, occasionally putting a bit of lettuce in his mouth. He twice dried the lettuce in a salad spinner and wrapped it in a clean kitchen towel. And to make it tastier and crunchier, he then put the lettuce in the lower drawer of his refrigerator. Once the salad preparations were finished, he started to clean another shallot and rinse a head of broccoli, a red chili pepper, and spring onions under streaming cold water and dried these with a kitchen towel. Cut into bite-sized pieces, the broccoli florets and peeled and sliced stems were steamed in a saucepan with a bit of water from his boiling water tap. In between he sliced another shallot, cut the red chili pepper into small rings, and together with thinly sliced garlic bulbs put it into a bowl and ground a bit of white pepper on top. He prefers white pepper, because black pepper tends to dominate the color of the dish. Using a small knife, he removed the skin of a small piece of frozen ginger and then used a small stainless steel ginger grater (Japanese, brand Muji) to grate the ginger over the bowl with the onions and chili pepper.

Jan's style of food preparation and cooking does not involve measuring and spoons and cups. After displaying the ingredients and in between cutting and slicing, he tastes several of the ingredients and judges the right quantity by looking at the cutting board or at the bowls and plates with the ingredients. Before he took the chicken breast out of the refrigerator in his pantry, he took out a yellow plastic cutting board and cleaned a knife. After cutting the chicken breast into pieces he ground white pepper on top, sprinkled them with fine sea salt, scooped some Japanese rice flour from a plastic bag in the palm of his hand, and used his fingers to coat the chicken pieces. In between he stirred and tasted the marinade for the salad with salad cutlery and heated the wok on the fast burner of the stove. Once it was smoking hot, he added two large tablespoons of coconut oil from a jar; while shaking and stirring the wok with a wok spoon, he added the chicken pieces. While stir-frying, Jan paid much attention to their color and tested their resistance and doneness by pressing on the pieces. Once the chicken pieces had a light brown color, he took out a larger piece, cut it in half, looked at the inside color, put it in his mouth, and removed the other pieces from the wok with a wok spoon. After putting the seasoning—shallot, chili pepper, garlic, and ginger—in the wok, within two minutes he added the broccoli. While quickly stir-frying, he added the chicken pieces and pulled out two bottles of soy sauce and oyster sauce from a drawer beneath the stove.

Splashing some sauce in the wok, after tasting the broccoli he added a bit of boiling hot water and gave the dish a final stir and tasting. After the fire was closed and the hood was turned off, he put the stir-fried chicken on a dinner plate and sprinkled the spring onions on top. He then dressed the lettuce with two large tablespoons of marinade and put the dishes on the dinner table, already set with a white plate, knife and fork, a water glass, and a bottle of white Chardonnay wine.

Jan doesn't like pots and pans and too much fuss on the dinner table. It is only on special occasions that he uses a tablecloth and napkins. Tableware, he believes, should be functional and at the same time look good. Because it is multi-interpretable and most parts can be used as a plate, bowl, or serving dish, for many years in the kitchen and on the dinner table he has used white Arabia tableware (Teema) from the 1950s. Whether it is beer or wine, he prefers to drink from straightforward Itala water glasses designed by the Finnish designer Aino Alto and likes to eat with his simple stainless steel German cutlery. According to Dutch custom, he put a knife on the left side and a fork on the right side of the flat white plate serving as a place mat, and while his left hand was holding a book, he used his right to eat with a fork. Although he used salad cutlery to prepare and stir the salad, he didn't use it to put salad on his plate but instead ate the salad straight from the salad bowl by pricking it with his fork. Whereas preparing dinner took him about 30 minutes, he ate it in about 10 minutes, on and off taking a sip from his wine. After dinner he put the dirty dishes in the dishwasher, inspected the kitchen, cleaned the countertop and dinner table with a cleaning cloth, and went straight back to his computers in his workspace. Living alone for many years and because of his above-average interest in food and cookery books, Jan has a style of food preparation that is superorganized and very functional. Unlike many Dutch people, he isn't bothered much about cooking a meal for one and eating it alone.

Stir-Fried Chicken Breast with a Marinated Salad

1 person

Marinated Salad

Cos lettuce	White pepper
½ banana shallot or any shallot variety	Maldon sea salt
1 preserved lemon, walnut-sized	1 tablespoon white balsamic vinegar
¼ fennel bulb	2 tablespoon extra virgin olive oil

1. Prepare the marinade for the cos lettuce by thinly slicing the shallot and fennel and cutting the lemon in thin pieces.
2. Put these in a bowl and grind a bit of white pepper on top.
3. Sprinkle with the balsamic vinegar and olive oil.
4. Mix and set the marinade aside for at least 30 minutes.
5. Meanwhile, clean a handful of cos lettuce leaves with cold water and tear these in roughly 2-inch pieces by hand. Use a salad spinner (tosser) to remove the excess water, dry the pieces with a clean kitchen towel, put the lettuce in the refrigerator loosely wrapped in a kitchen towel.
6. To serve, put the cos lettuce in a salad bowl and sprinkle the marinade over the top. Use salad cutlery to mix the salad.

Stir-Fried Chicken Breast

1 medium (about 6 ounces) chicken breast

1 head of broccoli

1 banana shallot

1 red chili pepper

4 or 5 thin spring onions

2 single garlic bulbs (solo garlic)

½-inch piece of fresh ginger

1 tablespoon soy sauce (all-purpose Kikkoman)

1 tablespoon oyster sauce (Chinese)

Japanese rice flour

White pepper

Fine sea salt

2 tablespoon extra virgin coconut oil

1. Rinse the broccoli, chili pepper, and spring onions under cold, streaming water.
2. Use a sharp knife to cut the stalk of the broccoli; peel and discard the outer skin of the stalk. Cut the stalk in slices and the individual florets in bite-sized pieces.
3. Place the broccoli in a saucepan with a steamer with about an inch of boiling water. Bring to a boil, put the lid on top, and cook the broccoli crisp-tender on medium heat for about 4 minutes, until you can pierce the thickest pieces with a knife.
4. As soon as the broccoli can be pierced with a knife, discard a bit of the water and steam the broccoli for about 1 minute without the lid. Put the broccoli in a bowl.
5. Remove the outer skin of the banana shallot and cut it in thin slices.
6. Cut the chili pepper in very small rings.
7. Remove the outer skin of the garlic bulbs, cut the bulbs in half, and slice very thinly.
8. Put the chili pepper and garlic on top of the broccoli.

9. Use a sharp knife to peel the ginger, then use a fine grater to grate the ginger on top of the broccoli. Grind a bit of white pepper over the top and sprinkle with a pinch of salt.

10. Put the chicken breast on a plastic cutting board. Use a clean sharp knife to cut it (horizontally) in bite-size pieces. Grind a bit of white pepper over the pieces and sprinkle with a bit of salt. Sprinkle Japanese rice flour over the chicken pieces and mix by hand until all the pieces are covered with flour.

11. Heat the wok over very high heat, add the coconut oil, and stir-fry the chicken pieces about 4 minutes until light brown. Use a slotted spoon to remove the pieces from the wok and set aside.

12. Add the broccoli, shallot, chili pepper, garlic, and ginger to the wok and stir-fry for about 2 minutes over high heat.

13. Add the chicken pieces, stir, add the soy and oyster sauce, and stir well. Eventually add 1 or 2 tablespoons of boiling water.

14. Put the stir-fried chicken on a plate, sprinkle with the spring onions, and serve immediately.

Meal prepared by Bert van der Veen, Enschede, the Netherlands.

FURTHER READING

Mohamed, Hiba. "Real Dutch No More?" Join Magazine, 2013, http://www.joinmagazine.nl/article/real-dutch-no-more/.

Otterloo, Anneke van. *Eten en Eetlust in Nederland, 1840–1990* [Food and Appetite in the Netherlands, 1840–1990]. Amsterdam: Bert Bakker, 1990.

Vaneker, Karin "The Netherlands." In *Encyclopedia of Food Cultures of the World,* Vol. 4, edited by Ken Albala, 245–257. Santa Barbara, CA: ABC-CLIO, 2011.

Nicaragua

Jennifer Moran

SOPA DE PESCADO

Tucked away deep in the barrio in the capital city of Managua, a huge aluminum pot bubbles with rich sustenance—an amalgamation of water, fire, agriculture, transportation, hunting, trade, cooperation, cooking skills, and traditions: *sopa de pescado*.

As the sun rises behind their backs, men with nets quietly haul in fish on the beaches of the Pacific. Along the rivers, men are busy with harpoons and poles. Some of the bounty from the waters will end up on their tables; the rest will be carted to markets.

Farther inland, after hot cups of local coffee and before the Managua sun climbs high in the sky and simmers the city, Mami and her niece walk up the dirt road and wait for the bus to the market.

The bus pulls up and rushes to a stop. Mami climbs aboard with her niece and swipes her card across the scanner, and it takes away another 5 *cordobas* (about 20 cents) from the balance. It is standing room only on the bus, filled with mothers cradling babies, students with backpacks, police officers in blue uniforms, construction workers with buckets of tools, vendors, hawkers, shoppers, artists. This city bus, like others, is owned by its driver and is uniquely outfitted with tassels, decals, stenciled graphics, paintings, and fans. Velvet curtains are ready for the midday sun, and the little glass windows have been pushed open as much as possible. *Ranchera* music fills the tight, close air.

The women hang onto the bars overhead and gaze out the windows for the 20-minute, three-mile trek to the Mercado Oriental: the country's largest, wildest, best-priced, and most popular and notoriously dangerous open-air market.

The bus stops, and the women push their way gently to the side door with a dozen other passengers. They step out onto the dusty, muddy, and colorful market streets. To the left: tires, toilets, and doors. To the right: tortillas, speakers, sprockets, hair clips, used clothes, shoes, Christmas lights, cobblers, vegetables, rice, fruit, flowers, and herbs. Beyond sight in every direction, the market continues as a vast labyrinth of passageways and shops, already brimming with people, music, and food even though it is still early morning.

Mami and her niece make their way toward the fish stands, stepping carefully over mud and rocks, concrete steps and rubbish, feet and tires. They're sharing the

A bowl of Nicaraguan fish soup, *sopa de pescado*, with the local catch of the day and market vegetables. (Courtesy of Jennifer Moran)

passageways with throngs of people and the occasional wooden cart, pushed by men or pulled by horses, hauling vegetables or fruits from neighboring pueblos and departments near and far. Earlier, the fishermen similarly arrived with Mami's savory *mixto* (seafood mixture).

It is still cool out at 7:00 a.m., only about 78 degrees Fahrenheit, and the fish are fresh and firm. Vintage weight scales dangle here and there for the vendors' use, and the scene is cast in a mix of shadow and light under a patchwork of new and rusty tin roof panels. The women act quickly, selecting fish with bright eyes, shimmering scales, and firm flesh. They move to the next stall, with shrimp, crabs, clams, and turtle eggs piled into little mountain ranges along the tables. Again Mami and her niece act quickly and leave with packages of freshwater and saltwater fish heads and filets as well as shrimp and crabs.

On the way out of the market, the women stop at a friend's stand for carrots, tomatoes, celery, *culantro* (similar to cilantro in taste and use but with a broader dandelion-like leaf), onion, and green bananas. Everything they buy is packed into thin, colorful plastic bags, nicknamed the "flowers of Nicaragua" because they are so numerous and colorful and often end up peppering the streets, plants, and trees. The packages are placed into the women's gigantic woven recycled plastic market bags, and everything is gently hauled through the market, back onto the bus, and down the dirt road home.

Managua is a city of dirt roads and developed highways, electronic club music and acoustic marimba-rich traditional sounds, aristocrats and barefoot peddlers, clapboard houses and vast estates, hunger and obesity, fresh whole foods falling from the trees, and *fritangas* (fried food stands) with everything dripping in grease. Back in barrio Jonathan Gonzales, children are playing in the street, kicking up dirt as they pass a soccer ball back and forth. Music pipes into the street from someone's kitchen, while a woman pats tortillas into small disks at the tortilla shop next door.

Mami's niece stops at the little *pulpería* (convenience store) across from their homes for cold milk, while Mami heads into her house with the fish and vegetables. The fish is placed in the fridge, and the veggies are placed on the table. A few hours flicker by, and family trickles in from down the path, next door, and across the city. Conversation naturally moves to hungry bellies, and Mami pulls together the ingredients: catfish, tilapia, crab, shrimp, sunfish, carrots, onions, celery, *culantro,* rice, green banana, tomato, salt, and a seasoning packet of *Maggi de camarón* (shrimp bouillon).

The rich fish stock starts with water piped into the neighborhood from the city's freshwater lagoon. With a twist of a knob, the water flows from the house's singular faucet into the huge aluminum pot and over the chopped onions and whole crabs that Mami has already added. This little faucet is used for cooking, washing dishes, doing laundry, watering the cats and dogs and plants, and brewing coffee in the morning—all of the household's needs. Mami walks back through the garden and breezeway with her pot of onions, crabs, and water.

She sets the pot on the new gas stove she bought and opens the valve on the tank. Gas is common and valued and is used with careful measure. Some homes still use wood or use both, as wood smoke is an important flavor component in traditional dishes such as *frijoles cosidos* (cooked red beans). A local utility delivers gas from a truck piled with tanks. Cooking wood is delivered by impoverished men, women, and children driving horse carts piled with bundles of wood from the countryside. Some of the cooking wood is grown for that purpose; some is gathered from streets, salvaged from landscaping work and storm waste; and some is sourced from the wild, a contributing factor in deforestation, droughts, and erosion in the region.

Flames lick the pot, and soon the stock is simmering. As a working grandmother in her 60s, Mami has been cooking like this for her family and for restaurants for many years. She moves swiftly, each movement productive and measured, with a smile on her face. Vegetables are chopped and tossed into the pot, water from a bucket is added, bony fish and fish heads are tossed in, rice is started in another pot, and those pretty green bananas are sliced and simmered in water in a third pan, next to the rice. In a few minutes, Mami will add more vegetables and tender fish, finishing with *culantro,* milk, and a pinch of salt just before serving.

Meanwhile out in the garden, music is playing, and the plantain trees sway in the breeze. When the weather is ideal, shared meals are often enjoyed outdoors in the garden between their houses, where there is ample space for everyone. Today is one of those days, and Mami's son and grandson bring out tables and tablecloths of silk and lace. The sofa is covered in a cotton tapestry under the avocado tree. A niece brings out a bowl of spoons, and another niece brings out the first bowl of soup. Cats lick their lips and dogs wag their tails in the shade, in joyful anticipation of the fishy leftovers.

Mami explains that *sopa de pescado* is rich in nutrients such as calcium and phosphorous, good for the brain and for enhancing sex drive and fertility, increasing energy, sustaining general health, and healing those who are ill. Although not an everyday food for most Nicaraguans, fish is a favored source of sustenance and protein. It is enjoyed in many forms, from ceviche to grilled or fried whole fish to *maiz* (corn) and fish patties to *sopa*.

Mami's son explains that at restaurants the price is marked up exponentially, but when the ingredients are bought at the market, the soup is much more economical. From market to table, the pot for a family of 7 or 8 costs about $5, or 127 *cordobas*. While pricier than the Nicaraguan staple *gallo pinto* (pan-fried rice and beans) and tortillas, it is affordable and typical for Mami's middle-class family.

Because her family loves her *sopa de pescado* and because it is good for health and relatively economical to make, Mami prepares the soup almost every week or upon request. Mami's family has a strong spirit of sharing their bounty, whether food or money. Work and a steady income are generally hard to come by in Nicaragua, and families often pool their resources. (Mami has worked washing and mending clothes and cooking since she was a teenager. Her nieces work at home and help maintain their homes. Her son has a business, painting and refinishing windows and doors, and he is often helped by his own 14-year-old son.)

The table is set: a bowl of rice to share among the group is placed on the table next to a bowl of sliced boiled green bananas. A niece serves cold glasses of *refresco de cacao* (a homemade chocolate milk made with cacao beans) or water or beer. One by one the bowls of *sopa* are brought out, each customized for the eater's preferences: Crab or catfish? Tilapia or sunfish? Snapper or shrimp? As the bowls are brought out, the family begins to sip, slurp, and share the soup with gusto. Fish head? Crab claw? More *culantro*? Sprinkle of salt? Mami finally sits down and takes a sip herself. Everyone is together now. The family holds hands, forming a circle around the table. A niece offers a prayer as everyone gives thanks to God for the bounty, the meal, and their blessings, culminating with a quiet chorus of "Amen."

Grace

Giving formal thanks at the table, usually to a higher power, is embedded in some cultures. We may be familiar with the practice among Christians in the West or among observant Jews who say a formal prayer before every meal, often specific to individual foods such as bread and wine. But in other cultures, recognizing God or the gods before eating is essential. In East Africa, pouring some drink onto the floor is a way of honoring the ancestral gods, and elsewhere a libation serves the same purpose. A sacrifice or offering is merely an extension of this practice, which in ancient times served to feed the gods but today can be an integral part of every meal.

The prayer is followed seamlessly by steel spoons clanking the ceramic bowls; fingers pulling tender fish flesh from bone; and hands, lips, and tongues working hard for precious crab meat, bites of juicy tomatoes and tender onions, and satisfying and sustaining bites of green bananas. The soup is savory and satisfying. The broth is light, with an element of velvety richness from the milk. A niece mentions that sometimes coconut milk is used in place of cow's milk especially in the country, where the fish is pulled from the river and the coconuts are pulled from the trees. Bright bits of *culantro* add a grassy, herbal flavor. The onions are sweet and tender, and the sliced carrots have a soft heft to the bite. A spoonful of salty rice and a few slices of green banana add another dimension and texture to the soup, and the starch extends the meal. The table is mostly quiet as everyone focuses on eating and sharing today's *sopa*.

As each bowl is finished, each family member steps up without ceremony and brings his or her bowl of bones to the singular sink, just behind today's dining table in the dusty tropical garden. Instead of throwing the bones in the garbage, they are tossed to the whisker-licking cats, who are waiting nearby and dine like royalty on the tiny bits of fish and cartilage. Any veggies and pieces of fish without bones are tossed to the less graceful dogs, who might swallow the dangerous little fish bones whole. Some diners then wash their dishes, and some simply start a stack on the corrugated concrete basin. A niece lingers at the sink after she washes her bowl and briskly deconstructs the stack of dishes every time it starts with solid dish soap, a woven plastic cleaning cloth, and cold water from the tap. Before long the animated garden table is once again clean and quiet, ready for the next family meal.

Barriga Llena, Corazón Contento (Full Stomach, Content Heart)

Sopa de Pescado

Water	Tomato, chopped
Assorted fish and seafood, such as catfish, tilapia, crab, shrimp, sunfish	Milk or coconut milk
	Salt
Carrots, chopped	Seasoning packet of *Maggi de camarón* (any seafood bouillon can be used)
Onions, chopped	
Celery, chopped, stalk and leaves	Rice, cooked
Culantro, chopped	Green (unripe) banana, sliced and boiled tender

1. Chop onion and add to a large pot with crabs. Fill pot halfway with water and bring to a boil.
2. Add chopped carrots and celery and simmer for 15 minutes.
3. Add fish and tomatoes.

4. Add water to cover, and simmer for 15 minutes or until fish is cooked.
5. Finish with milk, *culantro, Maggi,* and salt to taste.
6. Serve in bowls with cooked rice and boiled sliced green bananas at the table as optional additions.

FURTHER READING

Cuadra-Morales, Norma, Sheila Santos, and Maria Eugenia Fonseca de Lacayo. *Hospitalidad Nicaragüense: Tradiciones.* Managua: n.p., 2002.

Espinoza-Abams, Trudy. *Nicaraguan Cooking: My Grandmother's Recipes.* Philadelphia, PA: Xlibris, 2003.

Poland

Dorota Dias-Lewandowska

In recent years Poland has experienced many social and political changes, the reflection of which can be found on the Polish table. The end of communism in 1989, numerous economic crises accompanying the system transformation, and adjusting to the new type of economy have changed the dietary patterns of many Poles to a great extent. Poland's accession membership in the European Union in 2004 also influenced Polish food traditions.

In the last 30 years Poland has made a transition from simple cuisine, which clearly indicates lack of food products, caused by the policy of the state in the period of communism (Burrell, 2003), to the openness to new foreign products and cuisines, which have become a frequent guest on Polish tables. The contemporary meal of a Polish family is to a great extent a result of the aforementioned factors. It demonstrates love for the traditional, homey cuisine, which, however, slowly loses its hermetic character and welcomes new elements. Over the past few years there has been a fashion among the Poles to be interested in anything connected with cooking. Television airs many well-known culinary programs, but original Polish culinary shows are being produced too, and television stations have extended their offerings with thematic channels dedicated to cuisine and cooking. The publishing industry has been dominated by culinary magazines and cookery books, and the Internet has become a space for developing culinary blogs (IRCenter.com, 2014). Cooking has become a fashionable hobby in Poland, just like going to taste festivals or buying at ecological marketplaces. The interest in what we eat is becoming more and more common, yet due to the economic difficulties, many families limit their interest in cooking according to their economic level, and the main factor in deciding about preparing a given meal is the price of the ingredients.

At present, Polish family meals are a fusion between the old cuisine of the communist era (Smith, 2007), the period of fascination with prepared convenience foods and food concentrates, and the return to natural products. In the everyday meals, we may observe a few characteristic features of consumer behaviors that are typical of Polish society. First of all, the Polish cuisine is seasonal. A great emphasis is put on using products that are currently available and much cheaper than those imported and nonseasonal. At the same time, in comparison to other European countries, Poles eat little fruit, preferring vegetables, mainly potatoes. It is the Poles who still eat the most potatoes in Europe despite a drop in the 1990s, when

The Nawrocki's family dinner, second course—*gołąbki* with mashed potatoes, peas, and carrots. This meal was served in December, just few days before Christmas Eve when the most celebrated and traditional polish meal is served. (Courtesy of Dorota Dias-Lewandowska)

potatoes were partly replaced by pasta and rice (Adamczyk, 2002, 33). Although the Polish table is based on seasonal products, there is little variety of garden food products. The diet of the majority of the Poles is still rich in meat, which is the most important and the most desirable element of a meal.

The number of meals eaten during the day is typically three or four. Breakfast usually takes place at about 6:00 or 7:00 a.m. before going to work or school. A second breakfast is eaten at about 11:00 a.m. and as a rule consists of sandwiches prepared at home. Dinner, the largest meal of the day, is served in the afternoon between 3:00 and 4:00 p.m. It usually consists of two courses and sometimes a dessert, the latter served more often on holidays. During the week the dinner can be one course only; on the weekends it's mostly more developed. Soups are very popular here and are usually served as the first course during dinner. The second course is most often a piece of meat with a large amount of cooked potatoes and side dishes in the form of salads, raw vegetable and fruit salads, or cooked vegetables or pickles, depending on the season. The dessert is typically a homemade cake. Drinks served with the meal are mainly compotes made from seasonal fruits or tea, which in Poland is a drink served with practically every meal from breakfast to supper. Water, juices from concentrates, and fizzy drinks are less common and are usually chosen by the younger generation.

There are still few immigrants in Poland; thus, society is quite homogenous as far as nationality and religion are concerned (the dominant religion is Catholicism). The strict Catholic fasts that used to be obligatory in Poland in early modern and modern times had an enormous impact on the character of the old Polish cuisine, which to a great extent was based on fish. Today's fasts are an element of the Polish tradition. Usually at every home but also in many canteens and restaurants, there is a meatless meal on Fridays available. Friday is the day when it is fish that reigns on the table. On other days it is usually pork that is eaten, although its consumption has dropped quite significantly in recent years in favor of the cheaper poultry.

A special meal is the Sunday dinner, which often gathers more of the family. Important meals are also the ones connected with the most important Catholic feasts: Easter and Christmas. During these holidays people prepare traditional dishes, mainly meatless, that are not eaten on an ordinary day. Over the last few years there has been a growing interest in the old and forgotten traditions connected with holiday meals. One of the most important of these is the tradition of eating goose meat on November 11, Saint Martin's Day, which is also the day on which Poles celebrate the regaining of independence in 1918. Thanks to the promotional campaigns conducted, among other things, by self-governments that support the "Goose meat for Saint Martin's Day" campaign, this meat, which used to be popular in the past, slowly returned to Polish tables.

The family whose meal we shall present is that of Anna and Piotr Nawrocki and their children, Antoni and Helena. Anna is an amateur of homely Polish cuisine. She was raised in the countryside; her parents had a farm and a vegetable garden. Anna prepares many dishes from scratch; at home she learned how to make preserves, and her mother and grandmother taught her to cook. Anna cooks at home just like her parents do. Piotr spent all his childhood in a big city and ate dinners at a school canteen and afterward quite often at a milk bar (*bar mleczny*). When he was a child the kitchen was women's domain, and he never had the opportunity to learn how to cook. He likes home cooking, but he rarely cooks. However, he takes care of the adjacent garden in which he planted the most necessary vegetables and herbs. The whole family lives in a city of 50,000 inhabitants in the center of Poland.

The main meal of Anna, Piotr, Antoni, and Helena is dinner, usually served after 4:00 p.m., when the parents come back from work and children come back from school. Cooking is mainly Anna's job. Although the division of duties is becoming more and more popular in families, it is mainly women who take care of preparing meals for the whole family. The Nawrocki family usually eats home-prepared meals and only occasionally goes to restaurants. Takeaway food is not very popular here. In this category pizza is the most popular choice, although it is usually ordered during a friend's visit in the evening during film watching rather than at dinnertime.

Preparing all meals at home is connected with purchasing fresh products on an ongoing basis. The Nawrockis' cuisine is first of all seasonal, dominated by vegetables that are available at marketplaces and by dishes adapted to what is currently in season. It is usually Anna who takes care of this. After work she does the shopping in various shops, depending on the products she wants to buy. Over the last few years it has been popular to do the shopping in discount food stores; they are chosen also by middle-class people. Anna likes to buy products of well-known brands produced specially for a given store in such places. She often buys larger amounts of particular products when they are on sale in order to use them later for preparing meals. Sometimes she puts these products in the freezer and uses them much later.

Anna does the major part of her shopping at the marketplace. She has her favorite sellers there; she has known them for a long time and trusts them when it comes to the selection of products. Shopping at a marketplace has lots of advantages. Anna knows where the vegetables and fruit come from, and the prices are also very reasonable. Vegetables are not the only food products that can be bought at the marketplaces; there are many stands with dairy products and meat there. Sometimes sellers from the countryside go there to sell products from their own farms: eggs, cheese, and preserved fruits and vegetables. Food marketplaces can be found practically everywhere in Poland. Despite the competition from big supermarkets and discount stores, food marketplaces still enjoy great popularity. Recently there have been more and more special new marketplaces with products coming from the ecological farms, including farmstead cheeses, vegetables, ready-to-cook products, and homemade sourdough bread. Traditional food is more and more appreciated, and despite the fact that it is quite expensive, there are more and more enthusiasts of it, especially in big cities. Apart from regular fairs, there are also occasional sellers who come to smaller and bigger localities. They can be seen at the street corner by building units, especially in the seasons for particular fruit or vegetables. In June there are lots of strawberry sellers who sell the fruit directly from their fields. Autumn, in turn, is the time when we can notice stands with apples and plums.

This seasonality is also very noticeable in the kitchen. Seasonal products are readily purchased also due to their price. In autumn and winter the table is full of side dishes that are subject to pickling such as cucumbers or cabbage, which replace fresh vegetables as a side dish. In the Nawrockis' house it is Anna who cooks all the dishes; she also prepares preserves for winter, such as all kinds of pickles, salads, and jams, herself. Such products are quite rarely purchased in shops. Few semifinished products are used in the kitchen; soups are cooked of meat and vegetable stock and sometimes are seasoned with ready-made spices, yet Polish cuisine is still based on few semifinished products. Hence, cooking takes Anna quite a long time, for she spends from one to two hours in the kitchen. She usually prepares a two-course dinner, which consists of a soup and the second course, which is a portion of meat with potatoes and other side dishes. After dinner she sometimes serves a dessert—a homemade cake with seasonal fruit, usually an apple pie.

Anna's children, Antoni and Helena, help her to prepare the table for the meal; they set the table and help to take the dishes from the kitchen. The meal begins with the soup. When the Nawrockis have guests the soup is served in a tureen, and each person takes a helping. When they are just by themselves, Anna puts pasta and then soup into the soup plates in the kitchen and brings them to the family members. Soup is an important element of the meal; the dinner seems incomplete without it. Once the first course is finished, Antoni and Helena take the plates to the kitchen, while Anna serves the second course, a platter of *gołąbki* (cabbage rolls), boiled potatoes, and carrots with green peas. On Sundays, holidays, or during guests' visits there are usually several kinds of meat and dishes on the table at the same time, while there is typically only one type of meat served on an everyday basis.

Once everything has been put on the table, everybody takes a helping of potatoes and meat. Anna remembers that when she was a little girl she had to eat a large helping of potatoes with a small piece of meat and that she couldn't leave any food on the plate. Today, although she teaches children not to squander food, she lets them take as many vegetables, side dishes, and meat as they want. From his childhood Piotr remembers his father who, as the head of the family, began the dinner and was the first to take his helping. Today their family is governed by more liberal rules, and everybody takes as much food as they want in any order. An exception is made when guests come; they are then the ones who are asked to start the meal.

The tableware depends on the occasion. During ordinary, everyday meals there is an ordinary dinner service bought at a supermarket. Not much importance is attached to the way the table looks; it is more the functionality and practicality that matters. The situation changes on holidays, during guests' visits, and other special occasions, when Anna and Piotr serve the meal on white porcelain they got for their wedding. There is also a beautiful tablecloth and linen napkins laced by Anna's mother. On such days Anna uses a silver sugar bowl she got from her grandmother. It is the centerpiece of the table and is only put there on special occasions. The supper is eaten by candlelight, which makes the atmosphere more sublime. It is particularly noticeable at the Christmas Eve supper and the Easter breakfast. The whole family then dresses up, even if there are no other people apart from the family members present.

Today the family dines in the sitting room, where they have a wooden table as well as a TV set, bookshelves, family photos and memorabilia, and a glass case in which Anna keeps her best porcelain tableware, tablecloths, and napkins. The time of Christmas has begun so the Christmas tree is already there, and in a few days they will prepare a special fasting dinner, *wigilia* (Christmas Eve dinner), containing 12 traditional dishes.

The everyday meals are eaten in a quite loose atmosphere; in the family circle the Nawrockis are quite at ease. There are no really strict rules at the table; more attention is paid to the behavior of children, who shouldn't pick at their food. What is also unwelcome is choosing better helpings of food, hesitating for too long before choosing a helping, and leaving leftovers on one's plate.

The TV is often playing in the background, though it is not watched during the meal. The members of the family have lively discussions on various topics at the table, yet they avoid discussing the current family problems. The Nawrockis have a dog and two cats. Although pets shouldn't be fed during the meal, the children very often give them some bits from their plates in secret. The dinner usually doesn't take long—about 30 minutes up to an hour. On holidays and weekends the common meals may last several hours. The real marathons are Easter and

Christmas. On such occasions the family spends practically the whole day at the table eating and talking. It is also then when alcohol, a cordial or stronger vodka, drunk after the meal, arrives on the table. During everyday dinners Anna and Piotr drink tea sweetened with two teaspoons of sugar, while the children prefer mineral water or juices. After dinner the whole family readily eats something sweet, such as homemade cake or a sugar confectionary purchased in a shop.

After a finished meal, Anna clears the table. The leftovers from the plates are for the pets. The meat left on the platter is put into containers and then into the fridge. It will be used for tomorrow's dinner or, if Anna prepared a lot of it, frozen and served another day.

Gołąbki

1 pound minced pork, preferably from the shoulder	2 cloves garlic
1 cabbage head	1 onion
¾ cup rice	Butter
Salt and pepper	4¼ cups broth
Marjoram	Oil

1. Take the core out of the cabbage head.
2. Prepare a quite big pot that can hold the entire cabbage head. Fill the pot with water and bring it to a boil.
3. Put the cabbage into the boiling water. Wait a few minutes and remove the external cabbage leaves, which have already gotten soft in the course of the cooking. Continue this, removing the next soft leaves every few minutes. Of all the leaves choose the ones that are the biggest and prettiest. Cut the thickening of the main nerve out from them.
4. Next, prepare rice, which should be boiled a bit less time than usual. Once it's ready, add it to the raw minced meat and add spices: salt, pepper, marjoram, and garlic squeezed through a press.
5. Chop up the onion small, fry it in butter, and add it to the meat too.
6. Knead the mass with your hands until all the ingredients are nicely mixed together.
7. Once the filling is ready, put it on cabbage leaves and form cabbage rolls just like any other rolls. Fold the sides of the leave to the inside and then form the roll. This will prevent the cabbage rolls from unfolding during the cooking.
7. Put the cabbage leaves you didn't use at the bottom of the pot. The cabbage rolls should be placed one next to another so they lie against one another and fill the whole pot. You can put them in layers. Then the rolls have to be covered completely with broth; you may add some water.

8. Cook them over a low flame for about 40 minutes.
9. Once they are taken from the pot, they should be left for a while to cool down. You may also fry them in oil. Serve with potatoes, raw vegetable salad, and tomato sauce.

FURTHER READING

Adamczyk, Grażyna. "Wybrane aspekty zachowań konsumpcyjnych i wzorców spożycia żywności w polskich gospodarstwach domowych w latach dziewięćdziesiątych." *Roczniki Akademii Rolniczej w Poznaniu* 343 (2002): 31–41.

Bellows, Ann. "Gender, Utilitarianism and Poland: 100 Years of Women and Urban Agriculture." *Women and Environments International,* no. 44–45 (1998): 36–39.

Bellows, Ann. "One Hundred Years of Allotment Gardens in Poland." *Food & Foodways: Explorations in the History and Culture of Human Nourishment* 12(4) (2004): 247–276.

Burrell, Kathy. "The Political and Social Life of Food in Socialist Poland." *Anthropology of East Europe Review* 21(1) (2003): 189–194.

Culture.pl, http://culture.pl/en/tag/culinary-art-0.

Gulbicka, Bożena. *Wyżywienie polskiego społeczeństwa w ostatniej dekadzie XX wieku.* Warszawa: IERiGŻ, 2000.

Kowrygo, Barbara. *Studium wpływu gospodarki rynkowej na sferę żywności i żywienia w Polsce.* Warszawa: Wydawnictwo SGGW, 2000.

Krzysztofek, Kazimierz. "Poland: Cuisine, Culture and Variety on the Wisla River." In *Culinary Cultures of Europe: Identity, Diversity and Dialogue,* edited by Darra Goldstein and Kathrin Merkle, 333–346. Strasbourg: Council of Europe, 2005.

Kwasek, Mariola. *Wzorce konsumpcji żywności w Polsce.* Warszawa: IERiGŻ, 2012.

Smith, Jonathan, and Petr Jehlicka. "Stories around Food, Politics and Change in Poland and the Czech Republic." *Transactions of the Institute of British Geographers* 32(3) (2007): 395–410.

"Zachowania Żywieniowe Polaków." Centrum Badania Opinii Społeczne, August 2014. http://www.cbos.pl/SPISKOM.POL/2014/K_115_14.PDF.

Puerto Rico

Melissa Fuster

It's a mid-August late afternoon in San Juan, Puerto Rico. Victoria, a woman in her early 60s, returns home from the day's errands. She turns the air conditioner on, enters the kitchen, and gets ready to prepare dinner along with her husband Felipe. The menu for the evening: *Bistec empanado* (fried breaded steak), brown rice, *habichuelas* (beans), salad, and *sorullitos de maíz* (corn fritters). Except for the *sorullitos,* tonight's menu is no different than what they usually have any night. The menu was mostly planned by Victoria although influenced by my cravings. As her daughter recently arrived home for a visit from *allá afuera* (out there), referring to the United States, Melissa was longing for the type of home-cooked meals that only one's mother can make.

The meal itself is the result of remembered family recipes and traditional Puerto Rican staples with a healthy twist. The *bistec empanado* is prepared following the recipe of Victoria's mother. who died several years ago. The traditional combination of rice and beans (colloquially known as *casamiento,* or "marriage") is changed with the substitution of brown rice instead of the traditionally used white rice. Salad is always present at their table. Felipe will make the *sorullitos de maiz,* following his mother's recipe.

Cooking starts promptly at 4:00 p.m. Melissa sits attentively, ready to take her notes, at the granite breakfast counter that separates the kitchen from the dining area. The cooking space is big enough for only one person to move around freely, leaving Felipe out to wait while Victoria prepares her dishes first. The kitchen is modern and well equipped. The refrigerator is stainless steel with a water filtering system and ice maker. The stove is electric with induction technology, four hotplates, and an integrated oven. On top of the stove is a microwave with air extraction, which Victoria always turns on to avoid the accumulation of cooking smells inside the apartment. Despite their newly constructed apartment having windows, these usually remain shut to avoid the outside heat and onlookers from the street. The kitchen itself does not have a window but does have a door to access a small side patio full of potted plants and a small grill.

Victoria starts with the brown rice. She pours one cup of rice, along with 1¾ cups of water, sea salt, and olive oil, into her rice cooker. The salt and the oil are not measured but added instinctively *a ojo* (eyeballed). She reaches for a plastic spoon, mixes, and closes the rice cooker. While the rice cooks, Victoria opens the

Victoria and Felipe enjoying the evening meal: *empanadas de bistec* (breaded steak), rice and beans, salad and *sorullitos de maiz* (corn fritters). (Courtesy of Melissa Fuster)

refrigerator and takes out a plastic container with peeled garlic cloves bought at a wholesale store. "They are from China," she remarks, lamenting about not being able to find garlic from the United States or a closer location. Using the Quick-Chop, an "as seen on TV" gadget bought at the local pharmacy, she quickly chops a few garlic cloves with several loud and quick taps. The chopped garlic is saved in a repurposed glass jar with olive oil, which she will later use for the rice and the salad dressing.

Contrasting with the electric rice cooker used to prepare the rice are the traditional tools used to prepare the *bistec empanado*. Central in the process is the *pilón*, the traditional wood mortar and pestle found in most Puerto Rican kitchens (along with the *tostonera*, to make fried mashed plantains we call *tostones*). This particular *pilón* is made from cedar wood and has been part of Felipe's kitchen for several decades, passed on from his grandfather. Victoria uses the *pilón* to crush soda crackers for the *bistec* breading. As a recent modification from her mother's original recipe, she substituted the regular soda crackers with a whole wheat version, which they buy in bulk from a wholesale market. These soda crackers come in aluminum packets of four, and she pounded about one and a half packets. Once the crackers are ready, she takes out the steak from the refrigerator. The night's meat is a cube steak labeled "from the USA," bought at the nearest supermarket. She takes two eggs from the refrigerator also "from the USA" and bought from the same supermarket. She pounds the steak with the *pilón's* pestle. The meat is seasoned with *adobo* Goya light, a low-sodium version of the ever-present powder mix of dried

Supermarkets

The supermarket is a phenomenon only a century old and differs in certain key features from other food retail outlets. The size of the floor space and the range of goods carried is the most obvious, but so too is the fact that the vast majority of products are prepackaged, preweighed, and prepriced. Produce and the meat and deli sections are the exception. Most important, customers serve themselves, and wide aisles accommodate shopping carts that can hold a week's worth of food. Piggly Wiggly, A&P, King Kullen, Kroger, and Safeway were among the earliest supermarkets in the United States. The concept eventually spread to Europe and around the world, increasingly making small or specialized shops obsolete.

spices including garlic and onion powder, salt, and oregano, and fresh garlic. The *adobo* is sprinkled liberally *a ojo*, alternating between pounding and seasoning. Once the steaks are seasoned, or *adoba'os*, Victoria sets them aside and washes her hands in the sink. She then beats the eggs in a glass bowl, immerses the steaks in the egg bath, and coats them with the crushed crackers. She prepares about five pieces of meat, setting them aside for frying right before dinnertime.

After hand washing and clearing the space, Victoria continues on to prepare the salad. Like all of the ingredients of this meal, its components come from either the supermarket or a wholesale store—none are grown in Puerto Rico or measured. These include Roma tomatoes from Canada, iceberg lettuce (because it was on sale; they prefer Romaine), strawberries from the United States, jarred pimento-stuffed olives, carrots, sesame seeds, and an energy blend of nuts and dried fruits from the wholesale store. She chopped the lettuce and placed it in a medium-size crystal bowl. The carrot is peeled and washed, and then using the peeler, thin slices are added to the lettuce. The tomatoes are cut to quartered slices and added to the bowl along with chopped strawberries. The olives are added whole, followed by a sprinkle of sesame seeds and a small handful of the nut and dried fruit energy blend. She sets the bowl aside to prepare the dressing separately. Victoria prefers to make her "Arab" dressing passed on from a recipe of her older sister, who learned it from her Lebanese mother-in-law. The dressing is an unmeasured mixture of extra virgin olive oil, garlic, lime, sea salt, and balsamic vinegar, the latter a recent modification from her sister's recipe. These ingredients are mixed in a repurposed small glass jar that already contained a small quantity of previously mixed dressing from last night's dinner.

With the rice almost cooked, the steak ready for frying, and the salad served at the table, Victoria continues on to her last item on the menu: the *habichuelas*. While traditional bean recipes call for overnight-soaked dried beans boiled for at least two hours, in this urban home dried beans are seldom used. These are substituted by canned ones, as in an ever-increasing number of Puerto Rican households.

For this meal Victoria uses pink beans, also from the Goya brand. The canned beans and their liquid are added to the pan, followed by water, measured using the can (about one-third). With the stove set on low, she adds about one tablespoon of olive oil, a big spoon of store-bought *sofrito* (the traditional mixture of peppers, onion, garlic, *culantro* [long coriander], and sweet peppers), canned tomato paste (as "Canned tomato sauce has too much sodium," she explains), pieces of ham, and half of a cubed medium-size potato. She does not add salt, noting that the ham already adds that saltiness, but finishes with a pinch of *sazón,* a powdered dehydrated condiment with *culantro* and *achiote* (annatto), usually added to meals for color and a hint of flavor. The beans cook for about 15 minutes, or until the potato is tender. After this last step, Victoria cleans the area, leaving the counter free for Felipe, who has eagerly waited to get started with the *sorullitos.*

Felipe takes out the deep fryer stored under the kitchen sink, already prepped with clean canola oil. As the oil heats, he uses a metallic bowl to mix about two cups of very fine corn flour, along with a teaspoon of *adobo,* garlic powder, and sea salt. Next, he stirs in pregrated store-bought Parmesan cheese (about three tablespoons) and tastes the mix, making sure the seasoning is just right. Then, he heats one and a half cups of water in the microwave, adding slowly to the dry mix until a consistency similar to cookie dough is reached.

Using a plastic cutting board, Felipe cuts several two-inch pieces of white *queso de papa* (meaning "potato cheese" but better known as Gouda). "The important thing is to use sharp cheese," he says, while shaping the *sorullos.* These are best explained as having the shape of a very thick cigar, about two and a half inches long and half an inch wide. Then, Felipe inserts a piece of cheese and drops them in the already hot oil in the deep fryer for about 10 minutes. Now it is Victoria's turn to fry the breaded steak. She uses a medium-size frying pan with canola oil and cooks the steaks about 5 minutes on each side. The fried steaks are placed in a plate lined with paper towels to take the excess oil off before serving.

While the empanadas are cooking, Melissa sets the table with the usual everyday fabric place mats, paper napkins, and the silverware. The table setting is informal, with the place mats covering most of the round glass-top table. The silverware is set on the right, and glassware is placed on the left. Only the salad and the *sorullitos* are served at the table. The plates stay in the kitchen, along with the main meal components. This mode of serving is a recent modification in this household. Before, food used to be brought to the table family style, whereby each person would serve themselves and repeat if desired. In order to avoid overeating, Victoria and Felipe recently decided to leave the main dish components in the kitchen, bringing only the salad and any small side dish (in this case the *sorullitos*) to the center of the table.

Salad is a constant and important component for Victoria and Felipe. Victoria enjoys experimenting with different vegetable and nut combinations, resulting in creations that are a far cry from many other salads found in Puerto Rican households and restaurants: a bowl of iceberg lettuce served with a slice of tomato and a splash of Thousand Island dressing on top. Victoria explains that aside from liking the taste of the different combinations she comes up with, colorful salads such as the one prepared tonight are important, especially given her husband's diabetes and her own high blood pressure.

Felipe brings a pitcher full of iced water to the table and sits. Meanwhile, a few steps away in the kitchen, Victoria serves the main meal, starting with Felipe's plate. She serves the empanada, about a cup of rice with the beans on top, and leaves space on the side for the salad. Dinner is served on their everyday dinnerware, a set of circular leaf-shaped crystal plates. She brings his plate to the table and proceeds to serve herself, using equal portions but a smaller quantity. Finally, Melissa serves herself and joins them at the table.

Felipe and Victoria have usual spots on the round table. There is no clearly defined "head of the table" spot. Victoria sits in the spot closest to the kitchen, allowing easier access in case anything else is needed. We eat and talk, initially recounting the day's activities and plans for the next day. We instinctively start with the *sorullitos de maiz*. Felipe's recipe always results in a delectable treat, with the melted cheese pulling out of the dough with the very first bite. Next the main dish: the fried steak, rice, and beans joined together in a single mouthful. The crunchiness of the steak complements the soft texture of the rice and beans, bringing comfort and happiness to Melissa's stomach. The salad is placed on the side, enjoyed alongside the other dishes until the bowl is empty.

The food at the table inspires most of the dinner conversation. Felipe and Victoria recount stories about the recipes, the original cooks (their mothers), and their own upbringing. They both share memories of different dinner experiences growing up in Puerto Rico. He was raised having family dinners at the table at preset times and carries that tradition with him to this day. He eats meals and snacks at roughly the same time each day: breakfast at around 8:00 a.m., lunch at noon, dinner at 6:00 p.m., and a small snack right before bed. While this reflects his upbringing, he also cites his diabetes as a major motivation for his disciplined eating pattern. This contrasts with Victoria's upbringing, as she was raised in a home with divorced parents not really carrying the tradition of sitting down at the table for dinner. Her mother, much like herself, worked outside the home taking care of her own business, leaving little time for cooking. In her own life, Victoria has learned to maneuver her day to always have dinner ready on time, often achieved by preparing as much as possible beforehand, usually early in the morning.

Victoria's daily eating routine does not follow a scheduled pattern as that of Felipe. As her business depends on her client's schedules, she seldom eats breakfast or lunch at set times. Dinner, however, is another story. Felipe's 6:00 p.m. dinnertime is observed, as this is the only meal they routinely eat together on a daily basis. In this household, each meal has its own nuances. Felipe usually takes care of breakfast, and lunch is often eaten separately during the week as each of them engage in different daily errands. Food procurement is also a shared task, as they often visit the wholesale market together, but they also take turns making smaller trips to the nearest supermarket. It is only at dinnertime when more traditional gender roles are observed, as the wife is in charge of all or most of the cooking as well as serving and cleaning up afterward.

The sharing of traditional roles may be a sign of the changing gender roles in Puerto Rican society. At the same time, this is not a traditional couple. They have been married for about five years—the second marriage for both of them. They each had previous long-term marriages, both resulting in adult daughters. While not traditional, this couple's situation is common in today's Puerto Rican society. They share the experience of divorce and of having their grown children living abroad in the United States. This reality is shared by many Puerto Ricans, given the recent and increasing trends of out-migration from the island, a situation also discussed as part of our dinner conversation.

Our time eating and talking extends to almost an hour. The family finishes the salad and the *sorullitos,* not getting seconds of the main dish. Conversation lingers as Victoria takes the empty dishes and used silverware back to the kitchen, leaving them in the kitchen sink. Everyone leaves their plates clean, accounting for how good the meal was. Still, there is room for dessert. And tonight, as usual, there are different offerings, ranging from fruits (mostly oranges and apples) to a few sweet snacks. While Victoria is still in the kitchen, Felipe asks her to bring him the lemon crackers his daughter sent him via mail a few days ago. Like Melissa, she also lives *afuera.* Mirroring Felipe's preference for a daughter's gift, Victoria decides to have a piece of the *brazo gitano* that Melissa brought home from a trip to a western town in the island the day before. The *brazo gitano* (gypsy's arm), is a sponge cake, filled in this case with guava paste and cheese, rolled, and then topped with powdered sugar. Outside of Puerto Rico, this dessert is also known as Swiss roll, among other names. The family eats their desserts with water, while the conversation turns to the daughters who gifted these treats to them and their lives in the United States.

The cleanup after the meal is quick and easy. The table setting is practical, with the fabric place mats protecting the glass round table from scratches and other damage. The paper napkins are favored over cloth to avoid the necessity of washing them afterward. This table arrangement is not uncommon in this household, demonstrating perhaps a preference for a quick and convenient table setting for this daily meal. Right after the meal finishes, the table is cleaned, and the decorative table runner and ceramic vase are quickly restored to the center of the table.

It's almost 8:00 by the time the meal ends. Melissa returns to her spot at the kitchen counter, accompanying Victoria as she finishes washing the dishes and storing the leftover food (tomorrow's lunch or dinner) in the refrigerator. Despite having a dishwasher, they seldom use it, as it is mostly just the two of them at the dinner table every night. On occasion, dinner is followed by a movie at the nearby theater or sitting down on the couch to watch the evening news. Tonight Melissa joins them on the couch, completely satiated and happy while continuing to digest the splendid evening meal and sharing a few more moments after this family gathering.

Empanadas de Bistec (Breaded Steak) for Two

2 cubed steaks

1 garlic clove, minced

Adobo Goya (preferably with
  pepper)

½ package (about two) Export soda
  crackers (no salt added)

1 egg

Canola oil

1. Season the steaks with the minced garlic and *adobo* and set aside.
2. Crush the crackers until you have mostly powder and small pieces.
3. Add the crackers to a shallow plate and set aside.
4. In a second container, beat the egg and set aside.
5. Add enough canola oil to a frying pan to create a shallow pool (about ½ inch). Turn the heat on medium.
6. While the oil heats enough for frying, bread the steaks, one at a time. First, dip in the egg, enough to cover. Take the egged steak and cover with the crushed crackers. Ideally, the oil will be hot enough by now (you can test by adding a tiny drop of water). Add the steak to the pan. Quickly bread the second steak and add to the pan. Fry until crackers are browned and crunchy on each side.
7. Place the cooked steak on a plate with paper towels to drain the excess oil. Serve and enjoy! *Buen provecho.*

FURTHER READING

Díaz de Villegas, J. L. *Puerto Rico: Grand Cuisine of the Caribbean.* San Juan: University of Puerto Rico Press, 2004.

Ortiz Cuadra, C. M. *Eating Puerto Rico: A History of Food, Culture and Identity.* Chapel Hill: University of North Carolina Press, 2013.

Romania

Simona Dinu

Most of the food in Simona Dinu's Romanian household is cooked on a gas range, although an electric oven is also part of the weekly cooking. Simona and her family use nonstick pans and stainless steel pots, stainless steel and wooden spoons, and all sorts of silicon utensils. For this particular meal, she did the cooking using slow-cooking methods, which are common in her house, although they buy carefully chosen convenience food as well and cook quick recipes quite often. Slow-cooking methods are the same used by Simona's mother and grandmothers, and the quick recipes come mostly from specialized television programs. Slow cooking doesn't necessarily take a lot of time, as she relies a lot on good organization, such as boiling the whole animal or part of it and using it for several dishes, sometimes even freezing part of it. Most of the meat they eat comes from animals raised by their grandparents (poultry, pork) or from the butcher Simona knows well (beef). Her family buys fish from the supermarket and fruits and vegetables either fresh from the farmers' market or fresh or frozen from the supermarket. This is a normal Sunday early dinner served together with close relatives, including Simona's brother and his spouse.

For serving, Simona's family doesn't normally use a big table, nor do they use special cutlery but rather use the ones they would use any other day of the week.

With small children in Simona's life, serving meals is very casual. The food is brought to the table, and everybody helps himself or herself. They consider it nice to invite guests to help themselves first, and they usually expect this, but nobody gets offended if the guests or even one of the hosts just starts eating. If older people are at the dinner table, Simona and her family would make sure they are having a good time and perhaps would set a proper table with chairs, being a bit more formal with the details.

To serve, Simona uses ordinary stainless steel cutlery (purchased from IKEA), simple white plates, and big juice glasses, the same her family uses every day. They don't use special expensive cutlery for guests, although this is still done in some more conservative families. Fingers are sometimes used for meals that include polenta, such as the one today. Her family uses paper napkins and opts for nicely colored ones. A tablecloth was used for this meal, which is not necessarily the norm—place mats or nothing at all is just as common for this family, but again, in more conservative families, a tablecloth is used most of the time and, depending on the occasion, can be cotton or plastic. Simona used a tablecloth today, as she used the children's play table, the only table in the room.

A relaxed Sunday, family dinner. (Courtesy of Daniel Robert Dinu)

The manners at the table are simple; there is no special protocol. Guests are served first. Simona makes sure they are comfortable and have everything they need handy. They are encouraged to let Simona know if they need anything else at any time. Sometimes Simona insists a bit too much that the guests eat—this is the influence of her parents and grandparents, which sometimes leads to excess eating, and most people at the table are so full that they need to rest a bit before leaving. This was not the case today; everybody estimated how much they wanted to eat and filled their plates accordingly. The guests typically praise the food (sometimes even if they don't particularly like it) and often ask for the recipe. They appreciate the efforts that the host made to cook for them.

For this meal, everybody is dressed casually and comfortably. This time dinner lasted about an hour, and then for another hour or so the family and friends enjoyed the dessert and continued chatting. Most of the time there is coffee at the end of the dinner if it is served early enough. After 6:00 p.m. Simona typically doesn't have coffee, as she knows that this might affect the night's sleep. Some of guests stayed at the table, and some moved around while eating; in this family, there are no rules such as everyone sitting until the end of the meal. Everybody looked after the kids and offered them food and hugs.

Children can explore the food while playing or moving around. They learn how to use the cutlery, and Simona hopes they are careful not to throw food on the floor or on the table while eating, but they are encouraged to try all the foods. Sometimes they only eat a little, especially if the recipes are new for them, and sometimes Simona has to feed them after the guests leave or while they have the dessert. Cell phones are not banished from the table, but normally no one uses them unless

TV Dinners

TV dinners are an invention that grew indirectly out of wartime rations, which were sealed in metal trays and could be easily heated as a complete meal, not unlike early airline food. After World War II, it occurred to manufacturers such as Swanson that they could sell similar frozen foods on a tray with the novelty of being well suited to watching TV from a portable tray-table. For many critics these marked the symbolic breakdown of the family dinner, since conversation was curtailed by the TV, each diner eating alone or merely in proximity, with attention fixed on the screen. Aesthetically, it also marked the nadir of cooking, since it required nothing but heating or eventually by the 1980s microwaving. The descendants of these, although rarely marketed with TV in mind, still survive as complete frozen dinners.

someone calls or if someone at the table has to make an important call. When there are more people invited for dinner, some might get bored and check their Facebook account or call someone to check on how they are doing.

The TV is playing in the background most of the time Simona has guests—they watch news, music, or cartoons with the kids. When they have guests, they serve the meals in the living room or the kitchen. Tonight they chose the living room, as it is bigger and there is more natural light. Her home has simple minimalist furniture, colored walls with a few paintings, and carpets on part of the floor. At the windows there are roller blinds and no curtains. Part of the living room is empty at the moment, as her family is renovating.

After entering the house, the guests left their coats in the entrance dressing, took off their shoes, and washed their hands in the bathroom. Simona invited them in the living room. They sat on the couch, and they turned on the TV and started talking about various things, sharing their latest experiences at work, with kids, with parents, etc. Simona told them what they were going to eat and that she enjoyed cooking for them (to make them feel welcome).

Today the family served two dishes and a dessert. The first dish was a warm pasta, vegetable, and meat salad. The recipe was inspired by a famous British chef. For the salad Simona used medio orzo pasta, which she boiled in beef stock; frozen vegetables and grains (some purchased from the supermarket—peas and corn—and some grown in her parents' garden, minced and frozen by her mother for winter use); some dried tropical fruit (papaya and pineapple) purchased from a spice store; some local honey purchased from Simona's parents' small town; pancetta; and some traditional pork and beef sausage and various spices (pepper, paprika, a little five-spice mix). Vegetables and grains dominated the dish; meat was used rather sparingly for taste. They prefer it this way, as the second dish was heavier with lots of meat and fat.

The second dish is a very familiar, comforting one for Simona and her brother (the man in the photo). It is a dish they grew up with, and they like it so much that they tried and managed to make their spouses love it too. As described in the recipe, it contains duck meat and bones and onions. They enjoyed it with hot polenta or, as it is called in Romania, *mamaliga*.

Typically Simona's family does not usually have a nice dessert after dinner, even on weekends. For this meal, however, she did prepare a dessert, as she typically does when she has guests. The choice for the dessert tonight was a chocolate mousse cake, again inspired by a famous chef. Simona knew that all her guests like chocolate, so she chose to surprise them with a delicious cake they never ate before.

As usual, they sat at the table randomly and even moved around and changed seats. The guests didn't snack or drink before Simona and her husband set the table, so Simona made sure she had the food nice and warm, ready to be served, shortly after they arrived. Everybody at the table started with the first dish, which they enjoyed and praised.

The diners person put onto their plates the amount of food they estimated to eat, knowing they could add more if they wanted to. The small quantity of leftovers is normally thrown away. If there are more leftovers, Simona's family may choose to eat them later if they get hungry again after the guests have left, but they rarely eat leftovers the next day.

Simona estimated how much the group was going to eat and also thought about what recipes everyone would all enjoy and cooked accordingly. She cooked everything in advance, as she prefers to stay with the guests and with the kids at the table rather than spend time in the kitchen. The children tried all the dishes at the table; they were not forced to eat, but they noticed what adults were doing and asked for whatever they wanted.

The group drank water and good-quality orange juice purchased from the supermarket. The hosts put the juice bottle out and filled the guests' glasses shortly upon their arrival, and then everybody helped themselves if they wanted more. Nobody drank alcohol this time, as they were going to drive afterward, but if they were going to consume alcohol, beer would have been the first choice and wine (homemade or purchased from the supermarket) the second choice. Usually men drink alcohol, and women drink juice.

The hosts cleared the table and cleaned the dishes. Sometimes the guests try to help, but Simona politely refuses and invites them to relax and leave it to her. In her house, it is either Simona or her husband who clears the table, and usually her husband puts the dishes into the dishwasher while Simona watches the children and serves the guests with more juice, dessert, or whatever else they want. After the second dish today they chose to clean the table to prevent the children from making a mess. They continued to watch TV, chat, and enjoy the dessert, and then some of adults had coffee. While drinking coffee and eating the dessert, women may gather and talk more about kids, while men talk more about cars, politics, and sometimes sports.

Good-quality food is important for Simona and her family, and its accessibility is relatively easy. They normally have the freezer full of various kinds of meats (mostly poultry and pork) from animals grown by their grandparents during

A much enjoyed family recipe and an exotic dish. (Courtesy of Daniel Robert Dinu)

summer and autumn, which they eat until late winter. There are supermarkets only five minutes away by foot where they can buy anything else they need. There is a temperate continental climate, and her family eats differently according to the seasons (more meat and fat during the cold season and more fruits and vegetables during summer).

Simona and her family are Orthodox Christians. Religion doesn't impact the dining habits in her house, though; they don't fast or have any other rules imposed by the church, although a lot of people in Romania, especially in the countryside, do fast for long periods of time.

Duck with Onions

1 duck, whole
4 medium onions, thinly sliced
1 bay leaf

2 tablespoons of homemade tomato paste
Salt and pepper to taste

1. Cut the duck into pieces and put in a pot with cold water just enough to cover it, then put it on the stove on low to medium heat.
2. As soon as it starts boiling, remove the foam on the top.

3. Now add the bay leaf and ½ teaspoon of salt and leave it to boil for 2 to 2½ hours. If necessary, add a little water once in a while so it doesn't completely evaporate from the pot.
4. When the meat is easily removable from the bones and really tender, add the onions, salt, and pepper to taste and the tomato paste.
5. Let everything cook together on low heat for another 15 minutes. Taste and season again if necessary. Serve with polenta, boiled rice, or mashed potatoes.

FURTHER READING

Bacalbasa, Constantin. *Dictatura gastronomica: 1501 Feluri de Mancari din 1935.* Bucharest: Trei Lifestyle Publishing, 2009.

Klepper, Nicolae. *Taste of Romania.* New York: Hippocrene, 2011.

Roman, Radu Anton. *Bucate, vinuri si obiceiuri romanesti.* 1998; reprint, Bucharest: Paideia, 2001.

Sperber, Galia. *Art of Romanian Cooking.* London: Pelican, 2002.

Teodoreanu, Alexandru Osvald. *De re culinaria.* Bucharest: Agora, 1977.

Teodoreanu, Alexandru Osvald. *Gastronomice.* Bucharest: Agora, 1973.

Russia

Katrina Kollegaeva

This was a Sunday afternoon dinner that took place in the house of a Russian couple who are originally from Moscow and moved to London some 10 years ago. They were joined by their grown-up daughters, including one from the wife's previous marriage. As this was during the festive period, in the run-up to New Year's Eve and Christmas celebrations, the family invited the wife's cousin, who is also of Russian descent but grew up in Estonia before moving to Britain. Both the wife (KB) and the cousin (KK) really enjoy cooking and are known within their families and circles of friends for taking pleasure in having people around: entertaining and feeding them. Both women have turned to food as their source of comfort and inspiration, especially after they had migrated, wanting to both maintain the links with their culture and build an understanding in the new country.

Enjoying New Year's Eve celebrations with a "de-constructed" Napoleon cake—the cake of festivities during the Soviet era, and still today. (Courtesy of Natasha Nestman)

Drinking Customs

Customs governing the consumption of alcoholic beverages at the table vary widely across cultures. In some places, people will regularly help themselves to whatever they like. In most Asian cultures someone else must always pour for you, and it would be considered impolite not to drink thereafter. Toasting is even more complex, and in some cultures such as the Republic of Georgia, it is an integral part of the meal, with people making long speeches. Some societies consider it very uncouth to become drunk at the table, though interestingly in some settings and among some cultures it is rude not to drink heavily. Rarely is the family dinner such a setting, though it can be if guests are present or if it is a festive occasion.

The Menu

Oladushki pancakes served with salmon caviar and sour cream
Sauerkraut with dill
Zucchini "caviar"
Marinated mushrooms
Sweet-cured herring with beetroot
Salami
Borsch with Borodinsky bread
De-constructed Napoleon cake of phyllo pastry, whipped cream, pomegranate
    seeds, and almonds
Drinks: vodka Belochka and black tea with lemon

The dinner consisted of several *zakuski* (sing. *zakuska*), traditional Russian small appetizers that often start the meal with an accompaniment of vodka (or other alcoholic drinks). These are served family style, likely in a combination of cold and warm *zakuski,* before the main course (*goryacheye,* meaning "hot course") is served, which in this case was simply bowls of soup. The meal was finished with a cake, enjoyed by all from one large platter, alongside black tea.

Russians to this day tend to favor "proper" hot meals consisting of two to three dishes for their afternoon meal. This dinner being on a weekend during the Christmas period was a little more elaborate, mainly in the number of *zakuski* served and the fact that a cake was made from scratch. Alcohol is not a standard addition to the meals of this family (or many Russian families in general), but because of the time of the year and the wife's cousin joining the table, a bottle of vodka was opened.

PREPARATION

The dishes that needed cooking were all made by KB and KK, mainly that day. KK arrived in KB's house early in the morning, and they cooked until others arrived at around 2:00 p.m. The women have asked others to bring some ingredients along, sometimes specifying what they needed. Some dishes were therefore quickly assembled together by others on arrival, about half an hour before the family sat down to the meal.

ON *ZAKUSKI*

Many Russians would joke that *zakuski* are in fact the main event of a meal, the *goryacheye* (main course) being almost an afterthought. As in many other cultures (e.g., mezes and tapas), these small plates are there in Russia to excite one's tastes, to get one's juices going before the main meal.

Russian *zakuski* often combine strong flavors, such as fermented or soured vegetables, pickled mushrooms, and marinated fish alongside baked or fried goods, which go particularly well with strong spirits such as vodka.

OLADUSHKI PANCAKES SERVED WITH SALMON CAVIAR AND SOUR CREAM

Oladushki are little plump pancakes normally made with wheat flour, kefir (a traditional Russian dairy product of soured milk that is sometimes translated as "buttermilk" in English), and a bit of baking soda as rising agents. The trick is to fry the *oladushki* in hot oil quite quickly so that they fluff up and the edges get crisp.

Russian kids absolutely love them, especially for breakfast with jam and sour cream. But here KB wanted a slightly more glamorous *zakuska* and served them as a savory course with salmon eggs.

As it happens, KB had made a batch of *oladushki* several weeks prior to this dinner, and as there were lots of leftovers, she frozen them. So on this occasion she just took the *oladushki* out of a freezer the night before to defrost and just before serving briefly reheated them in a microwave.

Kefir that is used for this recipe is particularly dear to the hearts of Russians. Even though the ingredient has many counterparts in other cultures, such as *ayran* in Turkey, kefir's special sour flavor cannot be matched, many would say. Kefir's health properties are also legendary, and the drink is considered to be really good for all ages (kefir with sugar was a popular drink of children in Soviet times in particular).

Until recently kefir was difficult to source in London, but now it is stocked by many Russian shops. In the last year one start-up business even began making kefir in the southwest of England using local and organic milk and is now selling the product through such retailers as Whole Foods. KB bought this kefir for her *oladushki*, swearing by its special properties and "just as we remember it" flavor.

Caviar was also bought in a Russian shop that is often frequented by the hostess—this red salmon variety being a much more modestly priced type of caviar. Caviar is of course still very much associated with luxury and celebrations. During the Soviet era, caviar was among the top ingredients in deficit and could be obtained only on the black market, referred to as *blat*.

Sour cream topped the *oladushki* with caviar. The brands bought in East European shops are particularly favored because the cream has a much higher fat level, a thicker consistency, and a more intensely sour flavor—as opposed to the sour cream sold in British supermarkets.

SAUERKRAUT WITH DILL

Sauerkraut is another of those products that many Russians, including this family, seem to crave on a regular basis. Again, regarded of as highly *vitaminnaya* (i.e., full of vitamins), fermented cabbage used to be one of the few vegetables available to the Slavs in the centuries before refrigeration. To this day many women would make sauerkraut at home, fermenting it in buckets on small balconies in high-rise apartment buildings.

KB asked one of her daughters to buy some sauerkraut in a Russian shop she often goes to, making a point to look for the "right stuff"—the instruction somewhat difficult to convey that refers to the cabbage that is very crunchy, not too salty, and often sold in *na razves* (loose, in bulk) from wooden buckets or not particularly attractive plain plastic bags.

The daughter was then instructed to add some raw chopped onion to the sauerkraut and some flavorful Ukrainian unrefined sunflower oil that KB was given as a special gift by a friend.

MARINATED MUSHROOMS

The girl also bought some marinated mushrooms, on this occasion a jar of *opyata* (honey agaric). Wild mushrooms are a very significant part of Russian food and folkloric culture. Foraging for mushrooms is still an important pastime for many Russians and an activity that those living in London often remark as missing. KB and her husband tried at the beginning of their life in London to gather groups of family and friends to *po griby* (go on mushroom forage trips) but never found the experience satisfying. Either they had to travel quite a long distance outside of London to find suitable woods or were confused by local varieties of mushrooms to the extent that they didn't feel confident about picking any; they were also uncertain about the regulations for foraging more broadly in the United Kingdom.

The oldest daughter simply washed the marinated mushrooms under tap water (if not washed the mushrooms retain their gloopy consistency otherwise, something that some Russians really love but others—as well as most Westerners—cannot stomach) and added some chopped raw onions, parsley, and olive oil.

ZUCCHINI "CAVIAR"

This "caviar" used to be among the only products always available in the "good old days" of the Soviet Union, KK was explaining to everyone around the table excitedly. Sold in giant jars, it was nevertheless always popular. The caviar's color is dark red/brown because of the long stewing, the addition of tomatoes, and the all-important allspice (called "aromatic pepper" in Russia).

As with the *oladushki*, this dish had been made in advance and was frozen by KK. She defrosted it the night before and brought it along with her, then simply put it in a bowl, added a swirl of olive oil, and sprinkled some parsley.

They ate the caviar by putting some onto slices of Borodinsky rye bread. This bread has quite an iconic status back in Russia. Legend has it that the recipe was invented during the Napoleonic Wars by the widow of General Alexander Tuchkov, who perished in the Battle of Borodino. The widow set up a convent and created a bread recipe to serve at mourning events—hence, arguably, the bread's dark, solemn color and round coriander seeds representing gunshots.

Kefir (and dairy products more generally) and rye bread are the two items that migrants from the former Soviet Union often name as the top products they miss when moving to Britain. Even a decade ago, these ingredients were very difficult to source, but with the food revolution in London, especially around good-quality bread, many bakeries have started to sell breads made using North European recipes.

KB and KK normally buy Borodinsky in the Russian shops from a bakery that is run by a Lithuanian Belorussian family. Borodinsky is KB's favorite bread.

SWEET CURED HERRING WITH BEETROOT

Another dish based on the product bought in the Russian shop is sweet cured herring. This particular brand is made in Lithuania. The product is really quite different from Scandinavian rollmops sold widely in British supermarkets that have a more sour taste. The Russian way of curing herring and then marinating it in oil means that it is much milder and slightly sweeter, and the texture is softer. KK in particular swears by this brand and claims to crave it on a regular basis.

KK assembled a *zakuski*, which is roughly based on the iconic Soviet dish herring under a fur coat (layers of herring covered by potato, beetroot, and mayonnaise). She cut the herring into large chunks, similar in size to beetroot that she had cooked earlier and cut into chunks; added sliced gherkins and lots of chopped dill; and dressed with olive oil and lemon.

SLICED SALAMI

The Russian *zakuski* table (most certainly its more formal celebratory version) almost always has a spread of cold meats. Here the family just had a plate of the Italian salami bought in a local supermarket "for the men amongst us," KK and KB joked. It is a norm for Russian men to favor meat during meals, so it is widely considered and thought of as proper. And even though this dinner was prepared solely by women and eaten mainly by women who didn't need much meat by their admission, they wanted to offer at least one dish based on animal protein (which they happily ate themselves later).

Zakuski were served family style, that is, in bowls and platters with extra forks and spoons so that each person could help themselves. Each person around the table had their own plate, a fork and a knife, and a paper napkin. There was no particular rule in terms of the order of serving dishes. At some point at the beginning KB brought a plate of *oladushki* with caviar, so it was easier for her just to take it around each person, offering the *oladushki*. With other *zakuski* people just helped themselves whenever they felt like adding more.

The exception to this rule is the alcohol. The bottle of vodka was bought by the husband a few days earlier and kept in a freezer together with shot glasses. (The vodka is the Russian brand Belochka, a name that means "little squirrel" and has a humorous play on words in Russian: *beloya gorachka* means "delirium tremens," the psychotic state that alcoholism can lead to. The term *belochka* is a shortened version of *beloya gorachka*.) He then was responsible for topping off the women's glasses at regular intervals (he himself was not drinking, as he was to drive in the evening) and taking the bottle off the table as soon as it was empty (a bad sign otherwise in popular superstition).

BORSCH WITH BORODINSKY BREAD

Soup is an integral part of a Russian meal to this day. Many grow up hearing from their mothers and grandmothers about the importance of hot liquid soup on a daily basis.

Normally soups form part of the first course and are then followed by a *goryacheye* (meat with grains and vegetables), but here KB and KK decided to serve borsch, effectively, as the main course just because it was a particularly cold weather spell and they "needed some hot soup in them."

KK made the borsch after arriving at KB's house in the morning. There are as many ways of making a borsch as there are cooks, but most recipes these days contain beetroot (although some research argues that the prototype of borsch was being made before beetroot arrived in Russia with the root called *borschevik*), potatoes, and cabbage of some kind. KK uses the recipe of her Ukrainian mother—the borsch is vegetarian with the addition of kidney beans (out of a can) and a bit of fresh chili. The latter is not traditional, but KK came to like spicier food after her arrival in the United Kingdom.

The soup was made in a big saucepan and ladled out into bowls in the kitchen by KK. KK and KB's daughters then brought the bowls to the dining room, starting with the father, then mother, and then the rest. Each person helped themselves to a dollop of sour cream and chopped herbs. But KB actually prefers mayonnaise with her borsch and lots of cracked black pepper.

DECONSTRUCTED NAPOLEON CAKE OF PHYLLO PASTRY, WHIPPED CREAM, POMEGRANATE SEEDS, AND ALMONDS

The Napoleon cake is another classic Soviet dish that had originated in France, where it is known as *mille feuille* (cake of a thousand layers).

KB's husband had asked for something "nice and sweet" for the end of the dinner, and as the mood was a bit more festive, KB and her cousin decided to assemble a version of the Napoleon cake. They call it "deconstructed" because it takes only the main elements of the classic cake but is so much easier to make. Instead of making pastry from scratch, KB bought phyllo dough, which KK baked quickly in the oven and then broke into pieces randomly (in fact, KB's daughters were later helping with the fun process). KK whipped some double cream (instead of the original custard cream) and interspersed layers of pastry with cream, roasted flakes of almonds, and topped with pomegranate seeds.

The whole family ended up helping themselves to the cake from one large platter by using spoons and then fingers. KB brewed some very strong tea in a pot—*zavarka* in Russian—that she brought to the table and poured into cups, topping it off with hot water depending on everyone's preferences. Eating the cake with dark tea with slices of lemon finished the meal.

THE CLEANUP

The meal was finished at about 5:00 p.m., which is longer than the usual Russian *obed* (lunch) would take, but this being a Sunday afternoon and only a few days before Christmas, the family lingered over more tea and crumbs of the cake.

The clearing of the plates was done in two stages. KK and KB, with some help from KB's daughters, cleared all plates and cutlery after the savory courses, just leaving glasses behind. KB has a dishwasher, so the girls helped with clearing the remnants of the food while KB put the dishes in the dishwasher.

After the cake was eaten, KK and KB took charge of clearing the rest of the plates. One of the daughters cleaned and tidied the table. Another daughter (who had lived in the house until very recently, before going to university) made sure all the leftover food was put in Tupperware containers. KK and the older daughter took some of the remaining zucchini caviar and bread back home with them. The husband took care of clearing the glasses and bottles at the end.

Courgette (Zucchini) Caviar

About 1½ pounds of courgettes (which is about three marrows—the variety traditionally used by Russians—or an equivalent to smaller courgettes), peeled and deseeded

2 carrots (about 1 cup), peeled and cubed

2 onions (a little less than 1 cup), sliced

3 tablespoons of tomato paste

4 garlic cloves, crushed

½ cup of celery sticks, chopped

Juice of ½ lemon

½ teaspoon allspice

| 2 teaspoons sugar | 2 teaspoons salt |
| 1 teaspoon black pepper | 1 bunch of fresh parsley, chopped |

1. Fry marrow in batches in vegetable oil until golden brown. Add 6 tablespoons of water and continue cooking covered until soft.
2. Meanwhile, fry onions, carrots, celery, and garlic and cook for about 10 minutes. Add 5 tablespoons of water and continue cooking until carrots are softened.
3. Mix both vegetable mixtures together. Blend the mixture with a hand blender in the pan, leaving some bits coarse. Add the tomato paste, lemon, and all the spices. Mix well and cook for another 10 minutes.
4. Add chopped parsley and mix through.
5. Cool the caviar down and keep in the fridge until needed. The caviar improves in flavor if left to steep for a day or two.

FURTHER READING

Baldry, Karina. *Russia on a Plate*. London: Stonewash DD&AG, 2010.

Burlakoff, Nikolai. *The World of Russian Borsch*. n.p.: CreateSpace, 2013.

Caldwell, Melissa. *Dacha Idylls: Living Organically in Russia's Countryside*. Berkeley: University of California Press, 2010.

Caldwell, Melissa. *Food and Everyday Life in the Post-Socialist World*. Bloomington: Indiana University Press, 2009.

Goldstein, Darra. *A Taste of Russia: A Cookbook of Russian Hospitality*. Montpelier, VT: Edward and Dee, 2013.

Ledeneva, Alena. *Russia's Economy of Favours: Blat, Networking and Informal Exchange*. Cambridge, MA: Cambridge University Press, 1998.

Von Bremzen, Anya. *Mastering the Art of Soviet Cooking*. New York: Black Swan, 2014.

Von Bremzen, Anya. *Please to the Table: Book of Russian Cooking*. New York: Workman Publishing, 1990.

Senegal

Chelsie Yount-André

A puff of spicy steam escaped as Penda Sy lifted the heavy lid of her family's five-gallon cooking pot. Cabbage, parsnip, and eggplant bobbed in a bubbling tomato-red broth. She surveyed the pot carefully, conscious of the many guests who would taste her cuisine that day. Her sister Awa had invited Chelsie and her husband to their home in Dakar for a goodbye meal before their return to France. As their neighbors and friends caught wind of the special lunch, the number of guests quickly swelled. Penda prepared *ceebu jën* for the occasion, a rice and fish dish that requires a list of tasks that appear daunting in recipe form but were automatic for her, ingrained in muscle memory.

Ceebu jën is called Senegal's national dish due to its sheer popularity among Senegalese. Families prepare it multiple times a week, alternating between red and white varieties. The dish promises a taste of Senegal difficult to find abroad. While one might find everything for a good *ceeb* in places with large African populations

The Sy family gathering around a communal platter of Ceebujen, Senegal's national dish of rice and fish. (Courtesy of Chelsie Yount-André)

such as Paris, Senegalese living in the United States, Spain, and Italy often have trouble finding ingredients such as the pungent smoked fish (*gejj*) and mollusks (*yeet*) that create the dish's singular flavor.

Ceebu jën is often prepared to welcome or bid farewell to visitors. More than three-quarters of households in Dakar include at least one member living abroad. Feasts of *ceebu jën* welcome migrants home like royalty. But the kindness offered can weigh heavy on returnees, well aware of their hosts' hopes that they remember this hospitality later when they receive phone calls requesting help with the costs of a wedding or other celebration. The foreign revenues that migrants send home keep the country afloat, often financing building projects in the capital. Construction of family houses takes place in a piecemeal fashion, because remittances can only be invested in building when they are not urgently needed to subsidize hospital bills or purchase a ram for sacrifice at a baptism according to Islamic custom. Some homes seem near completion, and others linger like cement skeletons, eroding in Dakar's sandy wind.

In the Sy family, the adult daughters take turns preparing the midday meal, typically the largest of the day. Once every four days, each woman spends two to three hours sweating next to the propane stove, cooking a rice-based dish for her mother, siblings, children, nieces, and nephews. The work is physical but not complicated for the sisters, who began learning to cook at their mother's side when they were only seven years old.

Meal preparation began that day at 10:00 a.m. with a trip to the market. Maman Sy, as even her neighbors affectionately call her, stopped cooking years ago. Leaving the laborious task to her daughters was a right of status that her age afforded. But she still enjoys walking each morning to the market five minutes from their home. Saleswomen stack mangos, carrots, and bitter African eggplants (*jakatu*) in small pyramids, creating swatches of color on the unfinished wooden tables. Meat vendors swat flies away from cuts of beef and mutton, and fishmongers' knives flash silver as they remove the scales from that morning's catch. In the capital, located on a peninsula jutting into the Atlantic, fresh fish is a daily staple. It is the cheapest and most accessible protein in Dakar, the westernmost point on the African continent.

Maman returned dutifully to her favorite vendors, who shouted greetings to her across the narrow aisles. The crowded passages and uneven paths did not faze her, having shopped there for decades. She enjoyed the challenge of finding the best ingredients for the day's asking price, but incessant price hikes frustrated her. Most days, she supplements beef with tripe and serves bony sardinella fish in *ceebu jën*. Her grandchildren have never tasted the marlin that is said to be best in the dish, which is now so heavily exported that it is too expensive for most Dakarois.

For the special meal that day, Maman made sure to get plenty of large fish and a wide variety of vegetables to add color and flavor to the dish. She collected onion, garlic, carrots, cabbage, eggplant, parsnip, okra, cassava, white sweet potatoes, bitter eggplant, chili pepper, and tamarind in a large plastic bowl. She pulled a faded franc CFA bill from the small change purse hidden in the pleats of her skirt and then moved on to a dry ingredients stand at the edge of the market. She leaned over barrels of chalky baobab fruit and red lentils to ask the salesman for two small packets of black pepper and red pepper flakes. He pulled the prefilled plastic bags from bundles that hung from the ceiling above his stand like bunches of pointy grapes. She bought a one-quart bag of vegetable oil and four bouillon cubes, balanced the overflowing bowl on her hip, and was on her way.

Once her mother returned home, Penda began washing the vegetables and heating oil to fry the fish. She wanted the dish to taste perfectly, but the crowd gathering for lunch did not intimidate her. Meals in Senegal are routinely prepared for big groups. Penda did not even need to modify her recipe. Senegalese families tend to be quite large, and Penda had been taught to cook making sure that there would always be leftovers. Households often include members of the extended family, particularly in Dakar, where cousins from rural areas often arrive in need of a place to stay while studying or looking for a job in the capital. "You never want your guests to have to scrape the bottom of the dish wanting more," her mother had warned, adding, "You never know when someone hungry might drop by!" Indeed, Penda had often put together a small bowl of leftovers for visitors who stopped by even hours after lunch.

In August, Dakar's heat is unrelenting. The air was heavy in anticipation of the rainy season that should have already begun. Penda wore an old wrap skirt and T-shirt to cook, wrapping a scarf around her head so that her braids would not smell of frying fish. She pounded garlic, pepper, parsley, and Maggi cubes in a wooden mortar and pestle. She stuffed the mixture in slits in the sides of three large red mullet and four small sardinella fish.

Every step of making *ceebu jën* takes place in the same pot. Penda fried the fish whole. She then removed them to add the onions and tomato paste to the oil in which she would cook the vegetables. Bubbles burst to the surface, interrupting the deep red of the oil, water, and tomato mixture. Senegalese describe this bright red-orange color as pleasing to the eye and the taste buds, linked to memories of the salty infusion of fish, tomato, and oil that the sauce contains. Some brands of bouillon even add red coloring to their spice packets. But these additives are no match for a well-dosed *ceebu jën*. An artificial pinkish hue gives away cooks who rely heavily on food coloring.

Penda dipped a large metal spoon in the pot, tapped the edge on her hand, and then licked the sauce from her palm. Content with the mixture, she added the peeled vegetables whole. She then measured 2 pounds of rice from their 110-pound bag of *riz brisé*, short-grained white rice broken into bits the size of coarse bulgur. She rinsed the rice three times before placing it inside a shallow metal steamer on top of the pot where the vegetables simmered. Once the vegetables were tender, she set them aside and added the steamed rice to the pot to absorb the liquid flavored by all the ingredients.

Awa sat with Chelsie and her husband, far from the heat of the kitchen, chatting and refilling their glasses with sweet hibiscus juice. She admitted to being relieved that it was her sister's turn to cook, freeing her to welcome the guests. As the rice absorbed the last of the sauce, Awa shook the wrinkles from an indigo and royal blue cloth that she set directly on the cool tiles near the side door. Once construction on their house is completed, special meals will take place in their large though currently empty living room. The entryway where she placed the cloth had a cross-current that pulls ocean breezes into the warm house, making it a perfect spot for everyday meals. Following their mother's cue, Awa's young sons scurried to get the low rectangular wooden stools from the closet. They placed them in a circle along the edge of the cloth. It was nearly 3:00 p.m., and they had been hungrily waiting an hour since coming home from playing at the beach.

In the kitchen, Penda took out the family's largest enamel serving tray. The paint was chipped on the wide round tray from frequent use on holidays, when it was the only dish large enough to fit all their guests. Penda covered the cartoonish stencils of pineapple, cherries, and pears with spoonfuls of red rice. She then filled a smaller bowl with rice for unexpected guests and for her husband and brother who would wait to eat when they returned home at 6:00 p.m. She spread the rice out evenly with the back of a wide metal spoon. The aluminum cooking pot vibrated as she scraped the bottom, collecting the crunchy rice (xoon) into a small serving bowl. Penda carefully placed the whole cooked fish at the center of each platter, then arranged a halo of vegetables around them. Dividing the ingredients equitably between the platters of different sizes was tricky. She hesitated before pinching the bitter eggplant in two and then broke the still firm cassava into large chunks with her spoon.

Twenty minutes later, finally content with the appearance of the meal, Penda carried the heavy platter downstairs. A three-inch circle of red rice showed along the perimeter of the dish. The rest was covered with whole carrots, cabbage, parsnips, eggplant, and fish that had been bubbling in the pot for the past three hours.

No one needed to be called to meal, having discreetly surveyed Penda's progress for the past hour. After urging their guests to take a stool, family members filled in empty spots, and everyone else sat directly on the cloth on the ground. The women leaned in close to the platter with their legs folded to the side, and the men hung back a bit. Crouching with one knee pulled to their chests, they left the space closest to the dish to the women, who would divide and distribute the ingredients. Children squeezed in close to their relatives, and 10-year-old Mouna passed out soup spoons to each person. Maman and her daughters declined, preferring to eat with their hands so they could easily pinch off bits of fish and vegetables to pass out and share during the meal.

Most days, the Sy family divides the meal into multiple platters, making the food easier to reach. When Maman was growing up in a village outside of Dakar, their family had three bowls: one for children, another for women, and a third for the men of the family. It was her job as the youngest child to hold the platter in place with her index finger. It was popular belief that if the dish rotated during the meal, it could cause stomachaches. Today most dismiss this as superstition, yet the task still falls to youngest children, reminding them to keep their eyes lowered on the dish, a respectful posture when eating.

Amid the commotion of settling down to eat, a neighbor slipped in through the open side door. She looked embarrassed to have dropped in at mealtime, anticipating the invitations that inevitably followed. Children's and adults' voices overlapped, urging her to "Kaay lekk!" (Come eat!). She thanked them and insisted that she was not hungry. She spoke quickly, offering multiple justifications as if she sensed that resistance was futile. Finally she complied, sitting between the dish and the door so she could slip out after politely tasting a few bites.

Once everyone was situated, Maman quietly said, "Bismillah." Her children repeated the utterance, which means "in the name of Allah," prompting the group to eat. Each person took a spoonful of the rice directly in front of them. The dent they made in the rice anchored each person's portion, dividing the circular dish into many imaginary slices. They ate only the food closest to them with the right hand, conforming to Islamic meal etiquette. Conscious of the guests present, the children were on their best behavior and were particularly careful to stick to their portions. Although adults can take from any fish and vegetables in their triangular section, children are forbidden from reaching for ingredients in the middle of the platter. Little hands that venture into the center of the dish often get slapped, scolded for not waiting to be served.

Each person scooped up tender fish along with the red rice. Maman, Penda, and Awa squeezed lime juice over the platter, passed around the spicy chili pepper, and spooned tamarind sauce and crunchy rice into each person's portion. Sharp flavors mingled with unexpected ease, like the vivid colors of the wax-print fabrics ubiquitous in West Africa. Tart tamarind sauce cut through the rich, salty rice. Sour lime juice accentuated the flavor of the white fish.

Toddlers perched in the crook of a relative's elbow opened their mouths wide, waiting for spoonfuls of rice like little birds. Adults expertly worked fish bones out of their mouths, while children's furrowed brows betrayed their concentrated efforts. Mouna's small hand quivered as she pressed the side of her spoon into the firm cassava, trying to cut through the stubborn root. Penda's and Awa's movements seemed choreographed with their mother's. Their right hands slipped past one another, extended fingers diving into the center of the dish, emerging to pass out morsels of fish and carrots with a flick of the wrist. They intermittently fed themselves, effortlessly shaping the unctuous rice into bite-size morsels with their right hands.

Penda, Awa, and their mother carefully surveyed the dish to make sure their guests had enough to eat, that their brothers received the protein necessary for their afternoon labors, and that their children got some of their favorite sugary carrots and sweet potatoes. The premeal confusion gave way to silence as the group ate hungrily. Only Penda and Awa spoke, asking if anyone would like a bit more chili pepper or lime. "Be careful!" they warned as they passed out a piece of fish stuffed with spices cooked inside. They moved uneaten ingredients around the platter, offering the cabbage and okra to those who could not reach it. They flipped over the fish to access the flesh on the opposite side and removed heads and skeletons from the bowl. Penda pushed the rice in the center down toward the edge of the dish, filling in the circular hollows that each person had carved into the rice.

The movements of the meal were mesmerizing. It seemed that they had only been eating for moments when the first family members began to rise and move away from the dish. Their voices overlapped with Maman's in a tug-of-war of hospitality as she insisted that they keep eating and they assured her that they had eaten their fill. As each person got up from the meal, they drank ice-cold water from a glass that immediately collected beads of condensation from the humid air. Family members poured water for one another from the repurposed plastic soda bottle that had been thawing while they ate, its core still frozen. A shallow dish of soapy water and a hand towel sat nearby for those who had eaten using their hands.

The sisters lingered around the bowl long after the men and children had moved on. They sucked on the tart tamarind pods and giggled as they swapped stories. Maman cleared the platter, and Awa and Penda lifted the cloth, carefully shaking it out to collect discarded fish bones. They reappeared carrying bottles of soda and juice and a platter of sliced mangos for dessert.

Meanwhile, their brothers gathered around a small coal-burning stove to make a sweet green tea called *attaaya*. The men placed the metal teapot directly on the stove, letting the tea infuse for 20 minutes as they mixed in sugar, pouring the liquid from one espresso-sized glass to another to create a frothy, syrupy mixture. They served the concentrated tea topped by a sweet foam in three rounds, each one sweeter than the last. Men in Senegal often spend hours chatting over *attaaya*, periodically passing out small glasses of tea to anyone in the vicinity.

Senegalese proudly remind visitors that Senegal is known as "the country of *teranga*" (the Wolof term for "hospitality"). Although tourists in Dakar might assume this hospitality to be related to their foreign status, *teranga* is a fundamental virtue that shapes all social relations in Senegal. Hospitality is not reserved for guests from abroad but is also routinely extended to neighbors who stop by unannounced and relatives from the village in need of a place to stay. *Ceebu jën* is a key vehicle of hospitality through which Senegalese create and confirm social relations around a shared dish.

Ceebu Jën (for 10–12 People)

12 cups of short white rice

3 pounds of large fish (marlin, sea bass, or large sardines)

2 cups of vegetable oil

1 onion, finely chopped

2 cloves of garlic

1 small spicy pepper (preferably a scotch bonnet pepper)

⅓-ounce piece dried or smoked fish such as cod or herring

2 tomatoes

2.5 ounces (about ⅓ cup) tomato paste

16 cups (4 quarts) water

4 carrots

2 parsnips

1 large white sweet potato

1 large piece of cassava

½ small cabbage, cut in half

1 small eggplant, cut in half

1 bitter African eggplant

6 okra

2 bouillon cubes

Salt

Black pepper

½ cup tamarind

2 limes

For *rof*:

3 cloves of garlic

Small bunch of parsley

½ bouillon cube

1 pinch of salt

½ teaspoon black pepper

¼ teaspoon of dried pepper flakes

For *nokos*:

6 cloves of garlic

2 onions, finely chopped

¼ teaspoon dried pepper flakes

1 bouillon cube

½ green bell pepper

1. Clean and salt the fish, leaving them whole (including heads).
2. Prepare the *rof* using a mortar and pestle or food processor. Grind garlic, parsley, pepper, bouillon, salt, pepper, and the red pepper flakes until it forms a paste. Cut 2 or 3 small slits in each fish and stuff them with the *rof* mixture.
3. Heat oil over medium heat in a large cooking pot for 10 minutes.
4. If using sardines or other smaller fish, flash fry the fish in the oil, cooking each side for 1–2 minutes. Remove and set aside. If using large pieces of fish such as marlin, skip this step.
5. When oil is hot, add 1 finely chopped onion, 2 cloves of garlic, half of the scotch bonnet pepper, dried fish, 2 tomatoes, and tomato paste. Stirring frequently, cook on medium heat until the sauce thickens, roughly for 20 minutes.
6. Add 1 gallon of water and 1 tablespoon salt and reduce heat to low.
7. Make *nokos* in mortar and pestle or food processor. Grind 6 cloves of garlic, 2 onions finely chopped, ¼ teaspoon dried pepper flakes, 1 bouillon cube, and the green bell pepper.
8. Add fish and *nokos* mixture to the pot. Let simmer on medium heat. Add 1 or 2 bouillon cubes to taste.
9. Peel the carrots, parsnips, sweet potato, and cassava. Gradually add the vegetables to the broth, adding softer vegetables such as eggplant, cabbage, and okra last. Let simmer on medium heat for 30 minutes or more. Gradually lower heat if the liquid comes to a rolling boil. Remove vegetables as they become tender and set aside. Remove fish and set aside when it is no longer translucent and

flakes off easily. Place vegetables and fish in one bowl to collect sauce that drips from them.

10. While vegetables are cooking, rinse the rice and place it in a steamer on top of the pot so that the vapor from the pot steams the rice.

11. Once vegetables and fish are cooked through and have been removed from the pot, add the steamed rice to the broth left in the pot and cover. Cook on medium heat for 5 minutes, then cook for 30–45 over low heat until the rice has completely absorbed the water, stirring after 20 minutes.

12. Add tamarind to the bowl containing the vegetables and fish to marinate in the sauce that drips from them.

13. Spread a thick layer of rice evenly on a large platter. Arrange the vegetables and fish in the middle on top of the rice.

14. Garnish with lime. Spoon the tamarind and sauce mixture over rice.

FURTHER READING

Bâ, Miriama. *So Long a Letter.* London: Heinemann, 1981.

Fall, Aminata Sow. *Un grain de vie et d'espérance, réflexion sur l'art de manger et la nourriture au Sénégal.* Paris: Françoise Truffaut Editions, 2002.

N'Dour, Youssou. *Senegal: La cuisine de ma mère.* Paris: Éditions de La Martinière, 2014.

Thiam, Pierre. *Yolele! Recipes from the Heart of Senegal.* New York: Lake Isle Press, 2008.

Slovenia

Ana Tominc

Thursday afternoon may not be the best day to visit a busy family during their meal together, but it is one of those weekdays when the weekend leftovers have been eaten and fast-cooked or convenience foods may appear on the menu. While trying to convince her four-year-old daughter Zala that the chocolates Ana just brought her are to be eaten only after she had finished all the soup, rice, chicken, and salad, Zala's mother Katja tells Ana that she had returned from work early, hoping to dine at 4:30 p.m. She had less than half an hour, but at that point she had already started cooking rice, which takes about half an hour, and had also cut the chicken breasts into small pieces.

Katja has come to the Italian/Slovene bilingual Adriatic coastal town of Koper/Capodistria from an inland town near the Slovene-Croatian border, where her

A young Slovenian family eating their evening meal. (Courtesy of Ana Tominc)

parents settled in the late 1970s as migrants from other former Yugoslav republics. The home food of her youth was a mixture of Ottoman cooking that her mother brought with her from the Serbian region of Vojvodina, such as oven-baked *pasulj* (beans in tomato sauce with pork), *sarma* (parcels of meat and rice wrapped in cabbage) and stuffed peppers, and the dishes she learned from women's magazines and her Slovene colleagues at work. Katja, the older of the two daughters, started cooking when she was 13 years old, mainly as help to her mother who, upon her arrival home, could simply finish the food Katja had started to prepare. Miha, her partner, on the other hand, was born in Koper to parents who also migrated to this coastal town some 30 years ago from a town in northeastern Slovenia in search for work. He can cook, though contrary to Katja, he learned on his own because in his home, he only cooked when they had "barbeque day" and even then only when his father wasn't at home.

Today, Katja no longer cooks the dishes that identified her family migrant home and instead embraces new recipes that she sees prepared on television or creates new variations from those learned from her mother. Similarly, Miha prepares only certain recipes that his mother would have cooked, such as polenta, buckwheat, or corn *žganci*, which are seen as "proper Slovene home cooking." He mainly prepares dishes such as pasta carbonara, roasted meat with potatoes, and pancakes that his mother would have regularly served too. According to him, his and Katja's cooking is much simpler than his mother's, who would have cooked dishes that require more time-consuming techniques, such as breading of steaks and marinating, while also adding that their cooking is "healthier" because they no longer use cream in sauces or cook with a lot of fat. Occasionally he still lunches at his parents', though mostly when Katja is at work and he doesn't want to waste time cooking for only him and their daughter. This also gives his parents an opportunity to see Zala more often, while she gets to taste "more complicated" dishes.

Katja and Miha are an example of how young people increasingly live in postsocialist Slovenia: with little job security and relatively unstable income, in rented accommodation or in a redesigned part of the house their parents built in the 1960s and 1970s when Yugoslav socialism still offered many opportunities for an ordinary worker. Like many of their generation, they are not formally married but live in a relationship recognized by the state as equal to marriage in rights. They represent the generation that lived their teenage years through the 1990s Balkan Wars after the breakup of Yugoslavia in 1991 and their 20s in the time when Slovenia joined the European Union (2004) and, after the start of the financial crisis in 2007, decided to start a family.

Their kitchen is a small U-shaped corner of a rented apartment, with stunning views of Koper Bay, that extends on one side toward a small rectangle dining table, which at the time of my arrival hosts a pile of papers and bills, toys, and a laptop playing Slovene and other international popular music. At the table, there are two chairs and a special height-adjusted child's seat. In the corner, there is a computer desk with a comfortable wheeled chair that is only used for dining if guests arrive.

While Katja cooks, their daughter plays in the attached living room with Buksi, their small mixed-breed dog. They run toward the door when Miha arrives home from what was a work shift longer than usual. "So do you cook every day?" Ana asks Katja, knowing that she too works in shifts. Katja, searching for noodles in one of the cupboards to finish the clear beef soup that she cooked on Sunday in expectation of a busy week, says that it all depends on who comes home first. Katja often prepares soup in advance and freezes it, because, as she says, it is the only way to have home-prepared soup during the week; she then defrosts it in the microwave and cooks in noodles that she buys in the supermarket. The clear beef soup—*juha*, or *župa* as it is called more commonly in the Slovene dialects (from German *die Suppe*, meaning "soup")—is a lunch starter that almost every person in Slovenia would recognize as an essential part of a Slovene lunch. Its preparation is certainly time consuming, as it requires cooking beef (or chicken) meat and bones in a large pot of water with vegetables and herbs for three to four hours. This yellow, watery soup with fatty rings floating on the surface is then strained into a smaller pot, and very thin noodles or tiny pasta are simmered in it until tender. On the day when it's cooked, soup beef is eaten as part of the main course together with roasted potatoes and vegetables, such as spinach, and, if there is anything left, in cold salad with onions.

In Slovenia, lunch (*kosilo*) is the heaviest and main meal of the day. The word refers to the meal that is eaten in the middle of the day and normally almost always traditionally contains soup and the main dish. Dinner (*večerja*, deriving from *večer*, meaning "evening") is always eaten in the evening and has no specified permanent structure. But as the working days are becoming longer and lunch is eaten later and later in the afternoon, the main meal of the day is becoming more of an evening meal (therefore dinner), which is often still structured as lunch, with soup as a starter and (normally) a meat dish to follow. This is increasingly changing, as week-day meals tend to only be composed of one course due to lack of time.

Katja's clothes reflect the informality of a family home. Wearing an old green T-shirt with pink tracksuit bottoms, she doesn't have to worry about "getting dirty" and hence wear an apron. These are the clothes in which she spends all her home time, which includes eating, cleaning, cooking, and watching TV. Likewise, her partner, who upon return first changes his work clothes to something more comfortable, believes that it wouldn't be practical to eat in work clothes for fear of food stains.

As the soup is slowly boiling and the noodles are being cooked in it, Katja also prepares chicken and rice, following a recipe she appropriated herself. She learned a simple chicken recipe with salt and pepper from her mother whereby chicken is simply fried in oil, adding the seasoning in the end. Now, she also adds rosemary because she has it growing on the balcony and coriander—a spice that is not regularly used in Slovenia—because she once accidentally bought it in the supermarket and now likes it. Instead of olive oil, which she would have normally used, she recently switched to coconut oil. She bought it in a local supermarket because she had read that it is healthier than olive oil. Two months ago she decided to lose some weight, so the whole family is now subjected to a more "healthy" diet, which also includes rice. She is preparing a special mixture of "three rice"—black, brown, and red rice—sold premixed by the local Zlato polje (Golden Field) as a healthier alternative to the usual white rice.

The ingredients for this meal were bought in the supermarket, though Katja tells Ana that often her in-laws bring them fruits and vegetables that grow in the garden surrounding their house and even meat—sausages and salamis—that they source from a farmer they know in the vicinity of Koper. In Slovenia, such (family) networks are an important safety net for young couples and families with modest incomes, as they provide not only free care (for example, for children) but also homegrown and home-produced food.

After half an hour when the soup with noodles, the rice, and the chicken are ready, Katja summons Zala, who is playing with the dog in the living room and occasionally stopping by in the kitchen to see whether the food will soon be done. She is now told to help set the table (but only after she washes her hands!) as the mother brings plates and cutlery from the cupboard and positions three sets of plates on the table: a deep plate for soup, which is laid on top of a flat plate for the main course. It is Zala's job to set the napkins, spoons, and forks, which she places without any rule, one to the right and one to the left of the plate, though both forks and spoons are laid to the same side of the plate. No tablecloth or mats are used except for a mat that is will be used to place a hot soup pot on and is laid in the middle of the table, accompanied with the ladle. No glasses are set, though the usual drink is either water or wine and beer.

As Katja brings the pot of soup—the same pot in which the soup was being cooked—to the table, she calls Miha, as the dinner is ready. The dog sits near or under the table, ready to catch any food that comes his way, but is told to go to the living room, an order he doesn't readily obey. Though he normally eats special dog food from the tin and "is not really hungry at any time," he loves begging for food under the table and won't move away until the table is cleared and there is no more hope for a taste of his family's meal. Any leftovers are eaten the next day from a lunch box.

Katja explains that she never brings all the dishes together to the table because the table is simply too small. And hence, there are days when she portions the meal onto plates in the kitchen just to avoid having to bring everything to the table. Today, however, she starts dividing the food onto plates before Zala and Miha are even seated; Katja only portions the food for the child, while Miha takes it for himself. This order, whereby whoever cooks also brings food to the table and serves it, is certainly not how it used to be in the primary families of both Miha and Katja. Miha, for example, tells Ana that it was his mother who used to cook and serve all the food unless it was "barbeque day," which was the duty of his father. To make it easier, his mother used to be seated closest to the kitchen so she could go to the kitchen easily. Unlike now, the seating order was fixed, with him always sitting opposite his brother and mother opposite their father.

Eating the soup brings to the forefront certain personal preferences. Like many children, Zala likes to eat her soup with *kroglice*, little crispy balls of fried dough that

Seating Arrangements

Formal dinners such as weddings and banquets are perhaps the last remaining place where we expect to be told where to sit, but it was once common practice to have name cards and seating arrangements decided by the host beforehand. The logic was that certain people would strike up a conversation or should be kept apart for some reason. In some cases, men and women were intentionally seated next to each other but not husbands and wives. On the other hand, even within families people will have their favorite spot where they always sit, and in many households it become a rule that people keep their accustomed places at the table.

soften once soaked in the soup. She adds them to her plate from a small bowl using her own spoon, which had been placed on the table by one of the parents, and is told to stop when her plate seems to contain almost nothing but balls. Miha, on the other hand, dislikes a soup that is too thick and complains that there are "too many noodles." As a consequence, she is the only one not to finish the soup. As they eat, they talk of the events of the day and other people they spent time with, such as coworkers in the job or brother's new scooter. Importantly, they also teach Zala how to behave at the table by either asking her questions they deem appropriate for such an occasion (Do you like the soup? What did you do in the kindergarten?) or correcting her behavior (Eat the soup with spoon, not hands. Put your leg down.).

As they finish, the soup dishes are cleared. Miha stacks them, and Katja takes them to the sink. Despite a relative flexibility of the rules and roles, certain rules still seem to apply. The soup is eaten from a soup plate, which is followed by a flat plate. Ana asks if they ever use the same plate for the soup and the main meal, to which Katja answers with a large amount of self-irony, "We never eat from the same plate—we are *fini* [posh] people." A large smile and an ironic look when she refers to their own "poshness" suggests that she is perfectly aware of the possible interpretation of this habit as a middlebrow attempt to appear sophisticated but does not seem to care: this is how they ate when she was young, and she is determined to teach her daughter the same manners.

The second course—chicken, rice, and salad—is brought to the table by both Katja and Miha while Zala played with her fork at the table. No specific tools are used for serving the dishes or indeed cooking them. A simple stainless steel spoon bought in a supermarket as part of a larger set is used for mixing the soup while cooking, and a similar fork is used for chicken. The mother places rice on Zala's plate and asks Miha, who is just searching for a spoon with which to serve the chicken, if he would portion it for her. And as with soup, there seems to be no general rule as to whose job this is: whoever sits closer to the pot gets to serve the food. For chicken, the task seems to fall to the father, who starts serving Zala and ends with himself. In the meantime, Katja announces that the rice is a bit overcooked but at the same time seeks for approval from her partner as to whether he likes it or not. Salad, made of seasonal vegetables such as tomato, cucumber, onion, and basil and dressed with vine vinegar, salt and pepper, is being placed at the center of the table. Despite Katja's insistence on changing plates for the main meal, the expectation for the salad is that it will be eaten from this common bowl, which includes Zala even though she can only just about stretch her hand to the center of the table. In Slovenia, portioning the salad to separate plates is often perceived as unnecessary work in terms of later dishwashing but also, more important, as a distancing from the comforting domesticity of everyday food sharing: allowing a guest to share the salad from the common bowl may suggest that the guest has been accepted into the family not merely as a newcomer but as part of the family.

In the background, pop music from the laptop plays almost unheard as the family eats, drinks, and negotiates over what to eat and how much—mostly with Zala, who finished eating all the chicken but none of the rice and refuses to continue. Both parents try to give convincing arguments as to why rice should also be eaten, from the idea that it is delicious to reminders of the fact that she does normally like it and examples of how "Mum and Dad also eat the rice" and that she would be hungry had she only eaten chicken. What finally wins is her mother's promise that if she only eats one forkful of rice she would be allowed to have chocolate at the end of the meal, which is a message consistent with her promise at the time she received the chocolate. Katja fills the fork with rice and passes it to the daughter's hand. Even though Zala makes faces, she finally manages to finish. She finally helps herself using fingers as she picks separate rice grains that have fallen from her fork to the plate in front of her.

There is an expectation that everyone should sit at the table until the end of the meal. In order to convey this message, Miha, who finishes his meal first, moves from his corner wooden chair to a more comfortable computer seat while still sitting close to the table, patiently waiting for Zala to finish her rice. When she is done, she immediately jumps off her chair and sets out to find her chocolate box while her parents both clear the table. She offers chocolates to everyone, even the dog, and is then told off for this, because "a dog should not eat sweets, and I have told you this one million times." Except for this no other dessert follows the main course, and the meal closes with a playful and rather funny argument as to who will clean the dishes since the dishwasher is broken. They are finally left in the sink, and Ana is offered a coffee: this is their way of finishing the lunch and of starting a relaxing evening with the family.

Clear Beef Soup with Noodles

1 pound of beef "for soup"	1 carrot
1 onion	Parsley
1 tomato	Salt and pepper

1. In a large pot with a capacity of 4 quarts, add all the ingredients and cover with 3–4 quarts of water.
2. Bring to boil and then cook slowly for about 3–4 hours.
3. Strain and add small pasta/noodles.

Herby Chicken and Tomato Rice

Chicken breasts cut in pieces	Rosemary
Salt and pepper	Coconut oil
Powdered garlic	Rice
Coriander	Tomato pulp

1. Fry chicken pieces in oil. Add salt, pepper, garlic, coriander, and rosemary and cook until done.
2. Add some water to create sauce.
3. In a separate pot, cook rice and tomato pulp in water until tender and all the water has evaporated.

Recipe reprinted with permission.

FURTHER READING

Bogataj, Janez. *Recipes from a Slovenian Kitchen: Explore the Authentic Taste of an Undiscovered Cuisine in over 60 Traditional Dishes.* London: Lorenz Books, 2014.

Godina Golija, Maja. "From Gibanica to Pizza: Changes in Slovene Diet in the Twentieth Century." *Glasnik Etnografskog Instituta: Bulletin of the Ethnographical Institute* 58(2) (2010): 117–130.

South Africa, Suburban

Yael Joffe

Dolly (age 62) and Robert (age 58) Maisurnam Madlala live in a two-bedroom house in KwaNdengezi, KwaZulu-Natal, South Africa. Robert is a house painter, and Dolly works as a domestic worker in Durban. KwaNdengezi, a semiurban area about 30 minutes outside the city of Durban, is populated by lower-income black South Africans, mostly Zulus. It has minimal infrastructure, schools, retail, and transport. KwaNdengezi is an example of a community experiencing both the nutrition and urban transitions that have resulted from the movement of black rural populations seeking employment in the city, often exchanging one level of poverty and food insecurity for another.

These communities are structured around a large number

Dolly Madlala together with her neighbor Mavis and Mavis's daughter Zodwa have prepared Sunday lunch for Dolly's friends and neighbors who stop by to eat after church. Dolly takes charge dishing up a generous plate of many dishes for her guests, who sit quietly with unspoken appreciation enjoying the generous meal. (Courtesy of Ciske Janse van Rensburg)

and variety of churches that play a strong role in the moral, material, and nutritional sustenance of the community. However, in contrast there is also a high incidence of substance abuse, violence against women and children, and crime. Sunday is for most the only day of rest and revolves around church services; as a result, the biggest meal of the week is lunch after church on Sunday. Dolly cooks for her and Robert but makes enough for any neighbor who may stop by. On this Sunday because Yael's family was joining Dolly and Robert for lunch, Dolly invited her church friends for lunch and asked her neighbor and her daughter to help come and cook. Mavis (age 57), also a domestic worker, and her daughter Zodwa (age 25) live next door to Dolly and helped with the cooking, each showcasing her own specialty. Dolly, Mavis, and Zodwa each had dishes they were responsible for and were proud of. They took the lead on those dishes, with the other two helping out in the preparation tasks.

Cooking started at 9:00 a.m. Yael was relegated to drinking tea out of Dolly's precious tea set, reserved for special guests and unpacked for the occasion. The tea was served with fresh milk rather than the long-life milk usually used. Yael was refused participation in the cooking and was to sit and drink tea as their guest. They spent the time talking and laughing. It was a time for the women to share their stories with Yael. They talked about their favorite foods and how no one ate pork but everyone loved lamb, which they couldn't afford. Dolly cooked turkey and lamb on Christmas Day, which was an extravagance she was proud of. They spoke about the church and how strict they were. Zodwa is young and was dressed in modern clothes with false eyelashes and painted fingernails, all of which were frowned upon in the church (and by her mother). They spoke about the kitchen as the domain of the women. Robert was described as one of the better and more helpful husbands, who on occasion will cook if Dolly is not around. He boils everything he cooks and thinks it an excellent cooking method. With the nutrition transition and accompanying aspiration to eat and live like the whites, boiling is often regarded as backward, whereas frying food is modern and more delicious. Men in the community do not shop, cook, or make any food decisions. The community remains traditionally patriarchal; men do not do "women's work." Women are responsible for the home; for sourcing, preparing, and serving the food; and for all child rearing. In South Africa, black women carry the greatest emotional, physical, and financial burden. Women will care for the children and the home and work full-time, but the men decide how and where to spend the money. There is also an alarming prevalence of violence against women and children in poor South African communities, fueled by the frustration of poverty, substance abuse, and traditional gender roles.

South Africa has a quadruple burden of disease, characterized by undernutrition and underdevelopment, found predominantly in children; emerging chronic diseases associated with increasing overweight and obesity; HIV/AIDs; and injuries (often crime related). The paradox of obesity in black African populations is the prevalence of overweight and obesity with malnutrition as a result of poor food choices that favor processed, refined, low-nutrient carbohydrates; sweetened foods and beverages; and fried foods. Neither Dolly, Mavis, nor Zodwa had any knowledge or interest in the health properties or nutritional content of foods. In conversation around the nutritional value of different foods over others, they were unable to discern a more healthy from a less healthy food. Their food choices were based entirely on affordability and access.

Neither family grew any vegetables, as they did not have time owing to their long commutes to the houses they cleaned—this despite Mavis expressing a love of gardening and her wish to be able to grow her own produce. The majority of South Africa's small-scale farmers are women. Black African women have a tradition of growing vegetables and maize (*mielies*) to provide basic sustenance for their families. Maize is eaten in numerous ways and forms the basis of all meals. With the move to semiurban overcrowded areas, there is little arable land, little time to farm, and an aspiration for cheap, processed, white flour, maize meal, rice, and sugar.

While poor food choices may partly explain the rising incidence of obesity in these communities, body size perception is still driven by tradition, culture, and to some degree superstition. Dolly, who would be defined as morbidly obese, expressed great satisfaction with her body weight and had no wish to look any different; she expressed pride in her corpulence. Mavis, who suffered from stomach ulcers and battled to eat, was very slim and wished she could be bigger. Zodwa was voluptuous and also expressed great satisfaction with her body weight. In black African populations, being bigger means being healthy, robust, and able to afford good food. Being obese is seen as a status of wealth. Being thin is to be sick, often thought to be due to HIV or AIDS. This poses a significant challenge to South African health authorities looking for ways to impact the growing prevalence of obesity.

In addition to a disinterest in and an ignorance of healthy foods, they also had no knowledge of or interest in organic food, pesticides, hormones, antibiotics, sustainable agriculture, or the environment. There was no understanding of ethical consumerism or consumption, and when these issues were raised they had no empathy for why these issues should be important to them.

A beef curry and a chicken curry were the main offers of the lunch. These were very mildly spiced and may be described more as a stew than a curry. Beef is seldom cooked because of the cost and is reserved for special occasions and celebrations. Rather than constituting the main part of the plate, chicken and meat are used as a flavoring for meals, and each person is dished only a few tablespoons of each. Often meat bones will be bought and used to flavor food such as beans or samp (dried corn kernels that have been stamped and chopped until broken but not as fine as *mielie* meal or *mielie* rice).

The beef was braised with onion, mild curry spices, fresh curry leaves, fresh garlic, and ginger. Powdered stock cubes, frozen mixed vegetables, and water were then added to the meat, and it was slow-cooked for an hour at least. The chicken curry was cooked in a similar way. The chicken was in portions and frozen, and Mavis washed the chicken and removed the random feathers and gristle. The starch foods make up the majority of the meal. This is true of all meals. In more food-insecure households, many meals will include only cooked *mielie* meal, such as *phutu* and *maas* (sour milk). *Mielie* meal is a relatively coarse flour (much coarser than cornflour or cornmeal) made from maize (called *mielies* or *mealies*). It is a staple food in South Africa and many other parts of sub-Saharan Africa, traditionally made into *uphuthu*, sour-milk porridge, *pap,* and also *umqombothi* (a type of beer). For this lunch there were three different starch foods served. *Phutu* is a cooked fine maize meal that is the staple carbohydrate dish for the South African black population, and it is made by mixing the maize meal with water and a little salt and stirring it until it forms a thick mix that can be molded by hand. *Phutu* is made to varying consistencies depending on what it is being served with and at which meal. White rice was also served. One of Mavis's specialties is steamed bread. Steamed bread is made from a yeast dough that has risen in a plastic tub covered with a large plastic bag. The dough is divided in two, and each portion is placed in a plastic carrier bag, which is knotted. A very large pot is placed on the stove with about two inches of water, and an upside-down plate is placed in the water. The plastic bags with the dough are placed onto the plate, a lid is placed over the pot that is not opened, and the bread is steamed in this way for 20 minutes. The bread is then taken out of the plastic bags, cut into slices, and plated.

A number of accompanying salads were also made. *Chakalaka* is made from a variety of grated and chopped vegetables, cooked beans, and a small amount of curry spice and chilli. It is a warm salad that is eaten like a relish alongside the meat and chicken dish or served with pap. Store-bought mayonnaise was used extensively. One salad included sliced processed sausages, a tin of baked beans, and mayonnaise. A coleslaw salad of finely cut green cabbage, grated carrot, and mayonnaise was made. A beetroot salad included chopped chunks of boiled beetroot mixed with a sweet store-bought chutney. Dessert was a very large bowl of pudding made from store-bought long-life custard, long-life tinned cream, a large tub of sweetened mixed fruit yogurt, and a tin of mixed fruit pieces. This was followed by a second dessert course that included a store-bought chocolate cake layered with cream and a berry-flavored "cold drink" (soft drink).

The majority of the preparation and cooking revolved around a small table and the stove with an array of very large aluminum pots. There was a microwave and also a food processor sitting on top of the fridge, but these items were not used and are probably not used at all. Everything was chopped by hand on wooden chopping boards, and there was a great deal of chopping done. Tins were opened with a knife, as the tin opener had long ago broken. Dishes and pots were washed and dried by hand by Dolly, Mavis, and Zodwa.

Dolly did the shopping a day or two before the lunch. Price was the primary determinant for foods bought, followed by accessibility. KwaNdengezi has no supermarkets. A few vendors sell soft drinks, sweets, and potato crisps on the side of the road. The majority of the ingredients were bought from two supermarkets (Shoprite and Cambridge) in the nearby town of Pinetown. Shoprite and Cambridge are the cheapest retail supermarket chains in South Africa. A few items such as the tomatoes, green pepper, and chilies were bought from street vendors, as they offer smaller quantities than the supermarkets, which means less waste of any fresh produce bought. These vendors are local and may be nothing more than a table on the side of the road or a shopping trolley piled high with produce. They buy bulk sizes from the supermarkets and then sell the fruit and vegetables individually or in small quantities. Food is bought daily to cook and only as much as is needed. Enough food will be cooked for that day and if possible leftovers for the next day lunch. Dolly and Mavis are very conscious of food waste. Their purchasing and cooking choices demonstrate a creative consideration for minimizing food waste.

The women cooked until lunch was served at around 1:00 p.m. There was no apparent starting time for lunch; the guests arrived slowly and quietly at different times. A table was set outside in the narrow cement driveway with plastic chairs up against the wall. A small gazebo and beach umbrella borrowed from a neighbor were erected over the table, as it was raining that day. There was no place for so many people to eat in the house. The table was covered with a tablecloth, and all the food except the desserts was placed on the table in the pots and dishes they were cooked or made in. Commercially manufactured white ceramic plates and metal cutlery (only spoons and forks) were laid out on the table in piles. A few glasses were placed on the table with colored paper napkins folded inside. These appeared to be for decorative purposes only, as no one used the napkins.

Yael and her family were encouraged to dish up for themselves first, but for the other guests Dolly dished up their plates. Robert was given a plate of food and ate his lunch inside, by himself. He was not expected to eat with the guests and removed himself from the gathering with no consequence. There was only one other man, who was younger and ate with the women. The older women were served before the younger women. Dolly dished up their plates, a small amount of each food, a few tablespoons, but because of the array of dishes the plates were full.

Each guest found a chair up against the wall and sat down to eat. There was a conspicuous silence, and manners were immaculate. Hardly any words were exchanged, and no one expressed any dietary or food preferences. Only a spoon was used to eat, and the *phutu* was eaten with a hand and used to dip into the food and mop up the sauces and gravies. The food was eaten in total silence with little eye contact, as if the food was shared among strangers. No one asked for second helpings, and no one helped himself or herself to more food. After the main course, the pudding was dished into glass bowls and handed around with spoons. As if agreed beforehand, the guests started talking to each other, transforming the lunch into a jovial animated gathering. After the pudding each guest was given a slice of the chocolate cake with a teaspoon and a poured glass of berry cold drink. This was clearly the highlight of the meal and was relished by everyone. The guests all stayed, perhaps waiting politely for Yael and her family to leave. When they did leave, the other guests all congregated in the driveway, waving goodbye to Yael with big smiles and loud farewells.

Chakalaka

6–7 medium-size carrots, grated

2 onions, chopped small

1 big green pepper, chopped small

2 green chilies, spilt open and seeds taken out

1 can of baked beans (beans in a tomato sauce)

2 teaspoons of curry powder

½ cup of sunflower oil

1 Knorex cube (a beef stock cube)

1. Fry the onion, green pepper, and whole chilies in oil until a little soft, then add carrots, beans, and stock cube.
2. Season to taste and cook until all the ingredients are well mixed throughout but retain their texture. Serve hot, warm, or at room temperature.

FURTHER READING

Battersby, J. "Beyond the Food Desert: Finding Ways to Speak about Urban Food Security in South Africa." *Geografiska Annaler: Series B, Human Geography* 94(2) (2012): 141–159.

Frayne, Bruce, et al. *The State of Urban Food Insecurity in Southern Africa.* Cape Town: AFSUN, 2010.

Joubert, L. S., and E. Miller. *The Hungry Season: Feeding Southern Africa's Cities.* Johannesburg: Picador, 2012.

South Africa, Urban

Lexi Earl

This is the story of one South African family's dinnertime. The family represents perhaps an example of South Africa's urban middle-class, but that is not to suggest that this family speaks for all South African families. There is a great amount of variety within the cuisine we might call "South African." South Africa's history is one of conquest, contest, and colonialism, and our food culture reflects this diversity.

South African food culture is a melting pot of Bantu-speaking people's foods (Zulu, Xhosa, and Sesotho people, for example) and our immigrant heritage. Waves of immigration, beginning in 1652 with Dutch settlers, has led to a food culture and heritage that features elements of Dutch, British, Jewish, Italian, Portuguese, Malay, Indian, and Chinese cuisines. Some would argue that a South African family dinner is a *braai* (barbeque), complete with *braaivleis* (barbeque meat) such

The family sits together to eat, a special treat for Mae who normally eats first. (Courtesy of Lexi Earl)

as *boerewors* (spicy sausage), *sosaties* (meat cooked on skewers, similar to kebabs), or *chops* and sides of *pap* (stiff porridge made from mealie meal) and *djelelo* (tomato and onion sauce). Others would say that such a dinner is a Cape Malay curry or *babotie* (curried meat and fruit with a savory egg custard topping) and that dessert would be *melktert* (milk tart) or *koeksisters* (deep-fried plaited dough, soaked in syrup) or *poffertjies* (small fluffy pancakes coated in sugar). These examples merely explain that in the global age, South Africans, like many others, eat a combination of traditional foods as well as adopted ones.

What is told here is the story of one family having dinner on an early summer night in the city of Johannesburg.

The kitchen in the Baker household forms a central part of their home. It is a thoroughfare, with people coming and going throughout the day. The kitchen's back door leads out into the driveway and along to the outbuildings, so the kitchen is the natural entry point to the house rather than the front door, which is located around the side. The kitchen is a large brightly lit space with terra-cotta tiled floors and large windows on three sides. The windows are fitted with cottage pane–style burglar guards. One window looks out over the garden, while the other two windows look out onto the driveway.

There is a large freestanding stainless steel fridge/freezer in one corner and a long row of countertops along one side. There is a double oven along one wall, with the range built into the countertop beside it. The kitchen has two sinks, a testament to the house's history. The house is located in a historically Jewish neighborhood, and the purpose of the two sinks is to keep dairy and meat products separate.

At the far end of the room is a large white wooden table with six white chairs around it. The table is covered with day-to-day debris—a bowl filled with bananas and *naartjies* (easy-peeling citrus fruit similar to a clementine or mandarin), a radio, a vase of flowers, and glasses of water.

Dinner preparation has begun early today—before 5:00 p.m. Mae, the Bakers' daughter, age three and a half years, is eating with her parents tonight. Usually Rose and Peter eat later in the evening, around 8:00 p.m., preparing their dinner while Mae eats hers. But Rose is heavily pregnant (their baby boy is born two weeks later) and tired, so they are planning to eat early, with Mae. They are therefore going to eat at around 6:30 p.m. Rose has begun preparation for the lasagna she is making before Peter returns home from work. She and Mae are in the kitchen when he arrives. Mae has been sitting at the table, with a green board placed in front of her. Rose has gathered various things for a salad—organic baby salad leaves, cucumber, black olives, black pepper feta, and rosa tomatoes (small plum tomatoes). When Peter comes in, Mae gets up to greet him and then returns to the table to help with the salad. Peter goes to put down his things and then joins the family in the kitchen.

The food for today has predominantly come from two large supermarkets—Woolworths and Pick 'n Pay. Woolworths is a higher-end store, providing not only food but also clothing and home goods (everything from kitchen equipment and crockery to bedding and lamps). Rose prefers their fresh produce—vegetables, fruit, and meat products—and the increasing variety; Woolworths now stocks heritage tomatoes and locally grown produce. Woolworths is regarded as a responsible retailer, with producers who use sustainable farming methods and give back to the community, but is reasonably more expensive, and so for staple items Rose shops at Pick 'n Pay.

Peter and Mae make the salad collectively while Rose cooks the lasagna sauce and béchamel at the stove behind them. She has set all the salad ingredients on the table. Peter tips the salad leaves into a white ceramic bowl and asks Mae if she wants to cut up the feta. She nods assent, so he extracts two rounds from the tub for her. When he puts it down onto the board and goes to fetch an ordinary knife for Mae, she exclaims, "We can't eat that! There are ants in it!" Peter laughs and says to her, "No, those aren't ants. That is black pepper." Mae draws her hands toward her and refuses to touch the feta. Peter slices the feta into cubes and tosses them onto the salad leaves. Rose suggests that he get a bowl of water for Mae. She can wash the tomatoes for the salad as well as some extra for her lunch box tomorrow.

Peter fetches the bowl of water and a Tupperware container to put the tomatoes into for Mae's lunch. Mae washes the tomatoes slowly, turning them over and over in the water and occasionally putting one in her mouth. Peter slices the tomatoes in half for her lunch and adds others whole to the salad. Then he slices the cucumber into pieces and saves some for Mae's lunch. Next he opens a jar of black olives. Olives are one of Mae's favorite foods at the moment, and he asks her if she would like to eat some now. She says that she would, and Peter pits several for her, placing them to one side on the board before taking more olives from the jar, draining them slightly, and adding them to the salad. He also snacks on a few as he works.

Peter fetches grapes and strawberries from the fridge. He asks Mae to wash some of these too, as they can be put into her lunch box now. She obeys, taking a strawberry to eat in the process. Peter then leaves the kitchen to pour drinks at their bar, and Rose comes to sit down at the table to supervise the washing of the fruit. Peter comes back with a glass of red wine for himself and a long glass of passion fruit cordial with soda and ice for Rose, who cannot drink alcohol due to the pregnancy. Mae requests some water, so he gets her water bottle—a green one with a purple lid and straw—fills it, and brings it to the table for her.

The family talks about the imminent arrival of their baby boy. They tell Mae that she will soon be a big sister, and she says she is going to be a good one. Once all the grapes and strawberries are washed, they are placed in a Tupperware container. The salad is placed in the center of the table.

While Mae and Peter have been making the salad, Rose has been busy making the lasagna. Peter and Rose often take turns cooking. They both like to cook, although Rose is more skilled. She took cooking at school, cooked with her mother and grandmother growing up, and is very interested in food. Part of her work entails teaching mothers ways to feed their children. She is also a baking enthusiast and likes to spend time in the kitchen. But Peter makes dinner fairly often, and he

Food Marketed to Kids

Baby food was an invention of the early 20th century in tandem with baby formula, developed by scientists who believed that they could feed infants better than with breast milk and puréed adult food after infants were weaned. Food marketed to kids came somewhat later and in many ways was more ingenious. Offering food that could be eaten with the fingers, such as pizza, hot dogs, chicken nuggets, and tater tots, and making an explicit connection between these foods and fun (since no utensils or manners were required), manufacturers invented a whole new category of food. Arguably, they also stunted the aesthetic development of young palates so that many children never learned to like the food their parents ate. Parents were forced to cater to their children's tastes in a way that would have been unthinkable a generation before.

is in charge of *braaiing*, as it is South African tradition. (Cooking meat over the fire is a particularly masculine activity in South Africa and one that remains severely gendered. While men will gather at the *braai* and remain outside cooking for most of the afternoon, the women will be primarily in the kitchen making sides and salads or sitting on the *stoep* [veranda] talking. Everyone gathers together at the table to eat when the *braaiing* is done.)

Rose sautés some sliced onions, carrots, celery, and leeks in a cream Le Creuset crock pot on the stove. Le Creuset is hugely popular in South Africa, and cooking enthusiasts often have at least one treasured pot that they use. Rose is no exception, and she uses the pot for the meat sauce. Once the onions are softened, she adds in some garlic. She then takes this mixture out of the pot, keeping it to one side while she browns the meat.

Rose uses a combination of beef mince, bacon, and pork sausage filling that she squeezes from the sausage casings, which she then discards. Once the meat is evenly browned, she adds the onion mixture back in, followed by some of Peter's red wine (a South African *pinotage*), some tomato paste, tinned tomatoes, and beef stock. The whole mixture is left to simmer and putter away on the stove until Rose has finished the béchamel.

Rose is making extra lasagna tonight so she can freeze the leftovers. She has prepared several ready-made meals for the freezer that Peter will be able to reheat in the few weeks following the new baby's birth. Perhaps because Rose likes to cook so much, the family hardly ever has instant meals or takeout. They eat out on the weekend, but during the week they eat freshly prepared made-from-scratch dishes. These dishes are often made using local products. Sometimes these are organic (such as the salad leaves), but elements may be bought already prepared.

South Africa's middle classes tend to eat a variety of semiprepared and ready-prepared dishes. Rose's cooking every night is therefore slightly atypical.

Woolworths provides middle-class families with high-quality freshly prepared meals, such as the rotisserie chicken that can be bought still warm and carved at home and ready-made salads. In the summertime, South Africans eat a lot of salad. The heat in the summertime entices people to eat cold foods, and because vegetables form a staple part of the South African diet, these are consumed in salad form in the summer. Salad may be eaten as a side dish—for example, with steak and chips or with a cooked piece of chicken—or as an entire main meal. In this sense, Rose's pairing of the lasagna with salad is very South African.

While the meat is simmering, Rose makes the béchamel. The béchamel is the first thing she can remember her grandmother teaching her to make, so there is a sense of comfort and continuity in its preparation. She does not weigh the butter, flour, or milk, having made béchamel so many times that the process is now second nature. She has two secret ingredients in her sauce—the mustard powder her grandmother insisted upon and an egg yolk. This innovation Rose saw once on a cookery program. It adds a silky richness to the sauce. Today she is using eggs given to her by friends who keep chickens in their backyard. She exclaims how orange the egg yolk is and keeps referring to its color as she whisks it into the béchamel.

Once the sauce is made, Rose layers the lasagna in a rectangular white baking dish. She uses green (spinach) lasagna sheets. She layers meat sauce and then béchamel and lasagna sheets until the meat sauce is finished. On the last layer she adds the béchamel, and she asks Mae if she would like to grate the cheese for the top. Mae says she would and goes to fetch her stool so she can reach the higher countertop. She grates the Parmesan slowly, with concentrated purpose. When she says she is done, Rose grates a little bit more onto the top and places the lasagna into the oven to bake. Mae and Peter go upstairs so that Mae can bathe.

Half an hour later, the family is ready to eat. Mae has changed into her pajamas. She takes her place at the head of the table. Rose has removed the lasagna from the oven, and it is cooling on a lower set of drawers next to the main counter on a potholder. She and Peter move around the kitchen, getting everything they need. Peter checks that they both still have drinks and asks Mae if she would like some juice. She says, "Yes please" and is given some apple juice in a clear plastic cup. She also has her water bottle on the table. Rose fetches two white china plates from a cupboard (their normal everyday crockery) and a colorful small plastic plate (pink and purple with butterflies) for Mae. Rose gets paper napkins with a floral design in a napkin holder from the counter. Peter gets the cutlery from the top drawer in the counter, a knife and fork each for himself and Rose and a special smaller spoon and fork set for Mae. Rose puts three florets of broccoli into the microwave to steam—this is Mae's favorite food, so she has some every night.

Peter dishes up for Mae first, and Rose sits down next to her at the seat by the window. The family has a more formal dining room with a dark oak dining table, but they only use that space for dinner parties or special meals. Peter dishes some lasagna for Mae and then passes the plate to Rose. She asks Mae if she would like some salad and then gives her some salad leaves, tomatoes, olives, and cucumber but no feta. Mae is allowed to begin eating before Peter sits down or either of her parents have their plates. Rose asks Peter to fetch the Greek salad dressing from the fridge door. Mae does not have salad dressing, but Peter brings her the steamed broccoli and places it on her plate. He then dishes up for Rose and himself.

Peter puts their plates on the table but then decides that the overhead light is too bright. He goes to the pantry to get two fat red candles and a silver candlestick holder with three tapered cream candles. He lights these and then switches the overhead light off. The light on the extractor fan above the stove is still on, and the room is cozy. It is dark outside already, although they have not drawn the blinds in the kitchen. Rose waits for Peter to sit down before beginning to organize her eating. She cracks black pepper onto the lasagna and dishes up salad for herself. Peter avoids the black pepper but takes salad. They both put dressing on their salad and begin to eat.

Mae is an exceptionally slow eater, and most of the meal is spent encouraging her to eat more. She eats a few elements of her salad—the olives and tomatoes—then switches to a broccoli floret before consenting to have some lasagna. Rose and Peter eat and talk in between encouraging Mae to eat. Peter feeds her some of the lasagna with her fork to entice her to eat more.

While they eat, the family's two cats come in via an open window. The first cat leaps onto the counter where the lasagna is still cooling and carefully steps around it to get onto the floor. Peter gets up and moves the lasagna to a higher counter, out of the way. Peter and Rose are both finished eating before Mae. They encourage her to eat a bit more, and eventually she finishes her lasagna and has one last broccoli floret. Peter helps himself to more lasagna and fetches an individual smooth strawberry yogurt from the fridge for Mae's dessert.

Peter finishes eating while Rose feeds the yogurt to Mae, who is tired now and yawns at the table. Once she and Peter are both finished, Peter clears the plates from the table, putting them all in the sink for the moment. There is a little leftover salad and quite a lot of lasagna. Peter takes Mae upstairs to brush her teeth, and Rose stays downstairs. She puts the salad into a Tupperware container, puts the salad dressing back in the fridge, and carries their glasses into the living room. Later, Peter will pack the dishwasher. Rose goes upstairs to say goodnight to Mae. When Mae is asleep, she and Peter return to the living room to finish their drinks.

This dinner is an example of middle-class South African eating. The choice of lasagna suggests the globalization of food—Italian dishes such as pizza and pasta are South African staples now. Table manners and habits are typically Western, and although it might be fairly common for people to adopt more informal eating spaces—in front of the television, for example—Peter and Rose eat at the table almost every night, in part because they are educating Mae on acceptable ways to eat but also because it keeps to the traditions in which they were raised and the kind of family life they are trying to build.

Rose spoons the egg-enriched béchamel atop the ragu and pasta layers before Mae grates the cheese on top. (Courtesy of Lexi Earl)

Lasagna with Egg-Enriched Béchamel

For the meat sauce:

Olive oil

Butter

1 white onion, diced

1 large carrot, finely sliced

2 sticks of celery, finely sliced

1 baby leek, finely sliced

3 large garlic cloves, chopped

1 pound of ground beef

3 strips of bacon, cut into cubes

3 pork sausages

⅓ bottle of red wine

2 tablespoons of tomato paste

1 can of cherry tomatoes

Approximately 2 cups of beef stock

Lasagna sheets

For the béchamel:

5 tablespoons of unsalted butter

5 tablespoons of plain flour

Approximately 2½ cups of whole milk

1 egg yolk

Generous pinch of mustard powder

Parmesan

This recipe is infinitely adaptable. As Rose explained when she made it, she cooks dishes like this by instinct and feel rather than according to a recipe and particular amounts.

For the meat sauce:

1. In a heavy-bottomed large pot, heat a generous pour of olive oil and a teaspoon of butter until the butter is foaming.
2. Add in the onion, carrot, celery, and leeks, stirring to coat, and cook over a medium heat until the onion is translucent and the vegetables are soft.
3. Add in the garlic and cook for several more minutes.
4. Remove the vegetables from the pot, keeping them to one side in a bowl.
5. Add the bacon to the pot and cook for a few minutes to release some of the fat.
6. Then add in the meat, breaking it up with your hands.
7. Squeeze the sausage meat out of the casings directly into the pot. Discard the casings.
8. Stir the meat, breaking up the sausages as you do so, and cook until the mince has browned all over. Add the vegetables back into the pot.
9. Increase the heat and add in the red wine, allowing some of the alcohol to boil away.
10. Then add in the tomato paste and canned tomatoes.
11. Stir the sauce and add in enough beef stock to cover the meat. Bring this all to a boil and then reduce the heat so that the sauce simmers and putters on the stove until thickened and reduced, about 45 minutes.
12. While the sauce is simmering, make the béchamel. Melt the butter in a saucepan. Add in the flour and stir until the flour and butter are emulsified.
13. In a separate saucepan, heat the milk until scalding.
14. Slowly add the milk into the flour and butter. It may be necessary to use a whisk to ensure that the sauce is smooth. Cook the sauce slowly, adding the milk a little at a time, until the sauce is thickened, smooth, and bubbling.
15. Turn off the heat, whisk in the yolk and the mustard powder. Set aside.
16. Heat the oven to 325 degrees F.
17. Into a large rectangular baking dish, spoon some of the meat sauce, followed by the béchamel. Then cover with a single layer of lasagna sheets, breaking them to fit if necessary. Then repeat—meat sauce, béchamel, and lasagna sheets—until all the meat sauce is used up. For the last layer, place the lasagna sheets on top of the meat sauce and then spoon over the last of the béchamel.
18. Grate Parmesan over the top of the béchamel, using as much cheese as you like.
19. Bake the lasagna in the middle rack of the oven for about 45 minutes, until the cheese is golden and the lasagna is bubbling.

FURTHER READING

Cheifitz, P. *South Africa Eats.* Johannesburg: Quivertree, 2009.
Essop, S. *Karoo Kitchen.* Johannesburg: Quivertree, 2012.
Joubert, L. *The Hungry Season.* Johannesburg: Picador Africa, 2012.
Trapido, A. *Hunger for Freedom.* Johannesburg: Jacana, 2008.

Spain

F. Xavier Medina

Spanish cuisine and gastronomy is probably among the most famous internation-ally: elements such as tapas, wine, and paella are very well known around the world. Nevertheless (and probably due to this same reason), information on Spain and Spanish gastronomy and food culture is usually made up of a number of ste-reotypes and preconceived ideas that, in most cases, have little or nothing to do with reality.

What really happens at a table in everyday life in Spain? The aim of this essay is to offer an overall view on the Spanish culture and society using a real picture, a real day-to-day image of a meal in Spain as a storyline.

Two young couples having an outdoor lunch at a restaurant terasse near the beach, during the autumn season in Barcelona, Spain. (Courtesy of F. Xavier Medina)

THE CONTEXT: THE PROTAGONISTS, THE PLACE, THE TABLE . . .

The picture in this entry shows two young couples at an outdoor lunch in a restaurant near the beach. The place: the city of Barcelona, capital of Catalonia, in the northern Mediterranean coastal area of Spain. The moment: a friend lunch on a Friday during the autumn season.

On the table, we can see a local variation of the popular paella, as a main dish, and a bottle of an also local and cold white wine. This rice, nevertheless, was not the only dish of this meal. Our four protagonists started with a selection of small dishes for tapas: clams, mussels, *patatas bravas* (fried potato cubes with spicy sauce), and fried calamari. After the rice, just coffee: one *café solo* (espresso) and three *cortados* (espresso with a very little milk, known also in Italian as a *café macchiato*).

About the restaurant, we have to say that this is a very popular one on the beach, specializing in different rice preparations. This kind of restaurant is not uncommon in Barcelona and throughout the Spanish Mediterranean coast but is also present in other big cities all over Spain. These restaurants were founded by a small entrepreneurial group, with different restaurants in Barcelona and all around Catalonia, and also another couple of them in Madrid. They define their cuisine as a creative one but based on tradition and always made with the best-quality products. In the kitchen, there is a mix of local and foreign-born workers (mainly from Latin America and North and Central Africa).

First, we will start with a short discussion about Spain and its present context. After that, we will analyze the different parts of our description, more than in an ethnographic way, looking for a comprehensive pattern to explain the country and its very complex food culture.

SPAIN WITHIN THE EUROPEAN-MEDITERRANEAN CONTEXT

Spain, a country of 46 million people in southwestern Europe, occupies most of the Iberian Peninsula. Spain borders Portugal to the east, France (and the very small principality of Andorra) to the north, and Morocco (Northern Africa) to the south. Spain boasts a wide variety of landscapes: a big central plain, some of the most important mountain ranges of Europe, and nearly 5,000 miles of coast. It is washed by the Mediterranean and the Cantabrian Seas and by the Atlantic Ocean and also has two archipelagoes: the Balearic (northwestern Mediterranean) and the Canary Islands (northwest African coast). There are four official languages: Spanish or Castilian (in all of Spain), Catalan, Basque, and Galician (in their own areas of origin).

An important aspect to take into account is the quality of Spanish products. Spain has been an agricultural country since the mid-20th century: the mild climate and the quality of the soil have facilitated the production of widely appreciated foods that are highly competitive on the international market. Admission (together with Portugal) to the European Union in 1986 was a major boost for the

Cutlery Proliferation

In certain periods in history, tableware became more varied and specialized. Thus, in the Victorian era there were special fish forks, marrow spoons, butter knives, and dozens of other items that were a mark of sophistication and wealth. In the 20th century the variety of items narrowed, with many serving several functions. At home especially, a complete set of cutlery might be only a knife, fork, and spoon. Eventually even these were combined into sporks, knorks, and many other all-purpose utensils, first found in fast-food outlets but gradually making their way into homes.

Spanish economy and marked the entrance of Spanish agriculture in the integrated European policies.

During the years after 2008, the Spanish economy has been strongly affected by the European debt crisis and the Great Recession. Even if Spain had a comparatively low debt level among advanced economies prior to the crisis, debt was largely avoided by the ballooning tax revenue from the housing bubble, and in 2013 the country suffered 27 percent unemployment. This important fact has affected significantly Spanish lifestyles until the present moment, including food consumption (quality and quantity) and eating out in restaurants and in other public food services and spaces. However, during the second half of 2014 and early 2015, the effects of the crisis seem to be giving way to some recovery, which has begun to be reflected again at all levels.

A PICTURE TAKEN IN BARCELONA . . .

The city of Barcelona is the second-largest city in the country (around 2 million inhabitants), after Madrid, the capital, and is probably the most internationally known and touristic city in all Spain. Barcelona is capital of one of the most important industrial and economic but also touristic poles of the state: the autonomous community of Catalonia.

Barcelona is actually among the most cosmopolitan cities in Europe and is also a very important culinary center. Just as the restaurant in the picture defined its own cuisine as a *creative one but based on tradition*, Barcelona and Catalonia's cuisines are also in between *innovation* and *tradition*. On one hand, the region is an important pole of concentration of the most innovative and creative cuisine in the international gastronomic panorama: Ferra Adrià was internationally recognized for the first time as the best cook of the moment in 2004; *Restaurant Magazine* judged his restaurant, *El Bulli*, to be number one on its Top 50 list of the world's best restaurants for a record five times (2002, 2006, 2007, 2008, and 2009) and second in 2010. Another Catalan restaurant, El Celler de Can Roca, founded by the

Roca Brothers, was also number one of the list in 2013 and second in 2011, 2012, and 2014.

On the other hand, Catalan traditional cuisine is also very important and recognized. This fact led to an effort for Catalan cuisine to be declared a World Intangible Heritage by UNESCO. This was the first proposal for a nonstate cuisine as an Intangible Heritage of Humanity.

THE PEOPLE AND THE MOMENT: AN OUTDOOR LUNCH NEAR THE BEACH

As mentioned before, our picture shows two young couples at an outdoor lunch in a restaurant near the beach during autumn. Food culture in Spain, unlike in some other European countries, has always been of capital importance. Eating is conceived of as a social act, as an activity that must be shared with others. Spaniards in general highly value eating with their family, friends, and colleagues, spending daily time on it. Sharing food fosters social relationships, and it is not uncommon for meetings to be articulated (or ended) around a dining table. It is not so common to see a person eating alone everywhere or drinking alone in a bar (unless he or she is forced by specific circumstances). As a matter of fact, such situations are avoided, which shows how socially important meals are.

In the last century, Spain changed from a prominently rural and agricultural country into a modern industrialized and mainly urban country that ranks among the top 15 world economies and is one of the pillars of the European Union. This process has brought along deep cultural and social transformations, which have affected the structure of families, the distribution of working and leisure time, and, consequently, the timing of all those activities related to food, both inside and outside the home.

To correctly interpret our picture, we have to say that these fast changes include the transformation of the familial unit traditionally made up of a married couple, children, and even grandparents into a wider variety of family forms: married and unmarried couples, one-parent families (singles, widows and widowers, divorcees), heterosexual and gay couples (Spain approved same-sex marriage in 2005, becoming one of the first countries in the world to do so, only behind the Netherlands, Belgium, and Canada) with or without biological or adopted children. (Incidentally, Spain has one of the lowest birthrates in all of Europe and is also the leading European country in international adoptions and one of the world's leaders.)

Keeping all this in mind, it is noteworthy that social change in Spain has been rapid and steady. While in other European countries this social change has been gradual over decades, in Spain, after the long period of Francisco Franco's dictatorship (1939–1975), all these changes took place in an accelerated manner after the late 1970s.

But back to the picture, we must remember also that we are talking about a lunch, one of the two main meals of the day (around 2:00 to 3:30 p.m.). Throughout history the timing of daily activities has also changed. Regarding the structure and timing of the meals, and as far as eating hours are concerned, these underwent significant changes in the 20th century; the most important ones concerned main meals (lunch and dinner), which were shifted to a later time of day.

Comida (lunch, between 2:00 and 4:00 p.m.) is, together with dinner, one of the two main daily meals. In Spain, unlike other European countries where very little time is devoted to lunch, lunchtime generally lasts from one to two hours, and the meal is usually a complete one (starter, main course, and dessert). Those who have time to return home for lunch habitually eat there, if possible with family. Nowadays, the working rhythm and the distance between working and living places make it difficult for people to have lunch in their homes. As a consequence, most restaurants offer the so-called midday menus (based on the three-course pattern described above, including coffee) that provide a complete enough meal at low cost. It is worth noting that this meal has been traditionally considered a social act, so it is common for people to meet for lunch with relatives, friends, or coworkers. Wine, together with water, is the most traditional drink (as we can see in our picture). Today, however, the consumption of beer and soft drinks has increased considerably.

An aspect worth highlighting is that Spaniards usually eat much later than other Europeans (such as Central and North Europeans but also French and Italians). The difference is particularly evident with regard to lunch and dinner, which are consumed about two hours later than in other European countries. Whereas in places such as France and the United Kingdom lunch is at about noon, in Spain it is around 2:00 or 3:00 p.m. (even a bit later sometimes, such as weekends and holidays). In the case of the protagonists of our picture, they are having lunch together on a workday, using the lunch break that allows them to have lunch between 2:00 and 4:00 p.m.

Likewise, while in certain European countries dinner is at about 6:00, 7:00 or 8:00 p.m. (even earlier in places farther north), in Spain dinner is between 8:30 and 10:30 p.m. (and even a bit later on holidays and weekends). The daily distribution of meals in Spain brings along a different distribution of working hours; Spaniards' workday may stretch until 7:00 or 8:00 p.m., yet they wake up at the same time as other European workers. In other words, Spanish people sleep fewer hours than other Europeans since they go to bed much later, and yet get up at the same time in the morning. This daily timing, however, is not as old as might be believed but has become established only recently. In the 19th century, lunch was around noon or 1:00 p.m. and dinner was at 7:00 or 8:00 p.m., depending on the season. These mealtimes progressively shifted into the current pattern during the 20th century.

Another feature of Spanish society that is worth highlighting, as we can see also in our picture, is that people like eating and drinking out. As we said before, the picture above shows an outdoor lunch in a restaurant in the Mediterranean area in autumn. The climate, with its mild temperatures, is typical of a South European country. It is very rarely extreme, and it allows outdoor celebrations and meals almost all year long (except, perhaps, in the harshest winter months). Eating out includes popular feasts, communal meals, or simple visits to restaurants, premises with outdoor tables, bars, cafés, etc.

A PAN ON THE TABLE: ON PAELLA, WINE, AND THE BUILDING OF A NATIONAL DISH

If we look at the picture, we can see on the table different interesting items. Near the viewer is a bottle of local white wine. There is a paella (the rice dish) for four people, served in a standard paella (the pan). This rice nevertheless was not the only dish of this meal. Our four protagonists started, as we said before, with a small selection of tapas: clams, mussels, *patatas bravas,* and fried calamari. After the rice, just coffee: one *café solo* and three *cortados.*

As the writer Manuel Vázquez Montalbán pointed out many years ago, in Europe probably only Spain and Italy developed a real culinary culture of rice. Spain is the second-largest producer of rice in the European Union after Italy, and both countries are also the biggest rice consumers on the continent. The Valencia region produces a big part of the rice cultivated in Spain, and it is one of the only rice-growing regions in Europe to have a designation of origin. The Valencian way of cooking rice spread to the whole country to the extent that a local dish such as paella and other similar rice dishes (such as the one in our picture, which is not the most typical paella) has come to be considered the Spanish national dish.

If a particular dish has come to be considered the Spanish national representative, it is the paella. Paella is one of those dishes without a long history but nevertheless is known virtually worldwide. Nowadays when most foreign gastronomes think about Spain they almost invariably link it with paella, although this dish originated only in the 19th century in a little coastal area, the Valencia countryside, in the east-central part of Spain. The growing and cooking of rice are admittedly ancient agricultural practices in almost all the Mediterranean coastal region of Spain, but the dish itself is a product of modernity. Appearing in a precise socioeconomic context at the end of the 19th century, paella gradually became an emblem of Spanish cookery more or less accepted as such by the Spaniards themselves, even though it is not really a *national* dish (all Spaniards know that this dish is originally from the Valencia area). Paella has become known internationally but has also been integrated into many of the different local food cultures in Spain, thanks to phenomena that are characteristic of the modern period, such as agricultural changes, Spanish recent history and demographic consequences, and the birth of mass tourism.

The name of the rice dish paella is, in fact, one of the dialectal names of the utensil (in the Catalan language) used for cooking it: the frying pan. Nowadays, the word "paella" (from the Latin "patella") or sometimes its derivation *paellera* is especially employed to designate the round, flat frying pan in which paella is usually cooked and also served—on the table, like in our picture, where one of the members will serve the plates or everyone will serve their own plate, or carried to the table, showed to the diners, and served by the waiter on individual plates.

But at this point, we must remember that our four protagonists started their lunch with a small selection of tapas. In different parts of Spain, some bars offer tapas menus with more than 100 specialties, which are eaten while consuming wine, beer (a *caña* is the typical size of a glass of beer in almost all Spain, normally around 5–6 ounces), or the drink that better suits each of these appetizers. Tapas are actually popular all over Spain but are particularly important in the central and southern regions.

In some areas such as Catalonia (northeast), especially over the last century, the tradition is more linked to *vermut* (vermouth) as an aperitif. This drink, made of herbs and wine and fortified with spirits, originated in Italy. In the Basque country (north), *pintxos* are the Basque version of tapas: small portions of various—and very elaborate—kinds of food (sometimes small culinary gems), placed normally on a slice of bread.

This is not so in our meal (because paella is a main grain-based dish), but normally we can also find on the table some bread as well as some oil and salt. Traditionally, bread has always been the population's principal food, and even if its consumption is actually decreasing significantly, it is normally omnipresent on Spanish tables. Made from various kinds of cereals, the most appreciated has always been white bread. On the other hand, a set with oil, vinegar, and salt (almost never butter) are present on Spanish tables (particularly in restaurants) at lunchtime or dinnertime.

Olive oil, which is nowadays so famous and appreciated, is extracted from olives and is very commonly used in Spain nowadays (and is the basic fat we use to sauté the ingredients of the paella). Over the centuries olive oil became the predominant edible fat and spread toward the inland and northern regions of the peninsula. Spain is the most important producer of olive oil in the world. In recent decades cardiovascular health and dietetic properties have been attributed to olive oil, which has turned into one of the pillars of the food regimen known and promoted as the Mediterranean diet. For some people, a slice of bread with olive oil and a bit of salt can be a nice appetizer. In our picture, nevertheless, no bread is on the table, because paella is made with rice (also a cereal). In this case also, olive oil is not needed.

Finally, we also have a bottle of cold white wine on the table. Spain is currently one of the main international producers and consumers of wine (red and white mainly but also rosé) and, together with France and Italy, has some of the most valued wine designations of origin in the world (such as Rioja, Ribera del Duero, Priorat, Jerez-Sherry, and Penedès). Wine has been historically the main alcoholic beverage in Spain, and its culture still is very significant throughout the country. On the other hand, beer became definitely (and strongly) established in the second half of the 20th century, and Spain is currently one of the largest beer consumers in the Mediterranean area.

But even if we can identify a kind of national dish such as paella or a popular and common way to eat *tapas*, we must also say that Spain is a country that boasts a great cultural, geographical, and gastronomical diversity. It is a country with high potential in terms of both cultural relationships and geographical and environmental resources: from the Mediterranean coast, with a mild climate, to the Atlantic coast, colder, wetter, and with more vegetation, and from the flat and dry Castilian *meseta* to the high mountainous ranges. These diverse features make each Spanish cuisine different and unique, since each of them specializes in specific products, flavors, and cooking methods.

In this context, most Spanish cuisines have evolved around strong identities and representative elements that have changed along the centuries. Historical, social, and cultural factors marked a particular evolution in the various Spanish cuisines, giving each of them a specific character and individual features that distinguish them from each other and from the cuisines of other countries.

More than a single Spanish cuisine, in Spain we can find a very rich mosaic of cuisines and gastronomes with very strong personalities: Galicia and the Cantabric area, the Basque area, Catalonia, the Levantine coast, Andalusia, and the two Castilles, the Balearic Islands and the Canary Islands. Every landscape, culture, language (in Spain there are, as we said before, four official languages), and lifestyle has contributed to create a particular cuisine, even a specific food culture, that is strongest at the regional level rather than a unified general Spanish cuisine.

Paella

Rice (a cup/handful per serving plus some extra ones)	1²/₃ tablespoons tender green beans, chopped
3 garlic cloves	Saffron (1 pinch)
1 onion	Salt to taste
1 tomato	Olive oil
2 pounds of meat (pork loin ribs)	Water (enough to double the quantity of the rice)
1 rabbit, chopped (or chicken)	
1²/₃ tablespoons peas	

1. Sauté the meat (ribs, rabbit, and/or chicken) in a *paella* (typical metal pan, round, flat, and with two handles) with some oil.
2. When the meat is golden brown, add the minced onion, peas, beans, whole garlic cloves, and finally the minced tomato.
3. When the mixture is ready, add the water and bring to a boil.
4. Add the rice, and turn to high heat. After a few minutes add the saffron.
5. The rice must cook for about 20 minutes until all the water has been absorbed.
6. Once ready, cover the paella with a cotton cloth, let it sit for 5 minutes, and then serve it.

Note: Paella is a flexible dish that can be made with several ingredients. The recipe above follows the traditional preparation with meat and vegetables, which is originally from Valencia.

Only ingredients that are more or less easy to find have been included, whereas regional ones such as local species of snails and *garrofons* (broad beans that have a floury texture and are larger than usual) have been omitted.

Different kinds of paella may be made using other ingredients: fish and shellfish paella, meat paella, vegetable paella, or even mixed paella, the most popular with tourists, which blends in one recipe all the other kinds (meat, vegetables, fish, and shellfish).

FURTHER READING

Duhart, F., and F. X. Medina. "An Ethnological Study of the Paella in the Valencian Area of Spain and Abroad: Uses and Representations of a Mediterranean Dish." In *Mediterranean Food: Concepts and Trends,* edited by P. Lysaght, 121–131. Zagreb: Institut za Etnologiju i Folkloristiku, 2006.

Gamella, J. F. "Spain." In *International Handbook on Alcohol and Culture,* edited by D. B. Heath, 254–268. Westport, CT: Greenwood, 1995.

González-Turmo, I. "Spain: The Evolution of Habits and Consumption (1925–1997)." *Rivista di Antropologia,* Supplement 76 (1998): 335–342.

Luján, N., and J. Perucho. *El libro de la cocina española: Gastronomía e historia.* Barcelona: Tusquets, 2003.

Martínez Llopis, M. *Historia de la gastronomía española.* Huesca: la Val de Onsera, 1995.

Medina, F. X. *Food Culture in Spain.* Westport, CT: Greenwood, 2005.

Millán, A. "Tapeo: An Identity Model of Public Drink and Food Consumption in Spain." In *Drinking: Anthropological Approaches,* edited by I. De Garine and V. De Garine, 158–168. Oxford: Berghahn Books, 2001.

Sweden

Gabriela Villagrán Backman

The Blomberg family lives in a trendy suburb on the outskirts of Stockholm, Sweden. Renata, Peter, and their two children, Joakim and Alexandra, along with a couple of cats live in a small three-bedroom apartment a few minutes on foot from the subway station. They enjoy living in the area since it has a small supermarket, coffee shops, a bakery, a drugstore, and a school just a few blocks from their home.

Renata and Peter met abroad when he was doing research for his thesis. They fell in love, married, and moved to Sweden, where Renata became a work-at-home mother since the birth of their two children. Since business is going well, she has recently hired a small office space on the same block where the family lives.

The Blomberg family enjoying their vegetarian Friday dinner while planning the rest of the weekend. (Courtesy of Gabriela Villagrán Backman)

Food as Entertainment

Food on TV in the 21st century has become less a means of teaching cooking than a form of passive entertainment. That is, the more people watch cooking shows on TV, mostly competitive, the less they actually cook. It may be that expert chefs pulling off impossible feats simply discourage people from cooking themselves. Likewise, ridiculous combinations of unlikely foods with unusual techniques have become the stock-in-trade of many cooking shows. Or it may simply be that foodies find cooking so entertaining that they have no intention of replicating what they see on TV and perhaps never had any intention of cooking. In any case, cooking has become a kind of spectator sport much like any other.

Like many families in Stockholm, the Blombergs do not own a car. They feel that it is imperative to live in an environmentally sustainable manner, and many of the choices they make are based on climate change issues. Many middle-class people in Sweden who live in one of the three large cities—Stockholm, Gothenburg, and Malmo—try to live according to climate-friendly recommendations. However, sometimes public transportation is not good enough, and the Blombergs borrow Peter's parents' car if needed. About once a month, Peter and Renata take the chance to visit one of the larger supermarkets in the suburbs in order to buy in bulk and fill their pantry and refrigerator. Sometimes Renata stays at home and lets Peter do the shopping, as is the case on this Friday evening.

Peter drives to a large discount supermarket a short distance away. He knows exactly what to purchase because he has a long detailed list of what his family needs to fill the kitchen. His wife and he spent most of the previous evening checking their pantry in order to write a comprehensive list of what they need. First, he must make a brief stop at Systembolaget, the liquor shop owned by the Swedish government. Since it is Friday, the Blomberg couple has decided to have a couple of beers with dinner this evening. Peter parks near the entrance to the supermarket. It is a very popular place because it offers low prices and a wide variety of produce, fresh fish and seafood, and all kinds of canned food. It is full with customers, many parents with children, some young couples, and quite a few lone men, also with shopping lists in their hands. Peter has planned a route in order to finish quickly. He grabs some fresh produce from the vegetable and fruit section, moves on to dairy and eggs, and passes by cans, rice, coffee, detergent, and magazines. After standing in line for a few minutes, he pays, packs his purchases, and drives home.

Renata is waiting for her husband to come home before starting to prepare dinner, because he is bringing home several ingredients she is going to use tonight. As soon as he arrives, the couple puts away the groceries and catches up on how the day has been. Peter pours some beer in a couple of glasses and offers one to his wife. Teenager Joakim is in his bedroom listening to music, and seven-year-old Alexandra is on the couch drawing.

The kitchen is small but organized and clean. It has a floor-to-ceiling pantry; an electric stove with four burners, the most common kind in Sweden; and a combined refrigerator and freezer. The appliances are included in the rent for the apartment. There are two medium-sized hardwood counters and a large sink made of stainless steel with a window above it that presents a view of a small forested area behind the building.

Friday dinner is one of the most important events for families in Sweden. It has become a concept, and the idea is to enjoy a cozy evening with the family as opposed to the stress of weekday life. This evening, Renata has decided to make a vegetarian chickpea stew inspired by a dish she tasted at an Indian restaurant nearby. She and her husband have cut down on their intake of meat, mostly beef and pork, because public opinion has been intense on how meat production affects climate change. They believe that vegetarian options, even though not completely made with organic ingredients, are a better choice for the environment than supporting the meat industry.

The Blombergs are very environmentally conscious and carefully choose everything they purchase. They have recently begun to acquire pots and pans made of sustainable materials and worry a lot about chemicals in their older appliances. They keep up with new findings about the dangers of certain kinds of plastics and materials. They also try to purchase organic food as often as they can, although it is quite expensive, and there is a limited range of produce in Sweden.

Renata and Peter like to cook together, though she leads the preparations and decides what Peter will help with. They each take a few ingredients to work with on different counters. Soft music is playing in the background as Peter takes one of several good sharp knives and a plastic cutting board and starts to chop tomatoes. At the same time, Renata grabs a wooden cutting board and places it on another counter. She peels an onion, two cloves of garlic, and a large piece of fresh ginger; chops them; and moves on to cutting a daikon radish into long, thin strips. She slices a yellow bell pepper and half a red bell pepper and cuts butternut squash into cubes. She pours a couple of tablespoons of organic coconut oil into a large red porcelain enamel pan and turns the heat on. When the coconut oil is hot, Renata adds the onion, garlic, and ginger and sautés them for about five minutes. She stirs using a wooden spoon. Renata asks Peter to add the chopped tomatoes to the pan and stirs well.

In a stainless steel pot from IKEA, Renata boils water for the brown rice. She places the brown rice kernels in a sieve and rinses them under cool running water. She then pours them into the boiling water, adds salt and turmeric, and covers with a lid. She lowers the heat to medium and relaxes. Peter asks if there is anything more that he can do, and Renata tells him that she will call him if she needs help. Peter leaves the kitchen and gets his laptop. He sits beside his daughter on the couch and checks his e-mail while making small talk with Alexandra. After a while, the girl goes into her bedroom and returns with a book. She asks her father to read to her.

Renata lets the chickpea stew simmer until the brown rice is cooked. In the meantime, she sets the table. Since the apartment is so small, the table only seats four people. It is placed by a narrow wall between the hallway and the door to the kitchen. The same room also serves as a living room, but only a couch and small table fit. There is no television set in the room, and several drawings that Renata has done hang on the walls. Renata spreads a turquoise tablecloth on the table and places four individual cloth place mats on it. She then folds paper napkins in half and puts them on the right side of the place mats. Stainless cutlery and blue IKEA glasses are placed on the table.

When the brown rice is cooked, Renata makes a quick salad. She rinses and shreds romaine lettuce leaves and puts them in a glass bowl. She cuts one half red bell pepper into thin strips and slices some cucumber and adds these to the lettuce. Renata then presses half a lemon and pours some olive oil on the lettuce and finishes by sprinkling a little bit of salt and tossing well. She puts the bowl on a wooden stand and sets them on the table.

Peter turns the laptop off and goes into the kitchen to get a pot coaster. He puts it on the table and waits for Renata to bring the chickpea stew. In the meantime, Alexandra washes her hands and dries them carefully. In the kitchen, Renata pours the cooked brown rice into a red porcelain serving dish and places it on the table. She also brings the pot with the stew and sits down. Peter calls his teenage son, but it takes a while before he comes out of his room. His parents and sister wait patiently until he is ready to sit down and eat.

Renata begins by serving Joakim a large portion of food. She then serves Alexandra, then serves her husband, and finally herself. The chickpea stew, brown rice, and salad are served at the same time and on the same plate. Suddenly Peter notices that they have forgotten to bring out the drinks, so he goes into the kitchen to get the beer for the grown-ups and water for the children. They make small talk during dinner, soft music still playing in the background, and discuss what movie they want to watch later on that evening. Teenager Joakim shrugs his shoulders often and says he does not care about watching movies with the family. The couple is very lenient with their children and makes no comments if Alexandra chews loudly or if Joakim talks with his mouth full. They believe that these are minor things that are not very important.

As soon as the family is done eating, Joakim disappears into his bedroom and shuts the door. Peter and Renata clear the table together and carefully store the leftovers. Peter will probably take some for lunch on Monday next week. It is a good way to save some money, and most of his colleagues usually eat leftovers at work instead of going out for lunch. Peter washes the dishes, while Renata begins to prepare a Friday night dessert that the family will eat while watching a movie on TV.

Renata wants to try a new recipe for raspberry pie. Quark is the main ingredient, and it has become very trendy to replace other dairy products such as cream and sour cream with it. Renata puts four cups of quark and half a pound of raspberries into a blender. She adds two tablespoons of Fairtrade organic cane sugar and blends the ingredients well. She then crushes 15 digestive cookies, blends them with three tablespoons soft butter, and spreads the mixture in a pie mold. Renata pours the quark and raspberry mousse on top of the pie bottom and puts the dessert in the refrigerator for about 30 minutes so that it will set a bit. Sometimes the family likes to add fresh berries on top of the pie, but berry season is over, and the only fresh berries available are imported from outside Europe.

While the raspberry pie is setting, Peter makes coffee. He boils some water and pours it into regular coffee mugs. He places a jar of instant coffee and a couple of teaspoons on the table. He usually likes to drink his coffee black, but his wife likes a bit of milk in hers. Thus, Peter puts a carton of organic low-fat milk on the table. Alexandra has gone back to the couch to read her book. Renata and Peter sit in silence for a while, sipping their coffee. Life is stressful in the big city, and a few quiet moments are worth everything. One of the cats hops on to the table, and the couple takes it as a sign that it is time to eat dessert and finally watch a movie.

Vegetarian Chickpea Stew Inspired by India

1 handful fresh cilantro, chopped

4 pounds tomatoes, chopped

2 cloves garlic, chopped

1 large onion, chopped

1 daikon radish, peeled and cut into thin strips

1 yellow bell pepper, chopped

½ red bell pepper, chopped

2 cups cooked chickpeas

1 bag (about 7 ounces) fresh baby spinach

1 red chili pepper, sliced into thin slices

fresh ginger, about 2 inches, peeled and finely chopped

2 tablespoons organic coconut oil

2 teaspoons turmeric

1 butternut squash, peeled and cut into 1-inch squares

Sea salt

1 romaine lettuce, shredded

½ red bell pepper, cut into strips

¼ cucumber, sliced

1 tablespoon lemon juice

1 tablespoon olive oil

Sea salt

4 portions brown rice

1. Heat the coconut oil in a large pan. Sauté the onion, garlic, and ginger until the onion is translucent, about 5 minutes. Stir often.
2. Add the tomatoes, daikon radish, yellow bell pepper, red bell pepper, red chili pepper, and butternut squash and stir well. Season with 2 teaspoons sea salt. Cover with lid, lower heat to medium, and let simmer for 20 minutes. Stir occasionally.
3. In a separate pan, boil rice according to instructions on package, but add turmeric to give the rice an Indian touch.

4. Rinse, dry, and tear romaine lettuce leaves. Put in a bowl, and sprinkle with lemon juice, olive oil, and salt.
5. Stir the chickpea stew and season with salt if needed. Serve with brown rice and salad.

FURTHER READING

Albala, K. *Food Cultures of the World Encyclopedia,* Vol 4. Santa Barbara, CA: ABC-CLIO, 2011.

Notaker, H. *Food Culture in Scandinavia.* Westport, CT: Greenwood, 2009.

Porterfield, J. *Sweden: A Primary Source Cultural Guide.* New York: Rosen Publishing Group, 2004.

Turkey

Aylin Öney Tan

Turkey is a country at the crossroads of many cultures with an ever-changing dynamic young population. It is not easy to pick a standard family to represent all, especially if one considers that the country is like a bridge connecting Asia to Europe, flanked by Iran on the east and Greece on the west. Even the regional differences and the seasons will pretty much alter what is on the table, not to mention the social background of that particular family. A rural countryside table might still be a low table on the ground with simple fare shared from central serving dishes eaten with spoons or wrapped in flat bread with no individual servings. However, in cities and towns, people have dining furniture as a main feature of the house; actually the life of a typical housewife revolves around the dining table and the kitchen. Religion does not really affect what is served on the table, but alcohol is nonexistent among devout Muslim families, which is actually a majority. Even if

A Turkish family in Ankara enjoys a weekday dinner after a day of hard work by the parents at the hospital and the boy at school. Everything on the table is home-cooked from scratch, and all ingredients are seasonal. The leftovers will probably extend to the next night's dinner. (Courtesy of Aylin Öney Tan)

the men have drinks outside home, drinking it is not generally a family thing except in bigger towns or coastal regions. Pork is not on the menu either; though it is not legally prohibited, it has never been a common food in this region even for non-Muslim communities.

Food to be put on the table is almost always prepared at home from scratch. Vegetables, salad greens, and fruits are often bought from weekly neighborhood markets or sometimes supermarkets in big towns and cities. The neighborhood markets are held on a certain day of the week, and besides vegetables and fruits, many items such as cheese and olives, household items such as kitchen utensils, and even clothing are available. Usually the market day is the day out for women, so simpler cooking is done at home. Canned products are not much used except for the wide use of canned tomato and pepper paste, which seems to appear in most dishes. In a typical family, whether the mother is working or not, the cooking is done by her, sometimes with the help of daughters. In extended big families, it would be all the women in the house who take care of the cooking; in cities, people tend to hire home help for cleaning, ironing, and cooking. It can be said that cooking at home is still confined to women, though men take pride in their open-air grilling skills, which is pretty much the same all over the world since the time of hunters and gatherers! The housewife also often buys the food, though men can take care of some special purchases such as meat and special sweets, including the much-loved *baklava*. Classically, in Turkey the women are the nurturing fertility goddesses, and the men are providers of the sustenance.

Our example is a bit different from the classical family pattern; it is an example of the changing society, a modern core family living in the city, with both parents holding university degrees and holding regular jobs. Uğur and Tuncay Özçelik are both medical doctors living in Ankara. The wife Uğur (often confused as being a man because Uğur is more of a male name) is a pediatrician working in the Hacettepe University Children's Hospital. Husband Tuncay is an ear-nose-throat doctor working in a private hospital. Neither owns a private practice, as is often the case with doctors, so they have a relatively modest budget compared to most doctors in private practice. Daughter Iraz is studying architecture (she is not in the picture), and son Can is still in middle school.

They recently moved to a bigger three-story house, leaving the 1,300-square-foot flat they used to live in. Irma, a Georgian young lady, works for them as a live-in maid, a new luxury they encountered recently. Irma used to be the caretaker for Uğur's mother, who unfortunately spent her last few years bedridden. After she passed away, Irma was so much a part of the family that they did not want to let her go to another job. Irma has worked with other families in Turkey before, sometimes like a caretaker, sometimes as a nanny; now here with the Özçelik family, she feels in the right place. Her presence has been a great relief for the couple; they no longer have think about preparing all the food for the family of four. Tuncay is also very helpful in the kitchen, being the son of a *meyhane* (a drinking tavern) owner; he surely knows how to cook and really enjoys it.

The dining table is situated at one end of the living room. Usually the dining room is not a separate room in Turkish homes but rather is like an extension of the living room, as in an L-shaped plan, or is just at one end of the long rectangular salon. The living room has comfy chairs, a big central coffee table, lots of plants, and oil paintings on the walls. The TV and music set are also in the living room, so the dining experience is not segregated from the rest of daily life. A cupboard with ornamental glassware backs the dining table. On one side is a piano, once bought for the children, hoping that they'd learn how to play it. Seemingly Can is not very much into music but is into playing basketball, and Iraz can rarely get her head up from the drafting table designing her assignment projects. The family does not have very strict rules for table etiquette regarding the electronic equipment; they most often leave the TV on, but nobody seems to watch unless there is a national soccer game on or some important breaking news. No one brings a tablet or laptop to the table, of course. Keeping away from games seems to be a problem for Can, and Iraz has an urge to check her iPhone now and then, but their habit is not up to an incurable addiction level, as is the case with many youngsters. Actually, in Turkey no one ever turns their cell phones off during dinner, so there is no such rule in this home either.

All the cutlery and table settings are the same that one would find in any contemporary Western country: individual plates and cutlery, normal drinking glasses, special *rakı* glasses if *rakı* is to be drunk, and wineglasses if wine is to be served. The 24-piece table set the family uses daily is not an elaborate, expensive one. Silver cutlery and fine porcelain are reserved for special occasions. Nowadays fancy cutlery does not even seem to be necessary, as most gatherings are casual rather than formal sit-down dinners. However, even if not a fine embroidered one, there is usually a table cover, not place mats. Besides salt and pepper, they have their two favorite spices on the table: sumac and crushed red pepper flakes. The breadbasket is full of sliced whole bread set aside together with a big jug of still spring water. The bread is bought on a daily basis, and spring water is delivered to homes in five-gallon plastic containers by the supplier company. The family is quite health conscious, so sugar-laden soft drinks are not consumed, but sometimes fruit juices or *ayran* is served, depending on the food. Turkey is a big producer of all kinds of fruit juices, the most popular being the sour cherry juice, followed by apricot and peach juices. *Ayran,* salty diluted yogurt, is the most beloved Turkish nonalcoholic drink. Apart from that, water is the usual drink, followed usually by freshly brewed black tea after meals. Turkish coffee is more of a morning thing or is taken a few times in between meals to enjoy a break from work. The adults in the family usually do not drink alcoholic beverages on a daily basis, but sometimes, usually on Saturday night, they have some wine or *rakı,* an anise-flavored grape spirit that is the ubiquitous Turkish national drink. Now and then, based on the type of food in a meal, Tuncay opts for a beer, usually one of the national blond lagers. However, if friends are in for a dinner, there are usually abundant drinks to be shared, sometimes white and red wine, *rakı,* and beer to fit everyone's preference.

Tonight the table is a bit more elaborate than a normal weekday supper, maybe more like a Friday or Saturday dinner. The family tends to take more time preparing the table on those nights, as there is no hard working day ahead. There is also the possibility of friends popping in, so better to have plenty than too little to share.

As a first course there is a range of cold appetizer olive oil dishes called generically *zeytinyağlı*. This category of dishes in Turkish cuisine needs to be explained. *Zeytinyağlı* simply translates as "with olive oil" and refers to any vegetable dish cooked with olive oil without any meat, poultry, fish, or dairy. The vegetables are sautéed with onions and braised until the cooking liquid is totally reduced. There is always a touch of sugar added to bring out the flavor of the vegetable and sometimes a handful of rice to absorb the cooking juices. Just to note, in this fashion winter and spring vegetables such as leek, celeriac, Jerusalem artichokes, artichokes, peas, and fava beans are seldom cooked with tomatoes. These olive oil dishes are not eaten as a main course but rather as a cold starter, or *meze*. However, in the hot summer months, they can easily substitute for a light lunch. In the past *meze* was consumed after the meat course like a refreshing light last course before the dessert, but this habit is now long forgotten. On today's dinner table, the table is stretched by a few of the most popular olive oil dishes, namely *zeytinyağlı fasulye* (green beans with olive oil), *zeytinyağlı barbunya* (borlotti beans with tomato and olive oil), *zeytinyağlı enginar* (artichoke bottoms with peas, carrots, potatoes, and olive oil); and finally the ubiquitous good old *zeytinyağlı yaprak sarma* or *yalancı dolma* (stuffed vine leaves with rice filling). The latter has a sweetish note flavored with Christmas spices, such as cinnamon and allspice, and also includes dried currants and pine nuts. These dishes are also regarded as typical *meze* dishes; that is, an array of small plates accompanying *rakı*. Seeing this, Tuncay is tempted to have a glass of *rakı* to start with, while Uğur goes for red wine made from local grapes, a blend of Öküzgözü and Boğazkere varieties.

Tonight's main dish is *karnıyarık*, served together with *pilav* (buttery rice pilaf) and *cacık* (cold cucumber-yogurt soup). *Karnıyarık* can be translated as "split belly"; it is longitudinally slit and twice cooked (fried and braised/baked) eggplant with a sautéed minced meat, tomato, and pepper filling. The combination of

Courses

The procession of courses, from appetizers to salad or soup to main course to dessert, was invented in European restaurants in the 18th and 19th centuries. To some extent the home meal replicates this basic structure, but it is by no means universal. Many cultures intersperse sweet dishes among the savory. In many there is no such thing as a course; everything comes out together, and diners are free to choose whatever they like in whatever order they please. Ostensibly the logic of courses is to move from lighter-tasting dishes to heavier ones so the palate doesn't tire, but this is rarely the way it plays out in an actual meal, as the appetizers might be the most fully flavored dishes.

karnıyarık-pilav-cacık is almost like a cliché in Turkish cuisine. This trio is a typical lunch or dinner menu, almost always followed by some cool watermelon slices in summer. Normally all eggplant dishes were once confined to summer months only, but with the advance of greenhouse agriculture in the southern province of Antalya, nowadays eggplants, tomatoes, green peppers, and many other typically summer produce is available throughout the year. *Pilav* is made with short-grain rice with plain water (or sometimes chicken stock) and butter. *Cacık* can be defined as a minty-garlicky cucumber-yogurt soupy salad served like a side salad. The cucumber is diced finely and mixed with diluted salted yogurt flavored with crushed dried mint and a little minced garlic. A drizzle of cold-pressed olive oil adds a final touch and is the most refreshing thing on Earth on a hot summer day. It is individually served in bowls, eaten with a tablespoon. When *cacık* is on the table there is no need for a salad, but tonight there is a big bowl of mixed salad as well: some torn romaine lettuce leaves, shredded carrots and red cabbage, and chopped spring onions and parsley garnished with pomegranate seeds and dressed with just salt, lemon juice, and extra virgin olive oil.

The dessert is *irmik helvası*, a simple semolina halvah sprinkled with cinnamon and made by sautéing semolina in butter and steeping in a syrup of milk and sugar. The result is grainy and tasty. There are also slices of watermelon for a refreshing finish and as a lighter alternative to the dessert.

There is no definitive order on who is served first, but generally it is the mother who makes the first service, portioning the food equally but always reserving some for second helpings. For the rest of the service, self-service is the norm; usually if one reaches out for more food from the serving plate, he or she passes it around so everyone can take another spoonful or two. However, when there are guests, serving the guests, urging them to have more and more food, and insisting repetitively is like a national sport for hosts in Turkey.

Toward the end of the dinner, Can shows signs of having had too much food and is restless to go back to his room. He asks permission to leave, mentioning all the homework he has to finish as an excuse. Actually that is accepted as normal, as kids in Turkey go through a very strenuous education system, with the stress of university entrance exams starting already in middle school. On the way to his room, Can takes his dirty dishes to the kitchen; the rest of the table is cleared by the parents and Irma together. If there were guests, they too would offer help, again insistently, as if like revenge for their hosts' repeated offers of more and more food.

Irma puts the dishes into the dishwasher, and all the leftovers are transferred into smaller containers to be eaten later. It is a fact that wasting food is like a taboo and is considered sinful, so even if there is no religious motivation, people in general are careful not to throw away edible food but instead give it to pets or even to wandering street dogs and cats. Even the stale breadcrumbs are often crumbled to be put on top of walls for birds to pick up.

The kitchen is quite roomy, fully equipped with a double-door big fridge complete with two freezer sections, a four-burner gas stove, an electric turbo convention oven, a microwave, and several kitchen appliances including a food processor or "robot," a Turkish coffee machine, a *friteuse,* and a yogurt machine as well as usual items such as a kettle, a toaster, and so forth. In addition to a toaster, there is a sandwich toaster for making grilled cheese sandwiches. Even if there is no ready-made food available (which is never the case) or if one is too lazy to re-heat and serve a dish, one can pop up a grilled cheese sandwich in an instant, which is what the children do when studying for exams. Over the weekend they enjoy giving barbecue parties in the garden; and from buying the meat and the booze to the actual grilling, this seems to be a man's job. Like elsewhere in the world, men never give up the hunter's role and are keen to grill the meat. In reality, though, most of the prep and all of the cleanup is done by women. These weekend gatherings are quite popular, and getting together for a long breakfast is also very common; friends take the place of families in urban families.

Karnıyarık (Split-Belly Eggplants with Meat Filling)

6–8 Japanese eggplants

1 cup oil for frying

Salt and sugar to sprinkle

For the filling:

2 large onions, finely chopped

3 tablespoons butter or oil

1 pound lean ground meat

4–6 ripe tomatoes, peeled and chopped

1 tablespoon tomato paste diluted in ½ cup water

1 handful flat-leaf parsley, finely chopped

1 teaspoon salt

½ teaspoon black pepper

1 cup water

For the garnish:

1 tomato sliced into 6–8 wedges

3–4 long green chili peppers, sliced longitudinally

1 handful flat-leaf parsley, finely chopped

1. Peel the eggplants in lengthwise alternate strips. Cut the stems off.
2. Heat the oil in a pan and shallow-fry whole eggplants until golden brown. Drain on paper towels.
3. Slit open eggplants lengthways not quite to the ends so that they remain intact. Sprinkle inside of each eggplant with a pinch of both salt and sugar.
4. To prepare the filling, fry onions in butter or oil until slightly browned; add the minced meat. Sauté the meat until it absorbs its own juices.
5. Add the chopped tomatoes, the diluted tomato paste, salt, and pepper.

6. Cook covered about 10–15 minutes. Add the parsley.
7. Arrange eggplants split side up in a large, shallow pan or oven-proof dish. Stuff the filling into the slits, making each eggplant resemble a boat. Garnish each eggplant with tomato wedges and green chili peppers and sprinkle with parsley. Pour water on the bottom of the pan. Either cook on the stove, covered for 40 minutes, or bake covered loosely with foil in a moderate oven for about 30 minutes. Serve with buttered rice *pilav* and *cacık*.

FURTHER READING

Peterson, Joan, and David Peterson. *Eat Smart in Turkey.* Madison, WI: Gingko, 1996.

Tan, Aylin Öney. "Turkey." In *Food Cultures of the World Encyclopedia,* Vol. 1, edited by Ken Albala, 305–306. Santa Barbara, CA: ABC-CLIO, 2011.

Uganda

Diana Caley

"YOU ARE MOST WELCOME" FOR LUNCH IN KAMPALA

"*Tugende*," Agnes calls, "come and we will show you how to press the water from the *matooke* now because it is halfway cooked." She invites Diana into a dimly lit hallway where Rose, her mother, is bent at the waist peering into a massive aluminum pot. "You are most welcome, *mzungu*," Rose sings, drawing my attention to a steaming bundle of green bananas. The starchy staple is a fixture of Ugandan and other tropical East African cuisines. Rose, the matriarch of the Mukaandi family, explains the importance of hand-smashing the individual banana "fingers" halfway through the steaming process in order to get the right consistency. Like many home cooks here, Rose uses the traditional method of steaming *matooke* in banana leaves even though plastic bags are a cheap, convenient alternative. After peeling back the top layer of

The kitchen and living room fall silent as the Mukaandi family finishes eating lunch, the main meal of the day in Uganda. (Courtesy of Diana Caley)

leaves, Rose plunges her bare hands into the steaming pot and carefully macerates the bananas into a starchy mass. "*Thick skin!*" she laughs, holding up her hands.

It is almost noon, and although the *matooke* pot has been perfuming the house with fragrant steam for over half an hour, Rose and her daughters have been preparing for lunch since early morning. Like many urban dwellers in Uganda, the Mukaandis shop for food each day at the local open-air market. Josephine, the family's second-oldest daughter, purchased everything for today's meal: massive purple-fleshed yams, white cassava with a thick brown skin, a small sack of polished white rice, a giant stalk of green bananas, chunks of beef on the bone, a whole dried fish, a small baggie of raw peanut paste, a handful of local greens (*dodo*); and a basket of tomatoes, onions, green bell peppers, and carrots.

Though the Mukaandis generally consider themselves to be Kampala natives now, Peter, the head of the household, fondly remembers growing up in a small village in western Uganda. "There was always something to do!" he recalls, pointing out rows of tall cassava plants and banana trees in the background of a treasured family photograph. The capital of Uganda and the country's largest metropolitan area, Kampala is rapidly urbanizing as more and more people abandon labor-intensive farming in search of work in the city. Making ends meet in Kampala isn't easy, however, and 6 out of 10 families here live in slums that lack basic necessities such as running water, electricity, and even toilets.

Like their parents, Agnes and her six brothers and sisters are busy with jobs and children of their own, so family meals always involve a rotating cast of characters. With the exception of holiday vacations, the young children eat midday meals at school, and the older Mukaandi sons and daughters typically eat with their own families or at work. Agnes discloses that she comes by only once or twice a month now that she is married, so she is excited for the opportunity to catch up on family gossip with her mom and sister in the kitchen. When Diana had first arrived earlier in the day, the three were laughing and trading stories in rapid-fire English and Luganda, so Diana instantly felt like an interloper intruding on intimate family time. When she admitted this to Agnes she kindly laughed, "Sister, you are most welcome." Her heartfelt response perfectly epitomizes the Ugandan spirit: everyone, even a relative stranger, is welcome not only at the proverbial table but also into the unadorned areas of the home where everyday tasks such as meal preparation take place.

In larger multiroom homes such as the Mukaandis', ingredients are stored and prepared in a dedicated kitchen, and the actual cooking takes place either outside or in a passageway near the door. Most families here do not have a kitchen, however, so countless streets and alleyways are lined with colorfully dressed women bent at the waist over small charcoal stoves. The Mukaandis, who are relatively well off by local standards, have a kitchen area that is separated from the living room by a thin lace curtain, so the women gather there to chat as ingredients are prepared. Josephine and Agnes adeptly peel tiny onions, tomatoes, and carrots using small kitchen knives, placing the prepared vegetables into large plastic bowls on the floor as they work. There are no chopping blocks, cutting boards, or large chef knives in sight, since everything is carefully and painstakingly prepared in their hands. The women rinse up with water from large yellow jerry cans, since there is no running water in the house.

Curls of steam rise from a quartet of massive aluminum pots tucked into a small closet like corridor leading to the back door. To crank up the heat on the traditional charcoal stoves, Rose fans glowing wood briquettes with a piece of cardboard long since liberated from the top of a box. Once-turquoise walls are black with soot and blemished with smudges of grease and light gray ash. Rose identifies the contents of each pot: unseasoned white rice, still boiling; a leaf-wrapped bundle of *matooke*; thick raw peanut paste sauce dotted with chunks of dried fish; and bitter *dodo* greens. Lifting back the lid from a large pot of boiling beef stock, Rose carefully drops in two handfuls of finely chopped vegetables. In order to make the beef "sauce" properly, she explains, you must first boil the meat until it is firm and then add the vegetables. In Uganda, the term "sauce" refers to a wide range of dishes from thick legume-based gravies to thin stock-based soups that are served alongside starchy staples such as *matooke*, maize, cassava, yams, potatoes, rice, millet, and sorghum.

As the beef sauce finishes cooking, Josephine unrolls two brightly colored straw mats on the floor of the kitchen, along with a massive grain-storage bag made from woven plastic. Rose sits on the bag, which she has reappropriated as a clever food-and water-resistant alternative to the traditional straw mats. She wipes clean a stack of plastic and ceramic plates and places them haphazardly on the floor around her. A handful of small glass drinking cups materialize from a back room, and Agnes fills each one from a colossal aluminum kettle. "Already boiled," she offers, immediately registering my inadvertent look of concern about the safety of municipal tap water. Since none of the cooking vessels are adorned with handles, Josephine uses a thin towel to retrieve the massive pot of *matooke* and place it directly on the concrete floor next to her mother. Next comes the pot of rice, then the fish in peanut sauce, then the *dodo* greens, then the beef sauce, and then a tray of steamed cassava and yams that had been prepared earlier.

Starchy, bland, and dull yellow in color, the center of today's meal is *matooke*. Ugandans throughout the central and western regions generally prefer *matooke*, but food preferences vary by region (and climate zone), so Ugandans from other areas favor other staples. In the Mukaandi home, a variety of starches comprise the bulk of the midday meal: *matooke* is served alongside purple and white wedges of yam, fibrous wedges of cassava, and white rice. All four are unseasoned and relatively dry, so Rose's sauces add much-needed flavor and moisture to the meal. The thicker of the two sauces, similar in color and texture to soupy refried beans, is made from raw peanut paste mixed with water and pieces of dried fish. The beef sauce is made from industrially produced packets of sodium-saturated Real Beef Flavor and sinewy chunks of meat on the bone. Long-cooked *dodo* greens, similar in bitterness and texture to dandelion, serve as a condiment to cut the richness of the sauces.

As lunchtime arrives, Peter pulls aside the lace curtain and guides his wheel-chair into the kitchen, greeting his wife with a broad smile. Flipping through a local newspaper, he selects several pages and hands these to his daughter, who in turn places them on the ground in front of each family member. Folded in half, the sheets are transformed into a set of place mats that perfectly epitomize Ugandan pragmatism and ingenuity. Similarly, there is little formality or ceremony to signal the start of the meal. Rose begins by preparing a Tupperware container of food for her middle son, who is at work. (She later brings the meal to him on her way out of the house.) Josephine uses a pliant plastic soup bowl as a serving utensil to carve up and maneuver portions of *matooke* onto each large plate. Adults receive a piece of *matooke* about the size and shape of a pair of hands pressed loosely together in prayer. Rose adds a fist-sized spoonful of rice and wedges of yam and cassava to each plate. Joseph, the only young child present, receives a full portion of rice and yam but no *matooke* or cassava. (Children, they explain, cannot eat such firm, dry foods.) Rose portions out generous servings of sauce into small soup bowls and places these in front of each person. Presumably in an effort to reduce postmeal cleanup, she serves the sauces directly onto the plates of her family members. In keeping with local custom and hospitality, Diana is presented with her meal first, followed by Peter and then the children.

Rose finishes preparing her plate last, and by then the other family members have commenced eating. Like the use of newspaper place mats, dining etiquette in Uganda is guided by practicality: you eat when your plate arrives so that your food is hot, and there are few rules when it comes to mealtime manners. The family talks freely to each other over the sound of a tiny television that fills the empty living room with familiar baselines and drumbeats characteristic of East African popular music. Peter takes a short phone call at the beginning of the meal. There is neither pomp nor circumstance when dining at home in Kampala, so individuals can come and go during meals, sometimes lingering to catch up on family news and other times dashing back to busy lives.

Efficiency and adaptability also seem to characterize feeding practices for the young. Babies are fed breast milk or formula, and once they are old enough to eat solid food, young children receive primarily the same foods as adult family members. Children tend to eat sweeter and softer foods such as fried breads, buns, cakes, yams, orange-flesh sweet potatoes, and rice, while firm and dry staples such as cassava, *matooke*, and white-flesh sweet potatoes are reserved for adults. Specially prepared or industrially processed baby foods are rarities even among wealthier Ugandan households, which embrace Western tastes and foods.

In addition to being highly practical and utilitarian, many food-related practices in Uganda are also egalitarian, as is the case with certain aspects of Ugandan society. Both young boys and girls are expected to perform well in school and to help with household tasks such as fetching water and cleaning up after meals. Typically all family members—regardless of gender, employment status, or household position—receive approximately equal portions of food. When resources are scarce,

Eating with Hands

In many places around the world, hands are the preferred way to get food from plate to mouth, as it was in Europe before the 16th century. There is definitely a sensual appeal of directly bringing food to the mouth without the interference of cold metal utensils. In most settings one must only use the right hand, since the left is reserved for matters of personal hygiene. Thereafter customs differ widely. In some places such as India, only the fingertips are to scoop up food, or a piece of flat bread is used for this purpose. In other places a big handful is perfectly acceptable or perhaps, as in Africa, a big ball of *fufu* made from grain to scoop up the food with the hand. In many places people eat off of a communal plate or out of one big bowl as well, which in many respects seems closer and more sociable than everyone getting a separate private plate. Although eating with hands seems to be increasingly common in the West where hamburgers, pizza, and portable food proliferate, there are some countries where it is strictly off limits, as in Chile.

everyone eats less (or else parents and grandparents reduce their portions so youngsters have enough). Though many families will present nonfamily guests with utensils, when dining at home most Ugandans—from babies to grandparents—eat with their hands. (Agnes once justified her preference for eating with her fingers by holding up a sauce-laden chunk of cassava and stating simply, "It's more satisfying when you eat like this.") It is also the task of the youngest teenage or preteen household member, regardless of gender, to present a small basin and carafe of water to each family member and guest in order to wash up prior to a mealtime. Food sharing and borrowing are also widely accepted in Uganda particularly in urban slums, where people recognize that hard times can befall anyone at any time. Perhaps because poverty is so entrenched and so pervasive, Ugandans tend to be exceptionally empathetic and hospitable, especially when it comes to sharing food.

Other aspects of Ugandan food practices and norms are distinctly hierarchical and gender biased. Earlier in the day, Rose had laughed when Diana inquired as to whether any men she knew could properly prepare *matooke*. The idea that an adult male, aside from street food vendors and restaurant cooks, could (or, more accurately, *would*) cook any kind of proper meal seemed preposterous. Meal budgeting, planning, shopping, and preparation all fall distinctly within the sphere of female responsibility. Young men in Kampala who are unmarried and living on their own tend to patronize street vendors and cheap restaurants for most or all of their meals. Unmarried women, on the other hand, typically remain at home and contribute to meal preparation and other domestic tasks until they wed or attend school out of town. Uganda's adherence to traditional gender roles seems to be static, since many men and women view their respective positions with apathy and perhaps even complacency. Men come out ahead in the trade-off of responsibility and power: while they may feel a societal pressure to be providers, they also enjoy decision-making power within the home. Most women expect to be taken care of by men in their lives but are also obligated to perform myriad domestic and maternal responsibilities without complaint. While children of both sexes are required to perform certain domestic tasks, this equitable distribution of labor diminishes with adolescence. Today there are huge gender disparities in school enrollment, for example, particularly in rural areas where girls are forced to drop out in order to share the incredible burdens of domestic labor with their mothers and sisters.

As lunch in the Mukaandi house comes to an end, the room falls silent as everyone scrapes up last smudges of sauce from their plates. Josephine gathers up the constellation of dishes from the floor and carefully separates uneaten chunks of cassava, yam, and *matooke* from fish bones and smashed bits of food. The scraps will become chicken feed, and intact leftovers will be kept until supper. Diana asks the two daughters if they ever get tired of eating the same thing for lunch and dinner or of eating the same foods over and over. "Nope!" they chime in unison. One of the most remarkable aspects of food and eating culture here is a general aversion to trying varied, new, or exotic foods. Even in relatively cosmopolitan cities such as Kampala, Ugandans tend to stick to what is referred to as "local food," or the traditional diet of grains, tubers, and bananas garnished with vegetable-, legume-, or meat-based sauces. Street foods and restaurant foods—from grilled meats and grasshoppers to samosas and chapatti—are also considered local and therefore safe to eat (despite the decidedly Indian origin of the latter two examples).

Encircled by myriad pots and dishes, the lady of the house portions out servings of dried fish in peanut sauce. (Courtesy of Diana Caley)

Today Kampala boasts dozens of "international" restaurants as well as those with slapdash combinations of various global cuisines. (Kampala's most popular pizza chain also serves a smattering of Thai and Indian dishes.) Kampala residents also welcomed the opening of the country's first Kentucky Fried Chicken in December 2013. One might interpret the growing number and popularity of such restaurants as signs that food tastes and preferences are quickly changing here. In reality, most "international" and Western food establishments cater almost exclusively to small but growing subpopulations of expatriates, immigrants, elite locals, and young university students (who are generally more adventurous eaters). And though many home cooks are slowly adopting various time- and labor-saving products and techniques, overt signs of systematic cultural homogenization remain to be seen across the Ugandan food landscape. This country's strong ties to authentic "local" food will likely continue to stem the tide of globalization, at least for a little while.

Steamed *Matooke* (Green Bananas) with Dried Fish in Peanut Sauce and Bitter Greens

The small green bananas used to make authentic *matooke* are not widely available outside of East Africa, so green plantains are a suitable alternative. Banana leaves are used to regulate the moisture of the dish and to impart a distinct flavor, but if these are unavailable a metal or bamboo steamer can be used instead. If using peanut butter instead of raw peanut paste, make sure it does not contain sugar or salt.

Serves 4 to 6

4–5 whole banana leaves (if available)

6–8 green plantains, peeled and quartered

1 medium-sized dried or smoked and dried fish, broken into pieces

2 cups of raw peanut paste or unsalted peanut butter

1 tablespoon vegetable oil

3 cups chopped dandelion greens (or other dark leafy greens)

Salt to taste

1. Remove the stalk and woody rib of each banana leaf and place the stalks and ribs in the bottom of a large pot along with 3 to 4 cups of water. Place 2 banana leaves in the pot crosswise and arrange the plantain pieces on top of the leaves. Place 2 banana leaves in a crisscross pattern on top of the plantains, tucking the edges of each leaf down against the edge of the pot. Heat over medium-high heat until the plantains begin to steam. Lower the heat to low and cook

until banana leaves have turned completely brown, about 30–45 minutes. Check periodically to ensure that a small amount of water remains in the bottom of the pot, adding more if necessary.

2. In the meantime, prepare the fish and peanut sauce. In a small saucepan, cover the fish pieces in water and simmer on low until the fish is soft, about 30 minutes. In a separate saucepan, whisk the peanut paste or peanut butter with 1 cup of warm water. Once the fish is soft, drain and then add to the peanut sauce. Season to taste and set aside.
3. Turn off the heat under the plantains. Carefully pull aside the top layer of banana leaves. Using a potato masher, carefully mash the plantains. Replace the top layer of banana leaves, using a fresh leaf if necessary. Add about 1 cup of water to the bottom of the pan. Steam for an additional 30 minutes on medium-low heat until the plantains are soft (about the consistency of dry mashed potatoes).
4. In the meantime, heat a skillet on medium heat. Add the vegetable oil and chopped greens. Cook over medium-low heat until soft, about 10 minutes, and add water if necessary. Season to taste.
5. Serve the peanut-fish sauce and greens over the mashed plantains.

FURTHER READING

Gonahasa, Jolly. *Taste of Uganda: Recipes for Traditional Dishes.* Kampala: Fountain Books, 2002.

Henson, Erika. *The Food Holiday Uganda.* Atlanta, GA: Echo Media, 2010.

Montgomery, Bertha Vining, and Constance R. Nabwire. *Cooking the East African Way.* Minneapolis, MN: Lerner Publishing Group, 2001.

United States

Ken Albala

Many people believe that family dinner in the United States is a threatened institution. They imagine that it is deeply connected to if not substantially responsible for the breakdown of the American family. They insist that because of hectic schedules (especially for children's activities), long commutes, and a general lack of time, eating dinner together is the first thing sacrificed. Or they claim that even if people eat together, they are distracted by the television, cellular phones, or electronic games. Many of the social ills of the nation are blamed on the demise of the family dinner as a place not only where children learn manners and social skills but also as a regularly scheduled time to communicate, learn about each other's daily activities, and even learn the skills of compromise necessary in a democratic society.

A mother and her sons sit down to a dinner of penne, broccoli, and sausage. (Courtesy of Christine Larson)

Moreover, adding to the difficulty, it seems like no one eats the same foods anymore. There is a special category of children's food, often breaded and fried and laden with sugar—things such as chicken nuggets, tater tots, fish sticks, pizza, hot dogs, and spaghetti. Children's palates have been altered not by giving them bland food but exactly the opposite. It is mostly industrial mass-produced food specially designed to incite them to eat more because it causes a spike in flavor that fades away quickly. It is no wonder, many claim, that there is an obesity epidemic, especially among children. And it is also no wonder that fruits and vegetables are not appealing to young palates; they have no chance compared with flavor-enhanced industrial food. The whole situation is further complicated when adults might go on a weight-loss diet, might be avoiding wheat, or might have become vegetarian. It appears impossible to serve one set of foods that will please everyone.

There is also a general fear that home cooks have become de-skilled because of the proliferation of convenience foods and junk foods. Routine procedures that any housewife could have performed half a century ago are now obsolete. Even if these skills can been seen on TV in cooking shows, no one would think of actually doing them anymore. They are merely watched passively for entertainment value. Or if someone does cook, it is often the husband in the family as a leisure activity or for special occasions, rarely for an ordinary weekday dinner.

This at least is the perception among many Americans, and despite the fact that we have become obsessed with food, we don't actually cook much anymore. Cooking programs are mostly outlandish competitions rather than instructional guides, as in the day of Julia Child. We may read about food in cookbooks and magazines or watch shows about food on TV, but cooking is no longer a routine part of the day. Prepared foods, convenience foods, takeout, and simply eating out all the time have replaced the home-cooked meal, it seems.

Food Deserts: United States

Inner cities and sometimes even rural areas without grocery stores in the United States are described as food deserts. This means that people have little access to fresh fruits and vegetables as well as other nutritious whole foods. They are forced to resort to quick convenience stores, where everything is either packaged or simply junk food. Often fast food is the only other option. The situation is created when retailers either can't afford the high rents in downtown districts or simply imagine that they can't make a profit in low-income areas. Or sometimes a location is so remote or has become depopulated with the loss of farming jobs so that groceries don't have enough customers to stay in business. Subsidizing food outlets and helping small retailers stock more fresh produce have been considered as solutions, but neither has been completely successful.

The reality is actually much more complex. First, the traditional family of 2 heterosexual parents and 2.5 children never really was the statistical norm. Nor can we be very certain that cooking a full meal at home every night was routine in the past. While it is true that most people would rather cut corners and, say, use canned stock rather than make it from scratch, it is not entirely certain that many people in the past could whip up a hollandaise or bake a cake. It is not at all clear that anyone but professionals had complex skills from which they could become de-skilled. The example below will illustrate that the dinner table has not disappeared in the United States. It may have changed, the definition of a family may be slightly different, and the dynamics of the table might be different than in the past. But the family dinner has not yet become extinct.

Meg Carlson is a single divorced mother with twin 9-year-old boys named Alan and Jack who attend school nearby. She is 46 years old, and after many years with a distinguished career in journalism and coauthoring many books, she decided to return to graduate school for a PhD in communications at the University of California in Berkeley. She intends to eventually get a job in academia.

She and her boys live in graduate school housing on campus. The two-level apartment has a narrow, cramped kitchen with little counter space and few cabinets, some of which are too high to reach. There is a step stool in the middle of the cooking space. The washing machine and dryer are also in the kitchen, making for an even more than usually busy work space, and sometimes dishes and cooking utensils end up on top of the dryer. On the counter there is a knife block with several well-sharpened knives and cutting boards stacked out of the way. Meg recently bought an electric sharpener for her knives. She has a Keurig coffee machine, a microwave, and a large white fridge that is usually well stocked during the week. The fridge is really too small for a busy family of three, so they constantly finds themselves rummaging in the fridge and moving out milk and other products to get to what they need. The freezer is also too small, since Meg often freezes leftovers and keeps a constant supply of frozen fruit for smoothies as well as different frozen desserts for each family member: a few times a month there's a freezer avalanche, with ice cream bars cascading to the floor.

They have only been in the space a few months, so she is still decorating, and a few interesting items have begun to adorn the walls. She recently bought a monoprint from a local art fair for the kitchen. There is also a sign that says "The glass is always full, half water and half air," which reflects her generally optimistic demeanor. Pictures and school notices naturally grace the refrigerator, as they do in most American households. In some respects the fridge is the center of the American household, vying for attention with the TV and increasingly nowadays with the computer. Another sign on the wall shows a cheeky 1950s housewife and reads "The house was clean yesterday. Sorry you missed it!" A giant calendar dominates one wall so the family can keep track of events. Various sheets listing household rules and chore schedules surround the calendar.

Since the kids spend most weekends with their father, meals are usually fit in around homework and other activities during weekdays. The cabinets always contain Wheat Thins, some canned soup, and just a few items that can be put together quickly. Cooking is usually done quickly, though normally from fresh ingredients. While Meg enjoys cooking, especially pizza and bread, she often finds herself strapped for time, being tugged between her demanding schoolwork, including writing a dissertation, and the kids. Dinner is almost always cooked fresh, and she is definitely health conscious, but it is usually fairly quick.

There is a small space for a dining table, where she and the boys spend much of their time doing homework, writing, and playing games. The table is covered with a new cheery tablecloth that Meg bought at World Market, a store that carries international housewares, packaged food, and wine. She would prefer to have the formal dining table that her mother bought her as a present, but it's too big for the space, so it stays in a storage unit. Meg tries her best to keep the dining table clear, but sometimes papers and toys end up there. They usually eat off of stoneware dishes bought from Macy's. The dishes are 15 years old and were a wedding present that she took after the divorce, likewise the silverware. The kids usually set the table, taking turns each time, and they both clear it as well after dinner.

The family doesn't have a dishwasher, so they rotate doing dishes. The boys take turns doing the dinner dishes, everyone washes their own breakfast dishes, and Meg takes care of pots, pans, and other food-prep items. At the table they usually chitchat about their day, or someone gets excited and talks about the latest science or art project. Sometimes Meg will read a book just so their attention is focused at the table. Sometimes there will be music on, but never the TV while they eat.

The adjacent living room space always has some toys around, which she doesn't allow at the table during dinner. Nor does she let the kids play video games or watch TV at that time, though once in a while they will eat in front of the TV as a special treat and sit on the big comfortable couches. Jack tends to get distracted and often wants to wander from the table, so keeping him there is sometimes an effort.

Dinner this weeknight consisted of pork chops that were marinated in Trader Joe's Island Soyaki and then sautéed in a pan. She still cuts up the meat for the boys, who sometimes eat with their hands. Choosing her battles wisely, she has decided that it is more important that they are well fed. Propriety can come later. The broccoli was blanched in salted water, and then a little butter was added afterward. There was also a salad of kale and lettuce dressed with Annie's Goddess dressing. The kids actually weren't that hungry, since they had In And Out burgers with their dad earlier in the day before they were dropped off, but everyone ate whatever they pleased of the food put out. It was more important that they actually sit down and eat together and talk about their day. Lately Jack has been eating nearly twice as much as Alan; Jack is either going through a growth spurt or he's ravenous from all the training he's doing for an upcoming 5K run. So tonight was a little unusual, as neither of them ate a lot.

For tonight's dinner, the vegetables are organic and came from a community-supported agriculture box that arrives twice a month. Meg orders a "no cooking" option, so there is no prep work. The company is Farm Fresh to You, which delivers throughout California and is based northwest of Sacramento. The medium-sized box she orders costs $33 per delivery and might contain mandarin oranges, pink lady and fuji apples, kiwis, carrots, butter lettuce, green onions, bell peppers, and celery. All of these can be eaten raw and out of the hand. She also hopes to get a space in the cooperative gardens adjacent to her townhouse complex where students grow vegetables. Growing food seems like time well spent, but in truth Meg dislikes shopping so much that she does most of her regular shopping online, one of the boons of living in the Bay Area. She says she'll do anything to avoid going to the store.

The delivery service she uses costs about $130 a week and comes from the supermarket Safeway. This particular week she bought apples, pears, blueberries, carrots, broccoli, cauliflower, onions, celery hearts, whole grain spaghetti, a bean soup mix, two jars of grilled marinated artichokes, and two cans of whole plum tomatoes. There is also a package of Mexican Style Four Cheese blend, shredded, as well as Parmesan for pizza and crumbled blue cheese for salads.

Meg ordered ground beef, smoked pork hocks for soup, boneless pork loin chops, and Italian sausages. As usual, she always buys a variety of yogurts, which they all eat for breakfast. They especially like fruit smoothies, which she also serves to the kids' friends when they come over. She uses a Ninja blender because it was highly rated in Consumer Reports, and she can't imagine spending several hundred dollars for the trendy high-end blender all her friends have. She's gotten a reputation for being the smoothie lady, and once in a while neighbors' children will stop by asking for a one.

In this week's order there were also Wheat Thins as usual and Cheddar Gold Fish Crackers, which the boys like for lunch. She ordered Capri Sun 25 percent reduced-sugar lemonade juice pouches, which they also like for lunch. The delivery also included flour tortillas, a jar of basil leaves, and craisins, which are sweetened cranberries.

Finally, there are organic vanilla ice cream sandwiches and Weight Watchers Giant Fudge Ice Cream Bars. She eats one almost every night. This past week she decided to go on a Weight Watchers diet, since she gained five pounds over the holidays and is very careful about her lithe figure. She has tried many diets in the past, usually with success. She also exercises about three times a week, usually running three miles or so.

From the shopping list, it is clear that Meg does actually cook the majority of their meals from raw ingredients, and there is little in the way of convenience foods or instant meals, frozen or canned. Putting these ingredients together without fuss does take a little time, but it is worth the effort in the interest of health, she firmly believes. It is rarely complicated cooking, but it is cooking nonetheless. For special occasions or parties she might roast a pork loin, and she uses a meat thermometer to gauge the exact cooking temperature. She really likes tri-tip, which is an unusual cut of beef common in California though less so elsewhere in the United States. She would normally throw steaks on the barbecue, though they don't have one at this rental unit. She loves to entertain, even in her cramped space (the apartment is only 850 square feet), and she invites friends over to dinner at least twice a week. Spring and summer make for easier entertaining because of her outdoor patio, overlooking a large pretty communal courtyard. She's planning to buy a grill (even though they're not permitted in her student housing) so she can make her favorite grilled vegetables and salmon wrapped in foil with ginger and lemon.

Meg has also perfected a no-knead bread from the *New York Times* for which, incidentally, she has written many articles on health, finance, and a range of topics. The bread uses a little yeast and gets a long rise on the countertop, sometimes overnight. It is then placed in a preheated iron Dutch oven, which gives it a lovely crust and big irregular holes. She often bakes for parties or important occasions if she has the time. Recently Jack has been working on a science project for school to figure out the effect of kneading on bread, and as it turns out it doesn't actually make much of a difference. Kneaded bread looks a little smoother and has regular-sized holes, but the unkneaded loaf looks more rustic and appealing. In any case, there is sometimes fresh bread on the table, and everyone in the family agrees that a pizza is just about as good as food gets, so Meg makes the dough from scratch.

For most meals, Jack drinks orange juice or sparkling water with juice; Alan drinks milk; and Meg drinks water or sparkling water with lemon. She has a seltzer machine that makes really good sparkling water. A couple of nights a week she might have a glass of wine. She also has a weakness for good port but rarely keeps it on hand.

She tries to get the boys involved in cooking, but right now that mostly involves having them pack their own lunches occasionally. She helps them make a week's worth of peanut butter and jelly sandwiches, and she keeps a bin full of lunch snacks (jerky, goldfish crackers, juice boxes) in a cupboard. She'll slice apples or another fruit and squeeze lemon on them in the morning and usually include carrots or celery in their lunches as well. Making lunches takes a valuable 10–15 minutes at night when everyone is tired, but it makes the mornings smoother. On Thursdays, the boys buy pizza for lunch at school. Occasionally they'll buy lunch on other days, especially if corn dogs are on the menu.

This family and their dinner could not in any way be said to represent the average American household, and of course one example statistically proves nothing about the viability of the family dinner. But it does highlight many current trends and perhaps ways in which the practice of eating together will change in the coming years. Although the family itself may transform in unexpected ways and the way people eat certainly will change, most likely toward convenience foods and prepared foods, there are small elements of this vignette that are encouraging. People do still like to cook, even though their time is increasingly eaten up by other activities. It is still an activity that can generate personal value and give meaning to expending labor for the benefit of others. Most important, eating dinner together can still be a venue for meaningful communication and social exchange whereby we learn to cooperate. It is still the place where we tell stories and practice expressing ourselves as members of a wider community, where we learn both civility and how to engage with our fellow beings. If there is any promise in the future of our civilization, it is manifest in the fact that we still can muster the energy to break bread and share with others around the dinner table.

Penne with Broccoli and Sausage

1 box whole wheat penne	3 tablespoons oil
Water to boil	2–3 cloves garlic, minced
2 heads of broccoli, florets separated from stalk	1 pound chicken sausage, Italian flavored, chopped

1. Boil penne it in salted water until almost but not quite done.
2. Blanch broccoli florets in boiling water and drain.
3. In a big saucepan, heat olive oil.
4. Add garlic.
5. Then add blanched broccoli.
6. Add chicken sausage and brown lightly.
7. Next add a little of the pasta water and simmer it all together for a few minutes.
8. Then add the almost-done penne (use a slotted spoon; do not drain or rinse).
9. Cook on the stove top a few minutes until the pasta is cooked through but still slightly al dente. Add salt and pepper to taste. Add a lot of shredded Parmesan before serving.

FURTHER READING

Biltekoff, Charlotte. *Eating Right in America: The Cultural Politics of Food and Health.* Durham, NC: Duke University Press, 2013.

Brewer, Priscilla J. *From Fireplace to Cookstove: Technology and the Domestic Ideal in America.* Syracuse, NY: Syracuse University Press, 2000.

Carroll, Abigail. *Three Squares: The Invention of the American Meal.* New York: Basic Books, 2013.

Cromley, Elizabeth Collins. *The Food Axis: Cooking, Eating and the Architecture of American Houses.* Charlottesville: University of Virginia Press, 2010.

Flammang, Janet. *The Taste for Civilization.* Urbana: University of Illinois Press, 2009.

Freeman, June. *The Making of the Modern Kitchen: A Cultural History.* New York: Berg, 2004.

Gabbaccia, Donna R. *We Are What We Eat: Ethnic Food and the Making of Americans.* Cambridge, MA: Harvard University Press, 1998.

Levenstein, Harvey. *Paradox of Plenty: A Social History of Eating in Modern America.* New York: Oxford University Press, 1993.

Mudry, Jessica. *Measured Meals: Nutrition in America*. Albany: State University of New York, 2009.

Nestle, Marion. *Food Politics: How the Food Industry Influences Nutrition and Health*. Berkeley: University of California Press, 2007.

Schenone, Laura. *A Thousand Years over a Hot Stove: A History of American Women Told through Food, Recipes and Remembrances*. New York: Norton, 2003.

Shapiro, Laura. *Something from the Oven: Reinventing Dinner in 1950s America*. New York: Viking, 2004.

Visser, Margaret. *The Rituals of Dinner: The Origins, Evolution, Eccentricities, and Meaning of Table Manners*. New York: Harper Perennial, 1991.

Recipe Index

Below is a listing of the recipes that appear in *At the Table*.

Index

About the Editor and Contributors

Ken Albala is professor of history at the University of the Pacific and director of the Food Studies MA program in San Francisco. He has authored or edited 23 books on food, including *Eating Right in the Renaissance; Food in Early Modern Europe; Cooking in Europe, 1250–1650; The Banquet, Beans* (winner of the 2008 IACP Jane Grigson Award); *Pancake; Grow Food, Cook Food, Share Food;* and *Nuts: A Global History.* He was coeditor of the journal *Food, Culture and Society* and has also coedited *The Business of Food, Human Cuisine, Food and Faith* and edited *A Cultural History of Food: The Renaissance* and *The Routledge International Handbook of Food Studies.* Albala was editor of the Food Cultures around the World series and the four-volume *Food Cultures of the World Encyclopedia* and is now series editor of Rowman and Littlefield Studies in Food and Gastronomy, for which he wrote *Three World Cuisines* (winner of the Gourmand World Cookbook Awards best foreign cuisine book in the world for 2012). He has also coauthored cookbooks, including *The Lost Art of Real Cooking* and *The Lost Arts of Hearth and Home.* His latest works are a *Food History Reader* and a translation of the 16th-century *Livre fort excellent de cuysine.* His course *Food: A Cultural Culinary History* is available on DVD from the Great Courses. Albala has also edited the three-volume *Sage Encyclopedia of Food Issues.* He is now working on a book about noodle soups.

Lara Anderson is senior lecturer in the School of Languages and Linguistics at the University of Melbourne. Dr. Anderson's main research focus is Spanish culinary culture, from the role of gastronomy in Spain's fin de siècle identity formation to Spanish cookery television shows as a site for gender critique. She also has emerging expertise in Australian food culture and has written on food multiculturalism and culinary xenophobia.

Gabriela Villagrán Backman has lived in Sweden for over 20 years and is an independent researcher with a deep passion for food. She contributes regularly to publications that focus on the world's food cultures and is currently working on her next cookbook.

Sally M. Baho is a researcher at the Naval Postgraduate School in Monterey, California, and an aspiring scholar. Her interests include food as it relates to identity, culture, immigrants, diaspora communities, and memory and nostalgia and its dynamic nature in the 21st century. She loves to travel and experience all that life has to offer, especially the food.

Scott Barton is a doctoral candidate in food studies. He has worked for more than 25 years as an executive chef, restaurant and product development consultant, and culinary school teacher. *Ebony* magazine named Barton among of the top 25 African–African American chefs. He is an alumnus of the School for American Chefs. Barton has been a fellow of Instituto Sacatar in Salvador da Bahia, Brazil, and the Tepoztlán Institute for Transnational History of the Americas in Tepoztlán, Mexico, and is a fellow of Fundaçao Cultural Palmares, the Brazilian nongovernmental organization for Afro-Brazilian folkloric cultural heritage practices. His doctoral work is focused on the intersection of secular and sacred cuisine as a marker of ethnic and cultural identity in northeastern Brazil, using documentary film and written text. He has been featured as a chef on BayCafe TV, the *CBS Early Show* segment "Chef on a Shoestring," and the TV Food Network and in the magazines *Gourmet* and *Food Arts*. His recipes are included in the *Jocelyn Diabetes Cookbook*, *The Southern Foodways Community Cookbook*, and Tavis Smiley's *Pass It Down Cookbook*. Barton was recently featured on the PBS program *A Chef's Life*. He currently is an adjunct professor at New York University and a culinary instructor at the Institute for Culinary Education.

Diana Caley is a scholar and practitioner in the field of global food security and international development. She is a PhD candidate in food studies at New York University and holds a BA in international affairs from George Washington University.

Judy Corser is a Vancouver, Canada, novelist with an interest in domestic foodways and household arts. She has a master's degree in food culture and communication from Universita degli studie science gastronomiche in Parma, Italy.

Charlotte De Backer is assistant professor of interpersonal communication in the Department of Communication Studies at the University of Antwerp. Among other topics in the field of interpersonal communication, she studies the impact of media on eating habits and the impact of eating habits on prosocial behavior. In the past few years she has published several articles about eating habits, commensality, and meat reduction in Belgium in international scientific journals.

Dorota Dias-Lewandowska is a lecturer in the Faculty of Enology at Jagiellonian University in Cracow. She holds a PhD in history from the Michel de Montaigne Bordeaux 3 University and Nicolas Copernicus University in Toruń. Dias-Lewandowska's PhD dissertation is titled "Cultural History of French Wine in Poland from the Middle of the Seventeenth Century to the Beginning of the Nineteenth Century." She is a member of the Research Centre for the History and Culture of Food (Polish History Association scientific base) and is involved in the project Old Polish culinary recipes. She also cooperates with the Museum of King Jan III's Palace at Wilanów regarding the history of 17th- and 18th-century cuisine.

Simona Dinu is a former health coach who is passionate about food anthropology and history. At present she works as a small-scale entrepreneur.

Lexi Earl is a PhD researcher at the University of Nottingham. Her research explores the diverse nature of school food experiences, focusing on the ways policies are enacted and taken up within schools. Earl works to rupture understandings of good food and seeks to draw attention to the increasing problem of childhood hunger in the United Kingdom. She works as a pastry chef and blogs at Philosophy and Madeleines.

Melissa Fuster is a food policy and nutrition scholar with an interest in the historical, social, and cultural factors surrounding food selection and consumption. Her community-based research has focused on minority underserved populations in the United States, Central America, and the Spanish Caribbean. Using interdisciplinary approaches and methods, Fuster's research underscores the importance of sociopolitical and cultural factors that affect culinary and nutritional outcomes, with a current emphasis on Cuba and Puerto Rico. She holds a PhD in food policy and applied nutrition from the Tufts University Friedman School of Nutrition Science and Policy.

Jonell Galloway grew up on Wendell Berry and food straight from a backyard Kentucky garden. She is a freelance writer. Galloway attended Le Cordon Bleu and La Varenne cooking schools in Paris, worked for the *GaultMillau* restaurant guide and *CityGuides* in France and Paris, and collaborated on *Le tour du monde en 80 pains/Around the World with 80 Breads* in France, *André Raboud, Sculptures 2002–2009* in Switzerland, *Ma Cuisine Méditerranéenne* in France, and a biography of French chef Pierre Gagnaire. Galloway gives taste awareness workshops and cooking classes and is working on a book, *What to Eat in Venice*.

Alessandra Grasso, MSPH, is currently a U.S. Borlaug Fellow in Global Food Security in Kenya, where she is undertaking research on biodiversity for food and nutrition. She completed her master of science degree in public health with a concentration in international health and human nutrition at the Johns Hopkins Bloomberg School of Public Health in 2015. Before pursing her master's degree, Alessandra completed her bachelor of science degree in nanomedicine engineering at the University of Virginia in 2012 and traveled and worked on farms in Europe for almost a year. Alessandra spent three months in Addis Ababa, Ethiopia, for her master's degree, where she supported endeavors to enhance the capacity of academic institutions to provide quality nutrition education for a more competent health and agriculture workforce to combat malnutrition in Ethiopia. Alessandra quickly fell in love with the Ethiopian landscapes, food, coffee, dance, and culture, and she hopes to return soon for a longer period of time.

Saman Hassibi is a doctoral student in management in the Department of Business and Law at the University of Canterbury, New Zealand. She received her MSc from the Norwegian Hotel School at the University of Stavanger, Norway, where she worked on a project on Norwegian food culture with cooperation from the Norwegian Cookbook Museum. Her doctoral research is on New Zealand cuisine, and her other research interests mainly focus on food studies, food culture, culinary media, and gender studies. She is also interested in the history of food and is currently working on a project on Persian culinary history.

Ursula Heinzelmann, independent scholar and culinary historian, was twice awarded the prestigious Sophie Coe Prize. A trained chef, sommelier, and ex-restaurateur, she works as a freelance wine and food writer and is based in Berlin, Germany. Her most recent work in English is "Beyond Bratwurst: A History of Food in Germany."

Shawn M. Higgins is a doctoral candidate of English at the University of Connecticut, where he specializes in 19th- and 20th-century American literature, American studies, Asian American studies, and comparative ethnic studies. Shawn also teaches English and American studies at Temple University's Japan campus in Tokyo.

Máirtín Mac Con Iomaire is a lecturer in culinary arts in the Dublin Institute of Technology. He is an award-winning chef, food historian, broadcaster, and ballad singer. Iomaire has been a regular contributor at the Oxford Symposium on Food and Cookery. He is chair and cofounder of the biennial Dublin Gastronomy Symposium and coeditor of *"Tickling the Palate": Gastronomy in Irish Literature and Culture* (2014). In 2009 he completed a PhD on the history of Dublin restaurants. Iomaire has authored over 30 peer-reviewed papers, book chapters, and conference papers and currently is forming a cluster of doctoral candidates at the Dublin Institute of Technology to investigate Irish food history and critical success factors for restaurants.

Yael Joffe is a registered dietician in South Africa who specializes in nutrigenomics and functional nutrition. Together with Dr. Ruth DeBusk, Joffe coauthored the book *It's Not Just Your Genes*. Yael obtained her PhD from the University of Cape Town, exploring the genetics and nutrition of obesity in South African women. She is currently an adjunct assistant professor teaching nutrigenomics at Rutgers University and has developed an online translational nutrigenomics training course for all health practitioners.

Judith Klinger is the founder and director of World-Eats.org, an international nonprofit food organization that promotes dialogue and exploration of culinary culture and food policy. She is also a food writer, food organization manager, personal chef, and home cooking activist. Klinger has served on the board of directors and as director of operations for the International Association of Culinary Professionals. She is the creator of Aroma Cucina, a private chef and event service company in the United States and Italy. She is also an award-winning blogger and cookbook author.

Katrina Kollegaeva graduated with an MA in the anthropology of food from the University of London, completing her dissertation on the social and cultural roles of the Ukrainian *salo* (lard). In early 2011 Kollegaeva started a supper club focusing on food from the former Soviet Union and later founded Russian Revels, designers of dining experiences aimed at transforming the image of Russian food and culture in London. Now a long-term Londoner, she was born in Soviet Estonia to a Ukrainian mother and a dad from Crimea.

Annie Levy lives in Wales and writes on cooking and food politics, large and small, at Kitchencounterculture.co.uk.

F. Xavier Medina holds a PhD in social anthropology from the University of Barcelona. He is academic and programs director in the Department of Food Systems, Culture and Society in the School of Health Sciences, Universitat Oberta de Catalunya, Barcelona; director of the UNESCO Chair in Food, Culture and Development; and chair of the European section of the International Commission on the Anthropology of Food and Nutrition.

Jennifer Moran is a lifestyle photographer specializing in food; chefs and kitchens; products; individual, family, and group portraits; and urban, nature, and farm life. She is also a blogger, cook, gardener, illustrator, and crafter.

Amanda Katili Niode is the chair of the Omar Niode Foundation (www.omarni ode.org), a nonprofit organization working to raise awareness about the quality of education and human resources in the fields of agriculture, food, and culinary arts. She is a certified culinary travel professional and also a certified ambassador for Indonesia at the World Food Travel Association.

Katerina Nussdorfer (née Pejovska) is currently finishing her doctorate degree on the topic of food as ethnic identity in contemporary American memoirs of immigrants from Iran, Jordan, China, and Singapore. She has contributed to several conferences, journals, and edited volumes on topics such as street food in Austria and the Balkans, immigrant foodways in Vienna, cooking and technology, and food advertisements in American women/food magazines, etc. Her main interests are Macedonian cuisine, advertising of food, and Austrian culinary traditions during the Habsburg Empire under Franz Joseph I of Austria.

Caroline Nyvang works as a researcher at the Royal Library, Denmark.

Nafsika Papacharalampous is currently a PhD researcher in the anthropology of food at the School of Oriental and African Studies (SOAS), University of London.

She is writing her dissertation on Greek traditional foods and markets, focusing on national identity, memory, *terroir,* and heritage. She is also collecting oral histories in Athens, focusing on food and the economic crisis. Nafsika holds an MA in anthropology of food from the SOAS and an MBA from the Athens University of Economics and Business. She is a food blogger at www.NafsikaCooks.com, where she indulges her passion for both cooking and writing. She has written for the online food market Love Your Larder and is the recipe editor for the SOAS recipe book. Nafsika also cooks professionally for restaurants in London and Athens.

Cristina Potters, born in America, is a writer and blogger living in Morelia, Michoacán. Her blog is the most compelling and well-informed blog about Mexican food and culture to be found on the Internet. Cristina writes weekly about food and drink, art, culture, and travel.

Nanna Rögnvaldardóttir was born in 1957 and brought up on a farm in northern Iceland, where her ancestors have lived for 280 years, and learned food history and traditions from her mother and her extended family. Rögnvaldardóttir later moved to Reykjavík, where she studied history at college, and has worked in the publishing industry for almost 30 years. Her first book on food was published in 1998 and was short-listed for the Icelandic Literary Prize. Since then, she has published almost 20 cookbooks and books on food and food history. In addition, she writes food columns and articles for several magazines and newspapers.

Helen Saberi is a London-based food writer. She married an Afghan and lived in Afghanistan for nine years. Saberi is the author of *Noshe Djan: Afghan Food and Cookery,* first published in 1986. She has regularly attended the Oxford Symposium on Food and Cookery, where she has presented several papers about Afghan food and culture. Her other published books include *Trifle* (coauthored with Alan Davidson), *The Road to Vindaloo: Curry Cooks and Curry Books* (coauthored with David Burnett), and *Tea: A Global History.*

Amir Sayadabdi is a doctoral student in the anthropology of food in the Department of Language, Social and Political Sciences at the University of Canterbury, New Zealand. His geographic specialization is Iran, and his current research focuses on food and national identity of Iranian communities in diaspora. Sayadabdi's other areas of scholarly interest are food in Persian literature, food in Zoroastrianism, and the food history of Iran. He has been writing and translating articles about food for Anthropology and Culture, the official web journal of the Iranian Institute of Anthropology and Culture. Sayadabdi is currently engaged with a project on Persian culinary history.

Colleen Taylor Sen is a Chicago-based food writer and historian specializing in South Asia. She is the author of many articles and six books, including *Curry: A*

Global History; How to Eat in an Indian Restaurant; and *Food Culture in India.* Sen is a regular contributor to the Oxford Food Symposia. She has a BA and an MA from the University of Toronto and a PhD from Columbia University, all in Slavic languages.

Jennifer Shutek received her BA in history with a minor in English from Simon Fraser University and studied Arabic at the Arabic Language Institute in Fez and the Hebrew University of Jerusalem. Her love of food influences her academic interests, which include food semiotics and the importance of food and agriculture in identity construction. She has worked as a coeditor of the Israel/Palestine and Levant pages for *Muftah* and lectured on culinary Orientalism and gastronationalism in Palestine/Israel. Shutek is completing her MPhil in modern Middle Eastern studies at the University of Oxford, where she is researching identity politics in Palestinian/Israeli cookbooks.

Aylin Öney Tan is an architect turned food writer. She is a columnist for the *Hurriyet Daily News* and writes for *Gastro Yemek Külütür* and is a culinary guide-traveler and the leader of Slow Food Ankara.

Ana Tominc is a lecturer in gastronomy on a new MSc gastronomy program at Queen Margaret University, Edinburgh, Scotland. Tominc's background is in social anthropology, cultural studies, and (critical) discourse analysis. She is also book review editor for the *Journal of Language and Politics.*

Karin Vaneker graduated from the AKI Academy of Visual Arts in Enschede, the Netherlands, and later attended Sint-Lukas, Higher Institute for the Arts, in Brussels, Belgium. Since 1999 she has written articles about food for numerous Dutch newspapers and magazines, specializing in the cultural and other histories of ingredients and cuisines. In recent years Vaneker has written books and contributed to several publications and reference works, including the *Encyclopedia of Food Cultures of the World* (ABC-CLIO), *They Eat That?* (ABC-CLIO), *Reimagining Marginalized Foods: Global Processes, Local Places* (University of Arizona Press), *Oxford Encyclopedia of Food and Drink in America* and *Encyclopedia of Food and Agricultural Ethics* (Springer), *Ethnic American Food Today Encyclopedia* (AltaMira), *The Encyclopedia of World Street Food* (ABC-CLIO), and *Food: An Atlas* (UC Berkeley). In 2003, Vaneker started researching edible aroids (taro), a venture that in 2007 resulted in an exhibition in Amsterdam and several presented papers and publications.

Stephen R. Wooten is a sociocultural anthropologist whose research interests include political economy and ecology, local food systems, and expressive culture. Dr. Wooten has been conducting ethnographic field research in Mali since 1992 and has recently begun a study of urban agriculture in Eugene. His research publications include "Colonial Administration and the Ethnography of the Family in the French Soudan" in *Cahiers d'etudes africaines,* "Antelope Headdresses and Champion Farmers: Negotiating Meaning and Identity through the Bamana Ci-wara Complex" in *African Arts,* and "Losing Ground: Gender Relations, Commercial Horticulture and Threats to Local Plant Diversity in Rural Mali" in an edited volume titled *Women and Plants: Gender Relations in Biodiversity Management and Conservation.* His book *The Art of Livelihood: Creating Expressive Agri-Culture in Rural Mali* explores the creativity of rural Bamana people. Dr. Wooten has been at the University of Oregon since 2001.

Chelsie Yount-André is a PhD candidate in cultural and linguistic anthropology in the dual doctoral (*cotutelle*) program at Northwestern University and l'École des Hautes Études en Sciences Sociales in Paris. Her research examines food sharing in Senegalese households in Paris and Dakar to shed light on the role of children in the reproduction and transformation of economic moralities, normative expectations of material obligation and entitlement. Yount-André analyzes everyday verbal and material exchanges to shed light on the ways transnational families negotiate expectations of how one ought to earn, spend, and redistribute resources. Her dissertation illustrates how immigrants reinforce stratification among transnational populations in their attempts to demonstrate integration into French society. Yount-André is a member of the Centre Edgar Morin and has taught at Northwestern University and the School of the Art Institute Chicago.

Willa Zhen is a lecturing instructor in liberal arts at the Culinary Institute of America in Hyde Park, New York. Trained as a social anthropologist, she teaches courses on the anthropology of food, food studies, and gastronomy.

Printed in the USA
CPSIA information can be obtained
at www.ICGtesting.com
LVHW010912011123
762637LV00011B/428